A Sequence for Academic Writing

A Sequence for Academic Writing

Laurence Behrens
University of California,
Santa Barbara

Leonard J. Rosen

Bonnie Beedles

Longman

New York • San Francisco • Boston
London • Toronto • Sydney • Tokyo • Singapore • Madrid
Mexico City • Munich • Paris • Cape Town • Hong Kong • Montreal

Senior Vice President/Publisher: Joseph Opiela
Acquisitions Editor: Lynn M. Huddon
Executive Marketing Manager: Carlise Paulson
Supplements Editor: Donna Campion
Production Manager: Charles Annis
Project Coordination, Text Design, and Electronic Page Makeup: Pre-Press Co., Inc.
Cover Design Manager: John Callahan
Cover Designer: Laura Shaw
Manufacturing Buyer: Al Dorsey
Printer and Binder: R. R. Donnelly and Sons Co.
Cover Printer: Lehigh Press, Inc.

Library of Congress Cataloging-in-Publication Data
Beedles, Bonnie.
    A sequence for academic writing / Bonnie Beedles, Laurence Behrens, Leonard
    J. Rosen.
        p. cm.
    Includes index.
    ISBN 0-321-08133-1 (alk.paper)
        1. English language—Rhetoric. 2. Academic writing. I. Behrens, Laurence. II.
        Rosen, Leonard J. III. Title.

PE1408 .B44 2001
808'.042—dc21

                                                                        2001050436

ISBN 0-321-08133-1

DOC—04 03 02

10 9 8 7 6 5 4 3

Brief Contents

Detailed Contents

Chapter 3
Writing as a Process: Steps to Writing Theses, Introductions, and Conclusions   91

Chapter 4
Explanatory Synthesis   135

Chapter 5
Argument Synthesis   177

Preface for Instructors

A Sequence for Academic Writing evolved out of another text, *Writing and Reading Across the Curriculum* (WRAC). Through seven editions over the last twenty years, WRAC has helped hundreds of thousands of students prepare for the writing done well beyond the freshman composition course. WRAC features a rhetoric in which students are introduced to the core skills of summary, critique, and synthesis, and a reader that presents readings in the disciplines to which students can apply the skills learned in the earlier chapters. Because the skills of summary, critique, and synthesis are so central to academic thinking and writing, many instructors—both those teaching writing-across-the-curriculum and those using other approaches to composition instruction—have found WRAC a highly useful introduction to college-level writing. We therefore decided to adapt the rhetoric portion of WRAC into a separate book that instructors could use apart from any additional reading content they chose to incorporate in their writing courses. *A Sequence for Academic Writing* is both an adaptation of WRAC and an expansion: we have added the core skill of *analysis* to the mix because it, too, is an assignment type often encountered throughout the curriculum and beyond.

We proceed through a sequence from "Summary, Paraphrase, and Quotation" to "Critical Reading and Critique," to "Explanatory Synthesis" and "Argument Synthesis" to "Analysis," concluding with a chapter on "Research." This final chapter presents the research process as the culmination of all the skills previously covered in the text. Along the way, we also include a chapter on "Writing as a Process," which offers extended treatment of writing *theses, introductions,* and *conclusions.* We reinforce this emphasis on writing as process in all chapters through examples of student writing processes and exercises encouraging engagement with various steps in the processes.

Key features in *A Sequence for Academic Writing* include *boxes,* which sum up important concepts in each chapter; brief writing *exercises,* which prompt individual and group activities; *writing assignments,* which put each chapter's skills into practice, and *model essays,* which provide examples of student responses to writing assignments discussed in the text. An *Instructor's Manual* and *Companion Website* provide further resources for teaching with this text.

While we are keenly aware of the overlapping nature of the skills on which we focus and while we could all endlessly debate an appropriate order in which to cover these skills, a book is necessarily linear. We have chosen the sequence that makes the most sense to us, though individual instructors may choose to cover these skills in their own sequence. Teachers should feel perfectly free to use these chapters in whatever order they feel is most useful to their individual aims and philosophies. Understanding the material in a later chapter does not, in most cases, depend on students having read material in the earlier chapters.

ACKNOWLEDGMENTS

We would like to thank the following reviewers for their help in the preparation of this text: Cora Agatucci, *Central Oregon Community College*; Clinton R. Gardner, *Salt Lake Community College*; Susanmarie Harrington, *Indiana University and Purdue University Indianapolis*; Georgina Hill, *Western Michigan University*; Jane M. Kinney, *Valdosta State University*; Lyle W. Morgan, *Pittsburg State University*; Joan Perkins, *University of Hawaii*; Catherine Quick, *Stephen F. Austin State University*; William Scott Simkins, *University of Southern Mississippi*; Marcy Taylor, *Central Michigan University*; Zach Waggoner, *Western Illinois University*; Heidemarie Z. Weidner, *Tennessee Technological University*; and Betty R. Youngkin, *The University of Dayton*.

Thanks to Lynn Huddon, our editor at Longman Publishers, for seeing this project through from conception to completion. We are also grateful to Robin Gordon, project manager at Pre-Press Co., for her careful and attentive handling of the manuscript throughout the production process.

Laurence Behrens
Leonard J. Rosen
Bonnie Beedles

Introduction

In your sociology class, you are assigned to write a paper on the role of peer groups in influencing attitudes toward smoking. Your professor expects you to read some of the literature on the subject as well as to conduct interviews with members of such groups. For an environmental studies course, you must write a paper on how one or more industrial plants in a particular area have been affecting the local ecosystem. In your film studies class, you must select a contemporary filmmaker—you are trying to decide between Martin Scorsese and Spike Lee—and examine how at least three of his films demonstrate a distinctive point of view on a particular subject.

These writing assignments are typical of those you will undertake during your college years. In fact, such assignments are also common for those in professional life: scientists writing environmental impact statements, social scientists writing accounts of their research for professional journals, film critics showing how the latest effort by a filmmaker fits into the general body of his or her work.

Core Skills

To succeed in such assignments, you will need to develop and hone particular skills in critical reading, thinking, and writing. You must develop—not necessarily in this order—the ability to

- read and accurately *summarize* a selection of material on your subject;
- determine the quality and relevance of your sources through a process of *critical reading* and assessment;
- *synthesize* different sources by discovering the relationships among them and showing how these relationships produce insights about the subject under discussion;
- *analyze* sources by applying particular perspectives and theories to your data;
- develop effective techniques for (1) discovering and using pertinent, authoritative information and ideas and (2) presenting the results of your work in generally accepted disciplinary formats.

A Sequence for Academic Writing will help you to meet these goals. You will learn techniques for preparing and writing the summary, critique, analysis, and synthesis because we have found that these are the core skills you must master if you are to succeed as a writer, regardless of your major. In conversations with faculty across the curriculum, time and again we have been struck by a shared desire to see students thinking and writing in subject-appropriate ways. Psychology, biology, and engineering teachers want you to think, talk, and write like psychologists, biologists, and engineers. We set out, therefore, to learn the strategies writers use to enter conversations in their respective disciplines. We discovered that four readily learned strategies—summary, critique, synthesis, and analysis—provided the basis for the great majority of writing in freshman- through senior-level courses, and in courses across disciplines. We therefore made these skills the centerpiece of instruction for this book.

Applications Beyond College

While summary, critique, synthesis, and analysis are primary critical thinking and writing skills practiced throughout the university, these skills are also crucial to the work you will do in your life outside the university. In the professional world, people write letters, memos, and reports in which they must summarize procedures and the like. Critical reading and critique are important skills for writing legal briefs, business plans, and policy briefs. In addition, these same types of documents—common in the legal, business, and political worlds, respectively—involve synthesis. A business plan, for example, will often include a synthesis of ideas and proposals in one coherent plan. Finally, the ability to analyze complex data, processes, or ideas, to apply theories or perspectives to particular subjects, and then to effectively convey the results of analysis in writing is integral to writing in medicine, law, politics, business—in short, just about any of the professions in which you may later find yourself.

Emphasis on Process

Our focus upon these four core skills culminates in a chapter on Research, in which you will draw upon your work in the previous chapters to write a research paper. This chapter leads you through the research process, from finding a subject and developing a research question, to conducting research and drafting a paper, complete with in-text and end citation in the most common formats (MLA and APA). In fact, all of the chapters include a focus upon the *processes* of summary, critique, synthesis, and analysis. We emphasize that these skills involve steps in a process, and we break the processes into their constituent steps. Thinking, reading, and writing are all different—although interconnected—processes, and throughout this text you will find references to the processes involved in these tasks. Further, we devote an entire chapter to writing itself as a process, and to crucial elements of that process for college writers: theses, introductions, and conclusions.

It is important to emphasize that while we have broken down the reading, thinking, and writing processes into steps, we don't mean to imply that there is only one way to approach these processes. Instead, our experience as instructors shows us that students who are presented with suggestions for engaging in the processes of academic writing can then go on to adapt these suggestions to their own learning and working styles. We encourage you to try our approaches, modifying and revising them as suits your particular needs and abilities.

Many key features in *A Sequence for Academic Writing* should enhance your understanding of the material. Scattered through the chapters are brief writing *exercises*, as well as longer *writing assignments*. *Boxed* material provides useful summaries and hints relating to points covered at greater length in the text. *Model student papers* provide specific examples of student responses to writing assignments discussed in the text.

Students often view introductory college writing courses as unnecessary and irrelevant distractions from their subject-oriented courses. But success in these disciplinary courses is directly correlated to the ability to perform assigned reading and writing tasks. Professors in disciplinary courses generally do not teach reading and writing skills, though they do take such skills for granted in their students. (And if your college professors expect you to possess solid reading and writing skills, just imagine the expectations of your future employers, co-workers, and clients!) Beyond the need for developing your writing skills, however, don't underestimate the sense of satisfaction, even enjoyment, you will derive from becoming a more skillful reader and writer. You may not have chosen to enroll in your present writing course, but it could well become one of the most valuable—and interesting—of your college career.

A Sequence for Academic Writing

Summary, Paraphrase, and Quotation

WHAT IS A SUMMARY?

The best way to demonstrate that you understand the information and the ideas in any piece of writing is to compose an accurate and clearly written summary of that piece. By a *summary* we mean a *brief restatement, in your own words, of the content of a passage* (a group of paragraphs, a chapter, an article, a book). This restatement should focus on the *central idea* of the passage. The briefest of all summaries (one or two sentences) will do no more than this. A longer, more complete summary will indicate, in condensed form, the main points in the passage that support or explain the central idea. It will reflect the order in which these points are presented and the emphasis given to them. It may even include some important examples from the passage. But it will not include minor details. It will not repeat points simply for the purpose of emphasis. And it will not contain any of your own opinions or conclusions. A good summary, therefore, has three central qualities: *brevity, completeness*, and *objectivity*.

CAN A SUMMARY BE OBJECTIVE?

Of course, this last quality of objectivity might be difficult to achieve in a summary. By definition, writing a summary requires you to select some aspects of the original and to leave out others. Since deciding what to select and what to leave out calls for your personal judgment, your summary really is a work of interpretation. And, certainly, your interpretation of a passage may differ from another person's. One factor affecting the nature and quality of your interpretation is your *prior knowledge* of the subject. For example, if you're attempting to summarize an

1

anthropological article and you're a novice in the field, then your summary of the article might be quite different from that of your professor, who has spent 20 years studying this particular area and whose judgment about what is more significant and what is less significant is undoubtedly more reliable than your own. By the same token, your personal or professional *frame of reference* may also affect your interpretation. A union representative and a management representative attempting to summarize the latest management offer would probably come up with two very different accounts. Still, we believe that in most cases it's possible to produce a reasonably objective summary of a passage if you make a conscious, good-faith effort to be unbiased and not to allow your own feelings on the subject to distort your account of the text.

USING THE SUMMARY

In some quarters, the summary has a bad reputation—and with reason. Summaries often are provided by writers as substitutes for analyses. As students, many of us have summarized books that we were supposed to *review* critically. All the same, the summary does have a place in respectable college work. First, writing a summary is an excellent way to understand what you read. This in itself is an important goal of academic study. If you don't understand your source material, chances are you won't be able to refer to it usefully in an essay or research paper. Summaries help you to understand what you read because they force you to put the text into your own words. Practice with writing summaries also develops your general writing habits, since a good summary, like any other piece of good writing, is clear, coherent, and accurate.

Second, summaries are useful to your readers. Let's say you're writing a paper about the McCarthy era in America, and in part of that paper you want to discuss Arthur Miller's *Crucible* as a dramatic treatment of the subject. A summary of the plot would be helpful to a reader who hasn't seen or read—or who doesn't remember—the play. (Of course, if the reader is your American literature professor, you can safely omit the plot summary.) Or perhaps you're writing a paper about nuclear arms control agreements. If your reader isn't familiar with the provisions of SALT I or SALT II, it would be a good idea to summarize these provisions at some early point in the paper. In many cases (a test, for instance), you can use a summary to demonstrate your knowledge of what your professor already knows; when writing a paper, you can use a summary to inform your professor about some relatively unfamiliar source.

Third, summaries are required frequently in college-level writing. For example, on a psychology midterm, you may be asked to explain Carl Jung's theory of the collective unconscious and to show how it differs from Freud's theory of the personal unconscious. The first part of this question requires you to *summarize* Jung's theory. You may have read about this theory in your textbook or in a supplementary article, or your instructor may have outlined it in his or her lecture. You can best demonstrate your understanding of Jung's theory by summarizing it. Then you'll proceed to contrast it with Freud's theory—which, of course, you must also summarize.

THE READING PROCESS

It may seem to you that being able to tell (or to retell) exactly what a passage says is a skill that ought to be taken for granted in anyone who can read at high school level. Unfortunately, this is not so: For all kinds of reasons, people don't always read carefully. In fact, it's probably safe to say that usually

---

WHERE DO WE FIND WRITTEN SUMMARIES?

Here are just a few of the types of writing that involve summary:

Academic Writing

- **Critique papers.** Summarize material in order to critique it.
- **Synthesis papers.** Summarize to show relationships between sources.
- **Analysis papers.** Summarize theoretical perspectives before applying them.
- **Research papers.** Note-taking and reporting research require summary.
- **Literature reviews.** Overviews of work presented in brief summaries.
- **Argument papers.** Summarize evidence and opposing arguments.
- **Essay exams.** Demonstrate understanding of course materials through summary.

Workplace Writing

- **Policy briefs.** Condense complex public policy.
- **Business plans.** Summarize costs, relevant environmental impacts, and other important matters.
- **Memos, letters, and reports.** Summarize procedures, product assessments, expenditures, and more.
- **Medical charts.** Record patient data in summarized form.
- **Legal briefs.** Summarize relevant facts of cases.

they don't. Either they read so inattentively that they skip over words, phrases, or even whole sentences, or, if they do see the words in front of them, they see them without registering their significance.

When a reader fails to pick up the meaning and the implications of a sentence or two, usually there's no real harm done. (An exception: You could lose credit on an exam or paper because you failed to read or to realize the significance of a crucial direction by your instructor.) But over longer stretches—the paragraph, the section, the article, or the chapter—inattentive or haphazard reading creates problems, for you must try to perceive the shape of the argument, to grasp the central idea, to determine the main points that compose it, to relate the parts of the whole, and to note key examples. This kind of reading takes a lot more energy and determination than casual reading. But, in the long run, it's an energy-saving method because it enables you to retain the content of the material and to use that content as a basis for your own responses. In other words, it allows you to develop an accurate and coherent written discussion that goes beyond summary.

Given the often large quantity of reading they are asked to do in college, many students skim through their assignments. Skimming can be a useful way of managing some kinds of course material. For example, textbooks that outline broad concepts that a professor elaborates upon in a lecture might be skimmed before the lecture, then read more carefully later to fill in gaps in your understanding. However, for the most part you should truly read and understand the readings you are assigned.

One effective strategy with which to approach course readings is to ask yourself how the reading fits into the course—both thematically and in terms of its *purpose*. Why is the reading assigned? How do different readings relate to one another? For example, many college courses will require you to read chapters from a textbook as well as essays selected from a reader or anthology. Textbooks usually provide general overviews, laying out and defining important concepts. Essays often follow up by narrowing the focus, by showing the concepts in action, critiquing them, or providing more in-depth discussion of some key concept or issue. When you understand the purpose of the reading you're doing, you will benefit more from it.

A useful way to approach reading assignments is to think of reading as a process, and try to enjoy it as you're doing it, rather than focusing entirely on the result and just powering through to the end. Try to think of reading as a circular movement through a text rather than a linear movement. In other words, when you start at the beginning of an essay or chapter, rather than moving through it in a straight, uninterrupted path to the end of the reading, stop reading periodically to sum up in your mind, flag difficult passages with notes or question marks in the margin, and circle back to reread those passages after you've read further and gained more understanding. Use paraphrase (see pages 33–38) to sum up difficult points in your own words and record them in the margins or in reading notes.

As you read, pay attention to the different stages of thought contained in a piece. Some readings are separated into sections with subheadings, which specifically identify the stages of thought. Other readings won't be sectioned off in this way, and you'll have to be alert to the shifts in focus that occur throughout a piece. If you're reading a difficult piece and find yourself confused, ask yourself not only what the author is *saying*, but also what he or she is *doing* in that portion of the reading. In other words, why is the author discussing this now? Is the writer providing examples, discussing opposing arguments, further elaborating an earlier point? By looking at what an author seems to be doing as well as saying, you'll have a better sense of how the different parts of a reading make up the whole. Paying close attention to transitional words and phrases such as "on the other hand," "for example," "therefore," and "conversely," will also help you locate the shifts in thought that occur in a piece of writing.

Read actively. Don't just passively internalize the ideas on the page, but stop and think, question, and write notes of agreement, disagreement, confusion, or identification in the margin. Underline key points, but try not to go crazy with the highlighter as you read. Often the first time you read something, it's tempting to overdo the highlighting, as every point strikes you as a potentially key idea. You end up with pages that are almost entirely covered in fluorescent yellow or pink, and this can be really distracting—and misleading—later on when you review your reading. Underlining with a pencil, or making marks in the margin, can be more effective, for several reasons. First, when you underline with a pencil, you have to focus more upon the actual words than you do when you quickly whisk a highlighting pen over the words; therefore, you'll be further comprehending the ideas as you underline them. Second, your first impression of which points are important is likely to be a little off the mark. If you underline with a pencil you can erase things that prove unnecessary after you've read the entire piece.

These tips are meant to help you get the most out of reading. We've included more suggestions for critical reading and summary in the box on Critical Reading for Summary, on the next page. Now we turn to the next step—how you take what you've read and condense and rephrase it.

HOW TO WRITE SUMMARIES

Every article you read will present a different challenge as you work to summarize it. As you'll discover, saying in a few words what has taken someone else a great many can be difficult. But like any other skill, the ability to summarize improves with practice. Here are a few pointers to get you started. They represent possible stages, or steps, in the process of writing a summary. These pointers are not meant to be ironclad rules; rather, they are designed to encourage habits of thinking that will allow you to vary your technique as the situation demands.

CRITICAL READING FOR SUMMARY

- **Examine the context.** Note the credentials, occupation, and publications of the author. Identify the source in which the piece originally appeared. This information helps illuminate the author's perspective on the topic he or she is addressing.
- **Note the title and subtitle.** Some titles are straightforward, while other titles' meanings become more clear as you read. In either case, titles typically identify the topic being addressed, and often reveal the author's attitude toward that topic.
- **Identify the main point.** Whether a piece of writing contains a thesis statement in the first few paragraphs or builds its main point without stating it up front, try to look at the entire piece to arrive at an understanding of the overall point being made.
- **Identify the subordinate points.** Notice the smaller subpoints that make up the main point, and make sure you understand how they relate to the main point. If a particular subpoint doesn't clearly relate to the main point you've identified, you may need to modify your understanding of the main point.
- **Break the reading into sections.** Notice which paragraph(s) make up a piece's introduction, body, and conclusion. Break up the body paragraphs into sections that address the writer's various subpoints.
- **Distinguish between points, examples, counterarguments.** Critical reading requires careful attention to what a writer is *doing* as well as what he or she is *saying*. When a writer quotes someone else, or relays an example of something, ask yourself why this is being done. What point is the example supporting? Is another source being quoted as support for a point, or as a counterargument that the writer sets out to address?
- **Watch for transitions within and between paragraphs.** In order to follow the logic of a piece of writing, as well as to distinguish between points, examples, and counterarguments, pay attention to the transitional words and phrases writers use. Transitions function like road signs, preparing the reader for what's next.
- **Read actively and recursively.** Don't treat reading as a passive, linear progression through a text. Instead, read as though you are engaged in a dialogue with the writer: ask questions of the text as you read, make notes in the margin, underline key ideas in pencil, put question or exclamation marks next to passages that confuse or excite you. Go back to earlier points once you finish a reading, stop during your reading to recap what's come so far, move back and forth through a text.

GUIDELINES FOR WRITING SUMMARIES

- *Read* **the passage carefully.** Determine its structure. Identify the author's purpose in writing. (This will help you distinguish between more important and less important information.) Make a note in the margin when you get confused, or when you think something is important; highlight or underline points sparingly, if at all.
- *Reread.* This time divide the passage into sections or stages of thought. The author's use of paragraphing will often be a useful guide. *Label,* on the passage itself, each section or stage of thought. *Underline* key ideas and terms. Write notes in the margin.
- **Write** *one-sentence summaries,* on a separate sheet of paper, of each stage of thought.
- *Write a thesis: a one- or two-sentence summary of the entire passage.* The thesis should express the central idea of the passage, as you have determined it from the preceding steps. You may find it useful to keep in mind the information contained in the lead sentence or paragraph of most newspaper stories—the *what, who, why, where, when,* and *how* of the matter. For persuasive passages, summarize in a sentence the author's conclusion. For descriptive passages, indicate the subject of the description and its key feature(s). *Note:* In some cases, *a suitable thesis may already be in the original passage.* If so, you may want to quote it directly in your summary.
- *Write the first draft of your summary* by (1) combining the thesis with your list of one-sentence summaries or (2) combining the thesis with one-sentence summaries *plus* significant details from the passage. In either case, eliminate repetition and less important information. Disregard minor details or generalize them (e.g., George Bush, Sr. and Bill Clinton might be generalized as "recent presidents"). Use as few words as possible to convey the main ideas.
- *Check your summary against the original passage* and make whatever adjustments are necessary for accuracy and completeness.
- *Revise your summary,* inserting transitional words and phrases where necessary to ensure coherence. Check for style. *Avoid a series of short, choppy sentences.* Combine sentences for a smooth, logical flow of ideas. Check for grammatical correctness, punctuation, and spelling.

DEMONSTRATION: SUMMARY

To demonstrate these points at work, let's go through the process of summarizing a passage of expository material. Read the following passage carefully. Try to identify its parts and to understand how these parts work together to create an overall point.

The Future of Love: Kiss Romance Goodbye, It's Time for the Real Thing
Barbara Graham

Author of the satire Women Who Run With Poodles: Myths and Tips for Honoring Your Mood Swings *(Avon, 1994), Barbara Graham has written articles for* Vogue, Self, Common Boundary, *and other publications. She regularly contributes articles to the* Utne Reader, *from which this essay was taken.*

1   Freud and his psychoanalytic descendants are no doubt correct in their assessment that the search for ideal love—for that one perfect soulmate—is the futile wish of not fully developed selves. But it also seems true that the longing for a profound, all-consuming erotic connection (and the heightened state of awareness that goes with it) is in our very wiring. The yearning for fulfillment through love seems to be to our psychic structure what food and water are to our cells.

2   Just consider the stories and myths that have shaped our consciousness: Beauty and the Beast, Snow White and her handsome prince, Cinderella and Prince Charming, Fred and Ginger, Barbie and Ken. (Note that, with the exception of the last two couples, all of these lovers are said to have lived happily ever after—even though we never get details of their lives after the weddings, after children and gravity and loss have exacted their price.) Still, it's not just these lucky fairy tale characters who have captured our collective imagination. The tragic twosomes we cut our teeth on—Romeo and Juliet, Tristan and Iseult, Launcelot and Guinevere, Heathcliff and Cathy, Rhett and Scarlett—are even more compelling role models. Their love is simply too powerful and anarchic, too shattering and exquisite, to be bound by anything so conventional as marriage or a long-term domestic arrangement.

3   If recent divorce and remarriage statistics are any indication, we're not as astute as the doomed lovers. Instead of drinking poison and putting an end to our love affairs while the heat is still turned up full blast, we expect our marriages and relationships to be long-running fairy tales. When they're not, instead of examining our expectations, we switch partners and reinvent the fantasy, hoping that this time we'll get it right. It's easy to see why: Despite all the talk of family values, we're constantly bombarded by visions of perfect romance. All you have to do is turn on the radio or TV or open any magazine and check out the perfume and lingerie ads. "Our culture is deeply regressed," says Florence Falk, a New York City psychotherapist. "Everywhere we turn, we're faced with glamorized, idealized versions of love. It's as if the culture wants us to stay trapped in the fantasy and does everything possible to encourage and expand that fantasy." Trying to forge an authentic relationship amidst all the romantic hype, she adds, makes what is already a tough proposition even harder.

Barbara Graham, "The Future of Love: Kiss Romance Goodbye, It's Time for the Real Thing," <u>Utne Reader</u> Jan.–Feb. 1997: 20–23.

4   What's most unusual about our culture is our feverish devotion to the belief that romantic love and marriage should be synonymous. Starting with George and Martha, continuing through Ozzie and Harriet right up to the present day, we have tirelessly tried to formalize, rationalize, legalize, legitimize, politicize and sanitize rapture. This may have something to do with our puritanical roots, as well as our tendency toward oversimplification. In any event, this attempt to satisfy all of our contradictory desires under the marital umbrella must be put in historical context in order to be properly understood.

5   "Personal intimacy is actually quite a new idea in human history and was never part of the marriage ideal before the 20th century," says John Welwood, a Northern California-based psychologist and author, most recently, of *Love and Awakening*. "Most couples throughout history managed to live together their whole lives without ever having a conversation about what was going on within or between them. As long as family and society prescribed the rules of marriage, individuals never had to develop any consciousness in this area."

6   In short, marriage was designed to serve the economic and social needs of families, communities, and religious institutions, and had little or nothing to do with love. Nor was it expected to satisfy lust.

7   In *Myths To Live By,* Joseph Campbell explains how the sages of ancient India viewed the relationship between marriage and passion. They concluded that there are five degrees of love, he writes, "through which a worshiper is increased in the service and knowledge of his God." The first degree has to do with the relationship of the worshiper to the divine. The next three degrees of love, in order of importance, are friendship, the parent/child relationship, and marriage. The fifth and highest form is passionate, illicit love. "In marriage, it is declared, one is still possessed of reason," Campbell adds. "The seizure of passionate love can be, in such a context, only illicit, breaking in upon the order of one's dutiful life in virtue as a devastating storm."

8   No wonder we're having problems. The pressures we place on our tender unions are unprecedented. Even our biochemistry seems to militate against long-term sexual relationships. Dr. Helen Fisher, an anthropologist at Rutgers University and author of *Anatomy of Love*, believes that human pair-bonds originally evolved according to "the ancient blueprint of serial monogamy and clandestine adultery" and are originally meant to last around four years—at least long enough to raise a single dependent child through toddlerhood. The so-called seven-year-itch may be the remains of a four-year reproductive cycle, Fisher suggests.

9   Increasingly, Fisher and other researchers are coming to view what we call love as a series of complex biochemical events governed by hormones and enzymes. "People cling to the idea that romantic love is a mystery, but it's also a chemical experience," Fisher says, explaining that there are three distinct mating emotions and each is supported in the brain by the release of different chemicals. Lust, an emotion triggered by changing levels of testosterone in men and women, is associated with our basic sexual drive. Infatuation depends on the changing levels of dopamine, norepinephrine, and phenylethylamine (PEA), also called the "chemicals of love." They are natural—addictive—amphetaminelike

chemicals that stimulate euphoria and make us want to stay up all night sharing our secrets. After infatuation and the dizzying highs associated with it have peaked—usually within a year or two—this brain chemistry reduces, and a new chemical system made up of oxytocin, vasopressin, and maybe the endorphins kicks in and supports a steadier, quieter, more nurturing intimacy. In the end, regardless of whether biochemistry accounts for cause or effect in love, it may help to explain why some people—those most responsive to the release of the attachment chemicals—are able to sustain a long-term partnership, while thrillseekers who feel depressed without regular hits of dopamine and PEA, are likely to jump from one liaison to the next in order to maintain a buzz.

10   But even if our biochemistry suggests that there should be term limits on love, the heart is a stubborn muscle and, for better or worse, most of us continue to yearn for a relationship that will endure. As a group, Generation Xers—many of whom are children of divorce—are more determined than any other demographic group to have a different kind of marriage than their parents and to avoid divorce, says Howard Markman, author of *Fighting For Your Marriage*. What's more, lesbians and gay men who once opposed marriage and all of its heterosexual, patriarchal implications, now seek to reframe marriage as a more flexible, less repressive arrangement. And, according to the U.S. National Center for Health Statistics, in one out of an estimated seven weddings, either the bride or the groom—or both—are tying the knot for at least the third time—nearly twice as many as in 1970. There are many reasons for this, from the surge in the divorce rate that began in the '70s, to our ever-increasing life span. Even so, the fact that we're still trying to get love right—knowing all we know about the ephemeral nature of passion, in a time when the stigmas once associated with being divorced or single have all but disappeared—says something about our powerful need to connect.

11   And, judging from the army of psychologists, therapists, clergy, and other experts who can be found dispensing guidance on the subject, the effort to save—or reinvent, depending on who's doing the talking—love and marriage has become a multimillion dollar industry. The advice spans the spectrum. There's everything from *Rules*, by Ellen Fein and Sherrie Schneider, a popular new book which gives 90's women 50's-style tips on how to catch and keep their man, to Harville Hendrix's *Getting The Love You Want*, and other guides to "conscious love." But regardless of perspective, this much is clear: Never before have our most intimate thoughts and actions been so thoroughly dissected, analyzed, scrutinized and medicalized. Now, people who fall madly in love over and over are called romance addicts. Their disease, modeled on alcoholism and other chemical dependencies, is considered "progressive and fatal."

12   Not everyone believes the attempt to deconstruct love is a good thing. The late philosopher Christopher Lasch wrote in his final (and newly released) book, *Women And The Common Life:* "The exposure of sexual life to scientific scrutiny contributed to the rationalization, not the liberation, of emotional life." His daughter, Elisabeth Lasch-Quinn, an historian at Syracuse University

and the editor of the book, agrees. She contends that the progressive demystification of passionate life since Freud has promoted an asexual, dispassionate and utilitarian form of love. Moreover, like her father, she believes that the national malaise about romance can be attributed to insidious therapeutic modes of social control—a series of mechanisms that have reduced the citizen to a consumer of expertise. "We have fragmented life in such a way," she says, "as to take passion out of our experience."

13   Admittedly, it's a stretch to picture a lovesick 12th century French troubadour in a 12-step program for romance addicts. Still, we can't overlook the fact that our society's past efforts to fuse together those historically odd bedfellows—passionate love and marriage—have failed miserably. And though it's impossible to know whether all the attention currently being showered on relationships is the last gasp of a dying social order—marriage—or the first glimmer of a new paradigm for relating to one another, it's obvious that something radically different is needed.

Read, Reread, Underline

Let's consider our recommended pointers for writing a summary.

As you reread the passage, note important points, shifts in thought, and questions you may have in the margins of the essay. Consider the essay's significance as a whole and its stages of thought. What does it say? How is it organized? How does each part of the passage fit into the whole? What do all these points add up to?

Here is how the first few paragraphs of Graham's essay might look after you had marked the main ideas, by highlighting and by marginal notations.

psychic importance of love   Freud and his psychoanalytic descendants are no doubt correct in their assessment that the search for ideal love—for that one perfect soulmate—is the futile wish of not-fully-developed selves. But it also seems true that the longing for a profound, all-consuming erotic connection (and the heightened state of awareness that goes with it) is in our very wiring. The yearning for fulfillment through love seems to be to our psychic structure what food and water are to our cells.

fictional, sometimes tragic examples of ideal love   Just consider the stories and myths that have shaped our consciousness: Beauty and the Beast, Snow White and her handsome prince, Cinderella and Prince Charming, Fred and Ginger, Barbie and Ken. (Note that, with the exception of the last two couples, all of these lovers are said to have lived happily ever after—even though we never get details of their lives after the weddings, after children and gravity and loss have exacted their price.) Still, it's not just these lucky fairy tale characters who have captured our collective imagination. The tragic twosomes we cut our teeth on—Romeo and Juliet, Tristan and Iseult, Launcelot and Guinevere, Heathcliff and Cathy, Rhett and Scarlett—are even more compelling role models. Their love is simply too powerful and anarchic, too shattering and exquisite, to be bound by anything so conventional as marriage or a long-term domestic arrangement.

If recent divorce and remarriage statistics are any indication, we're not as astute as the doomed lovers. Instead of drinking poison and putting an end to our love affairs while the heat is still turned up full blast, we expect our marriages and relationships to be long-running fairy tales. When they're not, instead of examining our expectations, we switch partners and reinvent the fantasy, hoping that this time we'll get it right. It's easy to see why: Despite all the talk of family values, we're constantly bombarded by visions of perfect romance. All you have to do is turn on the radio or TV or open any magazine and check out the perfume and lingerie ads. "Our culture is deeply regressed," says Florence Falk, a New York City psychotherapist. "Everywhere we turn, we're faced with glamorized, idealized versions of love. It's as if the culture wants us to stay trapped in the fantasy and does everything possible to encourage and expand that fantasy." Trying to forge an authentic relationship amidst all the romantic hype, she adds, makes what is already a tough proposition even harder.

difficulty of having a real relationship in a culture that glamorizes ideal love

What's most unusual about our culture is our feverish devotion to the belief that romantic love and marriage should be synonymous. Starting with George and Martha, continuing through Ozzie and Harriet right up to the present day, we have tirelessly tried to formalize, rationalize, legalize, legitimize, politicize and sanitize rapture. This may have something to do with our puritanical roots, as well as our tendency toward oversimplification. In any event, this attempt to satisfy all of our contradictory desires under the marital umbrella must be put in historical context in order to be properly understood.

contradictions of ideal love and marriage

"Personal intimacy is actually quite a new idea in human history and was never part of the marriage ideal before the 20th century," says John Welwood, a Northern California-based psychologist and author, most recently, of Love and Awakening. "Most couples throughout history managed to live together their whole lives without ever having a conversation about what was going on within or between them. As long as family and society prescribed the rules of marriage, individuals never had to develop any consciousness in this area."

"personal intimacy" never considered part of marriage before 20th century

In short, marriage was designed to serve the economic and social needs of families, communities, and religious institutions, and had little or nothing to do with love. Nor was it expected to satisfy lust.

Divide into Stages of Thought

When a selection doesn't contain sections headed by thematic headings, as is the case with "The Future of Love," how do you determine where one stage of thought ends and the next one begins? Assuming that what you have read is coherent and unified, this should not be difficult. (When a selection is unified, all of its parts pertain to the main subject; when a selection is coherent, the parts follow one another in logical order.) Look, particularly, for transitional sentences at the beginning of paragraphs.

Such sentences generally work in one or both of the following ways: (1) they summarize what has come before; (2) they set the stage for what is to follow.

For example, look at the sentence that opens paragraph 10: "But even if our biochemistry suggests that there should be term limits on love, the heart is a stubborn muscle, and for better or worse, most of us continue to yearn for a relationship that will endure." Notice how the first part of this sentence restates the main idea of the preceding section. The second part of the transitional sentence announces the topic of the upcoming section: three paragraphs devoted to the efforts people make to attain, save, or reinvent romantic relationships.

Each section of an article generally takes several paragraphs to develop. Between paragraphs, and almost certainly between sections of an article, you will usually find transitions that help you understand what you have just read and what you are about to read. For articles that have no subheadings, try writing your own section headings in the margins as you take notes. Then proceed with your summary.

The sections of Graham's article may be described as follows:

> **Section 1:** Introduction—a yearning for "fulfillment through love" pervades our culture, and that yearning is shaped by myths and romantic fantasies. (paragraphs 1–3).

> **Section 2:** Marriage and love—we expect passionate love to lead to happy, lifelong marriage. This is a relatively new and unique practice in human history (paragraphs 4-7).

> **Section 3:** Biochemistry and love—love has a biochemical component, which complicates our abilities to sustain long-term relationships (paragraphs 8-9).

> **Section 4:** Marriage and love revisited—many people are currently trying to preserve and/or reinvent marriage and love (paragraphs 10-12).

> **Section 5:** Conclusion—the fusion of passionate love with the institution of marriage hasn't worked very well, and we need something "radically different" to replace it (paragraph 13).

Write a One- or Two-Sentence Summary of Each Stage of Thought

The purpose of this step is to wean you from the language of the original passage, so that you are not tied to it when writing the summary. Here are one-sentence summaries for each stage of thought in "The Future of Love" article's five sections:

Section 1: Introduction—a yearning for "fulfillment through love" pervades our culture, and that yearning is shaped by myths and romantic fantasies. (paragraphs 1–3).

> Most members of American culture crave romantic love, but we have unreal expectations based upon idealized images of love we learn from fantasies and fairy tales.

Section 2: Marriage and love—we expect passionate love to lead to happy, lifelong marriage. This is a relatively new and unique practice in human history (paragraphs 4–7).

> We expect the passionate love of fairy tales to lead to "happily ever after" in the institution of marriage, and when this fails, we move on and try it again. Ironically, the idea that marriage should be based on love—rather than upon social and economic concerns—is a relatively recent practice in Western history.

Section 3: Biochemistry and love—love has a biochemical component, which complicates our abilities to sustain long-term relationships (paragraphs 8–9).

> Biochemists are discovering that love and lust have hormonal causes, and their evidence suggests that our biological makeup predisposes us to seek the excitement of short-term relationships.

Section 4: Marriage and love revisited—many people are currently trying to preserve and/or reinvent marriage and love (paragraphs 10–12).

> Despite all the difficulties, we spend a lot of time analyzing the elements of relationships in order to preserve or perhaps reinvent marriage. We clearly want to make it work.

Section 5: Conclusion—the fusion of passionate love with the institution of marriage hasn't worked very well, and we need something "radically different" to replace it (paragraph 13).

> Because confining passionate love to the institution of marriage hasn't worked very well, we need to revise our model for human relationships.

Write a Thesis: A One- or Two-Sentence Summary of the Entire Passage

The thesis is the most general statement of a summary (or any other type of academic writing—see Chapter 3 for a more complete discussion of thesis statements). It is the statement that announces the paper's subject and the claim that you or—in the case of a summary—another author will be making about that subject. Every paragraph of a paper illuminates the thesis by providing supporting detail or explanation. The relationship of these paragraphs to the thesis is analogous to the relationship of the sentences within a paragraph to the topic sentence. Both the thesis and the topic sentences are general statements (the thesis being the more general) that are followed by systematically arranged details.

To ensure clarity for the reader, *the first sentence of your summary should begin with the author's thesis, regardless of where it appears in the article itself.* Authors may locate their thesis at the beginning of their work, in which case the thesis operates as a general principle from which details of the presentation follow. This is called a *deductive* organization: thesis first, supporting details second. Alternately, an author may locate his or her thesis at the end of the work, in which case the author begins with specific details and builds toward a more general conclusion, or thesis. This is called an *inductive* organization—an example of which you see in "The Future of Love."

A thesis consists of a subject and an assertion about that subject. How can we go about fashioning an adequate thesis for a summary of "The Future of Love"? Probably no two proposed thesis statements for this article would be worded identically, but it is fair to say that any reasonable thesis will indicate that the subject is the current state of love and marriage in American society. How does Graham view the topic? What *is* the current state of love and marriage, in her view? Looking back over our section summaries, Graham's focus upon the illusions of fairy tales and myths, upon the difference between marriage in the present day and its earlier incarnations, her references to the problems of divorce and "romance addiction," suggest she is not altogether positive in her assessment of the current state of affairs, so to speak. Does she make a statement anywhere that pulls all this together somehow? Her conclusion, in paragraph 13, contains her main idea: "our society's past efforts to fuse together those historically odd bedfellows—passionate love and marriage—have failed miserably." Moreover, in the next sentence, "it's obvious that something radically different is needed." Further evidence that this is Graham's main point can be found in the complete title of the essay: "The Future of Love: Kiss Romance Goodbye, It's Time for the Real Thing." Mindful of Graham's subject and the assertion she makes about it, we can write a thesis statement *in our own words* and arrive at the following:

> The contemporary institution of marriage is in
> trouble, and this may be due to our unrealistic
> expectations that passionate love leads to lasting

union; it may be time to develop a new model for love and relationships.

To clarify for our readers the fact that this idea is Graham's and not ours, we'll qualify the thesis as follows:

> In her article "The Future of Love: Kiss Romance Goodbye—It's Time for the Real Thing," Barbara Graham describes how our unrealistic expectations that passionate love leads to lasting union may be partly causing the troubled state of marriage today; thus she suggests we develop a new model for love and relationships.

The first sentence of a summary is crucially important, for it orients readers by letting them know what to expect in the coming paragraphs. The preceding example sentence provides the reader with a direct reference to an article, to its author, and to the thesis for the upcoming summary. The author and title reference also could be indicated in the summary's title (if this were a freestanding summary), in which case their mention could be dropped from the thesis. And lest you become frustrated too quickly, keep in mind that writing an acceptable thesis for a summary takes time—in this case, three drafts, or roughly seven minutes of effort spent on one sentence and another few minutes of fine-tuning after a draft of the entire summary was completed. That is, the first draft of the thesis was too vague and incomplete; the second draft was more specific and complete, but left out the author's point about correcting the problem; the third draft was more complete, but was cumbersome.

> **Draft 1:** Barbara Graham argues that our attempts to confine passionate love to the institution of marriage have failed.
> *(too vague—the problem isn't clear enough)*
>
> **Draft 2:** Barbara Graham ~~argues that our attempts to confine passionate love to the institution of marriage have fail~~ed. describes how the contemporary institution of marriage is in trouble, and this may be due, she thinks, to our unrealistic expectations that passionate love will lead to lasting union.
> *(Incomplete—what about her call for a change?)*
>
> **Draft 3:** In her article "The Future of Love: Kiss Romance Goodbye—It's Time for the Real Thing," Barbara Graham describes how ~~the contemporary in-~~

stitution of marriage is in trouble, and this may
be due, she thinks, to our unrealistic expectations that passionate love will lead to lasting
union may be causing the troubles in the contemporary institution of marriage today, so she argues
that perhaps it's time to develop a new model for
love and relationships.
(Wordy)

Final: In her article "The Future of Love: Kiss
Romance Goodbye—It's Time for the Real Thing,"
Barbara Graham describes how our unrealistic expectations that passionate love leads to lasting
union may be partly causing the troubled state of
in the contemporary institution of marriage today;
so thus she argues that perhaps it's time to suggests we develop a new model for love and relationships.
(Add 'partly.' Cut out wordiness. Replace 'so' with 'thus')

Write the First Draft of the Summary

Let's consider two possible summaries of the example passage: (1) a short
summary, combining a thesis with one-sentence section summaries, and
(2) a longer summary, combining thesis, one-sentence section summaries,
and some carefully chosen details. Again, realize that you are reading
final versions; each of the following summaries is the result of at least two
full drafts.

Summary 1: Combine Thesis Sentence
with One-Sentence Section Summaries

In her article "The Future of Love: Kiss Romance
Goodbye—It's Time for the Real Thing," Barbara
Graham describes how our unrealistic expectations
that passionate love leads to lasting union may be
partly causing the troubled state of marriage today; thus she suggests we develop a new model for
love and relationships. Most members of American
culture crave romantic love, but we have unreal
expectations based upon idealized images of love
we learn from fantasies and fairy tales.

We expect the passionate love of fairy tales
to lead to "happily ever after" in the institution
of marriage, and when this fails, we move on and

try it again. Ironically, the idea that marriage should be based on love—rather than upon social and economic concerns—is a relatively recent practice in Western history. While the romantic marriage ideal doesn't fit with tradition, biological evidence is mounting against it as well. Biochemists are discovering that love and lust have hormonal causes, and their evidence suggests that our biological makeup predisposes us to seek the excitement of short-term relationships.

Nonetheless, despite all the difficulties, we spend a lot of time analyzing the elements of relationships in order to preserve or perhaps reinvent marriage. We clearly want to make it work. Because confining passionate love to the institution of marriage hasn't worked very well, Graham ends by suggesting that we ought to revise our model for human relationships.

Discussion

This summary consists essentially of a restatement of Graham's thesis plus the section summaries, altered or expanded a little for stylistic purposes. The first sentence encompasses the summary of Section 1 and is followed by the summaries of Sections 2, 3, 4, and 5. Notice the insertion of a transitional sentence between the summaries of Sections 2 and 3, helping to link the ideas more coherently.

Summary 2: Combine Thesis Sentence, Section Summaries, and Carefully Chosen Details

The thesis and one-sentence section summaries also can be used as the outline for a more detailed summary. Most of the details in the passage, however, won't be necessary in a summary. It isn't necessary even in a longer summary of this passage to discuss all of Graham's examples—specific romantic fairy tales, ancient Indian views of love and passion, the specific hormones involved with love and lust, or the examples of experts examining and writing about contemporary relationships. It would be appropriate, though, to mention one example of fairy-tale romance, to refer to the historical information on marriage as an economic institution, and to explain some of the biological findings about love's chemical basis.

None of these details appeared in the first summary, but in a longer summary, a few carefully selected details might be desirable for clarity. How do you decide which details to include? First, since the idea that love and marriage are not necessarily compatible is the main point of the essay, it makes sense to cite some of the most persuasive evidence supporting this idea. For example, you could mention that for most of Western history, marriage was meant "to serve the economic and social needs of families, communities, and religious institutions," not the emotional and sexual needs of individuals. Further, you might explain the biochemists' argument that serial monogamy based on mutual interests, and clandestine adultery—not lifelong, love-based marriage—are the forms of relationships best serving human evolution.

You won't always know which details to include and which to exclude. Developing good judgment in comprehending and summarizing texts is largely a matter of reading skill and prior knowledge (see page 1). Consider the analogy of the seasoned mechanic who can pinpoint an engine problem by simply listening to a characteristic sound that to a less experienced person is just noise. Or consider the chess player who can plot three separate winning strategies from a board position that to a novice looks like a hopeless jumble. In the same way, the more practiced a reader you are, the more knowledgeable you become about the subject, and the better able you will be to make critical distinctions between elements of greater and lesser importance. In the meantime, read as carefully as you can and use your own best judgment as to how to present your material.

Here's one version of a completed summary, with carefully chosen details. Note that we have highlighted phrases and sentences added to the original, briefer summary.

In her article "The Future of Love: Kiss Romance Goodbye—It's Time for the Real Thing," Barbara Graham describes how our unrealistic expectations that passionate love leads to lasting union may be partly causing the troubled state of marriage today; thus she suggests we develop a new model for

(Thesis) love and relationships.

Most members of American culture crave romantic love, but we have unreal expectations based upon idealized images of love we learn from fantasies and fairy tales such as Beauty and the Beast and Cinderella. Tragedies such as Romeo and Juliet teach us about the all-consuming nature of "true love," and these stories are tragic precisely because the lovers never get to fulfill what we've been taught is the ideal: living happily ever

(Section 1, after, in wedded bliss. The idea that romantic
¶'s 1–3) love should be confined to marriage is perhaps the biggest fantasy to which we subscribe. When we are unable to make this fantasy real—and it seems that often we are unable to do so—we end that marriage and move on to the next one. The twentieth century

(Section 2,
¶s 4–7)

is actually the first century in Western history in which so much was asked of marriage. In earlier eras, marriage was designed to meet social and economic purposes, rather than fulfill individual emotional and sexual desires.

Casting further doubt on the effectiveness of the current model of marriage, biochemists are discovering how hormones and enzymes influence feelings of love and lust. It turns out that the "chemistry" a person newly in love often feels for another has a basis in fact, as those early feelings of excitement and contentment are biochemical in nature. When people jump from one relationship to the next, they may be seeking that chemical "rush." Further, these biochemical discoveries fit with principles of evolutionary survival, because

(Section 3,
¶s 8–9)

short-term relationships-and even adulterous affairs-help to more quickly propagate the species.

Nonetheless, despite such historical and biological imperatives, we don't seem interested in abandoning the pursuit of love and marriage. In order to preserve or perhaps reinvent marriage, we spend a lot of time scrutinizing and dissecting the dynamics of relationships. Self-help books on

(Section 4,
¶s 10–12)

the subject of love and relationships fill bookstore shelves and top best-seller lists.

While some argue that such scrutiny ruins rather than reinvigorates love, perhaps our efforts to understand relationships can help us to

(Section 5,
¶ 13)

invent some kind of revised model for human relationships—since trying to confine passionate love to the institution of marriage clearly hasn't worked very well.

Discussion

The final two of our suggested steps for writing summaries are (1) to check your summary against the original passage, making sure that you have included all the important ideas, and (2) to revise so that the summary reads smoothly and coherently.

The structure of this summary generally reflects the structure of the original—with one notable departure. As we noted earlier, Graham uses an inductive approach, stating her thesis at the end of the essay. The summary, however, states the thesis right away, then proceeds deductively to develop that thesis.

Compared to the first, briefer summary, this effort mentions fairy tales and tragedy; develops the point about traditional versus contemporary versions of marriage; explains the biochemical/evolutionary point; and refers specifically to self-help books and their role in the issue.

How long should a summary be? This depends on the length of the original passage. A good rule of thumb is that a summary should be no longer than one-fourth of the original passage. Of course, if you were summarizing an entire chapter or even an entire book, it would have to be much shorter than that. The summary above is about one-fourth the length of the original passage. Although it shouldn't be very much longer, you have seen (pages 17–18) that it could be quite a bit shorter.

The length as well as the content of the summary also depends on its *purpose.* Let's suppose you decided to use Graham's piece in a paper that dealt with the biochemical processes of love and lust. In this case, you might summarize *only* Graham's discussion of Fisher's findings, and perhaps the point Graham makes about how biochemical discoveries complicate marriage. If, instead, you were writing a paper in which you argued against attempts to redefine marriage, you might only need to summarize the points about biochemistry. To help support your view, you might summarize Graham's points in paragraph 10 about the persistent desire for lasting union found among members of Generation X and evidenced in the high numbers of marriages and remarriages. Thus, depending on your purpose, you would summarize either selected portions of a source or an entire source, as we will see more fully in the chapters on syntheses.

EXERCISE 1.1

Individual and Collaborative Summary Practice

Turn to Chapter 2 and read Lynn Olson's essay "An Avenue to High Academic Standards" (pages 77–79). Follow the steps for writing summaries outlined above—read, underline, and divide into stages of thought. Write down a one- or two-sentence summary of each stage of thought in Olson's essay. Then, gather in groups of three or four classmates, and compare your summary sentences. Discuss the differences in your sentences, and come to some consensus about the divisions in Olson's stages of thought—and the ways in which to best sum these up.

As a group, write a one- or two-sentence thesis statement summing up the entire passage. You could go even further, and, using your individual summary sentences—or the versions of these your group revised—put together a brief summary of Olson's essay, modeled upon the brief summary of Graham's essay, on pages 17–18 (Summary 1: Combine Thesis Sentence with One-Sentence Section Summaries).

SUMMARIZING A NARRATIVE OR PERSONAL ESSAY

Narratives and personal essays differ from expository essays in that they focus upon personal experiences and/or views, aren't structured around an explicitly stated thesis, and their ideas are developed through the description of events or ideas rather than upon factual evidence or logical explanation. A narrative is a story, a retelling of a person's experiences. That person and those experiences may be imaginary, as is the case with fiction, or they may be real, as in biography. In first-person narratives, you can't assume that the narrator represents the author of the piece, unless you know the narrative is a memoir or biography. In a personal essay, on the other hand, the narrator is the author. And while the writer of a personal essay may tell stories about his or her experiences, usually writers of such essays discuss thoughts and ideas as much as or more than telling stories. Personal essays also tend to contain more obvious points than do narratives. Despite these differences, summarizing personal essays or narratives presents certain challenges—challenges that are different from those presented by summarizing expository writing.

You have seen that an author of an expository piece (such as Graham's "The Future of Love") follows assertions with examples and statements of support. Narratives, however, usually are less direct. The author relates a story—event follows event—the point of which may never be stated directly. The charm, the force, and the very point of the narrative lies in the telling; generally, narratives do not exhibit the same logical development of expository writing. They do not, therefore, lend themselves to summary in quite the same way. Narratives do have a logic, but that logic may be emotional, imaginative, or plot-bound. The writer who summarizes a narrative is obliged to give an overview—a synopsis—of the story's events and an account of how these events affect the central character(s). The summary must explain the significance or *meaning* of the events.

Similarly, while personal essays sometimes present points more explicitly than do narratives, their focus and structure link them to narratives. Personal essays often contain inexplicit main points, or multiple points; they tend to *explore* ideas and issues, rather than make explicit *assertions* about those ideas. This exploratory character often means personal essays exhibit a loose structure, and they often contain stories or narratives within them. While summarizing a personal essay may not involve a synopsis of events, an account of the progression of thoughts and ideas is necessary and, as with a narrative, summaries of personal essays must explain the significance of what goes on in the piece being summarized.

In the following personal essay entitled "Why I Will Never Have a Girlfriend," Tristan Miller performs a statistical analysis that illustrates the low odds of his ever finding a girlfriend. While this piece portrays the frustration felt by many single people, at the same time it pokes fun at this focus on finding the one "right" person. If you were writing a paper on current attitudes toward relationships you might reasonably want to include accounts from a single person's point of view. You could quote parts of such personal essays or narratives, and you could summarize them.

Why I Will Never Have A Girlfriend
Tristan Miller

This piece comes from Tristan Miller's personal Web site, at www.nothingisreal.com. Miller is currently a graduate student in computational linguistics at the University of Toronto.

Why don't I have a girlfriend? This is a question that practically every male has asked himself at one point or another in his life. Unfortunately, there is rarely a hard and fast answer to the query. Many guys try to reason their way through the dilemma nonetheless, often reaching a series of ridiculous explanations, each more self-deprecating than the last: "Is it because I'm too shy, and not aggressive enough? Is it my opening lines? Am I a boring person? Am I too fat or too thin? Or am I simply ugly and completely unattractive to women?" When all other plausible explanations have been discounted, most fall back on the time-honoured conclusion that "there must be Something Wrong™ with me" before resigning themselves to lives of perpetual chastity.[a]

Not me, though. I, for one, refuse to spend my life brooding over my lack of luck with women. While I'll be the first to admit that my chances of ever entering into a meaningful relationship with someone special are practically non-existent, I staunchly refuse to admit that it has anything to do with some inherent problem with me. Instead, I am convinced that the situation can be readily explained in purely scientific terms, using nothing more than demographics and some elementary statistical calculus.

Lest anyone suspect that my standards for women are too high, let me allay those fears by enumerating in advance my three criteria for the match. First, the potential girlfriend must be approximately my age—let's say 21 plus or minus three or four years. Second, the girl must be beautiful (and I use that term all-encompassingly to refer to both inner and outer beauty). Third, she must also be reasonably intelligent—she doesn't have to be Mensa material, but the ability to carry on a witty, insightful argument would be nice. So there you have it—three simple demands, which I'm sure you'll all agree are anything but unreasonable. That said, I now present my demonstration of why the probability of finding a suitable candidate fulfilling the three above-noted requirements is so small as to be practically impossible—in other words, why I will never have a girlfriend. I shall endeavor to make this proof as rigorous as the available data permits. And I should note, too, that there will be no statistical trickery involved here; I have cited all my

---

Tristan Miller, "Why I Will Never Have a Girlfriend," online essay, 1999, 7 Sept. 2000 <http://www.nothingisreal.com/girlfriend/>.

[a] After a short period of brooding, of course, these males will eventually come to the realization that the real reason they were never able to get a girlfriend is that they were too discriminating with their attentions. They will consequently return to the dating scene, entering a sequence of blasé relationships with mediocre girls for whom they don't really care, until they finally marry one out of fear of spending the rest of their lives alone. I am convinced that this behavior is the real reason for today's alarmingly high divorce rate.

sources and provided all relevant calculations[b] in case anyone wishes to conduct their own independent review. Let's now take a look at the figures, shall we?

Number of people on Earth (in 1998)   5, 592, 830, 000

We start with the largest demographic in which I am interested—namely, the population of this planet. That is not to say I'm against the idea of interstellar romance, of course; I just don't assess the prospect of finding myself a nice Altairian girl as statistically significant. Now anyway, the latest halfway-reliable figures we have for Earth's population come from the United States Census Bureau's 1999 World Population Profile. Due presumably to the time involved in compiling and processing census statistics, said report's data is valid only as of 1998, so later on we'll be making some impromptu adjustments to bring the numbers up to date.

. . . who are female   2, 941, 118, 000[c]

I'd've thought that, given the title of this web page, this criterion goes without saying. In case anyone missed it, though, I am looking for exclusively female companionship. Accordingly, roughly half of the Earth's population must be discounted. Sorry, guys.

. . . in "developed" countries   605, 601, 000[d]

We now further restrict the geographical area of interest to so-called "first-world countries." My reasons for doing so are not motivated out of contempt for those who are economically disadvantaged, but rather by simple probability. My chances of meeting a babe from Bhutan or a goddess from Ghana, either in person or on the Internet, are understandably low. In fact, I will most likely spend nearly my entire life living and working in North America, Europe, and Australia, so it is to these types of regions that the numbers have been narrowed.

. . . currently (in 2000) aged 18 to 25   65, 399, 083[e]

Being neither a pedophile nor a geriatrophile, I would like to restrict my search for love to those whose age is approximately equal to my own. This is where things get a bit tricky, for two reasons: first, the census data is nearly two years old, and second, the "population by age" tables in WP/98 do not have a single listing for "16–23" but are instead quantified into "15–19" (of whom there are 39,560,000) and "20–44" (population 215,073,000). Women aged 15 to 19 in 1998 will be aged 17 to 21 in 2000[f]; in this group, I'm interested in dating those 18 or older, so, assuming the "15–19" girls' ages are uniformly distributed, we have

---

[b] Due to rounding, figures cited may not add up exactly.

[c] U.S. Bureau of the Census, Report WP/98, Table A-3.

[d] U.S. Bureau of the Census, Report WP/98, Table A-7.

[e] U.S. Bureau of the Census, Report WP/98, Table A-7.

[f] Lest anyone think me out of touch with temporal reality, I am aware that it is still 1999 at the time of this writing; however, given that there remain less than two weeks until the new year, it would be more mathematically correct to make calculations based on the year 2000.

$$39,560,000 \times \frac{[21-18] + 1}{[19-15] + 1} = 31,648,000$$

Similarly, of 1998's "20–44" category, there are now

$$215,073,000 \times \frac{[25-22] + 1}{[44-20] + 1} = 34,411,680$$

females within my chosen age limit. The sum, 66,059,680, represents the total number of females aged 18 to 25 in developed countries in 2000. Unfortunately, roughly 1% of these girls will have died since the census was taken[g]; thus, the true number of so-far eligible bachelorettes is 65,399,083.

. . . who are beautiful   1, 487, 838[h]

Personal attraction, both physically and personality-wise, is an important instigator of any relationship. Of course, beauty is a purely subjective trait whose interpretation may vary from person to person. Luckily it is not necessary for me to define beauty in this essay except to state that for any given beholder, it will probably be normally distributed amongst the population.[i] Without going into the specifics of precisely which traits I admire, I will say that for a girl to be considered really beautiful to me, she should fall at least two standard deviations above the norm. From basic statistics theory, the area to the left of the normal curve at z = 2 is

$$\frac{1}{2} - \frac{1}{\sqrt{2\pi}} \int_0^2 e^{-\frac{1}{2}z^2} dz \approx 0.02275$$

and so it is this number with which we multiply our current population pool.

. . . and intelligent   236, 053

Again, intelligence can mean different things to different people, yet I am once more relieved of making any explanation by noting that it, like most other characteristics, has a notionally normal distribution across the population. Let's assume that I will settle for someone a mere one standard deviation above the normal; in that case, a further

$$\frac{1}{2} + \frac{1}{\sqrt{2\pi}} \int_0^1 e^{-\frac{1}{2}z^2} dz \approx 84.1345\%$$

---

[g] WP/98 gives the annual death rate for developed countries as 10 per 1,000, but does not list death rates per age group. Presumably, the death rate graphs as a bathtub curve, but in absence of any numbers supporting this hypothesis, and for the sake of simplicity, I will conservatively estimate the death rate among this age group to be 1% biennially.

[h] U.S. Bureau of the Census, Report WP/98, Tables A-3 and A-7.

[i] Despite my efforts to research the matter, I could find no data on the distribution of beauty, either outer or inner, amongst the population. Perhaps attractiveness, being a largely subjective trait, does not lend itself to quantification. It is not unreasonable, however, to assume that like most other traits, it has a normal distribution. Indeed, this assumption seems to be backed up by informal observation and judgment—in any reasonably large group of people, most of them will be average-looking, and a tiny minority either exceedingly beautiful or exceedingly ugly.

= 84.1345%

of the population must be discounted.

. . . and not already committed   118, 027

I could find no hard statistics on the number of above-noted girls who are already married, engaged, or otherwise committed to a significant other, but informal observation and anecdotal evidence leads me to believe that the proportion is somewhere around 50%. (Fellow unattached males will no doubt have also noticed a preponderance of girls legitimately offering, "Sorry, I already have a boyfriend" as an excuse not to go on a date.) For reasons of morality (and perhaps too self-preservation), I'm not about to start hitting on girls who have husbands and boyfriends. Accordingly, that portion of the female population must also be considered off-limits.

. . . and also might like me   18, 726

Naturally, finding a suitable girl who I really like is no guarantee that she'll like me back. Assuming, as previously mentioned, that personal attractiveness is normally distributed, there is a mere 50% chance that any given female will consider me even marginally attractive. In practice, however, people are unlikely to consider pursuing a relationship with someone whose looks and personality just barely suffice. Let's make the rather conservative assumption, then, that a girl would go out with someone if and only if they were at least one standard deviation above her idea of average. In that case, referring to our previous calculation, only 15.8655% of females would consider someone with my physical characteristics and personality acceptable as a potential romantic partner.

Conclusion

It is here, at a pool of 18,726 acceptable females, that we end our statistical analysis. At first glance, a datable population of 18,726 may not seem like such a low number, but consider this: assuming I were to go on a blind date with a new girl about my age every week, I would have to date for 3,493 weeks before I found one of the 18,726. That's very nearly 67 years. As a North American male born in the late 1970s, my life expectancy is probably little more than 70 years, so we can safely say that I will be quite dead before I find the proverbial girl of my dreams. Come to think of it, she'll probably be dead too. So there you have it, my friends—finally, a cogent, scientific, non-self-deprecating argument for why I will never have a girlfriend. That said, if you happen to be a girl deluded enough to think that you and I have a chance together, feel free to drop me a line, but I warn you, you face odds of 157,060 to 1. I wouldn't bother if I were you.

Miller uses quantitative "data" to make light of his own search for a girl-friend—as well of the practice of statistical analysis itself. While he wants to find a girlfriend, his meticulous analysis of the numbers shows an ironic self-awareness about the ways in which that desire so easily slides into an obsessive preoccupation. This first-person account could be valuable in a paper otherwise dependent on newspaper and journal articles and on books explaining more factual elements of trends in modern romance. You might reasonably pause in your explanations to acknowledge the frustrations of those who want a relationship yet remain single (and the attempts these unfortunates make to understand their predicament), and Miller's piece could be useful for this. How would you refer to Miller's essay?

When you summarize a personal essay or a narrative, bear in mind the principles that follow, as well as those listed in the box.

HOW TO SUMMARIZE PERSONAL ESSAYS AND NARRATIVES

- Your summary will *not* be a narrative, but rather the synopsis of a narrative or personal account. Your summary will likely be a paragraph at most.
- You will want to name and describe the principal character(s) of the narrative and describe the narrative's main actions or events; or, in the case of the personal essay, identify the narrator and his or her relationship to the discussion.
- You should seek to connect the narrative's character(s) and events: describe the significance of events for (or the impact of events on) the character(s), and/or the narrator.

To summarize events, reread the narrative and make a marginal note each time you see that an action advances the story from one moment to the next. The key here is to recall that narratives take place *in time.* In your summary, be sure to re-create for your reader a sense of time flowing. Name and describe the character(s) as well. (For our purposes, *character* refers to the person, real or fictional, about whom the narrative is written.) The trickiest part of the summary will be describing the connection between events and characters. Earlier (page 2) we made the point that summarizing any selection involves a degree of interpretation, and this is especially true of summarizing narratives and personal essays. What, in the case of Miller, is the point of his statistical analysis? Is he really simply trying to prove why he'll never have a girlfriend? An answer belongs in a summary of this piece, yet developing an answer is tricky. Five readers would arrive at five different interpretations of his attitude toward the subject, would they not? Yes and no: yes, in the sense that these readers, given their separate experiences, will read from different points of view; no, in the sense that readers should be able to distinguish between Miller's attitude and their (the readers') attitude about the topic. A particular interpretation is only valid if textual details support it. For example, we should be able to agree that Miller's tone expresses an attitude not wholly serious, since he makes small jokes throughout his piece.

Noticing details such as the joking tone adopted by a writer is an example of the way you have to infer from clues in a personal essay or narrative the significance of events for a character; at other times, the writer will be more direct. In either case, remember that it is the piece's main character or narrator, real or imaginary, whose perspective should be represented in the summary. Here is a one-paragraph summary of Miller's essay. (The draft is the result of two prior drafts.)

> As the title of his essay suggests, Tristan Miller, in "Why I Will Never Have a Girlfriend," explores the reasons for his status as a single man. Providing a detailed, step-by-step breakdown of demographic data, Miller narrows down the number of eligible women available to him. He starts with the total population of the world and systematically reduces that number based on the actual number of women in the world, in his age group, and so on. Once arrived at his final number of eligible women, Miller offers an ironic argument that he's proven how statistical odds—rather than any deficiencies in him—are to blame for his lonely condition.

SUMMARIZING FIGURES AND TABLES

In your reading in the sciences and social sciences, often you will find data and concepts presented in nontext forms—as figures and tables. Such visual devices offer a snapshot, a pictorial overview of material that is more quickly and clearly communicated in graphic form than as a series of (often complicated) sentences. Note that in essence, figures and tables are themselves summaries. The writer uses a graph, which in an article or book is labeled as a numbered "figure," to present the quantitative results of research as points on a line or a bar, or as sections ("slices") of a pie. Pie charts show relative proportions, or percentages. Graphs, especially effective in showing patterns, relate one variable to another: for instance, income to years of education, or a college student's grade point average to hours of studying.

In the following sections, we present a number of figures and tables from two different sources, all dealing with topics related to romance and relationships. Figures 1.1, 1.2, 1.3, and Table 1.1 all come from a study of the criteria used by participants on television dating shows in the United States and Israel to pick dating partners.* The categories are self-explanatory, although we should note that the category "physical appearance" denotes features of height, weight, facial features, and hair, while "sexual anatomy and bedroom behavior" refers to specifically sexual features of physical appearance, as well as to "kissing technique," "foreplay tactics," and the like. Figure 1.1 shows the percentage of American and Israeli men (out of a total of 266) who chose the most important criteria they used to choose a potential date among members of the opposite sex. Study this pie chart.

---

*Amir Hetsroni, "Choosing a Mate in Television Dating Games: The Influence of Setting, Culture, and Gender," <u>Sex Roles</u> 42.1–2 (2000): 90–97

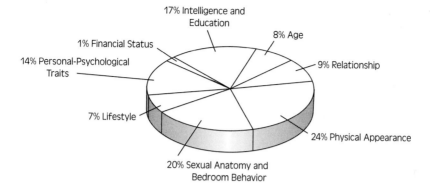

▌**FIGURE 1.1**   Categories Used by American and Israeli Males to Screen
▌Dating Candidates

Here is a summary of the information presented:

> Males rated the categories of "physical appear-
> ance" and "sexual anatomy and bedroom behavior"
> as most important to them. Combined, these two
> categories, which both center on external rather
> than internal characteristics, represent nearly
> half of males' chosen categories, at 44%. Inter-
> nal characteristics represented by the categories
> of "personal-psychological traits" and "intelli-
> gence and education" account for the next great-
> est amounts, for a combined 31%. Males rated "re-
> lationship," "lifestyle," and "age" at nearly
> equal percentages, with an average rating of 8%
> for the three; interestingly, "financial status"
> was rated at a negligible 1%.

Figure 1.2 shows the percentages for women's ratings of dating criteria.

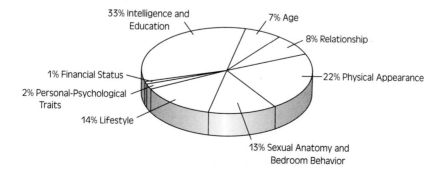

▌**FIGURE 1.2**   Categories Used by American and Israeli Females to
▌Screen Dating Candidates

Exercise **1.2**

Summarizing Charts

Write a brief summary of the data in Figure 1.2. Use our summary of Figure 1.1 as a model, but structure and word your own summary differently.

Bar graphs are useful for comparing two sets of data. Figure 1.3 illustrates this with a comparison of the male and female choices.

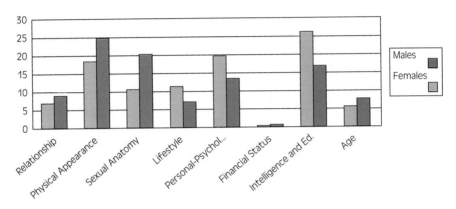

Figure 1.3   Comparison of Categories Used by American and Israeli Males and Females to Screen Dating Candidates

Here is a summary of the information in Figure 1.3:

> We find clear differences when comparing male and female choices of criteria for selecting a date. Males chose external characteristics such as "physical appearance" and especially "sexual anatomy and bedroom behavior" at significantly higher rates than did females. Conversely, females selected internal characteristics of "lifestyle," "personal-psychological traits," and "intelligence and education" at much higher rates than did males. There is virtually no significant difference between the male and female ratings of "relationship," "financial status," and "age"; all three of these criteria were rated at equally low levels of importance by both male and female participants.

A table presents numerical data in rows and columns for quick reference. Tabular information can be incorporated into graphs, if the writer chooses. Charts and graphs are preferable when the writer wants to emphasize a pattern or relationship; tables are used when the writer wants to emphasize numbers. While the previous charts and graphs combined all male and fe-

TABLE 1.1   Categories Used by American and Israeli Males and Females to Screen Dating Candidates

Category	American Males (%) (n = 120)	Israeli Males (%) (n = 146)	American Females (%) (n = 156)	Israeli Females (%) (n = 244)
Relationship	9.5	8.0	9.5	5.0
Physical appearance	18.5	30.0	12.0	22.0
Sexual anatomy and bedroom behavior	11.5	27.5	4.5	15.0
Lifestyle	9.0	6.0	11.0	11.5
Personal-psychological traits	20.0	8.0	27.0	15.0
Financial status	1.5	–	–	1.0
Intelligence and education	22.5	12.5	29.0	24.0
Age	7.5	8.0	7.0	6.0
Total	100.0	100.0	100.0	100.0

male data collected in the TV dating show study, Table 1.1 provides a breakdown of the categories chosen by males and females in the United States and in Israel. (Note: *n* refers to the total number of respondents in each category.)

Sometimes a single graph will present information on two or more populations, or data sets, all of which are tracked with the same measurements. Figure 1.4 comes from a study of 261 college students—93 males and 168 females. The students were asked (among other things) to rate the acceptability of a

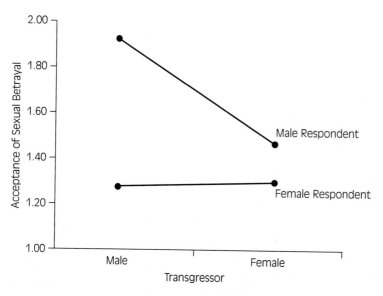

Figure 1.4   The Interaction of Sex of Respondent and Sex of Transgressor on the Acceptance of Sexual Betrayal

hypothetical instance of sexual betrayal by both a male and a female hetero-sexual romantic partner who has agreed to be monogamous. The graph plots the ways in which gender of the transgressor played into the acceptability ratings given by male and female respondents. The researchers established mean values of 1 to 4 (indicating ratings of "totally unacceptable" to "totally acceptable"). A "mean" indicates the average of the ratings or scores given by a population or, in numerical terms, the sum of the scores divided by the number of scores. When respondents in the study were asked to assign a numerical rating of acceptability to instances of sexual betrayal, they chose numbers on a scale from 1 to 4, and these choices were averaged into mean acceptability ratings. None of the scores given by respondents in this study surpassed a mean acceptability rating of 2, but differences are evident between male and female ratings. The male respondents were more accepting than the females, with an overall mean acceptability score of 1.63, whereas the females' mean score was 1.31.

A complete, scientific understanding of these findings would require more data, and statistical analysis of such data would yield precise information such as the exact amount of difference between male and female ratings. For example, in the original text of this study, the authors note that males were 11.6 times more accepting of sexual betrayal by male transgressors than were females. Even without such details, it is possible to arrive at a basic understanding of the data represented in the graph, and to summarize this information in simple terms. Here is a summary of the information reported in this graph:

> While males and females both rated sexual betrayal as unacceptable, males (with a mean rating of 1.63) were significantly more accepting overall than were females (with a mean rating of 1.31). Even more dramatic, however, is the difference between male and female ratings when the gender of the transgressor is factored in. Males rated male transgression as markedly more acceptable than female transgression, with approximate means of 1.90 for male transgressions and 1.43 for female transgressions. The males' ratings contrast sharply with those of females, who indicated a mean acceptability rating of approximately 1.25 for male transgressors, and 1.30 for female transgressors. Therefore, while both sexes found transgression by members of their own sex more acceptable than transgressions by the opposite sex, men were more accepting overall than women, and men believed male transgressors were significantly more acceptable than female transgressors. On the other hand, women found transgression overall less acceptable than males did, and women indicated far less difference in their ratings of male versus female transgressors than did the male respondents.

PARAPHRASE

In certain cases, you may want to *paraphrase* rather than summarize material. Writing a paraphrase is similar to writing a summary: It involves recasting a passage into your own words, so it requires your complete understanding of the material. The difference is that while a summary is a shortened version of the original, the paraphrase is approximately the same length as the original.

Why write a paraphrase when you can quote the original? You may decide to offer a paraphrase of material written in language that is dense, abstract, archaic, or possibly confusing. For example, suppose you were writing a paper on some aspect of human progress and you came across the following passage by the Marquis de Condorcet, a French economist and politician, written in the late eighteenth century:

> If man can, with almost complete assurance, predict phenomena when he knows their laws, and if, even when he does not, he can still, with great expectations of success, forecast the future on the basis of his experience of the past, why, then, should it be regarded as a fantastic undertaking to sketch, with some pretense to truth, the future destiny of man on the basis of his history? The sole foundation for belief in the natural science is this idea, that the general laws directing the phenomena of the universe, known or unknown, are necessary and constant. Why should this principle be any less true for the development of the intellectual and moral faculties of man than for the other operations of nature?

You would like to introduce Condorcet's idea on predicting the future course of human history, but you also don't want to slow down your narrative with this somewhat abstract quotation. You may decide to attempt a paraphrase, as follows:

> The Marquis de Condorcet believed that if we can predict such physical events as eclipses and tides, and if we can use past events as a guide to future ones, we should be able to forecast human destiny on the basis of history. Physical events, he maintained, are determined by natural laws that are knowable and predictable. Since humans are part of nature, why should their intellectual and moral development be any less predictable than other natural events?

Each sentence in the paraphrase corresponds to a sentence in the original. The paraphrase is somewhat shorter, owing to the differences of style between eighteenth- and twentieth-century prose (we tend to be more brisk and efficient, although not as eloquent). But the main difference is that we have replaced the language of the original with our own language. For example, we have paraphrased Condorcet's "the general laws directing the phenomena of the universe, known or unknown, are necessary and constant" with "Physical events, he maintained, are determined by natural laws that are knowable and predictable." To contemporary readers, "knowable and predictable" might be clearer than "necessary and constant" as a description of natural (i.e., physical) laws. Note that we added the specific examples of eclipses and tides to clarify what might have been a somewhat abstract idea. Note also that we included two attributions to Condorcet within the paraphrase to credit our source properly.

When you come across a passage that you don't understand, the temptation is strong to skip over it. Resist this temptation! Use a paraphrase as a tool for explaining to yourself the main ideas of a difficult passage. By translating another writer's language into your own, you can clarify what you understand and pinpoint what you don't. The paraphrase therefore becomes a tool for learning the subject.

The following pointers will help you write paraphrases.

HOW TO WRITE PARAPHRASES

- Make sure that you understand the source passage.
- Substitute your own words for those of the source passage; look for synonyms that carry the same meaning as the original words.
- Rearrange your own sentences so that they read smoothly. Sentence structure, even sentence order, in the paraphrase need not be based on that of the original. A good paraphrase, like a good summary, should stand by itself.

Let's consider some other examples. If you were investigating the ethical concerns relating to the practice of in vitro fertilization, you might conclude that you should read some medical literature. You might reasonably want to hear from the doctors themselves who are developing, performing, and questioning the procedures that you are researching. In professional journals and bulletins, physicians write to one another, not to the general public. They use specialized language. If you wanted to refer to a technically complex selection, you might need to write a paraphrase for the following selection:

In Vitro Fertilization: From Medical Reproduction to Genetic Diagnosis

Dietmar Mieth

[I]t is not only an improvement in the success-rate that participating research scientists hope for but rather, developments in new fields of research in in-vitro gene diagnosis and in certain circumstances gene therapy. In view of this, the French expert J. F. Mattei has asked the following question: "Are we forced to accept that in vitro fertilization will become one of the most compelling methods of genetic diagnosis?" Evidently, by the introduction of a new law in France and Sweden (1994), this acceptance (albeit with certain restrictions) has already occurred prior to the application of in vitro fertilization reaching a technically mature and clinically applicable phase. This may seem astonishing in view of the question placed by the above-quoted French expert: the idea of embryo production so as to withhold one or two embryos before implantation presupposes a definite "attitude towards eugenics." And to destroy an embryo merely because of its genetic characteristics could signify the reduction of a human life to the sum of its genes. Mattei asks: "In face of a molecular judgment on our lives, is there no possibility for appeal? Will the diagnosis of inherited monogenetic illnesses soon be extended to genetic predisposition for multi-factorial illnesses?"*

Like most literature intended for physicians, the language of this selection is somewhat forbidding to an audience of nonspecialists, who have trouble with phrases such as "predisposition for multi-factorial illnesses." As a courtesy to your readers and in an effort to maintain a consistent tone and level in your essay, you could paraphrase this paragraph of the medical newsletter. First, of course, you must understand the meaning of the passage, perhaps no small task. But, having read the material carefully (and perhaps consulting a dictionary), you might eventually prepare a paraphrase like this one:

> Writing in the *Newsletter of the European Network for Biomedical Ethics,* Dietmar Mieth reports that fertility specialists today want not only to improve the success rates of their procedures but also to diagnose and repair genetic problems before they implant fertilized eggs. Since the result of the in vitro process is often more fertilized eggs than can be used in a procedure, doctors may examine test-tube embryos for genetic defects and "withhold one or two" before implanting them. The practice of selectively implanting embryos raises concerns about eugenics and the rights of rejected embryos. On what genetic grounds will specialists distinguish flawed from healthy embryos and make a decision whether or not to implant? The appearance of single genes linked directly to specific, or "monogenetic," illnesses could be grounds for destroying an embryo. More complicated would be genes that predispose people

* Dietmar Mieth, "In vitro Fertilization: From Medical Reproduction to Genetic Diagnosis," <u>Biomedical Ethics: Newsletter of the European Network for Biomedical Ethics</u> 1.1 (1996): 45.

> to an illness but in no way guarantee the onset of
> that illness. Would these genes, which are only
> one factor in "multi-factorial illnesses" also be
> labeled undesirable and lead to embryo destruc-
> tion? Advances in fertility science raise diffi-
> cult questions. Already, even before techniques of
> genetic diagnosis are fully developed, legisla-
> tures are writing laws governing the practices of
> fertility clinics.

We begin our paraphrase with the same "not only/but also" logic of the original's first sentence, introducing the concepts of genetic diagnosis and therapy. The next four sentences in the original introduce concerns of a "French expert." Rather than quoting Mieth, quoting the expert, and imme-diately mentioning new laws in France and Sweden, we decided (first) to explain that in vitro fertilization procedures can give rise to more embryos than needed. We reasoned that nonmedical readers would appreciate our making explicit the background knowledge that the author assumes other physicians possess. Then we quote Mieth briefly ("withhold one or two" embryos) to provide some flavor of the original. We maintain focus on the ethical questions and wait until the end of the paraphrase before mention-ing the laws to which Mieth refers. Our paraphrase is roughly the same length as the original, and it conveys the author's concerns about eugenics. As you can see, the paraphrase requires a writer to make some decisions about the presentation of material. In many, if not most, cases, you will need to do more than simply "translate" from the original, sentence by sen-tence, to write your paraphrase.

Finally, let's consider a passage written by a fine writer that may, nonetheless, best be conveyed in paraphrase. In "Identify All Carriers," an article on AIDS, editor and columnist William F. Buckley makes the follow-ing statement:

> I have read and listened, and I think now that I can convincingly crys-
> tallize the thoughts chasing about in the minds of, first, those whose
> concern with AIDS victims is based primarily on a concern for them,
> and for the maintenance of the most rigid standards of civil liberties
> and personal privacy, and, second, those whose anxiety to protect the
> public impels them to give subordinate attention to the civil ameni-
> ties of those who suffer from AIDS and primary attention to the safety
> of those who do not.

In style, Buckley's passage is more like Condorcet's than the medical newsletter: it is eloquent, balanced, and literate. Still, it is challenging, con-sisting of another lengthy sentence, perhaps a bit too eloquent for some readers to grasp. For your paper on AIDS, you decide to paraphrase Buck-ley. You might draft something like this:

> Buckley finds two opposing sides in the AIDS de-
> bate: those concerned primarily with the civil lib-
> erties and the privacy of AIDS victims, and those
> concerned primarily with the safety of the public.

Our paraphrases have been somewhat shorter than the original, but this is not always the case. For example, suppose you wanted to paraphrase this statement by Sigmund Freud:

> We have found out that the distortion in dreams which hinders our understanding of them is due to the activities of a censorship, directed against the unacceptable, unconscious wish-impulses.

If you were to paraphrase this statement (the first sentence in the Tenth Lecture of his *General Introduction to Psychoanalysis*), you might come up with something like this:

> It is difficult to understand dreams because they
> contain distortions. Freud believed that these
> distortions arise from our internal censor, which
> attempts to suppress unconscious and forbidden
> desires.

Essentially, this paraphrase does little more than break up one sentence into two and somewhat rearrange the sentence structure for clarity.

Like summaries, then, *paraphrases* are useful devices, both in helping you to understand source material and in enabling you to convey the essence of this source material to your readers. When would you choose to write a summary instead of a paraphrase (or vice versa)? The answer to this question depends on your purpose in presenting your source material. As we've said, summaries are generally based on articles (or sections of articles) or books. Paraphrases are generally based on particularly difficult (or important) paragraphs or sentences. You would seldom paraphrase a long passage, or summarize a short one, unless there were particularly good reasons for doing so. (For example, a lawyer might want to paraphrase several pages of legal language so that his or her client, who is not a lawyer, could understand it.) The purpose of a summary is generally to save your reader time by presenting him or her with a brief and quickly readable version of a lengthy source. The purpose of a paraphrase is generally to clarify a short passage that might otherwise be unclear. Whether you summarize or paraphrase may also depend on the importance of your source. A particularly important source—if it is not too long—may rate a paraphrase. If it is less important, or peripheral to your central argument, you may choose to write a summary instead. And, of course, you may choose to summarize only part of your source—the part that is most relevant to the point you are making.

Summarizing and Paraphrasing

The following passage is excerpted from an article written in 1866 by Frederick Douglass, entitled "Reconstruction."* In this piece the famed advocate for African-American rights appeals to the Second Session of the Thirty-ninth United States Congress, as it considered issues of state and federal rights in the aftermath of the U.S. Civil War. Read this passage and write both a summary and a paraphrase.

> Fortunately, the Constitution of the United States knows no distinction between citizens on account of color. Neither does it know any difference between a citizen of a State and a citizen of the United States. Citizenship evidently includes all the rights of citizens, whether State or national. If the Constitution knows none, it is clearly no part of the duty of a Republican Congress now to institute one. The mistake of the last session was the attempt to do this very thing, by a renunciation of its power to secure political rights to any class of citizens, with the obvious purpose to allow the rebellious States to disfranchise, if they should see fit, their colored citizens. This unfortunate blunder must now be retrieved, and the emasculated citizenship given to the negro supplanted by that contemplated in the Constitution of the United States, which declares that the citizens of each State shall enjoy all the rights and immunities of citizens of the several States,— so that a legal voter in any State shall be a legal voter in all the States.

QUOTATIONS

A *quotation* records the exact language used by someone in speech or in writing. A *summary*, in contrast, is a brief restatement in your own words of what someone else has said or written. And a *paraphrase* also is a restatement, although one that is often as long as the original source. Any paper in which you draw upon sources will rely heavily on quotation, summary, and paraphrase. How do you choose among the three?

Remember that the papers you write should be your own—for the most part: your own language and certainly your own thesis, your own inferences, and your own conclusion. It follows that references to your source materials should be written primarily as summaries and paraphrases, both of which are built on restatement, not quotation. You will use summaries when you need a *brief* restatement, and paraphrases, which provide more explicit detail than summaries, when you need to follow the development of a source closely. When you quote too much, you risk losing ownership of your work: more easily than you might think, your voice can be drowned out by the voices of those you've quoted. So *use quotation sparingly,* as you would a pungent spice.

---

* Frederick Douglass, "Reconstruction," <u>The Atlantic Monthly</u>, 18. 1866: 761–765.

Nevertheless, *quoting just the right source at the right time can significantly improve your papers.* The trick is to know when and how to use quotations.

Choosing Quotations

You'll find that using quotations can be particularly helpful in several situations.

WHEN TO QUOTE

- Use quotations when another writer's language is particularly memorable and will add interest and liveliness to your paper.
- Use quotations when another writer's language is so clear and economical that to make the same point in your own words would, by comparison, be ineffective.
- Use quotations when you want the solid reputation of a source to lend authority and credibility to your own writing.

QUOTING MEMORABLE LANGUAGE

Assume you're writing a paper on Napoleon Bonaparte's relationship with the celebrated Josephine. Through research you learn that two days after their marriage, Napoleon, given command of an army, left his bride for what was to be a brilliant military campaign in Italy. How did the young general respond to leaving his wife so soon after their wedding? You come across the following, written by Napoleon from the field of battle on April 3, 1796:

> I have received all your letters, but none has such an impact on me as the last. Do you have any idea, darling, what you are doing, writing to me in those terms? Do you not think my situation cruel enough without intensifying my longing for you, overwhelming my soul? What a style! What emotions you evoke! Written in fire, they burn my poor heart!*

A summary of this passage might read as follows:

> On April 3, 1796, Napoleon wrote to Josephine, expressing how sorely he missed her and how passionately he responded to her letters.

You might write the following as a paraphrase of the passage:

> On April 3, 1796, Napoleon wrote to Josephine that he had received her letters and that one among all

---

* Francis Mossiker, <u>Napoleon and Josephine</u>, trans. (New York: Simon and Schuster, 1964): 437.

> others had had a special impact, overwhelming his
> soul with fiery emotions and longing.

How feeble this summary and paraphrase are when compared with the original! Use the vivid language that your sources give you. In this case, quote Napoleon in your paper to make your subject come alive with memorable detail:

> On April 3, 1796, a passionate, lovesick Napoleon
> responded to a letter from Josephine; she had
> written longingly to her husband, who, on a mili-
> tary campaign, acutely felt her absence. "Do you
> have any idea, darling, what you are doing, writ-
> ing to me in those terms? [. . .] What emotions
> you evoke!" he said of her letters. "Written in
> fire, they burn my poor heart!"

Quotations can be direct or indirect. A *direct* quotation is one in which you record precisely the language of another, as we did with the sentences from Napoleon's letter. An *indirect* quotation is one in which you report what someone has said, although you are not obligated to repeat the words exactly as spoken (or written):

> **Direct quotation:** Franklin D. Roosevelt said: "The only thing we have to fear is fear itself."

> **Indirect quotation:** Franklin D. Roosevelt said that we have nothing to fear but fear itself.

The language in a direct quotation, which is indicated by a pair of quotation marks (" "), must be faithful to the language of the original passage. When using an indirect quotation, you have the liberty of changing words (although not changing meaning). For both direct and indirect quotations, *you must credit your sources,* naming them either in (or close to) the sentence that includes the quotation or in a parenthetical citation (Note: We haven't included parenthetical citations in our examples here; see Chapter 7, pages 302–325 for specific rules on citing sources properly).

QUOTING CLEAR AND CONCISE LANGUAGE

You should quote a source when its language is particularly clear and economical—when your language, by contrast, would be wordy. Read this passage from a text by Patricia Curtis on biology:

> The honeybee colony, which usually has a population of 30,000 to 40,000 workers, differs from that of the bumblebee and many other social bees or wasps in that it survives the winter. This means that the bees must stay warm despite the cold. Like other bees, the isolated honeybee cannot fly if the temperature falls below 10°C (50°F) and

cannot walk if the temperature is below 7°C (45°F). Within the wintering hive, bees maintain their temperature by clustering together in a dense ball; the lower the temperature, the denser the cluster. The clustered bees produce heat by constant muscular movements of their wings, legs, and abdomens. In very cold weather, the bees on the outside of the cluster keep moving toward the center, while those in the core of the cluster move to the colder outside periphery. The entire cluster moves slowly about on the combs, eating the stored honey from the combs as it moves.*

A summary of this paragraph might read as follows:

```
Honeybees, unlike many other varieties of bee, are
able to live through the winter by "clustering to-
gether in a dense ball" for body warmth.
```

A paraphrase of the same passage would be considerably more detailed:

```
Honeybees, unlike many other varieties of bee
(such as bumblebees), are able to live through the
winter. The 30,000 to 40,000 bees within a honey-
bee hive could not, individually, move about in
cold winter temperatures. But when "clustering to-
gether in a dense ball," the bees generate heat by
constantly moving their body parts. The cluster
also moves slowly about the hive, eating honey
stored in the combs. This nutrition, in addition
to the heat generated by the cluster, enables the
honeybee to survive the cold winter months.
```

In both the summary and the paraphrase we've quoted Curtis's "clustering together in a dense ball," a phrase that lies at the heart of her description of wintering honeybees. For us to describe this clustering in any language other than Curtis's would be pointless since her description is admirably brief and precise.

QUOTING AUTHORITATIVE LANGUAGE

You will also want to use quotations that lend authority to your work. When quoting an expert or some prominent political, artistic, or historical figure, you elevate your own work by placing it in esteemed company. Quote respected figures to establish background information in a paper, and your readers will tend to perceive that information as reliable. Quote the opinions of respected figures to endorse some statement that you've made, and your statement becomes more credible to your readers. For example, in an essay on the importance of reading well, you could make use of a passage from Thoreau's *Walden:*

---

* Patricia Curtis, "Winter Organization," <u>Biology</u>, 2nd ed. (New York: Worth, 1976): 822–823.

> Reading well is hard work and requires great skill
> and training. It "is a noble exercise," writes
> Henry David Thoreau in *Walden,* "and one that will
> task the reader more than any exercise which the
> customs of the day esteem. It requires a training
> such as the athletes underwent [. . .]. Books must
> be read as deliberately and reservedly as they
> were written."

By quoting a famous philosopher and essayist on the subject of reading, you add legitimacy to your discussion. Not only do *you* regard reading to be a skill that is both difficult and important, so too does Henry David Thoreau, one of our most influential thinkers. The quotation has elevated the level of your work.

You can also quote to advantage well-respected figures who have written or spoken about the subject of your paper. Here is a discussion of space flight. Author David Chandler refers to a physicist and a physicist-astronaut:

> A few scientists—notably James Van Allen, discoverer of the Earth's ra-
> diation belts—have decried the expense of the manned space program
> and called for an almost exclusive concentration on unmanned scien-
> tific exploration instead, saying this would be far more cost-effective.
>   Other space scientists dispute that idea. Joseph Allen, physicist
> and former shuttle astronaut, says, "It seems to be argued that one
> takes away from the other. But before there was a manned space pro-
> gram, the funding on space science was zero. Now it's about $500
> million a year."

Note that in the first paragraph Chandler has either summarized or used an indirect quotation to incorporate remarks made by James Van Allen into the discussion on space flight. In the second paragraph, Chandler directly quotes his next source, Joseph Allen. Both quotations, indirect and direct, lend authority and legitimacy to the article, for both James Van Allen and Joseph Allen are experts on the subject of space flight. Note also that Chandler provides brief but effective biographies of his sources, identifying both so that their qualifications to speak on the subject are known to all:

> James Van Allen, *discoverer of the Earth's radiation belts . . .*
>
> Joseph Allen, *physicist and former shuttle astronaut . . .*

The phrases in italics are called *appositives.* Their function is to rename the nouns they follow by providing explicit, identifying detail. Any information about a person that can be expressed in the following sentence pattern can be made into an appositive phrase:

> James Van Allen is the *discoverer of the Earth's radiation belts.*
>
> He has decried the expense of the manned space program.

James Van Allen, *discoverer of the Earth's radiation belts,* has decried the
expense of the manned space program.

Use appositives to identify authors whom you quote.

Incorporating Quotations into Your Sentences

QUOTING ONLY THE PART OF A SENTENCE OR PARAGRAPH THAT YOU NEED

We've said that a writer selects passages for quotation that are especially
vivid and memorable, concise, or *authoritative.* Now put these principles into
practice. Suppose that while conducting research on college sports, you've
come across the following, written by Robert Hutchins, former president of
the University of Chicago:

> If athleticism is bad for students, players, alumni, and the public, it is
> even worse for the colleges and universities themselves. They want to
> be educational institutions, but they can't. The story of the famous
> halfback whose only regret, when he bade his coach farewell, was
> that he hadn't learned to read and write is probably exaggerated. But
> we must admit that pressure from trustees, graduates, "friends,"
> presidents, and even professors has tended to relax academic stan-
> dards. These gentry often overlook the fact that a college should not
> be interested in a fullback who is a half-wit. Recruiting, subsidizing
> and the double educational standard cannot exist without the knowl-
> edge and the tacit approval, at least, of the colleges and universities
> themselves. Certain institutions encourage susceptible professors to
> be nice to athletes now admitted by paying them for serving as "fac-
> ulty representatives" on the college athletic board.*

Suppose that in this entire paragraph you find a gem, a sentence with
quotable words that will enliven your discussion. You may want to quote
part of the following sentence:

> These gentry often overlook the fact that a college should not be in-
> terested in a fullback who is a half-wit.

INCORPORATING THE QUOTATION INTO THE FLOW OF YOUR OWN SENTENCE

Once you've selected the passage you want to quote, work the material into
your paper in as natural and fluid a manner as possible. Here's how we
would quote Hutchins:

> ```
> Robert Hutchins, former president of the Univer-
> sity of Chicago, asserts that "a college should not
> be interested in a fullback who is a half-wit."
> ```

---

* Robert Hutchins, "Gate Receipts and Glory," <u>The Saturday Evening Post</u> 3 Dec. 1983: 38.

Note that we've used an appositive to identify Hutchins. And we've used only the part of the paragraph—a single clause—that we thought memorable enough to quote directly.

AVOIDING FREESTANDING QUOTATIONS

A quoted sentence should never stand by itself—as in the following example:

> ```
> Various people associated with the university ad-
> mit that the pressures of athleticism have caused
> a relaxation of standards. "These gentry often
> overlook the fact that a college should not be in-
> terested in a fullback who is a half-wit." But
> this kind of thinking is bad for the university
> and even worse for the athletes.
> ```

Even if it includes a parenthetical citation, a freestanding quotation would have the problem of being jarring to the reader. Introduce the quotation with a "signal phrase" that attributes the source not in a parenthetical citation, but in some other part of the sentence—beginning, middle, or end. Thus, you could write:

> ```
> As Robert Hutchins notes, "These gentry often
> overlook the fact that a college should not be in-
> terested in a fullback who is a half-wit."
> ```

Here's a variation with the signal phrase in the middle:

> ```
> "These gentry," asserts Robert Hutchins, "often
> overlook the fact that a college should not be in-
> terested in a fullback who is a half-wit."
> ```

Another alternative is to introduce a sentence-long quotation with a colon:

> ```
> But Robert Hutchins disagrees: "These gentry often
> overlook the fact that a college should not be in-
> terested in a fullback who is a half-wit."
> ```

Use colons also to introduce indented quotations (as in the cases when we introduce long quotations in this chapter).

When attributing sources in signal phrases, try to vary the standard "states," "writes," "says," and so on. Other, stronger verbs you might consider: "asserts," "argues," "maintains," "insists," "asks," and even "wonders."

Incorporating Quotations

Go back to Tristan Miller's essay "Why I Will Never Have a Girlfriend," pages 23–26, and find some sentences that you think make interesting points. Imagine you want to use these points in an essay you're writing on contemporary attitudes toward dating. Write five different sentences that use a variety of the techniques discussed thus far to incorporate whole sentences as well as phrases from Miller's essay.

USING ELLIPSIS MARKS

Using quotations becomes somewhat complicated when you want to quote the beginning and end of a passage but not its middle—as was the case when we quoted Henry David Thoreau. Here's part of the paragraph in *Walden* from which we quoted a few sentences:

> To read well, that is to read true books in a true spirit, is a noble exercise, and one that will task the reader more than any exercise which the customs of the day esteem. It requires a training such as the athletes underwent, the steady intention almost of the whole life to this object. Books must be read as deliberately and reservedly as they were written.*

And here was how we used this material:

> ```
> Reading well is hard work, writes Henry David
> Thoreau in Walden, "that will task the reader more
> than any exercise which the customs of the day es-
> teem. [ . . . ] Books must be read as deliberately
> and reservedly as they were written."
> ```

Whenever you quote a sentence but delete words from it, as we have done, indicate this deletion to the reader by bracketing three spaced periods—called an "ellipsis mark"—in the sentence at the point of deletion. The rationale for using an ellipsis mark is that a direct quotation must be reproduced *exactly* as it was written or spoken. When writers delete or change any part of the quoted material, readers must be alerted so they don't think the changes were part of the original. Brackets around the ellipsis mark indicate that the ellipsis was added by the person quoting, and was not contained in the original source. When deleting an entire sentence or sentences from a quoted paragraph, as in the example above, end the sentence you have quoted with a period, place the bracketed ellipsis, and continue the quotation.

---

* Henry David Thoreau, <u>Walden</u> (New York: Signet Classic, 1960): 72.

If you are deleting the middle of a single sentence, use a bracketed ellipsis in place of the deleted words:

> ```
> "To read well [ . . . ] is a noble exercise, and
> one that will task the reader more than any exer-
> cise which the customs of the day esteem."
> ```

If you are deleting material from the end of a quoted sentence, add a period following the bracketed ellipsis:

> ```
> "It requires a training such as the athletes un-
> derwent [ . . . ]. Books must be read as deliber-
> ately and reservedly as they were written."
> ```

If you begin your quotation of an author in the middle of his or her sentence, you need not indicate deleted words with an ellipsis. Be sure, however, that the syntax of the quotation fits smoothly with the syntax of your sentence:

> ```
> Reading "is a noble exercise," writes Henry David
> Thoreau.
> ```

USING BRACKETS TO ADD OR SUBSTITUTE WORDS

In addition to using square brackets around ellipsis marks when you need to show that you've removed material, you also should use brackets whenever you need to add or substitute words in a quoted sentence. The brackets indicate to the reader a word or phrase that does not appear in the original passage but that you have inserted to avoid confusion. For example, when a pronoun's antecedent would be unclear to readers, delete the pronoun from the sentences and substitute an identifying word or phrase in brackets. When you make such a substitution, no ellipsis marks are needed. Assume that you wish to quote the underlined sentence in the following passage by Jane Yolen:

> Golden Press's *Walt Disney's Cinderella* set the new pattern for America's Cinderella. This book's text is coy and condescending. (Sample: "And her best friends of all were—guess who—the mice!") The illustrations are poor cartoons. And Cinderella herself is a disaster. She cowers as her sisters rip her homemade ball gown to shreds. (Not even homemade by Cinderella, but by the mice and birds.) She answers her stepmother with whines and pleadings. <u>She is a sorry excuse for a heroine, pitiable and useless.</u> She cannot perform even a simple action to save herself, though she is warned by her friends, the mice. She does not hear them because she is "off in a world of dreams." Cinderella begs, she whimpers, and at last has to be rescued by—guess who—the mice!*

---

* Jane Yolen, "America's 'Cinderella,'" <u>Children's Literature in Education</u> 8 (1977): 22.

In quoting these sentences, you would need to identify to whom the pronoun *she* refers. You can do this inside the quotation by using brackets:

```
Jane Yolen believes that "[Cinderella] is a sorry
excuse for a heroine, pitiable and useless."
```

If the pronoun begins the sentence to be quoted, as it does in this example, you can identify the pronoun outside of the quotation and simply begin quoting your sentence one word later:

```
Jane Yolen believes that Cinderella "is a sorry
excuse for a heroine, pitiable and useless."
```

Here's another example of a case where the pronoun needing identification occurs in the middle of the sentence to be quoted. Newspaper reporters must use brackets in these cases frequently when quoting sources, who in interviews might say something like the following:

> After the fire they did not return to the station house for three hours.

If the reporter wants to use this sentence in an article, he or she needs to identify the pronoun:

> An official from City Hall, speaking on the condition that he not be identified, said, "After the fire [the officers] did not return to the station house for three hours."

You also will need to add bracketed information to a quoted sentence when a reference essential to the sentence's meaning is implied but not stated directly. Read the following paragraphs from physicist Robert Jastrow's "Toward an Intelligence Beyond Man's":

> These are amiable qualities for the computer; it imitates life like an electronic monkey. As computers get more complex, the imitation gets better. Finally, the line between the original and the copy becomes blurred. In another 15 years or so—two more generations of computer evolution, in the jargon of the technologists—we will see the computer as an emergent form of life.
>
> The proposition seems ridiculous because, for one thing, computers lack the drives and emotions of living creatures. But when drives are useful, they can be programmed into the computer's brain, just as nature programmed them into our ancestors' brains as a part of the equipment for survival. For example, computers, like people, work better and learn faster when they are motivated. Arthur Samuel made this discovery when he taught two IBM computers how to play checkers. They polished their game by playing each other, but they learned slowly. Finally, Dr. Samuel programmed in the will to win by

forcing the computers to try harder—and to think out more moves in advance—when they were losing. Then the computers learned very quickly. One of them beat Samuel and went on to defeat a champion player who had not lost a game to a human opponent in eight years.*

If you wanted to quote only the underlined sentence, you would need to provide readers with a bracketed explanation; otherwise, the words "the proposition" would be unclear. Here is how you would manage the quotation:

> According to Robert Jastrow, a physicist and former official at NASA's Goddard Institute, "The proposition [that computers will emerge as a form of life] seems ridiculous because, for one thing, computers lack the drives and emotions of living creatures."

EXERCISE 1.5

Using Brackets

Write your own sentences incorporating the following quotations. Use brackets to clarify information that isn't clear outside of its original context—and refer to the original sources to remind yourself of this context.

From the Robert Jastrow piece on computers and intelligence:
(a) Arthur Samuel made *this discovery* when he taught two IBM computers how to play checkers.
(b) *They* polished their game by playing each other, but *they* learned slowly.

From the Jane Yolen excerpt on Cinderella:
(c) *This book's* text is coy and condescending
(d) *She* cannot perform even a simple action to save herself, though she is warned by her friends, the mice.
(e) She does not hear *them* because she is "off in a world of dreams."

Remember that when you quote the work of another, you are obligated to credit—or cite—the author's work properly; otherwise, you may be guilty of plagiarism. See pages 302–325 for guidance on citing sources.

Writing Assignment: Summary

Read "Body Body Double: Cloning Infants a Distant Fantasy" by Alexander M. Capron. Write a summary of the article, following the directions in this chapter for dividing the article into sections, for writing a one-sentence summary of each section, and then for joining section summaries with a thesis. Prepare for the summary by making notes in the margins. Your finished product should be the result of two or more drafts.

---

* Robert Jastrow, "Toward an Intelligence Beyond Man's," <u>Time</u> 20 Feb. 1978: 35.

WHEN TO SUMMARIZE, PARAPHRASE, AND QUOTE

Summarize:
- To present main points of a lengthy passage (article or book)
- To condense peripheral points necessary to discussion

Paraphrase:
- To clarify a short passage
- To emphasize main points

Quote:
- To capture another writer's particularly memorable language
- To capture another writer's clearly and economically stated language
- To lend authority and credibility to your own writing

Body Body Double:
Cloning Infants a Distant Fantasy
Alexander M. Capron

An attorney and professor of Law and Medicine at the University of Southern California, Alexander M. Capron codirects the USC Pacific Center for Health Policy and Ethics and has written numerous articles and books on law, ethics, and medicine. This article originally appeared in the "Focus" section of The Boston Sunday Globe, *January 11, 1998.*

San Francisco—Barely 10 months after researchers at Scotland's Roslin Institute amazed the world by cloning a sheep, Chicago physicist Richard Seed created a stir when he announced he was establishing the Human Clone Clinic and would use the Roslin technique to make human babies.

Are last week's headlines just one more instance of the breathtaking speed with which science can advance? Not at all.

Seed had no scientific breakthrough to announce. He doesn't have the credibility that might come from having run a fertility center. That, at least, would provide him with state-of-the-art experience in using the techniques of embryo cultivation and transplantation necessary for any realistic attempt at human cloning.

Maybe the attention Seed has managed to generate will help him raise the $2 million he claims he needs, but his planned clinic has more in common with Barnum & Bailey's Circus than with Brigham and Women's Hospital. Indeed, the only result he has produced so far is to spark a call from President Clinton yesterday to ban human cloning experiments.

Last February, the announcement that scientists had cloned Dolly the sheep was met with a nearly unanimous chorus of concern. The prospect that the techniques used to produce the first copy of an adult mammal could be used to create human genetic replicas struck scientists and politicians alike as dangerous.

Concerned about the "serious ethical questions" presented by the "possible use of the technology to clone human embryos," Clinton at the time asked the National Bioethics Advisory Commission to report within 90 days on how the government should respond. He quickly banned the use of federal money for cloning.

At subsequent congressional hearings, medical scientists took a skeptical view of the prospect of using the Roslin technique to create humans. Harold Varmus, director of the National Institutes of Health, labeled human cloning "repugnant." Ian Wilmut, the creator of Dolly, told senators that cloning people would be "quite inhuman."

Some of the concerns first expressed turned out to be overblown or wrongheaded. For example, two people having the same genetic makeup hardly negates the basic dignity of each individual, as the birth of identical twins makes clear. Furthermore, just as twins differ in many ways as they grow and develop, a genetic clone would exist in a different environment and have different experiences from his or her progenitor.

Anyone who made a clone of Michael Jordan expecting to get a great basketball player 20 years later would likely be disappointed, and Mozart's clone wouldn't be a brilliant composer simply because of his genes.

But the advisory commission concluded that other concerns about human cloning deserved to be taken very seriously. First, the process of creating Dolly made it clear that the technique used is much too risky to use with humans at this time. Roslin scientists tried 276 times to clone a sheep before they succeeded with Dolly. Many tries did not result in viable embryos or did not produce successful pregnancies once transferred to surrogate mothers. And, before Dolly, all the lambs that went to term had such severe problems that they were stillborn or died shortly after birth. This is not a circumstance in which any responsible person would consider moving the technique to human use.

Nor has anything occurred over the past year to alter that conclusion.

Safety concerns were the first reason the advisory commission concluded that it would be unethical to proceed with cloning a human at this time. The second reason was that the potential psychological harm to children and the adverse moral and cultural effects of cloning merit further reflection and deliberation.

Many reasons have been advanced for why people might want to have a cloned child: To replace a child who dies young. To provide a genetic copy who could donate a kidney, bone marrow, or other life-saving organ. To allow infertile couples to have a child who is genetically connected to at least one of them, or to allow a person without a mate of the opposite sex to have a child. To give a child a "good start in life" by using genes from people regarded as particularly outstanding according to such criteria as intelligence, artistic creativity, or athletic prowess.

Some of the ideas are mere fantasy, especially when they reflect a strong streak of genetic determinism, the notion that genes control the people we become. The fact that they are fantasy does not mean that they won't be acted on. The chance to have a cloned child may tempt parents to seek excessive control over their children's characteristics and to value them for how well they meet such overly detailed parental expectations.

Moreover, if cloning were used, arguments would soon be heard that it was actually a superior way to produce children since it would aim to avoid the disappointments that now result from the "genetic lottery" inherent in sexual reproduction. Responsible parenthood in the 21st century might come to include using "ideal types" as the bases for our children, and perhaps even doing some "genetic enhancement" of the clones to provide what would now be regarded as superhuman capabilities. Whether such developments arose voluntarily, as a result of social pressure, or through eventual legislation, they would amount to a form of eugenics more chilling than those contemplated by the Nazis, more akin to Aldous Huxley's *Brave New World*.

These are serious worries, though whether they are compelling enough to justify permanently forbidding cloning needs further debate. If some reasons for using cloning were accepted, could the procedure be limited to those uses? Designing a system of regulation that is ethically defensible and practically enforceable would not be easy, but it might be necessary if we concluded that the proper balance between ethical risks and personal liberties meant that society must allow human cloning under some circumstances.

Thus, the advisory commission concluded that while safety concerns are being addressed, deliberations should go forward to allow an informed public consensus to develop.

Meanwhile, the president has urged Congress to enact an immediate federal ban on human cloning experiments. While Seed is likely to remain a sideshow in the ultimate development of this technology, his announcement ought to prompt Congress to take action now.

2

Critical Reading and Critique

CRITICAL READING

When writing papers in college, you are often called on to respond critically to source materials. Critical reading requires the abilities to both summarize and evaluate a presentation. As you have seen in Chapter 1, a *summary* is a brief restatement in your own words of the content of a passage. An *evaluation*, however, is a more difficult matter.

In your college work, you read to gain and *use* new information; but as sources are not equally valid or equally useful, you must learn to distinguish critically among sources by evaluating them.

There is no ready-made formula for determining validity. Critical reading and its written analogue—the *critique*—require discernment, sensitivity, imagination, knowledge of the subject, and, above all, willingness to become involved in what you read. These skills cannot be taken for granted and are developed only through repeated practice. You must begin somewhere, though, and we recommend that you start by posing two broad categories of questions about passages, articles, and books that you read: (1) What is the author's purpose in writing? Does he or she succeed in this purpose? (2) To what extent do you agree with the author?

Question Category 1: What Is the Author's Purpose in Writing? Does He or She Succeed in This Purpose?

All critical reading *begins with an accurate summary.* Before attempting an evaluation, you must be able to locate an author's thesis and identify the selection's content and structure. You must understand the author's *purpose.* Authors write to inform, to

---

WHERE DO WE FIND WRITTEN CRITIQUES?

Here are just a few of the different types of writing that involve critique:

Academic Writing

- **Synthesis, Analysis, and Research papers.** Critique sources in order to establish their usefulness.
- **Literature reviews.** Critique some of the sources being reviewed.
- **Book reviews.** Combine summary with critique.
- **Essay exams.** Demonstrate understanding of course material by critiquing it.

Workplace Writing

- **Legal briefs and legal arguments.** Critique previous rulings or arguments made by opposing counsel.
- **Business plans and proposals.** Critique other, less cost-effective approaches.
- **Policy briefs.** Communicate failings of policies and legislation through critique.

---

persuade, and to entertain. A given piece may be primarily *informative* (a summary of the research on cloning), primarily *persuasive* (an argument on why the government must do something to alleviate homelessness), or primarily *entertaining* (a play about the frustrations of young lovers). Or it may be all three (as in John Steinbeck's novel *The Grapes of Wrath*, about migrant workers during the Great Depression). Sometimes, authors are not fully conscious of their purpose. Sometimes their purpose changes as they write. Also, more than one purpose can overlap—an essay may need to inform the reader about an issue in order to make a persuasive point. But if the finished piece is coherent, it will have a primary reason for having been written, and it should be apparent that the author is attempting primarily to inform, persuade, or entertain a particular audience. To identify this primary reason, this purpose, is your first job as a critical reader. Your next job is to determine how successful the author has been. As a critical reader, you bring different criteria, or standards of judgment, to bear when you read pieces intended to inform, persuade, or entertain.

Writing to Inform

A piece intended to inform will provide definitions, describe or report on a process, recount a story, give historical background, and/or provide facts and figures. An informational piece responds to questions such as the following:

What (or who) is _____ ?

How does _____ work?

What is the controversy or problem about?

What happened?

How and why did it happen?

What were the results?

What are the arguments for and against _____ ?

To the extent that an author answers these and related questions and the answers are a matter of verifiable record (you could check for accuracy if you had the time and inclination), the selection is intended to inform. Having determined this, you can organize your response by considering three other criteria: accuracy, significance, and fair interpretation of information.

Evaluating Informative Writing

Accuracy of Information If you are going to use any of the information presented, you must be satisfied that it is trustworthy. One of your responsibilities as a critical reader is to find out if it is accurate. This means you should check facts against other sources—sources you can locate by searching key terms in library databases, and by performing searches for related material on the Web. Since material on the Web is essentially "self-published," however, you must be especially vigilant in assessing the legitimacy of sources you find there. Government publications of data are often a good resource for verifying facts about political legislation, population data, crime statistics, and the like. In Chapter 7, on research, we provide a more detailed discussion of how you should approach Web sources; there is a wealth of useful information now available on the Internet—but there is also a tremendous amount of misinformation, distorted "facts," and unsupported opinion out there as well.

Significance of Information One useful question that you can put to a reading is "So what?" In the case of selections that attempt to inform, you may reasonably wonder whether the information makes a difference. What can the person who is reading gain from this information? How is knowledge advanced by the publication of this material? Is the information of importance to you or to others in a particular audience? Why or why not?

Fair Interpretation of Information At times you will read reports, the sole function of which is to relate raw data or information. In these cases, you will build your response on the two questions in category 1: What is the author's purpose in writing? Does she or he succeed in this purpose? More frequently, once an author has presented information, she or he will attempt to evaluate or interpret it—which is only reasonable, since information that has not been evaluated or interpreted is of little use. One of your tasks as a critical reader is to make a distinction between the author's presentation of facts and figures and his or her attempts to evaluate them. Watch for shifts from straightforward descriptions of factual information to assertions about what this information means, what its implications are, and so on. Pay attention to whether the logic with which the author connects interpretation with facts is sound. You may find that the information is valuable but the interpretation is not. Perhaps the author's conclusions are not justified. Could you offer a contrary explanation for the same facts? Does more information need to be gathered before firm conclusions can be drawn? Why?

Writing to Persuade

Writing is frequently intended to persuade—that is, to influence the reader's thinking. To make a persuasive case, the writer must begin with an assertion that is arguable, some statement about which reasonable people could disagree. Such an assertion, when it serves as the essential organizing principle of the article or book, is called a *thesis*. Here are two examples:

> Because they do not speak English, many children in this affluent land are being denied their fundamental right to equal educational opportunity.

> Bilingual education, which has been stridently promoted by a small group of activists with their own agenda, is detrimental to the very students it is supposed to serve.

Thesis statements such as these—and the subsequent assertions used to help support them—represent conclusions that authors have drawn as a result of researching and thinking about an issue. You go through the same process yourself when you write persuasive papers or critiques. And just as you are entitled to critically evaluate the assertions of authors you read, so your professors—and other students—are entitled to evaluate *your* assertions, whether they be encountered as written arguments or as comments made in class discussion.

Keep in mind that writers organize arguments by arranging evidence to support one conclusion and oppose (or dismiss) another. You can assess the validity of the argument and the conclusion by determining whether the author has (1) clearly defined key terms, (2) used information fairly, (3) argued logically and not fallaciously.

EXERCISE **2.1**

Informative and Persuasive Thesis Statements

With a partner from your class, write one informative and one persuasive thesis statement for three of the following topics. For example, for the topic of prayer in schools, your informative thesis statement could read this way:

> Both advocates and opponents of school prayer frame their position as a matter of freedom.

Your persuasive thesis statement might be worded as follows:

> As long as schools don't dictate what kinds of prayers students should say, then school prayer should be allowed and even encouraged.

See what thesis statements you can come up with for the following issues (and don't worry about taking a position that you agree with or feel you could support—the exercise doesn't require that you write an essay at this point!)

Gun control; sex education in schools; grammar instruction in English class; violent lyrics in music; teaching computer skills in primary schools; curfews in college dormitories; course registration procedures.

EVALUATING PERSUASIVE WRITING

Read the argument that follows: a proposal to exempt teachers from federal income tax. We will illustrate our discussion on defining terms, using information fairly, and arguing logically by referring to J. Morton Davis's argument. The example critique that follows these illustrations will be based on this same argument.

A Simple One-Step Plan to Solve the Education Crisis: A Message to the President and the Congress
J. Morton Davis

A Wall Street investment banker and entrepreneur, Davis is Chairman of the D.H. Blair Investment Banking Corporation. He is the author of Making America Work Again *(Crown Publishers 1983) and* From Hard Knocks to Hot Stocks *(William Morrow and Company 1998). This piece was originally published by the author as a full-page ad in the* New York Times, *January 18, 1998.*

1   Great teachers.

2   Thousands and thousands of great teachers.

3   We must attract our best and brightest to the one profession upon which truly rests our nation's freedom, security and future greatness—teaching. If we can enlist the best among us to train our children, we will surely have the best-prepared and best-educated students in the world, thereby assuring America's continued leadership.

4   *By enacting legislation to exempt teachers from all federal income taxes, Congress and the President can help assure that many of the best and brightest college students will choose to dedicate their careers and lives to teaching our children.*

5   Perhaps it could go without saying that the education crisis is the most important issue we as a nation face today, affecting daily our single most important natural resource—our children. Just as we as a nation could mount all of our resources and efforts for the Manhattan Project to win World War II, and, later, harness all of our best in industry and technology to win the race to put a man on the moon, today we must, with the same urgency, apply all our collective

energies to improving the deplorable state of public education. And just as we use our tax system to advance many positive societal goals, our tax system here too offers a single, one-step opportunity to solve the current crisis in our education system. By exempting teachers from federal income taxes we will instantly put in place a mechanism sure to produce more and more great teachers.

6   First, this tax exemption would immediately and substantially increase teachers' salaries, thus incentivizing many of our top college graduates to pursue a career in teaching. In the 30's and 40's, public education produced superior academic results because, during the Depression, many of our best were attracted to teaching as it was a relatively well paying and secure job in a time when few jobs were available. Teaching would again become an economically attractive career if it carried with it an exemption from federal income taxes. The cost to the Treasury would be small, and certainly any tax money invested in teaching will return many-fold as a generation of better-educated, more productive citizens enters the work force.

7   Second, and perhaps more importantly, an exemption from federal income taxes for teachers would distinctly and dramatically recognize the gifted dedication of those who devote their careers to inspiring the minds of our children and grandchildren. Freeing teachers from ever paying federal income tax would, in one grand gesture, symbolically designate teachers as the one professional group whom we respect, cherish and value above all others. This is not to devalue the life-and-death work of police officers and fire fighters, or the terribly important life-saving efforts of doctors, nurses and other medical professionals. But none is more important to our nation's future than teaching.

8   If we are going to produce the world's best-educated future generations, we must attract the best candidates to the job of teaching those generations. Professionally dedicated teachers will not only provide a basic education in the three R's and the sciences, but can also impart to our children values and visions, dreams and opportunities.

9   No profession is more important to society and the future of our country than teaching. Teaching should never be a fall-back position or a career compromise. It is the noblest of callings, and should be recognized as such—both in dollars and in respect. If our children and our nation are to succeed in an ever-more-competitive world, let us reward and upgrade the status of teachers so that the finest young minds will be drawn to the profession. This will undoubtedly produce the best-educated, most globally-competitive generation of Americans in our history.

10   Mr. President and members of the 105th Congress, a golden opportunity awaits you—a chance to cure the abysmal state of public education and go down in history as having made the nation and the world a better place. In a single, decisive, creative stroke you can solve the education crisis. By implementing a permanent income tax exemption for teachers you will raise their financial rewards and status to a level commensurate with their contributions, you will attract the best-and-brightest of our population to this noble profession, you will create a society in which "teacher" is the most exalted title in the land.

11   And you will leave a legacy that will endure forever.

Before continuing with the chapter's reading, look back at the Critical Reading for Summary box on page 6 of Chapter 1. Use each of the guidelines listed there to critically examine the essay by Davis; make notes in the margins of this reading, or on a separate sheet of paper, as you work out such things as the essay's main point, subpoints, use of examples, and the like.

PERSUASIVE STRATEGIES

Clearly Defined Terms. The validity of an argument depends to some degree on how carefully key terms have been defined. Take the assertion, for example, that American society must be grounded in "family values." Just what do people who use this phrase mean by it? The validity of their argument depends on whether they and their readers agree on a definition of "family values"—as well as what it means to be "grounded in" family values. If an author writes that in the recent past, "America's elites accepted as a matter of course that a free society can sustain itself only through virtue and temperance in the people" (Charles Murray, "The Coming White Underclass," *Wall Street Journal*, 20 Oct. 1993), readers need to know what, exactly, the author means by "elites" and by "virtue and temperance" before they can assess the validity of the argument. In such cases, the success of the argument—its ability to persuade—hinges on the definition of a term. So, in responding to an argument, be sure you (and the author) are clear on what exactly is being argued. Only then can you respond to the logic of the argument, to the author's use of evidence, and to the author's conclusions.

Early in his argument, Davis refers to attracting "our best and brightest" to the teaching profession. He repeatedly uses the phrase, so it's fair to ask what, exactly, he means. "Best and brightest" was an expression associated with John F. Kennedy's administration, in which highly educated, exuberant people flocked to Washington with an explicit assumption that in committing themselves to public service they would do an exemplary job (because they were bright and committed). The closest Davis comes to defining "best and brightest" is "[p]rofessionally dedicated teachers," people "who devote their careers to inspiring the minds of our children and grandchildren." Davis appears to be using a Kennedy-era definition of "best and brightest." The phrase refers to academically talented, inspired and inspiring college graduates. However, this same phrase took on an ironic twist when it was used by reporter David Halberstam as the title of a book about the tragic miscalculations made by these same talented and inspired people in getting the United States involved in the war in Vietnam.

Fair Use of Information. Information is used as evidence in support of arguments. When presented with such evidence, ask yourself two questions:

The *first:* "Is the information accurate and up-to-date?" At least a portion of an argument becomes invalid if the information used to support it is inaccurate or out-of-date. The *second:* "Has the author cited *representative* information?" The evidence used in an argument must be presented in a spirit of fair play. An author is less than ethical who presents only evidence favoring his views when he is well aware that contrary evidence exists. For instance, it would be dishonest to argue that an economic recession is imminent and to cite as evidence only those indicators of economic well-being that have taken a decided turn for the worse while ignoring and failing to cite contrary (positive) evidence. Davis seems to use information fairly and accurately in his essay; however, some of the cause-and-effect conclusions he draws based on that information are suspect, as we will see.

LOGICAL ARGUMENTATION: AVOIDING LOGICAL FALLACIES

At some point, you will need to respond to the logic of the argument itself. To be convincing, an argument should be governed by principles of logic—clear and orderly thinking. This does *not* mean that an argument should not be biased. A biased argument—that is, an argument weighted toward one point of view and against others—may be valid as long as it is logically sound.

Here are several examples of faulty thinking and logical fallacies to watch for:

Emotionally Loaded Terms. Writers sometimes will attempt to sway readers by using emotionally charged words: words with positive connotations to sway readers to their own point of view (e.g., "family values"); words with negative connotations to sway readers away from the opposing point of view. The fact that an author uses emotionally loaded terms does not necessarily invalidate the argument. Emotional appeals are perfectly legitimate and time-honored modes of persuasion. But in academic writing, which is grounded in logical argumentation, they should not be the *only* means of persuasion. You should be sensitive to *how* emotionally loaded terms are being used. In particular, are they being used deceptively or to hide the essential facts?

Davis uses the word "noble" throughout the argument—as in, teaching is a "noble" profession, "the noblest of callings" (paragraph 9). Our culture is quick to attach "nobility" to professions such as teaching that serve a necessary function but pay relatively low wages, as if the word itself could compensate teachers for lower salaries. Since American voters are unwilling to pay teachers more money but at the same time are eager to laud teachers as "noble," the word "nobility" has taken on a somewhat patronizing, disingenuous air among teachers. Some teachers comment: "Sure we're flattered to be called noble. But raise our pay if you really care!" Davis does seem to be an outsider (that is, not a teacher) using the word "nobility" to heap familiar praise on teachers. He isn't being patronizing with his use of the term, however, since he's arguing for boosting teacher salaries and prestige. So teachers might well think him sincere.

TONE

Related to "emotionally loaded terms" is "tone." When we speak of the tone of a piece of writing, we refer to the overall emotional effect produced by the writer's choice of language.

- Were a film reviewer to repeatedly use such terms as "wonderful," "adorable," "magnificent performance," when discussing a film and its actors, we might call the tone "gushing."
- If a columnist, in referring to a politician's tax proposal, used such language as "obscene," "the lackeys of big business fat cats," and "sleazeball techniques," we would call the tone "angry."
- If another writer were to use language like "That's a great idea. Let's all give three cheers," when he meant just the opposite, we would call the tone "sarcastic."

These are examples of extreme kinds of tone; but tone can be more muted, particularly if the writer makes a special effort *not* to inject emotion into the writing. Almost any adjective describing human emotion can be attached to "tone" to describe the mood that is conveyed by the writer and the writing: playful, objective, brutal, dispassionate, sly, apologetic, rueful, cynical, hopeful, gleeful.

As we've indicated above in "Emotionally Loaded Terms," the fact that a writer's tone is highly emotional does not necessarily mean that the writer's argument is invalid. Conversely, a neutral tone does not ensure an argument's validity. One who argues passionately is not necessarily wrong, any more than one who comes across as objective and measured is necessarily right. In either case, we have to examine the validity of the argument on its own merits. We should recognize that we may have been manipulated into agreeing or disagreeing largely through an author's tone, rather than through her or his arguments.

Keep in mind, also, that many college instructors are likely to be put off by student writing that projects a highly emotional tone, a quality they will often consider more appropriate for the op-ed page of the student newspaper than for academic or pre-professional work. (One giveaway indicator of inappropriate emotion is the exclamation mark, which should be used very sparingly.)

Ad Hominem Argument. In an *ad hominem* argument, the writer rejects opposing views by attacking the person who holds them. By calling opponents names, an author avoids the issue. Consider this excerpt from a political speech:

> I could more easily accept my opponent's plan to increase revenues by collecting on delinquent tax bills if he had paid more than a hundred

dollars in state taxes in each of the past three years. But the fact is, he's a millionaire with a millionaire's tax shelters. This man hasn't paid a wooden nickel for the state services he and his family depend on. So I ask you: Is *he* the one to be talking about taxes to *us*?

It could well be that the opponent has paid virtually no state taxes for three years; but this fact has nothing to do with, and is a ploy to divert attention from, the merits of a specific proposal for increasing revenues. The proposal is lost in the attack against the man himself, an attack that violates the principles of logic. Writers (and speakers) must make their points by citing evidence in support of their views and by challenging contrary evidence.

Faulty Cause and Effect. The fact that one event precedes another in time does not mean that the first event has caused the second. An example: Fish begin dying by the thousands in a lake near your hometown. An environmental group immediately cites chemical dumping by several manufacturing plants as the cause. But other causes are possible: A disease might have affected the fish; the growth of algae might have contributed to the deaths; or acid rain might be a factor. The origins of an event are usually complex and are not always traceable to a single cause. So you must carefully examine cause-and-effect reasoning when you find a writer using it. In Latin, this fallacy is known as *post hoc, ergo propter hoc* ("after this, therefore because of this").

Davis makes two assertions that reveal questionable cause-and-effect thinking. First, he claims that enlisting our "best and brightest" into teaching will result in improved education: "If we can enlist the best among us to train our children, we will surely have the best-prepared and best-educated students in the world [...] " (paragraph 3). The reader is entitled to ask: why *surely*? Where's the proof that teachers, alone, can effect so monumental a change? Davis also claims that a permanent exemption from federal taxes will result in more good teachers entering the classroom. Again, what assures this result? In both cases, Davis may be correct; but readers can legitimately expect support for such statements, and Davis offers none.

Either/Or Reasoning. Either/or reasoning also results from an unwillingness to recognize complexity. If an author analyzes a problem and offers only two courses of action, one of which he or she refutes, then you are entitled to object that the other is not thereby true. For usually, several other options (at the very least) are possible. For whatever reason, the author has chosen to overlook them. As an example, suppose you are reading a selection on genetic engineering and the author builds an argument on the basis of the following:

Research in gene splicing is at a crossroads: Either scientists will be carefully monitored by civil authorities and their efforts limited to acceptable applications, such as disease control; or, lacking regulatory guidelines, scientists will set their own ethical standards and begin programs in embryonic manipulation that, however well intended, exceed the proper limits of human knowledge.

Certainly, other possibilities for genetic engineering exist beyond the two mentioned here. But the author limits debate by establishing an either/or choice. Such limitation is artificial and does not allow for complexity. As a critical reader, be on the alert for either/or reasoning.

Hasty Generalization. Writers are guilty of hasty generalization when they draw their conclusions from too little evidence or from unrepresentative evidence. To argue that scientists should not proceed with the human genome project because a recent editorial urged that the project be abandoned is to make a hasty generalization. This lone editorial may be unrepresentative of the views of most individuals—both scientists and laypeople—who have studied and written about the matter. To argue that one should never obey authority because Stanley Milgram's Yale University experiments in the 1960's show the dangers of obedience is to ignore the fact that Milgram's experiment was concerned primarily with obedience to *immoral* authority. Thus, the experimental situation was unrepresentative of most routine demands for obedience—for example, to obey a parental rule or to comply with a summons for jury duty—and a conclusion about the malevolence of all authority would be a hasty generalization.

False Analogy. Comparing one person, event, or issue to another may be illuminating, but it may also be confusing or misleading. Differences between the two may be more significant than the similarities, and conclusions drawn from one may not necessarily apply to the other. A writer who argues that it is reasonable to quarantine people with AIDS because quarantine has been effective in preventing the spread of smallpox is assuming an analogy between AIDS and smallpox that (because of the differences between the two diseases) is not valid.

Early in his argument, Davis exhorts the president and Congress to "mount all of our resources and efforts" (paragraph 5) to enlist great teachers in the same way we marshaled our resources to put humans on the moon and to win World War II by building an atomic bomb. Davis is making an analogy: we rallied and succeeded then; we can rally and succeed now. Readers can reasonably question the extent to which the challenges we face in education are similar to the challenges faced in building a bomb or rocket. To accept the parallel, we would have to believe that solving a problem in a mathematical science is equivalent to solving a problem in the social settings of the classroom and school. Are the problems and their solutions equivalent? Readers are entitled to question the parallel.

Begging the Question. To beg the question is to assume as a proven fact the very thesis being argued. To assert, for example, that America is not in decline because it is as strong and prosperous as ever is not to prove anything: it is merely to repeat the claim in different words. This fallacy is also known as circular reasoning.

Throughout his argument, Davis assumes a point he wants readers to accept—that enlisting our "best and brightest" will result in better-educated students. This is a cause-and-effect relationship that needs proof, but Davis assumes the correctness of the position and does not argue for it. This begging the question is especially evident when Davis writes: "Teaching would again become an economically attractive career if it carried with it an exemption from federal income taxes. The cost to the Treasury would be small, and certainly any tax money invested in teaching will return many-fold as a generation of better-educated, more productive citizens enters the work force" (paragraph 6). To Davis, the end result of hiring bright teachers may be "certain," but readers are entitled to question his logic.

Non Sequitur. "Non sequitur" is Latin for "it does not follow"; the term is used to describe a conclusion that does not logically follow from a premise. "Since minorities have made such great strides in the last few decades," a writer may argue, "we no longer need affirmative action programs." Aside from the fact that the premise itself is arguable (*have* minorities made such great strides?), it does not follow that because minorities *may* have made great strides, there is no further need for affirmative action programs.

Oversimplification. Be alert for writers who offer easy solutions to complicated problems. "America's economy will be strong again if we all 'buy American,'" a politician may argue. But the problems of America's economy are complex and cannot be solved by a slogan or a simple change in buying habits. Likewise, a writer who argues that we should ban genetic engineering assumes that simple solutions ("just say 'no'") will be sufficient to deal with the complex moral dilemmas raised by this new technology.

Davis has likely never been a classroom teacher, which can be inferred both from his honorific use of the word "noble" (if teachers feel this way about themselves, they typically don't advertise it!) and from his failure to mention other possible sources of crisis in education aside from the lack of gifted teachers. Anyone with experience in public education knows, for instance, that school budgets are closely linked with successful student performance. Davis makes no mention of school budgets or of other factors such as economically depressed circumstances for students or political fights within school districts. Justifiably then, the later critique of Davis's letter objects that Davis oversimplifies the issue.

Understanding Logical Fallacies

Make a list of the nine logical fallacies discussed in the last section. Briefly define each one in your own words. Then, in a group of 3 or 4 classmates, refer to your definitions and the examples we've provided for each logical fallacy, and collaborate with your group members to find or invent examples for each of the logical fallacies (or for some of them that your instructor assigns to each group). Compare these with the other groups in your class.

Writing To Entertain

Authors write not only to inform and persuade but also to entertain. One response to entertainment is a hearty laugh, but it is possible to entertain without laughter: A good book or play or poem may prompt you to ruminate, grow wistful, become elated, get angry. Laughter is only one of many possible reactions. You read a piece (or view a work) and react with sadness, surprise, exhilaration, disbelief, horror, boredom, whatever. As with a response to an informative piece or an argument, your response to an essay, poem, story, play, novel, or film should be precisely stated and carefully developed. Ask yourself some of the following questions (you won't have space to explore all of them, but try to consider some of the most important): Did I care for the portrayal of a certain character? Did that character (or a group of characters united by occupation, age, ethnicity, etc.) seem too sentimentalized, for example, or heroic? Did his adversaries seem too villainous or stupid? Were the situations believable? Was the action interesting or merely formulaic? Was the theme developed subtly or powerfully, or did the work come across as preachy or shrill? Did the action at the end of the work follow plausibly from what had come before? Was the language fresh and incisive or stale and predictable? Explain as specifically as possible what elements of the work seemed effective or ineffective and why. Offer an overall assessment, elaborating on your views.

Question Category 2: To What Extent Do You Agree or Disagree with the Author?

When formulating a critical response to a source, try to distinguish your evaluation of the author's purpose and success at achieving that purpose from your agreement or disagreement with the author's views. The distinction allows you to respond to a piece of writing on its merits. As an unbiased, even-handed critic, you evaluate an author's clarity of presentation, use of evidence, and adherence to principles of logic. To what extent has the author succeeded in achieving his or her purpose? Still withholding judgment, offer your assessment and give the author (in effect) a grade. Significantly, your assessment of the presentation may not coincide with your views of the author's conclusions: You may agree with an author entirely but feel that the presentation is superficial; you may find the author's logic and use of evidence to be rock solid but at the same time may resist certain conclusions. A critical evaluation works well when it is conducted in two parts. After evaluating the author's purpose and design for achieving that purpose, respond to the author's main assertions. In doing so, you'll want to identify points of agreement and disagreement and also evaluate assumptions.

IDENTIFY POINTS OF AGREEMENT AND DISAGREEMENT

Be precise in identifying points of agreement and disagreement with an author. You should state as clearly as possible what *you* believe, and an effective way of doing this is to define your position in relation to that presented in the piece. Whether you agree enthusiastically, disagree, or agree with reservations, you can organize your reactions in two parts: first, summarize the author's position; second, state your own position and elaborate on your reasons for holding it. The elaboration, in effect, becomes an argument itself, and this is true regardless of the position you take. An opinion is effective when you support it by supplying evidence. Without such evidence, opinions cannot be authoritative. "I thought the article on inflation was lousy." Why? "I just thought so, that's all." This opinion is worthless because the criticism is imprecise: The critic has taken neither the time to read the article carefully nor the time to explore his own reactions carefully.

EXERCISE **2.4**

Exploring Your Viewpoints

Go to a Web site that presents short persuasive essays on current social issues, such as IntellectualCapital.com, opinion-pages.org, drudgereport.com, Speakout.com, or nonline.com/procon. Or go to an Internet search engine and type in a social issue together with the word "articles," "editorials," or "opinion," and see what you find. Once you've located an essay or Internet chat post that takes a position on the issue, write a paragraph or two articulating your agreement or disagreement with the position taken in this source. Be sure to explain why you feel the way you do and, wherever possible, cite relevant evidence—from your reading, experience, or observation. After stating your opinion, discuss what else you would need to know about the issue in order to make a convincing case for your viewpoint.

Explore the Reasons for Agreement and Disagreement: Evaluate Assumptions

One way of elaborating your reactions to a reading is to explore the underlying *reasons* for agreement and disagreement. Your reactions are based largely on assumptions that you hold and how these assumptions compare with the author's. An *assumption* is a fundamental statement about the world and its operations that you take to be true. A writer's assumptions may be explicitly stated; but just as often assumptions are implicit and you will have to "ferret them out," that is, to infer them. Consider an example:

> *In vitro* fertilization and embryo transfer are brought about outside the bodies of the couple through actions of third parties whose competence and technical activity determine the success of the procedure. Such fertilization entrusts the life and identity of the embryo into the power of doctors and biologists and establishes the domination of technology over the origin and destiny of the human person. Such a relationship of domination is in itself contrary to the dignity and equality that must be common to parents and children.*

This paragraph is quoted from the February 1987 Vatican document on artificial procreation. Cardinal Joseph Ratzinger, principal author of the document, makes an implicit assumption in this paragraph: that no good can come of the domination of technology over conception. The use of technology to bring about conception is morally wrong. Yet there are thousands of childless couples, Roman Catholics included, who reject this assumption in favor of its opposite: that conception technology is an aid to the barren couple; far from creating a relationship of unequals, the technology brings children into the world who will be welcomed with joy and love.

Assumptions provide the foundation on which entire presentations are built. If you find an author's assumptions invalid, i.e., not supported by factual evidence, or, if you disagree with value-based assumptions underlying an author's positions, you may well disagree with conclusions that follow from these assumptions. The author of a book on developing nations may include a section outlining the resources and time that will be required to industrialize a particular country and so upgrade its general welfare. Her assumption—that industrialization in that particular country will ensure or even affect the general welfare—may or may not be valid. If you do not share the assumption, in your eyes the rationale for the entire book may be undermined.

How do you determine the validity of assumptions once you have identified them? In the absence of more scientific criteria, validity may mean how well the author's assumptions stack up against your own experience, observations, reading, and values. A caution, however: The overall value of an article or book may depend only to a small degree on the validity of the author's assumptions. For instance, a sociologist may do a fine job of gathering statistical data about the incidence of crime in urban areas along the eastern seaboard. The sociologist also might be a Marxist, and you may disagree with the subsequent analysis of the data. Yet you may find the data extremely valuable for your own work.

---

*From the Vatican document <u>Instruction on Respect for Human Life in Its Origin and on the Dignity of Procreation</u>, given at Rome, from the Congregation for the Doctrine of the Faith, 22 Feb. 1987, as presented in <u>Origins: N.C. Documentary Service</u> 16.40 (19 Mar. 1987): 707.

In his open letter to the president and Congress, Davis makes several assumptions worth examining. The first is that we face a crisis in education. Davis assumes his readers agree and bases his entire proposal on this agreement. If we disagree with the assessment that America's schools are in crisis, then we're bound to reject the proposal. We may also believe America's schools face significant problems, but reject Davis's characterization of these problems as a "crisis." Davis's next assumption is implied: that the crisis in education is due, mainly, to the absence of good teachers. He never states this view directly; but we can reason that if the solution to the current crisis is to place our best and brightest into the classroom, then our current problems are due, mainly, to the absence of especially talented teachers. Davis does not offer support for this assumption, and the reader is entitled to suggest that there may be *other* reasons education is in crisis. (The critique that follows takes exactly this approach.) Davis assumes, as well, that a tax break will entice teachers—which it may. The underlying logic is that we are all motivated by personal gain. If we can boost pay to teachers, then we should be able to attract more candidates to the profession. Davis does not explain why an exemption will attract the best and brightest, as opposed to less inspired individuals looking for a stable career with decent pay. Finally, as discussed under "Begging the Question," Davis assumes the very point he wants to argue: that "If we can enlist the best among us to train our children, we will surely have the best-prepared and best-educated students in the world." Essentially, Davis asks readers to accept this conclusion on faith, for he offers no support. Readers are entitled to meet each of an author's assumptions with assumptions of their own; to evaluate the validity of those assumptions; and to begin formulating a critique, based on their agreement or disagreement.

CRITIQUE

In Chapter 1 we focused upon summary—the condensed presentation of ideas presented originally in another form. Summary is key to much of academic writing—even when we're not explicitly asked to summarize something, the reliance upon the works of others for support of claims made in the academic setting requires that we know how to summarize. It's not going too far to say that summarizing is the critical thinking skill from which a majority of academic writing builds. However, most academic thinking and writing does not stop at summary; usually we use summary to fully understand something, then we go on to do something else with it. The most direct activity following summary is critique. In critical thinking, we understand things, then we evaluate them. Critique is an essential element of critical thinking. Critique is also an important element of writing, and to address that fact, we now turn to writing critiques.

A *critique* is a *formalized, critical reading of a passage*. It also is a personal response; but writing a critique is considerably more rigorous than saying that a movie is "great," or a book is "fascinating," or "I didn't like it." These are all responses, and, as such, they're a valid, even essential, part of your understanding of what you see and read. But such responses don't help illuminate the subject for anyone—even you—if you haven't explained how you arrived at your conclusions.

Your task in writing a critique is to turn your critical reading of a passage into a systematic evaluation in order to deepen your reader's (and your own) understanding of that passage. Among other things, you're interested in determining what an author says, how well the points are made, what assumptions underlie the argument, what issues are overlooked, and what implications can be drawn from such an analysis. Critiques, positive or negative, should include a fair and accurate summary of the passage; they also should include a statement of your own assumptions. It is important to remember that you bring to bear an entire set of assumptions about the world. Stated or not, these assumptions underlie every evaluative comment you make; you therefore have an obligation, both to the reader and to yourself, to clarify your standards by making your assumptions explicit. Not only do your readers stand to gain by your forthrightness, but you do as well: In the process of writing a critical assessment, you are forced to examine your own knowledge, beliefs, and assumptions. Ultimately, the critique is a way of learning about yourself—yet another example of the ways in which writing is useful as a critical thinking tool!

How to Write Critiques

You may find it useful to organize your critiques in five sections: introduction, summary, analysis of the presentation, your response to the presentation, and conclusion.

The following box contains some guidelines for writing critiques. Note that they are guidelines, not a rigid formula. Thousands of authors write critiques that do not follow the structure outlined here. Until you are more confident and practiced in writing critiques, however, we suggest you follow these guidelines. They are meant not to restrict you, but rather to provide you with a workable method of writing critical analyses that incorporates a logical sequence of development.

DEMONSTRATION: CRITIQUE

The critique that follows is based on J. Morton Davis's open letter to the president and the 105th Congress (see pages 57–58). In this critique, you will see that it is possible to agree with an author's main point or proposal but disagree with his or her method of demonstration, or argument. Critiquing a different selection, you could just as easily accept the author's facts and figures but reject the conclusion he draws from them. As long as you carefully articulate the author's assumptions and your own, explaining in some

GUIDELINES FOR WRITING CRITIQUES

- *Introduction.* Introduce both the passage under analysis and the author. State the author's main argument and the point(s) you intend to make about it.

   Provide background material to help your readers understand the relevance or appeal of the passage. This background material might include one or more of the following: an explanation of why the subject is of current interest; a reference to a possible controversy surrounding the subject of the passage or the passage itself; biographical information about the author; an account of the circumstances under which the passage was written; or a reference to the intended audience of the passage.

- *Summary.* Summarize the author's main points, making sure to state the author's purpose for writing.

- *Analysis of the presentation.* Evaluate the validity of the author's presentation, as distinct from your points of agreement or disagreement. Comment on the author's success in achieving his or her purpose by reviewing three or four specific points. You might base your review on one (or more) of the following criteria:

   Is the information accurate?

   Is the information significant?

   Has the author defined terms clearly?

   Has the author used and interpreted information fairly?

   Has the author argued logically?

- *Your response to the presentation.* Now it is your turn to respond to the author's views. With which views do you agree? With which do you disagree? Discuss your reasons for agreement and disagreement, when possible, tying these reasons to assumptions—both the author's and your own.

- *Conclusion.* State your conclusions about the overall validity of the piece—your assessment of the author's success at achieving his or her aims and your reactions to the author's views. Remind the reader of the weaknesses and strengths of the passage.

detail your agreement and disagreement, the critique is yours to take in whatever direction you see fit.

The selections you will likely be inclined to critique are those, like Davis's, that argue a specific position. Indeed, every argument you read is an invitation to agreement or disagreement. It remains only for you to speak up and justify your position.

Model Essay:
A Critique of J. Morton Davis's Open Letter to
the President and Congress

1 On January 18, 1998, J. Morton Davis wrote an open letter in the *New York Times* to President Clinton and the 105th Congress. Titled "A Simple One-Step Plan to Solve the Education Crisis," the letter argues that teachers should be exempt from federal income taxes in order to entice our best and brightest into the profession. Few can deny what Davis, chairman of the D. H. Blair Investment Banking Corporation (and author of *Making America Work Again* and *From Hard Knocks to Hot Stocks*), calls the current "abysmal state of public education" (58). The problems in education are real, and Davis's proposal is both achievable and attractive—one that Congress could enact with relatively little political risk. So is a permanent federal income tax exemption for teachers a good idea? Davis's plan should be adopted; but, alone, it will not solve our crisis in education.

2   In his open letter, Davis argues that we must solve America's education problems if we are to assert "continued leadership" in the world (57). The best way to "cure" the problem is to "attract the best-and-brightest of our population to" teaching (58). Because teachers, like everyone else, are motivated by personal gain, we can entice prospective teachers into the profession with the incentive of a permanent exemption from federal income taxes. Aside from boosting take-home pay, an exemption also will confer on teachers special recognition and "would distinctly and dramatically recognize [their] gifted dedication" (58). With the inducements of a tax break and enhanced national respect, teachers would be more inclined to enter and remain in the profession. If we can attract and retain great teachers, writes Davis, we "can solve the education crisis" (58).

3   Teachers are paid less than are other professionals, and in our society a low salary translates into low stature. Davis's proposal to raise teachers' pay by enacting a permanent federal income tax exemption would, shrewdly, increase pay *and* prestige if teachers were the only tax-exempt professionals

in the nation. Now that the country is enjoying budget surpluses, if we can afford the exemption we should enact it. Davis correctly notes that the federal government routinely uses the tax system to promote social objectives—as in the case of high taxes that discourage cigarette use. So why not use the system to promote a social end that everyone can endorse: a continuing supply of effective teachers?

4   While Davis does not say so openly, he mistakenly suggests that our current problems exist because the best and brightest are not presently in our classrooms. They are elsewhere. "Teaching should never be a fall-back position or a career compromise," he claims (58). Is it now? Is that how we got into the mess we're in, because our classrooms are led by people who could not succeed elsewhere? In the absence of suggesting a single other cause for the current crisis in education, Davis apparently thinks so. There is no denying that poor teachers clog the system. But plenty of competent teachers exist who, while applauding Davis's proposed federal income tax exemption, would never agree that the poor teachers are the sole or even the main problem with education. Ask good teachers what ails the system and they will acknowledge deadwood colleagues, but also they will point to other problems: meager budgets, tensions within communities over how the schools should be run, and severe social and economic conditions within local school districts.

5   Bringing the best and brightest into America's classrooms cannot solve the problem of under-financed schools. State and local governments set expenditures for schools; while Davis's suggestion will help the cash flow of teachers already working, it will do nothing to increase the *number* of teachers now available. The only way to increase teachers in the system is to raise local or state taxes or to get federal support. In the first case, tax increases to local home owners are never welcome; in the second, the federal government is not likely to forego collecting taxes from teachers *and* boost education dollars to states at the same time. As long as annual budgets remain low, student-to-teacher ratios will remain high and present barriers to individualized instruction. Education suffers when there are too few teachers, a problem that Davis's tax exemption would not resolve.

6   Davis's open letter also avoids mention of structural problems within the educational community itself: bloated administrations in which levels of assistant principals and curriculum coordinators stay out of the classroom, where they could do some direct good, and instead over-manage the lives of teachers; unions that militantly guard against increasing teachers' hours and responsibilities, thereby causing students to suffer; curricula that do not change with the times or, conversely, change too easily, driven by fads more than by careful review; and elected school committees that clash with administrators over policy. At the beginning of any given school year, at least one major school system in America seems on the verge of meltdown, with problems due mainly not to lack of bright, dedicated teachers but to lack of consensus among teachers, administrators, and towns. Many of these problems are budgetary, and more money could resolve them. But other problems are related to the process of teaching itself, which is a social activity based on philosophical principles.

7   Teaching is not an exact science. And while Davis exhorts the president and Congress to mount a response to the education crisis in the same way our nation addressed the challenges of going to the moon or winning World War II (by building the atomic bomb), we could not with respect to teaching agree on a single course of action as we could (and did) with scientific and military challenges. Teaching is unlike physics and rocketry—sciences in which experts can isolate all factors that bear on a problem, predict how those factors will behave in any given circumstance, and then plan solutions accordingly. Teaching mixes contentious issues of politics, philosophy, and economics into a soup so complex that no one—not even well-meaning advocates in ideal circumstances—can agree on what, precisely, the problems are, let alone on how to solve them. Davis's hope for a national commitment to cure our schools is misinformed, because problems in education differ fundamentally from the problems to which he draws comparison.

8   Most seriously, Davis neglects the economic component of America's crisis in education. We have in this country a structural poverty that makes learning difficult for tens of thousands of students whose home environments foster neither

the pride in education nor the basic economic security needed for success in school. When America's poorest children look around their communities and see disrepair, unemployment, crime, and the availability (mostly) of unskilled jobs, these students will see little reason to excel in the classroom. The truly motivated will rise above their conditions. But that takes hard work, and too few have the support structures of a steady home to make the transition out of poverty. The problem of structural poverty therefore persists, and its impact on the education system is immense. Davis's "simple" solution of exempting teachers from federal income taxes does not acknowledge what is perhaps the most profound and intractable cause of problems in American education.

9   Would prospective teachers approve of Davis's proposal? Forget for the moment the challenges to this proposal that other public servants such as firefighters and police would make. If Davis's proposed income tax exemption passed Congress, we could expect that those contemplating a career in teaching but who were wavering because of the low salaries would say yes and would join the profession. That would be good news. But until other problems that plague education—such as meager budgets, conflicting educational agendas, inefficient school bureaucracies, and structural poverty—are resolved, proposals such as Davis's, though they are welcome and *should be* enacted, will not achieve their desired end. Davis's proposal is a step in the right direction, but it is only a step.

EXERCISE 2.5

Informal Critique of Sample Essay

Before reading the Discussion of this student essay, write your own informal response to the essay: what are its strengths and weaknesses? Does the essay follow the general guidelines for writing critiques that we outlined on page 70? Jot down some ideas for a critique that takes a different approach to Davis's essay; what points might you bring up if you were going to argue that Davis's proposal is an all around bad idea?

Discussion

- Paragraph 1 of this critique introduces the selection to be reviewed, along with the author, and sets a context for the reader. The paragraph ends with the writer's thesis: to adopt the proposed federal income tax exemption, even though that policy will not solve the educational crisis in America.

- Paragraph 2 summarizes Davis's letter. Note that the topic sentence clearly indicates that Davis has written a persuasive, rather than an informative piece.

- Paragraph 3 explains the writer's basic agreement with Davis's federal income tax exemption proposal.

- Paragraph 4 begins the critical evaluation of Davis's letter, indicating that Davis assumes the problem with our current system is the absence of good teachers. Note how the paragraph's final sentence offers readers three arguments against Davis's assertion. These arguments are developed, in turn, in the next three paragraphs.

- Paragraph 5 raises the first problem Davis has failed to recognize—low budgets for school systems. Davis's proposal does not address this problem.

- Paragraph 6 raises a second problem Davis has failed to recognize: structural issues within the education community that lead to difficulties.

- Paragraph 7 continues this discussion and points out Davis's faulty logic in comparing the problems of education to problems faced by scientists during World War II and in the race to the moon.

- Paragraph 8 raises the third and most significant problem Davis has not acknowledged: the dire circumstances of many students and the effect of these circumstances on learning potential.

- Paragraph 9, the conclusion, summarizes the overall position of the critique—to accept the federal income tax exemption proposal, but to reject the expectation that the crisis in education will be solved with a single, "simple" solution.

 ## Writing Assignment: Critique

Read the following two position statements on the current "school-to-work" debate. School-to-work is an educational strategy that places jobs, and the skills needed to excel in the workplace, at the center of the school curriculum. Bob Kolasky, assistant editor for IntellectualCapital.com, an online magazine, explains the approach this way:

Intended to do more than teach the three R's, school-to-work applies math, science and the humanities to the reality of today's workplace, both by explaining how the lessons being taught are related to real-world situations and providing a more interactive forum to teach them in. Educators hope to replace the passive days of lectures and textbook learning with a more modern, group-oriented [. . .] education.*

CRITICAL READING FOR CRITIQUE

- **Use the tips from Critical Reading for Summary on page 6:** Remember to examine the context; note the title and subtitle; identify the main point; identify the subpoints; break the reading into sections; distinguish between points, examples, and counterarguments; watch for transitions within and between paragraphs; and read actively and recursively.
- **Establish the writer's primary purpose in writing:** Is the piece primarily meant to inform, persuade, or entertain?
- **Evaluate informative writing on the basis of three main criteria:**

  Accuracy of information

  Significance of information

  Fair interpretation of information

- **Evaluate persuasive writing on the basis of such criteria as the following:**

  Clear definition of terms

  Fair use and interpretation of information

  Logical reasoning

- **Evaluate entertaining writing on the basis of some of the following criteria:**

  Interesting characters

  Believable action, plot, and situations

  Communication of theme

  Use of language

- **Decide whether you agree or disagree with the writer's ideas, position, or message:** Once you have determined the extent to which an author has successfully achieved his or her purpose, you should decide your position in relation to the writer's.

---

*Bob Kolasky, "Issue of the Week: Today's Students, Tomorrow's Workers," <u>IntellectualCapital. com</u> 4 Sept. 1997, 16 Jan. 1998 <http://www.intellectualcapital.com>.

The arguments that follow take opposing stands on the school-to-work debate. Read both, and then select one on which to write a critique, using the techniques introduced in this chapter. We provide two arguments— Lynn Olson's "An Avenue to High Academic Standards," and Phyllis Schlafly's "School-to-Work Will Train, Not Educate"—from which to choose because each identifies core assumptions of the other and will help you to think critically about the issues. Use (and give credit to) one author in critiquing the other. We've also included excerpts from an online threaded discussion provoked by each essay; these responses are intended to stimulate your thinking about the issues raised by Olson and Schlafly. Before reading, review the tips presented in the box *Critical Reading for Critique* on page 76.

When you're ready to write your critique, start by jotting down notes in response to the tips for critical reading and the earlier discussions of evaluating writing in this chapter. Review the logical fallacies and identify any of these in the essay you've chosen to critique. Work out your ideas on paper, perhaps producing a working outline. Then write a rough draft of your critique. Review the readings and revise your rough draft at least once before considering it finished. You may want to look ahead to Chapter 3, Writing as a Process, to help guide you through writing your critique.

An Avenue to High Academic Standards
Lynn Olson

Lynn Olson is a senior editor at Education Week, *a national newspaper that covers topics in K–12 education. Her 1998 book,* The School-To-Work Revolution: How Employers and Educators Are Joining Forces To Prepare Tomorrow's Skilled Workforce, *is published by Addison Wesley. This essay appeared originally in the online magazine IntellectualCapital.com, dated September 4, 1997.*

At age 16, Erika Pyne of Kalamazoo, Michigan, was a fairly typical high school student. "I had absolutely no idea of what I was going to do with my life, and that really frustrated me," she recalls. Enrolled in a high school program that emphasized science and mathematics, she did not see any connection between her courses and what she might do in the future.

Then, as a high school junior, she enrolled in a school-to-work program run by the Education for Employment Consortium in Kalamazoo. For the next two years, she spent part of each school day taking classes at Bronson Methodist

---

Lynn Olson, "An Avenue to High Academic Standards," IntellectualCapital.com 4 Sept. 1997, 16 Jan. 1998 <http://www.intellectualcapital.com>.

Hospital, learning about such topics as anatomy and medical terminology. She also spent time observing and talking with health-care professionals and getting hands-on work experience. As a senior in high school, Erika interned afternoons on the family-care unit at Borgess Medical Center, where she helped out in the delivery room. "It was great. I just loved it," she says. "I had all these wonderful experiences that most people my age couldn't talk about. I fell in love with health care."

When I last spoke with her, Erika was a patient-care assistant at Bronson and a junior at Western Michigan University, where she was enrolled in a nursing program. Eventually, she planned to earn a degree as a physician's assistant so that she would have more authority and flexibility than a nurse.

"Why Do I Have to Learn This?"

Erika was one of many students whom I met during a year spent researching school-to-work programs around the country. And her story is not atypical.

High-quality school-to-work programs combine learning in school and in the workplace. They teach students rigorous academic content as well as practical skills. They engage students in active, hands-on learning rather than teaching solely from textbooks. And they build bridges between high schools, higher education and the workplace to help young people prepare for both careers and college.

Studies suggest that school-to-work can help address one of the greatest problems in education: motivation. Many students don't think that what they learn in school really counts. A majority of American teenagers in national surveys describe their education as "boring." Although they think it's important to graduate, they don't think that doing well in school matters. In one 1996 survey, most students described themselves as sliding by in school. Two-thirds admitted they could do better if they tried.

School-to-work can help young people answer the question, "Why do I have to learn this?" by showing how what students learn in school can be used now and in the future. Research from Jobs for the Future, the Manpower Demonstration Research Corporation, the Office of Technology Assessment, and Mathematica Policy Research Inc. all reach basically the same conclusion: well-structured school-to-work activities can slash boredom and re-engage students in schooling.

Creating a Desire to Learn

A prominent misconception surrounding school-to-work is that it downplays intellectual achievement. But far from jettisoning academics, well-structured school-to-work programs can make learning come alive for students, by connecting the academic content that students learn in school with its use in the world outside the classroom.

Evidence suggests that school-to-work can encourage students to take more academic coursework—not less. A 1994 evaluation of Pro Tech, a school-to-work program in Boston, found that students who participated took more rigorous math and science courses than their peers, although their grades were not substantially better. In 1993, a study of the seven most improved sites that belong to the *High Schools That Work* consortium found that these schools had managed to significantly close the achievement gap between college-bound and career-bound students in just three years. High schools that belong to the consortium pledge to replace low-level, watered-down courses with a solid academic core. Similarly, at Roosevelt High School in Portland, Oregon, enrollment in physics, algebra 2, and chemistry classes has increased since the school launched its school-to-work efforts in the early 1990s.

While such results are hardly conclusive, they demonstrate the promise of well-structured school-to-work activities.

Finally, school-to-work can encourage young people to pursue education and training beyond high school. In sites ranging from Kalamazoo to Boston, high percentages of young people involved in school-to-work initiatives are choosing to pursue postsecondary education because they understand the connection between learning and a good job. Many of these programs report college-going rates among their graduates of about 80%, compared with about 62% nationally. Other studies have found that while school-to-work graduates do not attend college at higher rates, those who do are more likely to declare a college major and to earn more college credits.

Worth Doing . . . Worth Doing Right

In most of the communities that I visited, school-to-work was a grassroots effort. Sometimes educators began a program after they realized that many of their students were going straight into the workplace or to college without being prepared for that transition. Other times, employers approached schools because of specific labor shortages in their community, or because they were concerned that high school graduates lacked the skills to succeed. These grassroots efforts are spreading slowly, but steadily.

School-to-work needs to be done well, making sure the academics are rigorous. Improperly structured, school-to-work could offer low-level curricula and channel students into narrow job training. That is exactly what we don't need. We must always demand quality.

Today, both employers and colleges want people who can read and do math; frame and solve problems; communicate orally and in writing; use computers; and work in teams. Schools need to do a better job of preparing all young people for this future.

Not every school-to-work program is right for every student. But good school-to-work activities can provide choices and opportunities for young people, many of whom are not now well served by our education system. Done right school-to-work can be a powerful tool in the effort to achieve higher academic standards and a more educated citizenry.

*Related Links—An online discussion of issues raised in Olson's essay**

9/4/97 Brian Farenell

Who chooses for what job each kid will be trained, er I mean, schooled? I just hope whatever powers-that-be involved in the decision-making get it right. Asking a freshman in high school what he'd like to do for the rest of his life, seems a bit early to me. I understand that in Holland (and perhaps other countries, I don't know) they have such a system. I'd suggest that the Dutch model be studied VERY carefully and see what pitfalls may occur.

9/4/97 Tom

Sounds good to me. I wonder what happened to the Vocational Technical HS? Have we now moved too far away from technical training which will prepare one for a job? Most of today's youngsters are given college prep courses whether they have the will or ability to go to college or not. They lose interest, and if they graduate have to pay for technical school to prepare them for a job. This seems to me a waste of resources. Public School dollars should be used to prepare people for the world of work first and college training next for those who can cut it.

9/5/97 Tony Poldrugovac

To be honest with you, if you don't start teaching kids (and adults for the matter) the truth about God, all your educational plans will result in ruin . . . just look at the world around you. Education without God produces intellectual barbarians. I may be viewed as narrow-minded, but the evidence is all around you. Tony

9/5/97 Victor

Tony, The truth about God according to whom?

---

* These "related links" illustrate an online, threaded discussion. It is common in e-mail communications to find errors in spelling, grammar, and punctuation. The discussion messages that follow are reproduced exactly as they appeared online at Intellectual-Capital.com —Editors.

9/5/97 David Hoover

It should be kept in mind that a successful work/study program will keep the interference of the job to a minimum. It should be regarded as a hobby at best. With the pace of change being so rapid, it would be unreasonable to expect the requirements of a job to remain the same for more than a few years at most. Thus, it is difficult to envision such programs pumping out trained monkeys. A fundamental education in all subjects is more pertinent today than ever before, and for all students, not just the "college bound" or "elite" (by the way, what is there for people without some sort of post-high school degree anyway?). The only real danger in these programs is the heavy reliance on companies footing the bills, as they will very quickly request something in return. It should always be remembered that the well-being of the students is paramount, and not the well-being of the industries that cheap, focused labor would aid.

9/6/97 Margaret

Our son, a senior at Badger High School in Lake Geneva, WI has just been accepted into a youth apprenticeship program in the field of Graphic Design. He will earn 6-12 college credits and receives high school credit, a grade and a pay check while enrolled. He is profoundly talented in the computer generated design field and has been submitting designs for contest and payment for several years. A program like this will really motivate him to work hard toward his future and begin his college education while still in high school. How do you really know what you want to do until you try it? I believe all students should have such progressive opportunities and I salute those who support and maintain such programs.

9/6/97 John Siefert

What educational dribble? Our teachers are almost 40% illiterate, so how can they even teach children about history, math, science and reading? It does not surprise me that children and teenages are not interested in school, and the reason is because teachers don't know their subject matter. They don't have authority in the classroom. Federal regulators have taken control of our schools away from the citizenry. And now they are trying to recover their foolishness by trying to help the economy. That is a big bunch of baloney. It is the job of corporations to train their workers. Don't make us pay for it. This is just another way to get "big brother" into our classroom. I implore our teachers to teach substance, but that does not have to be done with entertainment or school-to-work programs. I don't want my daughter being told by some regulator somewhere what she is supposed to do for a living. I might as well move to Russia, where there is more freedom than there is here in the United States.

9/7/97 Richard Geib

School merely as a means for job preparation? What a shallow typically "modern" interpretation of education! What a superficial and tendentious idea of learning! In my opinion, an education should revolve around the following questions: How to live and what to live for. If teenagers think that is "boring," maybe we adults had better spend more time with them talking about what is really important in life. In my experience, learning how to read and write (AND THINK!) comes naturally after those earlier questions are resolved satisfactorily. On the other hand, if they not be resolved, a student will never get excited about themselves and their place in the world. If we want to call our country "educated," we need to put more vigor into the liberal arts and not look at school primarily as a vehicle for churning out efficient workers. As a professional teacher who looks for inspiration all the way back to Socrates, I read Olson's article, look at my country, and despair almost completely. This "jobs-to-work" idea will be the latest educational fad or "magic bullet" which will not cure the ills of our educational system—the root of the problem remaining unacknowledged.

9/8/97 Bri Farenell

Our teachers are "40% illiterate"? Where'd you get those numbers from? Rush Limbaugh? And even if that's the case, you have to wonder where all the best college graduates are going instead of teaching . . . and why?

School-to-Work Will Train, Not Educate
Phyllis Schlafly

Phyllis Schlafly is president of the organization Eagle Forum, whose mission is to promote conservative policies in education. She is author of Child Abuse in the Classroom *(1964), producer of a video documentary called* Crisis in the Classroom *(1996), and has been publisher of the monthly* Education Reporter *since 1986. This essay appeared originally in the online magazine IntellectualCapital.com, dated September 4, 1997.*

The School to Work Opportunities Act (STW) was signed by President Clinton in 1994 and is being implemented nationwide through STW state laws, federal and state regulations, and the federal mandates that control the granting of federal STW funds.

From the Cradle to the Grave

School-to-work is the implementation of Marc Tucker's "cradle-to-grave" plan outlined in his now-famous 18-page "Dear Hillary" letter written on November 11, 1992. It delineates a master plan "to remold the entire American [public school] system" into "a seamless web that literally extends from cradle-to-grave and is the same system for everyone," coordinated by "a system of labor market boards at the local, state and federal levels" where curriculum and "job matching" will be handled by counselors "accessing the integrated computer-based program."

Tucker, who is president of the *National Center on Education and the Economy,* boasts that he has written the "restructuring" plans for more than 50% of public school children. Designed on the German system, Tucker's plan is to train children in specific jobs to serve the workforce and the global economy instead of educate them so they can make their own life choices.

The traditional function of education was to teach basic knowledge and skills: reading, writing, math, science, history, etc. School-to-work deemphasizes or eliminates academic work and substitutes mandated vocational training to better serve the workforce. Instead of the focus being on developing the child, the focus is on developing a labor force.

Education versus Training

There's a big difference between educating a child and training him or her to work. According to the dictionary, to educate means to develop the faculties and powers of a person by teaching. Becoming skilled at reading, writing and calculating is essential to developing as a student and as a person and being able to fulfill the American dream.

To train means to cause a person or animal to be efficient in the performance of tasks by responding to discipline, instruction and repeated practice. That's what you do to your dog. And that's exactly what school-to-work is: "performance-based" training of students to move them into predetermined jobs.

Phyllis Schlafly, "School-to-Work Will Train, Not Educate" IntellectualCapital.com 4 Sept. 1997, 16 Jan. 1998 <http://www.intellectualcapital.com>.

To make matters worse, those predetermined jobs will not be selected by the student or his family. New bodies called workforce development boards—appointed not elected—will determine what jobs are needed in the coming years. The schools will then design the curriculum to meet these governmentally determined workforce needs, and use counselors and computers to do "job matching" of the students.

After they complete their vocational training, rather than receiving their high school diploma, students will get a Certificate of Mastery—they won't be able to get jobs unless they have one. This certificate will be comparable to green cards which must be possessed by resident aliens in order to hold a job.

The Wrong Kind of School Choice

STW laws and regulations require vocational training to start "at the earliest possible age, but beginning no later than middle-school grades." The federal STW statute says that "career awareness" should "begin as early as the elementary grades." How many elementary or even middle school children do you know that are capable of choosing their lifetime career? Obviously, these decisions will be made by the school, not by the child.

The goal is not to graduate highly literate individuals but to turn out team workers to produce for the global economy. In the STW scheme, individual grades are inflated or detached from academic achievement, individual honors and competition are eliminated or deemphasized, and instead we have such "team" techniques as group grading, cooperative learning, peer tutoring, horizontal enrichment, job shadowing, mentoring, and job site visits.

It is obvious that the several years we've suffered with Outcome-Based Education was preparation for the system in which children are taught to be "team workers" instead of achievers.

A Litany of Apologists

Some big businesses support school-to-work because they think that vocational courses in high school for illiterate or semi-literate students will train young Americans to compete in the global economy with people in the third world willing to work for 25 and 50 cents an hour. They think they'll get some free teenage labor and the schools will do some of their job training for them. But it's not the job of the taxpayers to do job training; that's the job of the corporations that hire them. It is the job of the schools to teach children how to read, write and calculate.

Some governors support school-to-work because it gives them control of a pot of money for which they don't have to account to the state legislature.

School-to-work is wrong because it eliminates accountability by bypassing elected representatives in state legislatures and school boards.

School-to-work is a direct threat to the individual student, his or her privacy, his or her goals and his or her acquisition of an education that can help him reach them. Furthermore, a planned economy, with bureaucrats trying to predict what jobs will be needed in the next five years and training students for specific jobs, is a failure all over the world. All those who value freedom must defeat and defund school-to-work.

*Related Links—An online discussion
of issues raised in Schlafly's essay.*

9/4/97 Don Wallace

School-to-work appears to be born out of pragmatism. Public school students are dumber than ever and functional illiteracy is the norm. Therefore, the thought goes, why not sacrifice the ideal of a liberal education—which does not 'work' in our public school system for the majority of students—and trade rampant illiteracy and unemployability for a narrow trade education? Since you can't get students to think or reason, you'd better get them busy with a wrench or hammer. I perceive school-to-work to be the creation of policy wonks whose agenda is to create a two-tier American society: 'worker' and 'professional'. Note that public schools today are poor at teaching basic skills. Vocational education at an early grade level will displace what little "3 Rs" education that now takes place. The 'worker caste'—most likely from a blue collar or middle class, unmoneyed background—"tracked" through public schools—will be barred from minimal entrance requirements of a university should he choose to later broaden his education. The manager/professional/anointed policy wonk—probably from a "better" background more similar to those parties who endorse this plan—would be 'tracked' through private school and a good university, to assume his or her "rightful" position of riding herd over vocationally specialized savages. In short, school-to-work appears to be completely contradictory to a free democratic society because it will create functional castes.

9/4/97 Brian Farenell

It's a sub-freezing day in West Africa when I agree with Phyllis Schlafly but I do. Perhaps not the entirety of her reasoning but certainly her opinion. First off, I think asking a freshman in high school to declare a major is way too early. If someone at that age is focused and is certain what he or she wants to do with the rest of his life,

---

*These "related links" illustrate an online, threaded discussion. It is common in e-mail communications to find errors in spelling, grammar, and punctuation. The discussion messages that follow are reproduced exactly as they appeared online at IntellectualCapital.com. —Editors.

accomodations should be made. But I think kids are
the exception not the rule. Secondly, maybe I'm
old-fashioned (at age 23), but I always felt that
the point of the secondary educational system was
to mold citizens who are well-rounded in a wide variety of areas. Not only in basics, like literacy
and numeracy, but also in being aware of civics,
our nation's history, how to express oneself and so
on. It seems to me that college is where one should
specialize. With the rapidity that our job market
is changing, let's get workers out there that are
flexible and well-rounded. Finally, the public
school sytem is being asked to do an impossible
job. It's being asked to repair the damage left by
apathetic or abusive parents and by a society with
screwed up mores. Schools are not parents and they
can not parent, but that's what they're expected to
do. You've got kids who have never learned to socialize. You have to teach them how to socialize
and to sit still for more than 10 sec. at a time
before you can teach them how to add.

9/4/97 Diann Harle

Ms. Schafly would probably argue equally as vehe-
mently for the abolition of welfare benefits as she
argues for the "traditional" educational system.
Interesting that we now must "train" all these people who are being dropped from the welfare rolls to
have "marketable" skills to make the transition to
independence from the welfare state. Of course,
being somewhat educated, I have come to realize
that for many people in this country "life choices"
are dictated long before education is received. In
schools today we see children of elementary school
age who have been subjected to enough cruelty, neglect, abandonment, and indifference to make the
thought of our benign efforts more accurately banal. We cannot insure nor guarantee every child the
luxury of Ms. Schafly's "education." Not because
we don't agree with the purity of the concept but
because for too many of our children today "the
American Dream" is not only unknown, but unteach-
able. Ms. Schlafly uses all the right buzzwords to
incite her fans. Unfortunately, she has no clue
about the reality of life for children in 1997.
Will school to work make a difference? I do not
know. I do believe that the politicians on both
sides of this issue will insure that what gets lost

in this dialogue will not be their propaganda but the needs of our children.

9/4/97 Karen Card

Schlafly's article contains some grains of truth, buttressed with many wild exaggerations. The programs which I have heard or read about are only intended to expose children to careers and the kinds of interests and skills they involve. Job shadowing, mentoring, and cooperative learning are not dirty words. What is wrong with students who visit a vet hospital if they are interesed in veterinarian medicine? The same applies to auto mechanics, radiology technicians, doctors, and lawyers. Team players can also be high achievers, and should be encouraged to be both. Big business wants a labor pool of well educated thinkers who are good at math, writing, and oral expression and who can use a computer. Finally, Schlafly and the rest of her "thinkalikes" use a lot of buzz words as a scare tactic, without carefully analyzing the actual broad scope and variety of school-to-work programs available today. John Ring decried the loss of local control of schools as part of the new programs discussed by Schlafly. My school district has completed a strategic planning process which involved over 800 members of the local community. However, our plan has been rejected by individuals who are proponents of Schlafly's ideology. They don't really want local control—only if that control is in agreement with their politics.

9/5/97 Tom

Schlafly's elitist view of education is what is wrong with it. Sure we have to teach kids the 3 Rs. This can easily be done in the first 8 grades. At that point, we must train the majority to go out into the world of work(vocational/technical). Only those of the higher intellect should be subsidized to go on to higher education and train for the professions. Countless dollars and resources are wasted on 'college prep' courses for those who are not intellectually suited for higher education. Schlafly, and others in the clouds, insist that all kids need the flavor of higher education courses to lead a full, productive, successful life. Balderdash!

9/5/97 George Willett

Phyllis might care to read of John Dewey, New England educational philosopher who suggests that greater learning occurred where the practical was aligned with the academic. This applies to work skills which entails, among other skills, the ability to work well with others. Everybody will enter the workforce in some manner, and the more refined the career choice the more productive and happier person. School-to-work is also career exploration where young people really learn of career fields rather than just specific occupations. Imaginative educators and school districts require career exploration (community service or even volunteerism) as a graduation requirement. This is done not for producing products for drudgery but to encourage young people to gain the benefits of a total educational system which also involves the community and other adults.

9/5/97 Mark Dawdy

How unfortunate that so many Americans are blinded to "principles" and "freedom." Phyllis is correct in her opinion of this ridiculous scheme for more "big government". As usual the dupes of "doom and gloom" cannot see the "true" issues from the "perceived" ones. What is at stake here is not a philosophical difference of education, but freedom. The U.S. has produced many great people and ideas. Washington, Jefferson, Edison, etc, never would have been who they were without the freedom to mold their characters and disclipline themselves through life's educational course. Who is so all-knowing to determine which course will exactly fit each lifestyle? There is no one qualified for such a task on this earth and there never will be. FREEDOM is at stake here. This country was founded on the God-given principles of the right to pursue happiness. The federal gov't is too big. It wastes more money and time than anything else in this country. It has already stripped too many people's rights. I'm not saying we should abandon any change or not implement a better skill training program. I say that anything the government does usually gets messed up, ie. the welfare program, education, etc. The current education system as administered by the govenerment is an excellent example—7 administrators to 1 teacher. WHY? Whether you agree with Phyllis or not, is not the issue. Our freedom is at stake.

9/6/97 Lloyd Smith

Finding myself in even partial agreement with Phyllis Schlafly is novel and unsettling. But she is correct when she notes the difference between education and training. The former should prepare one for life, while the latter should prepare one for the tasks of life. There is a difference, on which many advocates of narrow vocational training fail to understand. There is also a danger: Mere training does not prepare one to adapt to change. As Toffler wrote many years ago in Future Shock, one's "copeability" is more important than one's capability. Having said all of that, I disagree with Schlafly's assertions that school-to-work is some sort of big government conspiracy designed to enslave the masses. It's not, and in fact, we can have it both ways: We can create sound educational programs which also prepare students for their lives after they leave school. (One place it's being done is in Washington state.) After all, we need to remember that eventually, every student will leave the schools, and every one of them needs to be able to do something, whether it is going to college or trade school, going directly to work, joining the military, or working in the home. Good school to work programs are designed to recognize this obvious fact.

9/6/97 John Siefert

I am so glad Ms. Schlafly has spoken out about this terribly important, but much belittled issue. We have too much miseducation in our schools. There is not teaching going on in the classrooms. The teacher has lost control in the classroom. The federal government and its Education Department have taken the classroom away from the teacher, student and parent. Sad to say, we are rearing an illiterate generation of students. I know of a young man in Coos Bay Oregon who went to a school that majored in this school-to-work program. This young man was singled out to train to be a politician or public speaker. He has been expressly trained to do just that. Yet, this young man knows

nothing about history, math, English, or even
reading. For his whole life he will only be able
to relate to people what someone else says to him.
He will not have a mind of his own. He will forever be a subject of the state. His work will not
be his own, but that of a silent elite that structured our schools so he would fail in literacy,
but prosper in speaking and politicking. What a
farce this school-to-work is! We have to find some
way to recapture our public schools and their curriculum from the powers that be. This country has
in many ways ceased to be the country of the people, by the people and for the people.

9/8/97 Tom Havelka

The criticism of the School-to-work program hinges
on two unproven assumptions. First, that training
and education are somehow mutually exclusive and
secondly that there being "trained" somehow pre-
vents someone from ever becoming educated. Both
ideas are wrong. It is quite possible to train and
educate at the same time. There is no reason why
someone can not be taught technical skills that are
marketable in the workplace while obtaining a education, one does not have to preclude the other.
The second assumption is equally wrong. People can
and often do continue with their education (both
formally and informally) after learning a skill
and the skills learned have only served to enhance
their education. Too much time is wasted on the
tired old debate between education and training
both work hand-in-hand with each other. It is also
interesting to note that the author never produces
a copy of the Act that she indicts and the suppose
link to the alledged "letter" is merely to another
article that does not let us acutally see the letter but merely quotes excerpts from it.

3

Writing as a Process: Steps to Writing Theses, Introductions, and Conclusions

WRITING AS A THINKING PROCESS

Most of us are used to thinking of writing as a process that culminates in a product such as a paper, a letter to a friend, study notes, and the like. Our focus is upon the result, rather than the process of getting there. But how *do* we get there? In particular, how does the act of *thinking* fit in? Thinking is often conceptualized as something apart from writing, something in response to it, or in preparation for it. Perhaps you sit down to think about a paper topic, THEN you begin to write the paper. How many times have you found this task agonizing? You think and think and think, then try to write, and something just won't translate. If this sounds familiar, you might need to approach thinking in a different way. In Chapter 2 we discussed reading as a process that involves a lot of thinking; this chapter will focus upon writing as a process—both a process of thinking and a process that produces a finished piece of writing.

If you've ever written study notes, perhaps recopying messy, disorganized notes into a more organized form to help you study for an exam, then you've experienced a very simple form of writing as a thinking process. If you pay attention as you copy the notes, your brain processes the information. Of course, simply reading your notes also allows your brain to process the information, but when you write, you are processing more actively than when you just read.

Writing can be a powerful way to refine your thinking about complex topics, and there are a number of useful ways to approach this task. These different approaches help lead to clear thinking, but they also lead to finished products, whether that be an understanding of the economic factors that helped to cause the American Civil War, a paper that explains such factors, or more specific questions about the event.

STAGES OF THE WRITING PROCESS

Of course, there is no "one size fits all" approach to writing; so, our use of "the" in the title of this section is misleading if taken too literally. There is no single writing process. There are, however, some stages or steps that many writers find useful for refining their thinking, as well as for ending up with solid finished work. By breaking the process into stages, writers also turn the sometimes overwhelming task of writing a paper into manageable pieces, each piece requiring different actions that ultimately build to a final draft. We can break the process down into the stages of *data gathering, invention, drafting, revision, editing,* and *publication.* While these stages generally occur in the order we've just listed them, the writing process is recursive, or nonlinear. While basically following the trajectory from data gathering to publication, a writer will typically have to circle back and add to different stages of the process as insights gained in one stage cause a reevaluation and refinement of previous stages, or expose some inadequacy in an earlier stage. For example, you might find a number of source materials in the data gathering stage of the process, and after reading and taking notes on these sources, you may feel ready to move on to the invention stage—perhaps listing your ideas about the topic. This task can help point out gaps in the information you've collected, and you may have to return to more data gathering before proceeding to the next step.

GETTING STARTED

Stage 1: Data Gathering

Essentially, all academic writing relies upon source materials of some sort. Here the broad term "data" is used to encompass the large range of materials one may rely upon to write academic papers of different types.

UNDERSTANDING THE ASSIGNMENT

The very first part of data gathering involves understanding the assignment you are given. This seems obvious, but you might be surprised at the large number of student writers who turn in substandard work simply because they misread or misunderstand what is being asked of them. Read and reread the assignment, and be sure to question your instructor if you are confused about aspects of the assignment she or he gives you. Underline the key task(s) of the assignment. A typical assignment might contain a number of suggestions and questions, but usually there is one overall task, and you need to be sure you identify this. Look for the kind of *action* being asked of you: Most assignments will ask you to *analyze* something, to *compare and contrast* a set of things, to *describe, summarize, discuss, explore, argue, explain, critique*—or to perform some combination of these things. We've already discussed summary and critique in this textbook, and later chapters will deal with more complex activities commonly required in academic writing. Be sure you start your writing process by understanding the overall task of the assignment.

In addition to understanding the major task of the assignment, you should also clarify such paper guidelines as the assignment length and the documentation method expected of you. Page requirements help determine the extent of your data gathering and the scope of your thesis statement. What kinds of sources you're required or encouraged to use is important information for proceeding with this stage. For later reference, you should clarify the documentation method you are asked to follow, such as standard MLA format, APA, or CBE, or some variant of these. In addition to documentation format, what kind of manuscript format does your professor prefer? Clarify these issues if they're not spelled out explicitly in the assignment, and be sure to attend to them before submitting your final draft.

EXERCISE **3.1**

Assignment Analysis

Write a paragraph or two explaining what a specific writing assignment in one of your current or past courses is asking of you. What specific type of task are you being asked to perform? What content are you supposed to address? For example, you might be asked to explain some psychological theory; in this case, the task is explanation, and the content is the psychological theory. Write down what you feel you understand and do not understand about the assignment. What structure do you think your essay should follow? Do you know what documentation style to use? In short, this exercise asks you to practice critical reading strategies on an assignment.

Because the extent and type of data gathering depends upon the type of writing assignment you are given, the real work in the data gathering stage must proceed only after you have a thorough understanding of the assignment and its parameters. Clearly, you will have to spend more time gathering data for a lengthy research report than you will for an analytical paper using course materials such as lecture notes and textbook sources.

TYPES OF DATA

"Data" is a term used most often to refer to *quantitative* information, such as the frequencies or percentages of natural occurrences in the sciences or of social phenomena in the social sciences. But "data" also refers to *qualitative* information—the sort that is textual rather than numerical. Interviews or ethnographic field notes recorded by a social scientist are usually qualitative in nature, comprising in-depth interview responses or detailed observations of human behavior. In the humanities, the term "data" can refer to the qualitative observations one makes of a particular art object one is interpreting or evaluating. Generally, quantitative data encompasses issues of 'how many,' or 'how often,' while qualitative research accounts for such issues as 'what kind?' and 'why?'

PRIMARY AND SECONDARY SOURCES

When you as a writer collect either or both of these kinds of data yourself, you are generating *primary* data—data that is gathered directly by a researcher using the research methods appropriate to a particular field of study, such as experiments or observations in the sciences, surveys or interviews in the social sciences, and close reading and interpretation in the humanities. The more common types of data you will collect as an undergraduate, however, are *secondary* in nature, that is, information and ideas collected or generated by others who have performed their own primary and/or secondary research. The data gathering for most undergraduate academic writing will consist of library research and, increasingly, research conducted online via Internet databases and resources; you will rely upon secondary data more often than you will generate your own primary data.

Chapter 7 on research provides an in-depth discussion of conducting secondary research; you can consult that chapter for more discussion of the specifics involved in data gathering. You also ought to refer to the material presented in Chapters 1 and 2 on summary, critical reading, and critique. The techniques of critical reading and assessment of sources will help you make the best use of your sources.

Stage 2: Invention

The next stage of the writing process is called "invention" in order to signify the thought and imagination involved in writing. This stage can also be termed "brainstorming," or "predrafting." Regardless of what one calls it, this is perhaps the most important part of the process, as well as the one most frequently skipped over. The more time you as a writer spend writing about your ideas, working them out in writing *before* beginning to shape them into the form of a paper, the better that paper will ultimately be.

Stages 1 and 2 of the writing process typically overlap—data gathering informs invention; invention sends one back to gather more data. This relationship between the two stages is most evident when it comes to choosing a subject for an open-ended assignment.

CHOOSING AND NARROWING YOUR SUBJECTS

Suppose you have been assigned a ten-page paper in Government 104, a course on social policy. Not only do you have to choose a subject, but also you have to narrow it sufficiently and decide upon your thesis. Where will you begin? First, you need to select a broad area of interest and make yourself knowledgeable about its general features. What if no broad area of interest occurs to you? Don't despair—usually there's a way to make use of material you've read in a text or heard in a lecture. The trick is to find a topic that can become personally important, for whatever reason. (For a paper in your biology class, you might write on the digestive system because a relative has stomach troubles. For an economics seminar, you might explore the factors that threaten banks with collapse because your great-grandparents lost their life savings during the Great Depression.) Whatever the academic discipline, try to discover a topic that you'll enjoy exploring; that way, you'll be writing for yourself as much as for your instructor. Some specific data gathering strategies to try if no topics occur to you: Review material covered during the semester, class by class if need be; review the semester's readings, actually skimming each assignment. Choose any subject that has held your interest, if even for a moment, and use that as your point of departure.

Imagine that you've reviewed each of your classes and recall that a lecture on AIDS aroused your curiosity. Your broad subject of interest, then, will be AIDS. At this point, the goal of your research is to limit this subject to a manageable scope. Although your initial, broad subject will often be more specific than our example, "AIDS," we'll assume for the purposes of discussion the most general case (the subject in greatest need of limiting).

A subject can be limited in at least two ways. First, a general article such as an encyclopedia entry may do the work for you by presenting the subject in the form of an outline, with each item in the outline representing a separate topic (which, for your purposes, may need further limiting). Second, you can limit a subject by asking several questions about it:

Who?
What aspects?
Where?
When?
How?

These questions will occur to you as you conduct your research and see the ways in which various authors have focused their discussions. Having read several sources and having decided that you'd like to use them, you might limit the subject "AIDS" by asking *who*—AIDS patients; and *which* aspect— civil rights of AIDS patients.

Certainly, "the civil rights of AIDS patients" offers a more specific focus than does "AIDS"; still, the revised focus is too broad for a ten-page paper in that a comprehensive discussion would obligate you to review numerous particular rights. So again you must try to limit your subject by posing a question. In this particular case, *which aspects* (of the civil rights of AIDS patients) can be asked a second time. Six aspects may come to mind:

- Rights in the workplace
- Rights to hospital care
- Rights to insurance benefits
- Rights to privacy
- Rights to fair housing
- Rights to education

Any *one* of these aspects could provide the focus of a ten-page paper, and you do yourself an important service by choosing one, perhaps two, of the aspects. To choose more would obligate you to too broad a discussion and you would frustrate yourself: Either the paper would have to be longer than ten pages or, assuming you kept to the page limit, the paper would be superficial in its treatment. In both instances, the paper would fail, given the constraints of the assignment. So it is far better to spend ample time gathering data, brainstorming, gathering data, and brainstorming, in order to limit your subject before you attempt to write about it. Let's assume that you settle on the following as an appropriately defined subject for a ten-page paper:

- The rights of AIDS patients in the workplace

The process of narrowing an initial subject (invention) depends heavily on the reading you do (data gathering). The more you read, the deeper your understanding of a topic. The deeper your understanding, the likelier it will be that you can divide a broad and complex topic into manageable—that is, researchable—categories. In the AIDS example, your reading in the literature suggested that the civil rights of AIDS patients was an issue at the center of recent national debate. So reading allowed you to narrow the subject "AIDS" by answering the initial questions—the *who* and *which* aspects. Once you narrowed your focus to "the civil rights of AIDS patients," you read further and quickly realized that civil rights in itself was a broad subject that also should be limited. In this way, reading provided an important stimulus as you worked to identify an appropriate subject for your paper. Your process here is recursive—you move back and forth between Stages 1 and 2 of the process, each movement bringing you closer to establishing a clear focus *before* you attempt to write your paper.

EXERCISE 3.2

Practice Narrowing Subjects

In groups of three or four classmates, choose one of the following subjects, and collaborate on a paragraph or so exploring the questions we listed above for narrowing subjects: Who? What aspects? Where? When? How? See if you can formulate a more narrow approach to the subject.

- Downloading music off the Internet
- College sports
- School violence
- Internet chat rooms
- America's public school system

COMMON MISCONCEPTIONS ABOUT WRITING

Many students believe in a myth of inspiration, thinking that good writing comes primarily from a kind of magical—and unpredictable—formation of ideas as one sits down in front of blank paper or a blank computer document. The idea is that a writer must be inspired, as if given her or his ideas from some mystical source (such as a muse), in order to write. While some element of inspiration may inform your writing, most of the time, hard work is the more realistic inspiration. The old adage, "invention is one part inspiration, and 99 parts perspiration," is wholly applicable here.

Alongside the myth of inspiration, many inexperienced writers also believe in a myth of talent, the idea that either you have it or you don't, and if you don't have the "talent" of writing, then you are doomed to go through life as a "bad writer." Again, hard work, rather than talent, is the norm. Yes, some people have more natural verbal ability than others—we all have our areas of strength and weakness. But in any endeavor, talent alone doesn't ensure success, and with hard work, the seemingly untalented writer can achieve great results in writing. Spending time on the *invention* stage of the writing process is one of the keys to augmenting or compensating for one's natural abilities.

WRITING AND THINKING

A classic image: Attempting to write a paper, the writer stares glumly at a blank sheet of paper—or a blank screen. Usually, however, this is an image of a writer who hasn't spent time on invention. If you have ever completed some data gathering, and then sat down in front of a clean sheet of paper or a blank computer screen to begin the introduction of an essay, you've probably experienced frustration. Perhaps you thought about the assignment, maybe even jotted down a rough outline of ideas, and now you feel it's time to start writing. But then the task seems overwhelming. How to start? Or after starting, where to go from there? What is the thesis statement of the essay? Here's where student writers often feel they lack talent and inspiration, believing that "real" or "good" writers sit down after some initial thought, and the ideas just flow out in an organized and clear fashion. It's true that when writers are highly knowledgeable about a topic, they can often begin writing after very little planning. Such knowledge can help them formulate a thesis—or essay focus—thus helping them to establish clarity and organization in their first drafts. Even for highly knowledgeable writers, though, writing generally flows more smoothly if they've spent time on invention, for example, writing an outline to flesh out their ideas and plan their essay structure. For student writers whose knowledge of the academic topics on which they're writing is not likely to equal that of professionals, time spent on invention is key. Brainstorming and planning help prevent that blank feeling when faced with beginning the essay in Stage 3, drafting.

Of course, first and foremost, invention involves thinking. We can sit and think to ourselves, we can think as we discuss ideas with others, and we can also think through the act of writing. Very often, thinking while writing is a more efficient method of invention than is thinking to yourself. Using writing to think provides you with a record of your thoughts, whereas when sitting and thinking alone, it's easy to forget ideas that might prove useful or that might lead to other useful ideas. It is also usually easier to stay focused on the task at hand when one uses writing as a thinking aid. Our brains don't necessarily process things in a linear, one-track fashion; it's too easy to get distracted, to go off onto tangents unrelated to the task at hand, and to end up with half-baked ideas. Writing one's thoughts helps to keep things focused and on-track. So, while invention can mean simply thinking about your ideas, approaching it through writing can be a more productive strategy.

Invention primarily refers to the act of developing ideas, but planning the ensuing essay's structure can also be a matter of invention. However, the invention process usually works best if you work on your ideas before you try to fit them into some kind of outline or plan for your paper's structure. Paper structure—the number and order of points, and how you relate them to each other and to a main point—is dependent upon the ideas you're working with. Student writers run into trouble when they rush into planning their paper's introduction, body paragraphs, and conclusion before they've given enough thought to their ideas. Jumping the gun like this can lead to papers that follow a standard format, but don't clearly articulate a main point, or don't even have a main point, presenting instead a conglomeration of loosely related points. Focus as much time and attention as you can on invention of *ideas* before you decide on your paper structure or begin drafting.

When student writers spend too little time working out their ideas before drafting a paper, they often end up turning in work with the following features: a rambling or overly general introduction containing no clear thesis or main point; a number of body paragraphs that make several different, semi-related points, and a concluding paragraph attempting to pull the paper together. Sometimes in a paper like this, a student will state a main point in the conclusion—and sometimes it's an excellent point. While building up to a main point is a legitimate essay structure—an inductive rather than deductive approach to arguing a point—this approach often won't work if what precedes the main point is disorganized and unclear. When this kind of thing happens, the student has turned in some excellent "predrafting" or inventive writing, rather than a true final draft; the student has inadvertently used the writing process to arrive at a point or a conclusion, but hasn't gone back and done the necessary drafting and revising to arrive at a polished paper.

Writers use a number of successful strategies for thinking through ideas in writing—you may already use some invention strategies yourself. Some different methods you might find useful for invention are provided below.

INVENTION STRATEGIES

Directed Freewriting

To freewrite is to let your mind go and write spontaneously, often for a set amount of time or set number of pages. The process of "just writing" in a stream of consciousness can often free up thoughts and ideas about which we aren't even fully conscious, or that we haven't articulated to ourselves. In *directed freewriting,* you focus upon a topic, and let what you think and know about the topic flow out in a focused stream of ideas. As a first step in the invention stage, you might sit down with a paper assignment and write continuously for 15 minutes. Such efforts might seem sluggish at first, but if you stick with it and really try to let yourself write spontaneously, you might be surprised at what comes out—you might generate questions whose answers help lead to an argument, or logical connections between ideas that you hadn't noticed before. If you write for 15 minutes, and only one solid idea comes through, you have succeeded in using freewriting to help "free up" your thinking. As a second step, you might take that one idea and freewrite about it, shift to a different invention strategy to explore that one idea, or even begin to draft a thesis and subsequent rough draft, depending on the extent to which your idea is formed in your mind and in writing.

Listing

Some writers find it helpful to make lists of their ideas, breaking significant ideas into sublists and seeing where they lead. This strategy can be approached as a form of freewriting if you try to let your mind go and jot down words and phrases that are related. You can create lists by pulling related ideas out of your notes or your course readings. A caution: The linear nature of lists can lead you to prematurely jump into planning your paper structure before working out your ideas; list ideas as a way of brainstorming, and then you can make another list working out the best paper structure for your points.

Outlining

As more structured versions of lists, outlines group ideas in hierarchical order, with main points broken into subordinate points, and sometimes indicating evidence in support of these points. You might use outlines as a first stage in generating ideas during your invention process, or you can use outlines as a second step in invention: After freewriting and/or listing, you might refine and build on your ideas by putting them into an outline for a workable structure in which to discuss the ideas you've brainstormed.

Clustering and Branching

These two methods of invention are more visual, nonlinear versions of listing and outlining. With both clustering and branching, you start with an assignment's main topic, or with an idea generated by freewriting or thinking, and you brainstorm related ideas that flow from that main idea. Clustering involves writing an idea in the middle of a page and circling it. Then draw lines leading from that circle, or "bubble," to new bubbles where you write different subtopics of that central idea. Picking the subtopics that interest you most, draw lines leading to more bubbles wherein you note important aspects of the subtopics. Branching follows the same principle, but instead of placing ideas in bubbles, write them on lines that branch off to other lines, containing the related subtopics of your larger topic.

You might find this method a useful first step in invention, for it can help isolate the topics about which you are most knowledgeable. As you branch off into the subtopics of a main essay topic, the number of ideas generated in relation to these topics will help show where you have the most knowledge and/or interest.

Drafting

While drafting comprises the next full stage in the writing process, it's also possible to combine stages 2 and 3 of the writing process, using the act of drafting an essay to discover your ideas. Of course, this method requires that you have some notion of what you want to write about, and as you begin your first draft, you can discover what you want to say as you write. Such a method can be seen as a highly focused and directed form of freewriting. You might start drafting your body paragraphs first, or begin with the introduction. Typically, what you write at first will be junk. Your first paragraph or so serves as a kind of pump priming or throat clearing, but as you proceed you can warm up and start to generate more useful material. Later you must go back and completely revise the early paragraphs you drafted.

You can modify and combine different invention techniques in a number of ways. There is no one right way to generate ideas—or to write a paper— and every writer must try different methods to find those that work best for him or her. The main point here is that time spent on invention, regardless of the method with which it is approached, leads to better paper drafts.

TIME MANAGEMENT

This increased attention to invention as a stage in your writing process requires good planning and time-management skills. In general, college life involves juggling assignments and responsibilities—actually, all of life requires these skills—so the more you learn to manage multiple demands upon your time while in college, the better off you will be in the "real world" after college. Because you're given multiple assignments in different classes, it's easy to put off writing papers until the night before they are due, and this can cause you to spend too little time on invention and to end up making illogical or inconsistent points in your papers. Clearly, planning ahead and approaching paper writing as a series of steps to be completed in advance of the due date leads you to produce better writing. Using this approach will also help you to learn more about your courses' subject matter, so you will likely improve your performance on subsequent work in the courses for which you've written papers. Then you might actually be grateful to those professors who assign written work—they're giving you the opportunity to learn more because you are processing ideas through writing!

Practicing Invention Strategies

After completing the group exercise (Exercise 3.2, page 96) where you narrowed a subject, work individually to brainstorm ideas about the subject your group chose. Use one of the invention strategies listed above—preferably one that you haven't used before. After brainstorming on your own, meet with your group again to compare the ideas you each generated.

WRITING THE ESSAY

Stage 3: Drafting

It's often best to begin drafting a paper after you've settled on at least a working or preliminary thesis. While consulting your notes, lists, outlines, or whatever form your invention steps have produced, you have a number of choices about how to proceed with drafting your essay.

Some writers are ready to sit down and start writing at the beginning, putting their ideas into an orderly form as they write. Of course, this drafting method results in a completed *rough* draft—good writers rarely, if ever, produce an adequate piece of writing in one draft. A corollary to the myths of inspiration and talent we discussed earlier is the belief among less experienced writers that a good writer is able, or should be able, to sit down and produce an excellent finished paper in one draft. This belief can lead students to feel like bad writers if their rough drafts are rough—as, in reality, they should be!—or, conversely, to think their rough drafts are good enough, with minimal editing, to turn in as finished work. If you want to write well, you'll do better to accept the fact that first drafts are always going to be rough and will need serious revision if they are to be excellent, or even good, pieces of polished writing.

Although certain writers are able to sit down and write a complete rough draft starting with an introduction, body, and conclusion, others need to plan the structure of their ideas after they have spent time brainstorming them. Some writers tackle that issue as a second invention step, while others work out their essay structure as they draft or redraft their work. If you find yourself wrestling with issues of essay structure, try mapping out a rough plan for your paper by asking yourself such questions as the following:

- On what main point do I intend to focus my paper?
- What related subpoints do I need to cover in order to develop my main point?
- In what order should my points be arranged?
- Do certain subtopics or points lead naturally into other points? If so, they might fit next to each other in sequential sets of paragraphs.

If you have trouble seeing the logical connections between your points and then ordering them accordingly, these points may not go together in the same paper. Ask yourself whether (and how) the points relate to the main idea of the paper. If you find they do relate and are important to developing your paper's main idea, then you may be missing another point or set of points that would establish the link between the ideas. Approach the fruits of your invention process with questions like these in order to arrive at a preliminary plan for the structure of your paper.

At this stage, as you review your points and clarify their relationships, you ought to be able to formulate at least a preliminary thesis. Your thesis can be very rough, but if you don't have a sense of your main point, writing the first draft will be more difficult. On the other hand, sometimes writers arrive at their theses through the process of putting ideas together into paper form. Even in this case, the writer has to have narrowed his or her subject, as we discussed in the invention section.

As you can see so far, there is a lot of overlap between the drafting and invention stages. The amount of planning you do after working out your ideas and before drafting your essay is a matter of preference. Try different methods to see which work best for you, and keep in mind that different assignments may require new methods for invention and drafting.

For many writers, the drafting stage is the most difficult. Let's move now from our general and somewhat abstract discussion of drafting into a more concrete focus upon the three most important—and most difficult—elements of drafting a paper: writing theses, introductions, and conclusions.

Writing a Thesis

A thesis is a one-sentence summary of a paper's content. It is similar, actually, to a paper's conclusion (see page 113) but lacks the conclusion's concern for broad implications and significance. The thesis is the product of your thinking; it therefore represents *your* conclusion about the topic on which you're writing, and therefore you have to have spent some time thinking (invention) in order to arrive at the thesis that begins your actual essay.

For a writer in the drafting stages, the thesis establishes a focus, a basis on which to include or exclude information. For the reader of a finished product, the thesis anticipates the author's discussion. *A thesis, therefore, is an essential tool for both writers and readers of academic material.*

This last sentence is our thesis for this section. Based on this thesis, we, as the authors, have limited the content of the section; and you, as the reader, will be able to form certain expectations about the discussion that follows. You can expect a definition of a thesis; an enumeration of the uses of a thesis; and a discussion focused on academic material. As writers, we will have met our obligations to you only if in subsequent paragraphs we satisfy these expectations.

THE COMPONENTS OF A THESIS

Like any other sentence, a thesis includes a subject and a predicate, which consists of an assertion about the subject. In the sentence "Lee and Grant were different kinds of generals," "Lee and Grant" is the subject and "were different kinds of generals" is the predicate. What distinguishes a thesis from any other sentence with a subject and predicate is that *the thesis presents the controlling idea of the paper.* The subject of a thesis must present the right balance between the general and the specific to allow for thorough discussion within the allotted length of the paper. The discussion might include definitions, details, comparisons, contrasts—whatever is needed to illuminate a subject and carry on an intelligent conversation. (If the sentence about Lee and Grant were a thesis, the reader would assume that the rest of the paper contained comparisons and contrasts between the two generals.)

Bear in mind when writing theses that the more general your subject and the more complex your assertion, the longer your paper will be. For instance, you could not write an effective ten-page paper based on the following:

> Democracy is the best system of government.

Consider the subject of this sentence ("democracy") and the assertion of its predicate ("is the best system of government"). The subject is enormous in scope; it is a general category composed of hundreds of more specific subcategories, each of which would be appropriate for a paper ten pages in length. The predicate of our example is also a problem, for the claim that democracy is the best system of government would be simplistic unless accompanied by a thorough, systematic, critical evaluation of *every* form of government yet devised. A ten-page paper governed by such a thesis simply could not achieve the level of detail expected of college students.

LIMITING THE SCOPE OF THE THESIS

To write an effective thesis and thus a controlled, effective paper, you need to limit your subject and your claims about it. We discussed narrowing your subject during the invention stage on pages 94–96, and such a process should help you arrive at a manageable thesis. You can begin drafting your essay with a working thesis, and through drafting (and revising, in Stage 4), you will further limit the extent of your discussion.

START WITH A WORKING THESIS

Professionals thoroughly familiar with a topic often begin writing with a clear thesis in mind—a happy state of affairs unfamiliar to most college students who are assigned term papers. But professionals usually have an important advantage over students: experience. Because professionals know their material, are familiar with the ways of approaching it, are aware of the questions important to practitioners, and have devoted considerable time to study of the topic, they are naturally in a strong position to begin writing a paper. In addition, many professionals are practiced at invention; the time they spend listing or outlining their ideas helps them work out their thesis statements. Not only do professionals have experience in their fields, but also they have a clear purpose in writing; they know their audience and are comfortable with the format of their papers.

Experience counts—there's no way around it. As a student, you are not yet an expert and therefore don't generally have the luxury of beginning your writing tasks with a definite thesis in mind. Once you choose and devote time to a major field of study, however, you will gain experience. In the meantime, you'll have to do more work than the professional to prepare yourself for writing a paper.

But let's assume that you *do* have an area of expertise, that you are in your own right a professional (albeit not in academic matters). We'll assume that you understand your nonacademic subject—say, backpacking—and have been given a clear purpose for writing: to discuss the relative merits of backpack designs. Your job is to write a recommendation for the owner of a sporting-goods chain, suggesting which line of backpacks the chain should carry. Because you already know a good deal about backpacks, you may already have some well-developed ideas on the topic before you start doing additional research.

Yet even as an expert in your field, you will find that beginning the writing task is a challenge, for at this point it is unlikely that you will be able to conceive a thesis perfectly suited to the contents of your paper. After all, a thesis is a summary, and it is difficult to summarize a presentation yet to be written—especially if you plan to discover what you want to say during the process of writing. Even if you know your material well, the best you can do at the early stages is to formulate a *working thesis*—a hypothesis of sorts, a well-informed hunch about your topic and the claim to be made about it. Once you have completed a draft, you can evaluate the degree to which your working thesis accurately summarizes the content of your paper. If the match is a good one, the working thesis becomes the thesis. If, however, sections of the paper drift from the focus set out in the working thesis, you'll need to revise the thesis and the paper itself to ensure that the presentation is unified. (You'll know that the match between the content and thesis is a good one when every paragraph directly refers to and develops some element of the thesis.) Later in this chapter we'll discuss revision techniques that will be useful in establishing this kind of unity in your work.

This model works for approaching topics proper to your professor's territory, such as government or medieval poetry. The difference is that when approaching topics that are less familiar to you than something like backpacking, you will have to spend more time gathering data and brainstorming. Such labor prepares you to make assertions about your subject.

MAKE AN ASSERTION

Thesis statements arise out of essay subjects—they constitute an assertion or claim you wish to make *about* your essay's topic. If you have spent enough time reading and gathering information, and brainstorming ideas about the assignment, you will be knowledgeable enough to have something to say about the subject, based on a combination of your own thinking and the thinking of your sources.

If you have trouble making an assertion, do some more invention: Try writing your topic at the top of a page and then listing everything you now know and feel about it. Often from such a list you will discover an assertion that you then can use to fashion a working thesis. A good way to gauge the reasonableness of your claim is to see what other authors have asserted about the same topic. In fact, keep good notes on the views of others; the notes will prove a useful counterpoint to your own views as you write and think about your claim, and you may want to use them in your paper. Next, make several assertions about your topic, in order of increasing complexity (as an example, we'll make three assertions). The earlier example of a subject, "the rights of AIDS patients in the workplace" (see page 96), might lead you to produce the following list of assertions:

1. During the past two decades, the rights of AIDS patients in the workplace have been debated by national columnists.

2. Several columnists have offered convincing reasons for protecting the rights of AIDS patients in the workplace.

3. The most sensible plan for protecting the rights of AIDS patients in the workplace has been offered by columnist Anthony Jones.

Keep in mind that these are *working theses*. Because you haven't written a paper based on any of them, they remain *hypotheses* to be tested. You might choose one of these and use it to focus your first essay draft. After completing a first draft, you would revise it by comparing the contents of the paper to the thesis and making adjustments as necessary for unity. The working thesis is an excellent tool for planning broad sections of the paper, but—again—don't let it prevent you from pursuing related discussions as they occur to you.

USING THE THESIS TO PLAN YOUR ESSAY STRUCTURE

Establishing a working thesis helps you then move to the invention of your essay structure, because essay structure flows directly from the type of thesis contained in an essay.

Notice how the three statements about AIDS in the workplace differ from one another in the forcefulness of their assertions. The third thesis is *strongly argumentative*, or persuasive. "Most sensible" implies that the writer will explain several plans for protecting the rights of AIDS patients in the workplace. Following the explanation would come a comparison of plans and then a judgment in favor of Anthony Jones's plan. This thesis thus helps the writer plan the paper. Assuming that the paper follows the three-part structure we've proposed, the working thesis would become the final thesis, on the basis of which a reader could anticipate sections of the essay to come.

The first of the three thesis statements, by contrast, is *explanatory*, or informative:

> During the past two decades, the rights of AIDS patients in the workplace have been debated by national columnists.

In developing a paper based on this thesis, the writer would assert only the existence of a debate, obligating himself merely to a summary of the various positions taken. Readers, then, would use this thesis as a tool for anticipating the contours of the paper to follow. Based on this particular thesis, a reader would *not* expect to find the author strongly endorsing the views of one or another columnist. The thesis does not require the author to defend a personal opinion.

The second thesis *does* entail a personal, intellectually assertive commitment to the material, although the assertion is not as forceful as the one found in statement three:

> Several columnists have offered convincing reasons for protecting the rights of AIDS patients in the workplace.

Here we have an *explanatory, mildly argumentative* thesis that enables the writer to express an opinion. We infer from the use of the word *convincing* that the writer will judge the various reasons for protecting the rights of AIDS patients; and, we can reasonably assume, the writer believes in protecting these rights. Note the contrast between this second thesis and the first one, in which the writer was committed to no involvement in the debate whatsoever. Still, the second thesis is not as ambitious as the third one, whose writer implicitly accepted the general argument for safeguarding rights (an acceptance the writer would need to justify) and then took the additional step of evaluating the merits of those arguments in relation to each other.

As you can see, for any subject you might care to explore in a paper, you can make any number of assertions—some relatively simple, some complex. It is on the basis of these assertions that you set yourself an agenda in writing a paper—and readers set for themselves expectations for reading. The more ambitious the thesis, the more complex will be the paper and the greater will be the readers' expectations.

USING THE THESIS

Different writing tasks require different theses. The *explanatory thesis* often is developed in response to short-answer exam questions that call for information, not analysis (e.g., "List and explain proposed modifications to contemporary American democracy"). The *explanatory but mildly argumentative thesis* is appropriate for organizing reports (even lengthy ones), as well as essay questions that call for some analysis (e.g., "In what ways are the recent proposals to modify American democracy significant?"). The *strongly argumentative thesis* is used to organize papers and exam questions that call for information, analysis, *and* the writer's forcefully stated point of view (e.g., "Evaluate proposed modifications to health maintenance organizations").

The strongly argumentative thesis, of course, is the riskiest of the three, since you must unequivocally state your position and make it appear reasonable—which requires that you offer evidence and defend against logical objections. But such intellectual risks pay dividends, and if you become involved enough in your work to make challenging assertions, you will provoke challenging responses that enliven classroom discussions. One of the important objectives of a college education is to extend learning by stretching, or challenging, conventional beliefs. You breathe new life into this broad objective, and you enliven your own learning as well, every time you adopt a thesis that sets a challenging agenda both for you (as writer) and for your readers. Of course, once you set the challenge, you must be equal to the task. As a writer, you will need to discuss all the elements implied by your thesis.

To review: A thesis (a one-sentence summary of your paper) helps you organize and your reader anticipate a discussion. Theses are distinguished by their carefully worded subjects and predicates, which should be just broad enough and complex enough to be developed within the length limitations of the assignment. Both novices and experts in a field typically begin the initial draft of a paper with a working thesis—a statement that provides writers with structure enough to get started but with latitude enough to discover what they want to say as they write. Once you have completed a first draft, you test the "fit" of your thesis with the paper that follows. Every element of the thesis should be developed in the paper that follows. Discussions that drift from your thesis should be deleted, or the thesis changed to accommodate the new discussions. These concerns will be addressed more fully when we discuss the revision stage of the writing process. For now, let's move to a discussion of introductions and conclusions.

EXERCISE 3.4

Drafting Thesis Statements

After completing the group exercise where you narrowed a subject (Exercise 3.2, page 96), and the individual invention exercise (Exercise 3.3, page 101), work individually or in small groups to draft three possible theses in relation to your earlier ideas. Draft one *explanatory thesis,* one *explanatory but mildly argumentative thesis,* and one *strongly argumentative thesis.*

Writing Introductions

All writers, no matter how much they prepare, eventually have to face the question of writing their introduction. How to start? What's the best way to approach your subject? With high seriousness, a light touch, an anecdote? How best to engage your reader?

Many writers avoid such agonizing choices by putting them off—productively. Bypassing the introduction, they start by writing the body of the piece; only after they're finished the body do they go back to write the introduction. There's a lot to be said for this approach. Because you have presumably spent more time thinking and writing about the topic itself than about how you're going to introduce it, you are in a better position to begin directly with your presentation. And often, it's not until you've actually seen the piece on paper and read it over once or twice that a natural way of introducing it becomes apparent. Even if there is no natural way to begin, you are generally in better psychological shape to write the introduction after the major task of writing is behind you and you know exactly what you're leading up to.

Perhaps, however, you can't operate this way. After all, you have to start writing *somewhere,* and if you have evaded the problem by skipping the introduction, that blank page may loom just as large whenever you do choose to begin. If this is the case, then go ahead and write an introduction, knowing full well that it's probably going to be flat and awful. Write whatever comes to mind, as long as you have a working thesis. Assure yourself that whatever you put down at this point (except for the thesis) "won't count" and that when the time is right, you'll go back and replace it with something that's fit for eyes other than yours. But in the meantime, you'll have gotten started.

The *purpose* of an introduction is to prepare the reader to enter the world of your essay. The introduction makes the connection between the more familiar world inhabited by the reader and the less familiar world of the writer's particular subject; it places a discussion in a context that the reader can understand.

You have many ways to provide such a context. We'll consider just a few of the most common.

QUOTATION

Here is an introduction to a paper on democracy:

> "Two cheers for democracy" was E. M. Forster's not-quite-whole-hearted judgment. Most Americans would not agree. To them, our democracy is one of the glories of civilization. To one American in particular, E. B. White, democracy is "the hole in the stuffed shirt through which the sawdust slowly trickles [. . .] the dent in the high hat [. . .] the recurrent suspicion that more than half of the people are right more than half of the time" (915). American democracy is based on the oldest continuously operating written constitution in the world—a most impressive fact and a testament to the farsightedness of the founding fathers. But just how farsighted can mere humans be? In *Future Shock,* Alvin Toffler quotes economist Kenneth Boulding on the incredible acceleration of social change in our time: "The world of today [. . .] is as different from the world in which I was born as that world was from Julius Caesar's" (13). As we move into the twenty-first century, it seems legitimate to question the continued effectiveness of a governmental system that was devised in the eighteenth century; and it seems equally legitimate to consider alternatives.

The quotations by Forster and White help set the stage for the discussion of democracy by presenting the reader with some provocative and well-phrased remarks. Later in the paragraph, the quotation by Boulding more specifically prepares us for the theme of change that will be central to the essay as a whole.

HISTORICAL REVIEW

In many cases, the reader will be unprepared to follow the issue you discuss unless you provide some historical background. Consider the following introduction to an essay on the film-rating system:

Sex and violence on the screen are not new issues. In the Roaring Twenties there was increasing pressure from civic and religious groups to ban depictions of "immorality" from the screen. Faced with the threat of federal censorship, the film producers decided to clean their own house. In 1930, the Motion Picture Producers and Distributors of America established the Production Code. At first, adherence to the Code was voluntary; but in 1934 Joseph Breen, newly appointed head of the MPPDA, gave the Code teeth. Henceforth all newly produced films had to be submitted for approval to the Production Code Administration, which had the power to award or withhold the Code seal. Without a Code seal, it was virtually impossible for a film to be shown anywhere in the United States, since exhibitors would not accept it. At about the same time, the Catholic Legion of Decency was formed to advise the faithful which films were and were not objectionable. For several decades the Production Code Administration exercised powerful control over what was portrayed in American theatrical films. By the 1960s, however, changing standards of morality had considerably weakened the Code's grip. In 1968, the Production Code was replaced with a rating system designed to keep younger audiences away from films with high levels of sex or violence. Despite its imperfections, this rating system has proved more beneficial to American films than did the old censorship system.

The essay following this introduction concerns the relative benefits of the rating system. By providing some historical background on the rating system, the writer helps readers to understand his arguments. Notice the chronological development of details.

REVIEW OF A CONTROVERSY

A particular type of historical review is the review of a controversy or debate. Consider the following introduction:

The *American Heritage Dictionary*'s definition of civil disobedience is rather simple: "the refusal to obey civil laws that are regarded as unjust, usually by employing methods of passive resistance." However, despite such famous (and beloved) examples of civil disobedience as the movements of Mahatma Gandhi in India and the Reverend Martin Luther King, Jr., in the United States, the question of whether or not civil disobedience should be considered an asset to society is hardly clear cut. For instance, Hannah Arendt, in her article "Civil Disobedience," holds that "to think of disobedient minorities as rebels and truants is against the letter and spirit of a constitution whose framers were especially sensitive to the dangers of unbridled majority rule." On the other hand, a noted lawyer, Lewis Van Dusen, Jr., in his article "Civil Disobedience: Destroyer of Democracy," states that "civil disobedience, whatever the ethical rationalization, is still an assault on our democratic society, an affront to our legal order and an attack on our constitutional government." These two views are clearly incompatible. I believe, though, that

> Van Dusen's is the more convincing. On balance, civil disobedience is dangerous to society.*

The negative aspects of civil disobedience, rather than Van Dusen's essay, are the topic of this essay. But to introduce this topic, the writer has provided quotations that represent opposing sides of the controversy over civil disobedience, as well as brief references to two controversial practitioners. By focusing at the outset on the particular rather than the abstract aspects of the subject, the writer hoped to secure the attention of her readers and to involve them in the controversy that forms the subject of her essay.

FROM THE GENERAL TO THE SPECIFIC

Another way of providing a transition from the reader's world to the less familiar world of the essay is to work from a general subject to a specific one. The following introduction begins a paper on improving our air quality by inducing people to trade the use of their cars for public transportation.

> While generalizations are risky, it seems pretty safe to say that most human beings are selfish. Self-interest may be part of our nature, and probably aids the survival of our species, since self-interested pursuits increase the likelihood of individual survival and genetic reproduction. Ironically, however, our selfishness has caused us to abuse the natural environment upon which we depend. We have polluted, deforested, depleted, deformed, and endangered our earth, water, and air to such an extent that now our species' survival is gravely threatened. In America, air pollution is one of our most pressing environmental problems, and it is our selfish use of the automobile that poses the greatest threat to clean air, as well as the greatest challenge to efforts to stop air pollution. Very few of us seem willing to give up our cars, let alone use them less. We are spoiled by the individual freedom afforded us when we can hop into our gas-guzzling vehicles and go where we want, when we want. Somehow, we as a nation will have to wean ourselves from this addiction to the automobile, and we can do this by designing alternative forms of transportation that serve our selfish interests.†

FROM THE SPECIFIC TO THE GENERAL: ANECDOTE, ILLUSTRATION

The following paragraph quotes an anecdote in order to move from the specific to a general topic:

> In an article on the changing American family, Ron French tells the following story:

---

*Michele Jacques, "Civil Disobedience: Van Dusen vs. Arendt," unpublished paper, 1993: 1. Used by permission.

†Travis Knight, "Reducing Air Pollution with Alternative Transportation," unpublished paper, 1998: 1. Used by permission.

> Six-year-old Sydney Papenheim has her future planned. "First I'm going to marry Jared," she told her mother. "Then I'm going to get divorced and marry Gabby." "No, honey," Lisa Boettcher says, "you don't plan it like that." That's news to Sydney. Her mother is divorced and remarried, as is her stepdad. Her grandparents are divorced and remarried, as are enough aunts and uncles to field a team for "Family Feud." She gets presents from her stepfather's ex-wife. Her stepfather's children sometimes play at the house of her father. "You never know what is going to happen from day to day," says Sydney's stepdad, Brian Boettcher. "It's an evolution." It's more like a revolution, from Norman Rockwell to Norman Lear.*
>
> French continues on to report that by the year 2007, blended families such as the Boettcher's will outnumber traditional nuclear families. Yet most people continue to lament this change. We as a nation need to accept this new reality: the "till death do us part" version of marriage no longer works.†

The previous introduction went from the general (the statement that human beings are selfish) to the specific (how to decrease air pollution); this one goes from the specific (one little girl's understanding of marriage and divorce) to the general (the changing American family). The anecdote is one of the most effective means at your disposal for capturing and holding your reader's attention. For decades, speakers have begun their general remarks with a funny, touching, or otherwise appropriate story; in fact, there are plenty of books that are nothing but collections of such stories, arranged by subject.

QUESTION

Frequently, you can provoke the reader's attention by posing a question or a series of questions:

> Are gender roles learned or inherited? Scientific research has established the existence of biological differences between the sexes, but the effect of biology's influence on gender roles cannot be distinguished from society's influence. According to Michael Lewis of the Institute for the Study of Exceptional Children, "As early as you can show me a sex difference, I can show you the culture at work." Social

---

* Norman Lear (b. 1922): American television writer and producer noted for developing groundbreaking depictions of the American family in the 1970's, such as "All in the Family," "Sanford and Son," and "Maude." Ron French, "Family: The D-Word Loses its Sting as Households Blend," <u>Detroit News</u> 1 Jan. 2000, 17 Aug. 2000 <http://detnews.com/specialreports/2000/journey/family/family.htm>.

†Veronica Gonzalez, "New Family Formations," unpublished paper, 1999: 1. Used by permission.

processes, as well as biological differences, are responsible for the separate roles of men and women.*

Opening your essay with a question can be provocative, since it places the reader in an active role: He or she begins by considering answers. *Are* gender roles learned? *Are* they inherited? In this active role, the reader is likely to continue reading with interest.

STATEMENT OF THESIS

Perhaps the most direct method of introduction is to begin immediately with the thesis:

> Every college generation is defined by the social events of its age. The momentous occurrences of an era—from war and economics to politics and inventions—give meaning to lives of the individuals who live through them. They also serve to knit those individuals together by creating a collective memory and a common historic or generational identity. In 1979, I went to 26 college and university campuses, selected to represent the diversity of American higher education, and asked students what social or political events most influenced their generation. I told them that the children who came of age in the decade after World War I might have answered the Great Depression. The bombing of Pearl Harbor, World War II, or perhaps the death of Franklin Roosevelt might have stood out for those born a few years later. For my generation, born after World War II, the key event was the assassination of John F. Kennedy. We remember where we were when we heard the news. The whole world seemingly changed in its aftermath.†

This essay begins with a general assertion: that large-scale social events shape generations of college students. The advantage of beginning with a general thesis like this is that it immediately establishes the broader context and the point illustrated by the paper's subsequent focus on contemporary college students. Stating your thesis in the first sentence of an introduction also works when you make a controversial argument. Stating a provocative point right away, such as "Democracy is dead," for a paper examining the problems plaguing representative government in current society, forces the reader to sit up and take notice—perhaps even to begin protesting. This "hooks" a reader, who is likely to want to find out how your essay will support its strong thesis. In the example paragraph above, the general thesis is followed by specific examples of social events and their effects on college students, which prepares the reader to consider the experiences of current college students in comparison to those of earlier generations.

---

*Tammy Smith, "Are Sex Roles Learned or Inherited?" unpublished paper, 1994: 1. Used by permission.

†Arthur Levine, "The Making of a Generation," <u>Change</u> Sept.–Oct. 1993: 8.

One final note about our model introductions: They may be longer than introductions you have been accustomed to writing. Many writers (and readers) prefer a shorter, snappier introduction. The length of an introduction can depend on the length of the paper it introduces, and it is also largely a matter of personal or corporate style: there is no rule concerning the correct length of an introduction. If you feel that a short introduction is appropriate, use one. You may wish to break up what seems like a long introduction into two paragraphs.

EXERCISE **3.5**

Drafting Introductions

Imagine that you are writing an essay using the topic, ideas, and thesis you developed in the earlier exercises in this chapter. Choose one of the seven types of introductions we've discussed—preferably one you have never used before—and draft an introduction that would work to open a paper on this topic. Use our examples as models to help you draft your practice introduction.

Writing Conclusions

One way to view the conclusion of your paper is as an introduction worked in reverse, a bridge from the world of your essay back to the world of your reader. A conclusion is the part of your paper in which you restate and (if necessary) expand on your thesis. Essential to many conclusions is the summary, which is not merely a repetition of the thesis but a restatement that takes advantage of the material you've presented. The *simplest conclusion is a summary of the paper,* but you may want more than this for the end of your paper. Depending on your needs, you might offer a summary and then build onto it a discussion of the paper's significance or its implications for future study, for choices that individuals might make, for policy, and so on. You might also want to urge the reader to change an attitude or to modify behavior. Certainly, you are under no obligation to discuss the broader significance of your work (and a summary, alone, will satisfy the formal requirement that your paper have an ending); but the conclusions of better papers often reveal authors who are "thinking large" and want to connect the particular concerns of their papers with the broader concerns of society.

Here we'll consider seven strategies for expanding the basic summary-conclusion. But two words of advice are in order. First, no matter how clever or beautifully executed, a conclusion cannot salvage a poorly written paper. Second, by virtue of its placement, the conclusion carries rhetorical weight. It is the last statement a reader will encounter before turning from your work. Realizing this, writers who expand on the basic summary-conclusion often wish to give their final words a dramatic flourish, a heightened level of diction. Soaring rhetoric and drama in a conclusion are fine as long as they do not unbalance the paper and call attention to themselves. Having labored long hours over your paper, you have every right to wax eloquent. But keep a sense of proportion and timing. Make your points quickly and end crisply.

STATEMENT OF THE SUBJECT'S SIGNIFICANCE

One of the more effective ways to conclude a paper is to discuss the larger significance of what you have written, providing readers with one more reason to regard your work as a serious effort. When using this strategy, you move from the specific concern of your paper to the broader concerns of the reader's world. Often, you will need to choose among a range of significances: A paper on the Wright brothers might end with a discussion of air travel as it affects economies, politics, or families; a paper on contraception might end with a discussion of its effect on sexual mores, population, or the church. But don't overwhelm your reader with the importance of your remarks. Keep your discussion well focused.

The following paragraphs conclude a paper on George H. Shull, a pioneer in the inbreeding and crossbreeding of corn:

> [. . .] Thus, the hybrids developed and described by Shull 75 years ago have finally dominated U.S. corn production.
>
> The adoption of hybrid corn was steady and dramatic in the Corn Belt. From 1930 through 1979 the average yields of corn in the U.S. increased from 21.9 to 95.1 bushels per acre, and the additional value to the farmer is now several billion dollars per year.
>
> The success of hybrid corn has also stimulated the breeding of other crops, such as sorghum hybrids, a major feed grain crop in arid parts of the world. Sorghum yields have increased 300 percent since 1930. Approximately 20 percent of the land devoted to rice production in China is planted with hybrid seed, which is reported to yield 20 percent more than the best varieties. And many superior varieties of tomatoes, cucumbers, spinach, and other vegetables are hybrids. Today virtually all corn produced in the developed countries is from hybrid seed. From those blue bloods of the plant kingdom has come a model for feeding the world.*

The first sentence of this conclusion is a summary, and from it the reader can infer that the paper included a discussion of Shull's techniques for the hybrid breeding of corn. The summary is followed by a two-paragraph discussion on the significance of Shull's research for feeding the world.

CALL FOR FURTHER RESEARCH

In the scientific and social scientific communities, papers often end with a review of what has been presented (as, for instance, in an experiment) and the ways in which the subject under consideration needs to be further explored. If you raise questions that you call on others to answer, however, make sure you know that the research you are calling for hasn't already been conducted.

This next conclusion comes from a sociological report on the placement of elderly men and women in nursing homes.

---

* William L. Brown, "Hybrid Vim and Vigor," <u>Science</u> Nov. 1984: 77–78.

Thus, our study shows a correlation between the placement of elderly citizens in nursing facilities and the significant decline of their motor and intellectual skills over the ten months following placement. What the research has not made clear is the extent to which this marked decline is due to physical as opposed to emotional causes. The elderly are referred to homes at that point in their lives when they grow less able to care for themselves—which suggests that the drop-off in skills may be due to physical causes. But the emotional stress of being placed in a home, away from family and in an environment that confirms the patient's view of himself as decrepit, may exacerbate—if not itself be a primary cause of—the patient's rapid loss of abilities. Further research is needed to clarify the relationship between depression and particular physical ailments as these affect the skills of the elderly in nursing facilities. There is little doubt that information yielded by such studies can enable health care professionals to deliver more effective services.

Notice how this call for further study locates the author in a larger community of researchers on whom she depends for assistance in answering the questions that have come out of her own work. The author summarizes her findings (in the first sentence of the paragraph), states what her work has not shown, and then extends her invitation.

SOLUTION/RECOMMENDATION

The purpose of your paper might be to review a problem or controversy and to discuss contributing factors. In such a case, it would be appropriate, after summarizing your discussion, to offer a solution based on the knowledge you've gained while conducting research. If your solution is to be taken seriously, your knowledge must be amply demonstrated in the body of the paper.

> (1) [. . .] The major problem in college sports today is not commercialism—it is the exploitation of athletes and the proliferation of illicit practices which dilute educational standards.
>
> (2) Many universities are currently deriving substantial benefits from sports programs that depend on the labor of athletes drawn from the poorest sections of America's population. It is the responsibility of educators, civil rights leaders, and concerned citizens to see that these young people get a fair return for their labor both in terms of direct remuneration and in terms of career preparation for a life outside sports.
>
> (3) Minimally, scholarships in revenue-producing sports should be designed to extend until graduation, rather than covering only four years of athletic eligibility, and should include guarantees of tutoring, counseling, and proper medical care. At institutions where the profits are particularly large (such as Texas A & M, which can afford to pay its football coach $280,000 a year), scholarships should also provide salaries that extend beyond room, board, and tuition. The important thing is that the athlete be remunerated fairly and

have the opportunity to gain skills from a university environment without undue competition from a physically and psychologically demanding full-time job. This may well require that scholarships be extended over five or six years, including summers.

(4) Such a proposal, I suspect, will not be easy to implement. The current amateur system, despite its moral and educational flaws, enables universities to hire their athletic labor at minimal cost. But solving the fiscal crisis of the universities on the backs of America's poor and minorities is not, in the long run, a tenable solution. With the support of concerned educators, parents, and civil rights leaders, and with the help from organized labor, the college athlete, truly a sleeping giant, will someday speak out and demand what is rightly his— and hers—a fair share of the revenue created by their hard work.*

In this conclusion, the author summarizes his article in one sentence: "The major problem in college sports today is not commercialism—it is the exploitation of athletes and the proliferation of illicit practices which dilute educational standards." In paragraph 2, he continues with an analysis of the problem just stated and follows with a general recommendation—that "concerned educators, parents, and civil rights leaders" be responsible for the welfare of college athletes. In paragraph 3, he makes a specific proposal, and in the final paragraph, he anticipates resistance to the proposal. He concludes by discounting this resistance and returning to the general point, that college athletes should receive a fair deal.

ANECDOTE

An anecdote is a briefly told story or joke, the point of which in a conclusion is to shed light on your subject. The anecdote is more direct than an allusion. With an allusion, you merely refer to a story ("Too many people today live in Plato's cave . . ."); with the anecdote, you actually retell the story. The anecdote allows readers to discover for themselves the significance of a reference to another source—an effort most readers enjoy because they get to exercise their creativity.

The following anecdote concludes a political-philosophical essay. First, the author includes a paragraph summing up her argument, and she follows that with a brief story.

Ironically, our economy is fueled by the very thing that degrades our value system. But when politicians call for a return to "traditional family values," they seldom criticize the business interests that promote and benefit from our coarsened values. Consumer capitalism values things over people; it thrives on discontent and unhappiness since discontented people make excellent consumers, buying vast numbers of things that may somehow "fix" their inadequacies. We buy more than we need, the economy chugs along, but such material-

---

*Mark Naison, "Scenario for Scandal," <u>Commonweal</u> 109.16 (1982).

ism is the real culprit behind our warped value systems. Anthony de Mello tells the following story:

> Socrates believed that the wise person would instinctively lead a frugal life, and he even went so far as to refuse to wear shoes. Yet he constantly fell under the spell of the marketplace and would go there often to look at the great variety and magnificence of the wares on display.
>
> A friend once asked him why he was so intrigued with the allures of the market. "I love to go there," Socrates replied, "to discover how many things I am perfectly happy without." (27)*

The writer chose to conclude the article with this anecdote. She could have developed an interpretation, but this would have spoiled the dramatic value for the reader. The purpose of using an anecdote is to make your point with subtlety, so resist the temptation to interpret. Keep in mind three guidelines when selecting an anecdote: It should be prepared for (readers should have all the information they need to understand it), it should provoke the reader's interest, and it should not be so obscure as to be unintelligible.

QUOTATION

A favorite concluding device is the quotation—the words of a famous person or an authority in the field on which you are writing. The purpose of quoting another is to link your work to theirs, thereby gaining for your work authority and credibility. The first criterion for selecting a quotation is its suitability to your thesis. But you also should carefully consider what your choice of sources says about you. Suppose you are writing a paper on the American work ethic. If you could use a line by comedian David Letterman or one by the current secretary of labor to make the final point of your conclusion, which would you choose and why? One source may not be inherently more effective than the other, but the choice certainly sets a tone for the paper. The following two paragraphs conclude an essay examining the popularity of vulgar and insulting humor in television shows, movies, and other popular culture:

> But studies on the influence of popular culture suggest that cruel humor serves as more than a release in modern society. The ubiquitous media pick up on our baser nature, exaggerate it to entertain, and, by spitting it back at us, encourage us to push the boundaries even further. As a result, says Johns Hopkins' Miller, "We're gradually eroding the kinds of social forms and inhibitions that kept [aggressive] compulsions contained."

---

*Frances Wageneck, <u>Family Values in the Marketplace</u>, unpublished paper, 2000: 6. Used by permission.

> Before the cycle escalates further, we might do well to consider the advice of Roman statesman and orator Cicero, who wrote at the peak of the Roman empire: "If we are forced, at ever hour, to watch or listen to horrible events, this constant stream of ghastly impressions will deprive even the most delicate among us of all respect for humanity."*

The two quotations used here serve different but equally effective ends. The first idea provides one last expert's viewpoint, then leads nicely into the cautionary note the writer introduces by quoting Cicero. The Roman's words, and the implied parallel being drawn between Rome and contemporary culture, are strong enough that the author ends there, without stepping in and making any statements of her own. In other cases, quotations can be used to set up one last statement by the author of an essay.

There is a potential problem with using quotations: If you end with the words of another, you may leave the impression that someone else can make your case more eloquently than you can. The language of the quotation will put your own prose into relief. If your own prose suffers by comparison—if the quotations are the best part of your paper—you'd be wise to spend some time revising. The way to avoid this kind of problem is to make your own presentation strong.

QUESTION

Questions are useful for opening essays, and they are just as useful for closing them. Opening and closing questions function in different ways, however. The introductory question promises to be addressed in the paper that follows. But the concluding question leaves issues unresolved, calling on the readers to assume an active role by offering their own answers. Take a look at the following two paragraphs, written to conclude an essay on genetically modified (GM) food:

> Are GM foods any more of a risk than other agricultural innovations that have taken place over the years, like selective breeding? Do the existing and potential future benefits of GM foods outweigh any risks that do exist? And what standard should governments use when assessing the safety of transgenic crops? The "frankenfood" frenzy has given life to a policy-making standard known as the "precautionary principle," which has been long advocated by environmental groups. That principle essentially calls for governments to prohibit any activity that raises concerns about human health or the environment, even if some cause-and-effect relationships are not fully established scientifically. As Liberal Democrat MP [Member of Parliament] Norman Baker told the BBC: "We must always apply the precautionary principle. That says that unless you're sure of adequate control, unless you're sure the risk is minimal, unless you're sure nothing horrible can go wrong, you don't do it."

---

*Nina J. Easton, "The Meaning of America," <u>Los Angeles Times Magazine</u> 7 Feb. 1993: 21.

> But can any innovation ever meet such a standard of certainty—
> especially given the proliferation of "experts" that are motivated as
> much by politics as they are by science? And what about those mil-
> lions of malnourished people whose lives could be saved by trans-
> genic foods? [Is] the "precautionary principle" [really] so precaution-
> ary after all [?]*

Perhaps you will choose to raise a question in your conclusion and then
answer it, based on the material you've provided in the paper. The answered
question challenges a reader to agree or disagree with your response and
thus also places the reader in an active role. The following brief conclusion
ends a student paper entitled "Is Feminism Dead?"

> So the answer to the question "Is the feminist movement dead?" is
> no, it's not. Even if most young women today don't consciously iden-
> tify themselves as "feminists"—due to the ways in which the term
> has become loaded with negative associations—the principles of gen-
> der equality that lie at feminism's core are enthusiastically embraced
> by the vast number of young women, and even a large percentage of
> young men.

SPECULATION

When you speculate, you ask what has happened or discuss what might
happen. This kind of question stimulates the reader because its subject is the
unknown.

The following paragraph concludes "The New Generation Gap" by Neil
Howe and William Strauss. In this essay, Howe and Strauss discuss the differences among Americans of various ages, including the "GI Generation"
(born between 1901 and 1924), the "Boomers"(born 1943–1961), the "Thir-
teeners" (born 1961–1981), and the "Millennials" (born 1981–2000):

> If, slowly but surely, Millennials receive the kind of family protection
> and public generosity that GIs enjoyed as children, then they could
> come of age early in the next century as a group much like the GIs of
> the 1920s and 1930s—as a stellar (if bland) generation of rationalists,
> team players, and can-do civic builders. Two decades from now
> Boomers entering old age may well see in their grown Millennial chil-
> dren an effective instrument for saving the world, while Thirteeners
> entering midlife will shower kindness on a younger generation that is
> getting a better deal out of life (though maybe a bit less fun) than they
> ever got at a like age. Study after story after column will laud these
> "best damn kids in the world" as heralding a resurgent American
> greatness. And, for a while at least, no one will talk about a generation
> gap.†

---

*"Frankenfoods Frenzy," Reason 13 Jan. 2000, 17 Aug. 2000 <http://reason.com/bi/bi-gmf.html>.

†Neil Howe and William Strauss, "The New Generation Gap," Atlantic Monthly Dec. 1992: 65.

Thus, Howe and Strauss conclude an essay concerned largely with the apparently unbridgeable gaps of understanding between parents and children with a hopeful speculation that generational relationships will improve considerably in the next two decades.

EXERCISE 3.6

Drafting Conclusions

Imagine that you have written an essay using the topic, ideas, and thesis you developed in the earlier exercises in this chapter. Choose one of the seven types of conclusions we've discussed—preferably one you have never used before—and draft a conclusion that would work to end your paper. Use our examples as models to help you draft your practice conclusion.

REVISING THE ESSAY

Stage 4: Revision

Perhaps it sounds like stating the obvious to say that rough drafts need revision, but as we've noted, too often students skimp on this phase of the writing process. The word "revision" can be used to describe all modifications one makes to a written document. However, it's useful to distinguish between two different kinds of revision—large-scale changes to a piece of writing, and small scale, sentence-level changes. The large-scale changes fall within Stage 4 of the writing process, while the sentence-level changes are covered in Stage 5, editing.

Separating large-scale revision from editing sentences works well for the same reason that separating content development, in the invention stage, from questions about paper structure, in the drafting stage, works. The bottom line is that it's best to try not to do too much at one time. Different tasks require different cognitive functions. For example, when you are working on revising the structure and content of a paragraph within a paper, getting caught up in rewording an awkward sentence can completely distract you from the larger issue of paragraph structure and content. Putting editing off until later keeps you from wasting time working on sentences that may not even appear in your work after you've revised it. As much as possible, defer sentence-level concerns until you've spent time revising the major elements of a paper—content (your ideas), structure (the arrangement of your paragraphs), and paragraph structure (the arrangement of ideas within your paragraphs).

Admittedly, revision is difficult, especially since as a student, you may feel you don't know enough about writing to really revise a paper draft. While it's true that students generally have a lot to learn, you can apply the things you know to the task of revision.

You can think of revision as re-vision, meaning, "seeing anew," so you might find it useful to set your paper aside for a period of time and come back later to view your rough draft with a fresh eye, from a new perspective. When you revise, try focusing on a few important areas at a time.

One set of principles you can apply to the revision process is *unity, coherence,* and *development,* (see pages 122–123), since good papers generally have these characteristics.

THE REVERSE OUTLINE

One very useful revision technique for refining a working thesis, and for establishing unity between your thesis statement and your paper body, is the reverse outline.

Print out a hard copy of your rough draft and carefully review each of your body paragraphs. Write down the main point of each paragraph in the margin next to it. If you have difficulty identifying the main points of paragraphs, then you know you have a problem with that particular paragraph—perhaps it doesn't fit in that paper, perhaps it needs rewriting so that the main point is clear, or perhaps you've tried to cover too many important ideas in one paragraph. If you find these kinds of paragraph problems, flag them with a note to yourself and come back to them later. For now, whether they contain one or many main points, sum them up in a sentence or two in your paper's margin.

After doing this for the entire paper, list the points on a separate sheet of paper. You are thus writing an outline in reverse—putting points from an essay into a list form rather than (or in addition to) using a list of points to write a paper. Put the paper aside, and look at this list of ideas. To what do all these points add up? Which of your points clearly relate to an overall idea? Do these correspond to your working thesis, or do you seem to be focused on a different point? Whatever the answer, take the points that are all related and write a thesis that encompasses all of these ideas in the form of a sentence or two. Is this what you are trying to say overall?

If you find that your points don't support your working thesis, or if you have trouble seeing the point of all your subpoints, read your concluding paragraph, if you have one. Sometimes you will find that you've attempted to pull all your ideas together in the conclusion. Is there a sentence or two in this section of your paper that is similar to the thesis in your reverse outline? Or does your conclusion contain a better summation of your main point than you've managed to provide elsewhere so far?

Look at your points and at these different theses, and fashion a thesis that most sums up what you want to say. Then decide where you need to add or remove points in your paper, and note whether or not the points are in a logical order. When you're satisfied with the paper unity and coherence reflected in your outline, go back to your rough draft and make the changes contained in your outline. Then work on adding transitional sentences and developing your points.

The extent of your revisions will often depend both on the amount of time you've budgeted for your writing process overall, as well as on the quality of your work at the invention and drafting stages. Some work needs

CHARACTERISTICS OF GOOD PAPERS

Unity

A paper is unified when it is focused upon a main point. Papers that meander all over the place—whether they start with a main point or not—are hard to follow. The chief tool for achieving paper unity is the thesis: it's very hard to achieve unity in a paper when a central point remains unstated. Unity, however, doesn't stop at the thesis; the body paragraphs that follow must clearly support and explain that thesis. Examine your introduction and make sure you have a clear, identifiable thesis. Check your paper's body paragraphs to make sure your points all relate to that thesis. Ask yourself how your conclusion provides closure to your overall discussion.

Coherence

The word "coherence" has several related meanings, yet chiefly it means "logical interconnectedness." When things cohere, they hold together and make sense together. As applied to essay writing, coherence is very closely related to unity: Good papers must cohere, they must hold together logically. Coherent papers stay focused upon a main point; that is, all the subordinate points covered in body paragraphs clearly relate to the main point of the essay as a whole, AND all those subpoints are covered in a logical order, so the connections between them are clear. You could write a highly unified paper, but if your points are discussed in a haphazard order, the reader will still not have an easy time following your argument or staying focused upon your point. Instead, a reader should be led along by your writing; he or she should be able to see not only how subpoints relate to a main point, but also how the subpoints relate to one another.

Many think of the concept of coherence as "flow"; students will often sense that in rough drafts of their work, the writing doesn't "flow." The best way to ensure a paper's flow is to think carefully about how the points relate to each other, and place them in an order that most reflects that relationship. If you do this, then it becomes easier to use an important tool for aiding a paper's coherence: transitions. When you

such extensive revision that writers in this stage essentially write new drafts, using parts of their rough draft but incorporating them into a new paper. More commonly, however, if you've worked hard on brainstorming ideas and drafting them into paper form, you will be able to revise papers by modifying and moving rough material, and adding new writing to an existing draft. Word processors have greatly aided the revision process, and the more of your writing you can accomplish on the computer, the easier it is to rework that writing. Still, you might find yourself working on paper in ad-open paragraphs with sentences that refer to an important element of the last paragraph and show how that element relates to the point of the new paragraph, you are using transitions that help to keep the essay flow going. These transitional sentences are easiest to write when you have put your points in a logical order to begin with.

Development

In addition to unity and coherence, good papers tend to be well developed, meaning that their main points are fully explained and supported. A reader is not inside your head; thus, he or she may not fully understand many of your points unless you adequately explain them. A reader also may not be persuaded that your paper's main point is a valid one unless you provide sufficient support for your arguments by using examples, the opinions of authorities on the subject, and your own reasoning and logic.

Good development demands that you try to step outside of your own head; you know what you're trying to say, but is a reader likely to fully understand you? Could you aid the reader's understanding with more development of your points?

Use the three principles of unity, coherence, and development to analyze what you have written and make necessary revisions. Does your paper stay focused upon the main point? Do your paper's points clearly relate to each other? Are there places where you need better transitions between paragraphs so that the ideas flow more logically and smoothly? Have you fully explained and given adequate support for all your points? Make the necessary changes to ensure that your paper accomplishes these objectives.

These three principles for good papers also apply to the composition of good paragraphs. Paragraphs are "mini-essays"; they should stick to a main point and fully develop that point in an orderly flow of ideas. Transitional words or phrases such as "however," "thus," "on the other hand," and "for example," help make clear to a reader how the points in individual paragraphs relate.

dition to working on the computer: Whatever methods work best for you are fine, of course.

Stage 5: Editing

After revising a paper's large-scale characteristics—its content, overall structure, and paragraph structure—you are now ready to polish your paper by editing its sentences for style and correctness. At this stage you may be tired, and the temptation to merely correct a few glaring mistakes here and there may be strong. Resist that impulse: A paper with excellent ideas and structure can be ruined by mechanical, sentence-level errors when your reader gets distracted by the errors instead of focusing upon your ideas.

EDITING FOR STYLE

Developing an engaging writing style takes a lot of practice over a long period of time. It's beyond the realm of this book to teach you the complexities of writing style, and you can consult many fine books to help with this. (See, for example, William Zinsser, *On Writing Well.*) However, one important stylistic issue we will mention is the use of short, choppy sentences, which often occurs in student writing, resulting in a repetitive style that lacks coherence or "flow."

Perhaps out of fear of making sentence errors—such as run-ons or comma-splices (which we define on page 126)—many students avoid writing complex and varied sentences, preferring strings of simple sentence structures that are not clearly linked with the related sentences surrounding them. Watch for this in your own writing. A good place to start developing a good writing style is at the sentence level. Learn how different sentence structures work, how to link related ideas with subordinating conjunctions ("because," "since," "while," "although," etc.), commas and coordinating conjunctions ("for," "and," "nor," "but," "or," "yet," "so"), and semicolons and coordinating adverbs ("however," "thus," "therefore," etc.). Take a look at the following example of short, choppy sentences:

> Scientists have finally succeeded in decoding the human genome. This accomplishment opens up a whole new field of study. Researchers now have new ways to understand human biological functioning. We may also be able to learn new perspectives on human behavior. For centuries people have wondered about how much we are shaped by genetics, and how much environment shapes us. The age-old questions about nature vs. nurture may now be answered. Each individual's genetic heritage as well as his or her genetic future will be visible to geneticists. All of these discoveries may help us to improve and extend human life. Many diseases will be detectable. New treatments will be developed. These new discoveries open up a new area of ethical debate. Scientists and the public are going to have to decide how far to take this new genetic technology.

This paragraph illustrates the problems with choppy and repetitive sentences. First, the writer hasn't connected the ideas, and each sentence doesn't clearly flow to the next. Second, the same structure—simple sentence forms consisting of one independent clause—appears over and over, each sentence following the simple subject-verb-predicate form. The resulting repetition would put a reader to sleep if she weren't reading along, supplying the transitions the writer should have included. Compare the choppy sentences to this rewrite (which represents just one way this paragraph could be rewritten):

> Scientists have opened a whole new field of study following their recent decoding of the human genome. Armed with new ways of understanding human biological and behavioral functioning, researchers may someday sort out the extent to which we are shaped by our genes and by our environment. When geneticists can examine an individual's genetic past and future, they may also be able to alter these things, with the goal of improving and extending human life through early disease detection and the development of new treatments. However, such promise is not without its pitfalls: genetic research must be scrutinized from an ethical standpoint, and scientists and the public will have to decide the uses and the limits of this new technology.

As you can see, the edited version of this paragraph is more concise and clear, as well as more coherent. A number of sentences have been created by combining several related ideas that were separated in the first version. Brief sentences have been converted to clauses or phrases and incorporated into the structure of other sentences to form more complex, coherent units of meaning.

EDITING FOR CORRECTNESS

While many writers would agree on some basic elements of style, this area is largely subjective. Grammar and punctuation, on the other hand, follow more widely accepted, objective standards. Of course, grammar, like language in general, is socially constructed, so people alter the rules to meet changing social contexts; however, during particular periods of time and in particular geographical regions, most academics agree upon certain grammar and punctuation rules so that orderly communication can occur. You can find such agreed upon standards in up-to-date writing handbooks. Grammar and punctuation rules, despite how it sometimes appears, are (usually) not arbitrary rules designed to make your life more difficult; rather, they are analogous to the laws, road signs, and signal lights that aid the orderly movement of vehicles over the roadways: They help us navigate through our daily lives. People are more likely to understand what you are trying to say in your writing if you follow the rules, just as you are more likely to get to school on time and in one piece if you follow the road signs and the rules of driving.

After going over your writing style, you should look carefully at your sentences for grammatical errors, that is, errors in the way you have structured or worded your sentences. Check for punctuation errors and look for errors of usage. Lastly, check your spelling. Consult a writing handbook for review of the sentence errors you tend to make most often so that you can spot them and properly correct them. Review the list of common sentence-level errors on page 126.

COMMON SENTENCE-LEVEL ERRORS

Grammatical Errors:

Sentence fragments—incomplete sentences missing a subject or a predicate.

Run-on sentences—two independent clauses joined together without the proper conjunctions (connecting words) or punctuation.

Comma-splices—two independent clauses joined with only a comma when they need stronger separation such as coordinating conjunctions, conjunctive adverbs, semicolons, or periods.

Subject-verb agreement errors—the verb form doesn't match the plural or singular nature of the subject.

Pronoun usage—pronoun reference errors and errors of pronoun-antecedent agreement.

Punctuation Errors:

Misplaced commas, missing commas, improper use of semicolons or colons, missing apostrophes, and the like.

Word-Usage Errors:

Improper or incorrect use of a word or phrase.

SPELL-CHECK AND GRAMMAR-CHECK

A spell-checker is a useful tool provided by most word-processing programs, and you should run spell-check before printing your essay. Use this tool carefully, however, since you may be using a correctly spelled word inappropriately. For example, most spell-checkers can't distinguish the different uses of "their" and "there." Grammar-check programs also can be useful, but they are tricky for novice writers to use successfully. Unless you have a comprehensive grasp of grammar and punctuation, grammar- and style-check can be confusing and, in some cases, simply wrong. Many grammar-check programs, for instance, are designed to weed out long sentences—even if these are punctuated and worded correctly. If you choose to run grammar-check, don't take everything it tells you at face value. If the program flags a long sentence, check it for correctness and clarity, and if it makes sense, then leave it (that is, unless nearly all of your sentences are long—you want to have some sentence variety).

Rather than rely on grammar-check tools, you ought to carefully and slowly go over your sentences. Reading them aloud either to yourself or to a friend can be very helpful since sometimes you will *hear* sentence problems more often than you will *see* them. When reading your work aloud, don't stop reading each time you come upon a problem. Instead, just make a note or mark next to the problem, continue reading, and then come back and make corrections after you've read over the whole paper.

Do your best to correct your errors. If you notice sentences that "just don't sound right," but you can't quite identify the specific error, try rewriting the sentence. If you can't get it to sound right, make a note of it and when you can, ask your instructor to look it over, or try to locate the error in a writing handbook. All writers—even professionals—have problem areas in their writing. One difference between veteran and novice writers, however, is that experienced writers usually are more aware of their problem areas, so they watch for these and correct them before going public with their writing. Pay attention to your instructors' comments on material you've submitted, and notice your patterns of errors. Learn how to recognize and correct several of your key problem areas, and your writing will improve by measurable increments.

Stage 6: Publication

You've reached the last stage of the writing process—your work is ready to be handed over for evaluation. We use the term "publication" here in its broadest sense of "going public." Your work may not be published in some academic journal, campus newspaper, the Web, or any other public forum, but if you turn it in to a professor for grading, you have taken your work public, and for now, the writing process is over (or at least in remission).

When you get your written work back from your instructors, be sure to read it over carefully, reviewing the instructors' comments. Rereading each piece of writing you produce will help you improve for the next writing assignment. If there are comments on your paper that you don't understand (or can't read!), be sure to ask your instructor to explain. Visit him or her during office hours and ask how you can improve on the areas commented upon. Also, be sure to look for, or ask about, the parts of your papers that are well done—almost all work has some good elements. Find out where your strengths and weaknesses lie, and work to improve.

Writing well is hard work, there's no doubt about it. But it definitely gets easier with practice. Subsequent chapters of this book will build upon material we've covered thus far, by examining more specific kinds of writing common to college assignments. As you work through the book, keep in mind this discussion of writing as a process. Also, when completing writing assignments from this book or from any of your courses, try breaking your work down into the stages of *data gathering, invention, drafting, revision, editing,* and *publication,* and see how these strategies work for you.

DEMONSTRATION: THE PROCESS OF WRITING AND REVISING A CRITIQUE

Included in Chapter 2 is a finished critique (pages 71–74) written in response to J. Morton Davis's essay, "A Simple One-Step Plan to Solve the Education Crisis" (pages 57–58). Returning to Davis's essay and its critique, here is a demonstration of the stages followed by the student writer who produced the critique.

Stage 1: Data gathering

I read Davis's essay several times. The first time through, I wanted to get an overview of the paper, so I read without a pen in my hand. During the following readings I used a pen to underline and make notations next to parts of the essay—points I agreed with, places where I questioned his assertions, and so forth.

I see this part of the writing process as both data gathering and invention, because even before I start writing, I know I'm going to be critiquing the article. So I'm coming up with ideas for the essay even as I read.

Stage 2: Invention

After I felt I had a good grasp on the essay, I opened a new document in my word processing program and started jotting down ideas. Incidentally, I used to do my brainstorming and drafting on paper, then type in my essay once I was ready to revise it, but I've found that the more writing I can accomplish on the computer, the easier and less time-consuming the process is.

BRAINSTORMING IDEAS

Here is the first piece of writing I produced to generate ideas for my critique. I think my technique is a combination of freewriting and listing:

Davis—who is this guy? A teacher? If so, he has a high opinion of himself. Probably not a teacher, otherwise would sound too self-serving.
More money = more teachers? Better teachers? I've heard people say they're not interested in

teaching b/c of low pay. But—do we want people primarily concerned with pay to be teachers? Teachers *should* get paid more. Plumbers make more than teachers. Training involved should relate to pay. Teaching is important—is it <u>the</u> most important job, as D. says? Doctors more important . . . police, fire . . .

This point is a problem. But is this the main problem with his essay? Does his whole argument rest on this? No . . .

So what is his main argument, and does it rest on faulty premises?

There is a crisis in education. Okay, most people agree on this.

What is this crisis caused by? D. doesn't say, exactly. But since he's proposing to solve it by attracting better teachers, he's implying that the cause of ed. crisis is bad teachers.

Does he have any evidence to support this? No.

Is this the cause? I don't think so. Other causes: lack of money—not just to teachers but to schools overall. Remember those old textbooks in American History? Some schools have no computers, have even worse textbooks, buildings are falling down.

Okay, so D.'s assumption about cause of prob. is wrong (cause-effect problem). His solution is too simple. Plus, does his analogy between the way we got behind the Manhattan Project and the space program and working to solve the ed. crisis hold up? Not quite the same kinds of problems . . .

Does faulty cause-effect analysis wreck his whole argument? Not entirely . . . Teachers should get more money. They work hard. And we should try to attract the best students into the teaching profession. This would help education, just wouldn't solve the problem, as D thinks.

Could D's idea about federal tax exemption be a way to get more money to teachers? Yes, sounds good. So . . . I agree there's a problem in education, and that teachers should be paid more. D. has a good idea about how to give teachers more money, and this probably will help attract better people to teaching. But D. is wrong to think this will solve the problem with ed. because the prob is more complex than this.

[working] Thesis:

There are problems with education, and Davis makes a good proposal to attract better teachers to education. However, this won't solve the complex problems with education.

BRAINSTORMING STRUCTURE

I felt good about this beginning. I went back and reread parts of Davis's essay to make sure I was on the right track, and decided I was. Now I returned to my brainstorming, and took the thesis I was using and tried to outline an essay structure. As I did this, more ideas came to me, so inventing ideas and essay structure work together for me.

First, I saw that I could make my working thesis fit into one sentence by linking the two sentences with a semicolon. Then I proceeded to use my thesis to map out the structure of my paper.

> There are problems with education, and Davis makes a good proposal to attract better teachers; however, this won't solve the complex problems with education.

Outline:

Introduction

    I. Sum up Davis's argument here: There are problems with education, and we should give teachers a tax break in order to attract better teachers.

   II. Why giving teachers this financial bonus is a good idea.

  III. Why this won't solve the crisis in education.

      a. bad teachers are not the problem, so this incentive won't address the problem.

         1. some teachers are bad, but there are plenty of good ones too.

      b. the real problems with education are complex; they include a lack of funding for the schools overall, poverty among students so they can't focus on learning . . .

Here I realized I had a problem. As I worked out the subpoints I needed to make to support my thesis, it became clear to me that if I was going to claim bad teachers weren't the real problem, I needed to discuss what the real problems are with public schools. Unfortunately, I realized I didn't know enough about the issues at this point to be able to explain the real problems. Obviously, I couldn't address all the problems with education anyway, but I knew I needed to discuss several key problems, and would need to do more than just say what they were. I would have to develop these points by explaining them somewhat knowledgeably. I knew I had a good argument, so I didn't want to change that. Instead I went back to data gathering to find out a little more about the problems with education.

Stage 1: More data gathering

I went online and used a search engine to search for documents related to keywords and phrases such as "problems with public schools" and "educational crisis." I made sure the documents I looked at came from reputable sources and that the authors of the readings I used were identified and possessed proper credentials. The Web is a great resource, but there's also a lot of junk out there. I read some reports from newsmagazines and newspapers online, and I read a few opinion/style essays as well, taking notes on what seemed to me to be the most significant problems identified in the readings.

Then I went back to my outline and revised my third point, listing three items under point b., along with some details about them:

III. Why tax breaks for teachers won't solve the crisis in education

    a. bad teachers are not the problem, so this incentive won't address the problem.

        1. some teachers are bad, but there are plenty of good ones too.

    b. the real problems with education are complex.

        1. We need more teachers as well as better ones and that takes money no one wants to give. More teachers would be good, but money to hire more teachers is scarce and would have to be raised with higher taxes, which voters don't want. We could increase funding at the federal level, but if fed. gov. is losing revenue by giving tax breaks to teachers, will they also increase funding for more teachers and smaller class sizes? Unlikely.

        2. Structural problems with schools. Administrators make too much money; teachers

are overmanaged by bureaucrats; unions pose obstacles to change; curriculum changes are made for bad reasons; school committees and administrators battle over funding, curriculum, etc.

3. Poverty in many school districts. Poor families' home environments are sometimes not conducive to education; poor neighborhoods provide few models to motivate students academically.

As I wrote down these points, I made sure not to copy the wording or the sentence structure used in my sources, so as not to plagiarize. I wasn't quoting or paraphrasing any ideas directly, and these points are common knowledge, so I didn't need to cite my sources. I did write down the Web site URLs, however, in case I needed to refer back to the material to help me draft my essay.

My outline seemed complete enough, so I moved on to the drafting stage, feeling that I would further refine my ideas if I jumped in and began writing.

Stage 3: Drafting

I started drafting my essay by skipping the introduction and simply copying my working thesis statement at the top of my page. Then I began drafting the body paragraphs set up by my outline. As I wrote, I thought of an additional point that I felt needed treatment in the essay: The first reason Davis's plan wouldn't work is because giving teachers tax breaks won't increase the *number* of teachers employed in the schools. The numbers can only increase if school districts allocate more funding for hiring. This idea exposes another logical fallacy in Davis's argument, so I spent one paragraph discussing it before I went on to describe the real problems causing the educational crisis.

Stage 4: Revision

My rough draft was essentially a rougher version of the essay appearing on pages 71–74. After composing it, I went back and drafted the introduction, tightened up the wording of my thesis, rearranged some of my ideas to improve the paragraph coherence, and revised some of my topic sentences for better essay coherence. My initial explanation of the structural problems within the educational community (paragraph 6) was a little skimpy, so I consulted my notes again to improve the development there.

Stage 5: Editing

I carefully went over my sentences. I have a tendency to use commas incorrectly, so I was especially careful to look for comma errors. After cleaning up the wording and punctuation of my sentences, I made sure I had formatted the paper properly—with the right margins and such—and I was finished.

Stage 6: Publication

When I handed in my essay, I essentially "went public" with it, completing stage six of the process.

4

Explanatory Synthesis

WHAT IS A SYNTHESIS?

A *synthesis* is a written discussion that draws on two or more sources. It follows that your ability to write syntheses depends on your ability to infer relationships among sources—essays, articles, fiction, and also nonwritten sources, such as lectures, interviews, and observations. This process is nothing new for you, since you infer relationships all the time—say, between something you've read in the newspaper and something you've seen for yourself, or between the teaching styles of your favorite and least favorite instructors. In fact, if you've written research papers, you've already written syntheses. In an *academic synthesis*, you make explicit the relationships that you have inferred among separate sources.

The skills you've already learned and practiced from the previous three chapters will be vital in writing syntheses. Clearly, before you're in a position to draw relationships between two or more sources, you must understand what those sources say; in other words, you must be able to *summarize* these sources. It will frequently be helpful for your readers if you provide at least partial summaries of sources in your synthesis essays. At the same time, you must go beyond summary to make judgments—judgments based, of course, on your *critical reading* of your sources. You should already have drawn some conclusions about the quality and validity of these sources; and you should know how much you agree or disagree with the points made in your sources and the reasons for your agreement or disagreement.

Further, you must go beyond the critique of individual sources to determine the relationship among them. Is the information in source B, for example, an extended illustration of the generalizations in source A? Would it be useful to compare and contrast source C with source B? Having read and considered sources A, B, and C, can you infer something else—D (not a source, but your own idea)?

135

┌───┐
│ **WHERE DO WE FIND WRITTEN SYNTHESES?** │
└───┘

Here are just a few of the types of writing that involve synthesis:

Academic Writing

- **Analysis papers.** Sometimes several related theoretical approaches are synthesized and applied.
- **Research papers.** Research requires synthesis of multiple sources.
- **Argument papers.** Synthesize different points into a coherent claim or position.
- **Essay exams.** Demonstrate understanding of course material through comparing and contrasting theories, viewpoints, or approaches in a particular field.

Work-Place Writing

- **Newspaper and magazine articles.** Synthesize primary and secondary sources.
- **Position papers and policy briefs.** Compare and contrast different solutions for solving problems.
- **Business plans.** Synthesize ideas and proposals into one coherent plan.
- **Memos and letters.** Synthesize multiple ideas, events, and proposals into concise form.
- **Web sites.** Synthesize information presented in Web pages and related links.

Because a synthesis is based on two or more sources, you will need to be selective when choosing information from each. It would be neither possible nor desirable, for instance, to discuss in a ten-page paper on the American Civil War every point that the authors of two books make about their subject. What you as a writer must do is select from each source the ideas and information that best allow you to achieve your purpose.

PURPOSE

Your purpose in reading source materials and then in drawing on them to write your own material is often reflected in the wording of an assignment. For instance, consider the following assignments on the Civil War:

American History: Evaluate the author's treatment of the origins of the Civil War.

Economics: Argue the following proposition, in light of your readings: "The Civil War was fought not for reasons of moral principle but for reasons of economic necessity."

Government: Prepare a report on the effects of the Civil War on Southern politics at the state level between 1870 and 1917.

Mass Communications: Discuss how the use of photography during the Civil War may have affected the perceptions of the war by Northerners living in industrial cities.

Literature: Select two twentieth-century Southern writers whose work you believe was influenced by the divisive effects of the Civil War. Discuss the ways this influence is apparent in a novel or a group of short stories written by each author. The works should not be *about* the Civil War.

Applied Technology: Compare and contrast the technology of warfare available in the 1860s with the technology available a century earlier.

Each of these assignments creates for you a particular purpose for writing. Having located sources relevant to your topic, you would select, for possible use in a paper, only those parts that helped you in fulfilling this purpose. And how you used those parts, how you related them to other material from other sources, would also depend on your purpose. For instance, if you were working on the government assignment, you might possibly draw on the same source as another student working on the literature assignment by referring to Robert Penn Warren's novel *All the King's Men*, about Louisiana politics in the early part of the twentieth century. But because the purposes of these assignments are different, you and the other student would make different uses of this source. Those same parts or aspects of the novel that you find worthy of detailed analysis might be mentioned only in passing by the other student.

USING YOUR SOURCES

Your purpose determines not only what parts of your sources you will use but also how you will relate them to one another. Since the very essence of synthesis is the combining of information and ideas, you must have some basis on which to combine them. *Some relationships among the material in your sources must make them worth synthesizing.* It follows that the better able you are to discover such relationships, the better able you will be to use your sources in writing syntheses. Notice that the mass communications assignment requires you to draw a *cause-and-effect* relationship between photographs of the war and Northerners' perceptions of the war. The applied technology assignment requires you to *compare and contrast* state-of-the-art weapons technology in the eighteenth and nineteenth centuries. The economics assignment requires you to *argue* a proposition. In each case, *your purpose will determine how you relate your source materials to one another.*

Consider some other examples. You may be asked on an exam question or in instructions for a paper to *describe* two or three approaches to prison reform during the past decade. You may be asked to *compare and contrast* one country's approach to imprisonment with another's. You may be asked to develop an *argument* of your own on this subject, based on your reading. Sometimes (when you are not given a specific assignment) you determine your own purpose: You are interested in exploring a particular subject; you are interested in making a case for one approach or another. In any event, your purpose shapes your essay. Your purpose determines which sources you research, which ones you use, which parts of them you use, at which points in your essay you use them, and in what manner you relate them to one another.

TYPES OF SYNTHESES: EXPLANATORY AND ARGUMENT

In this and the next chapter we categorize syntheses into two main types: *explanatory* and *argument*. The easiest way to recognize the difference between these two types may be to consider the difference between a newspaper article and an editorial on the same subject. Most likely, we'd say that the main purpose of the newspaper article is to convey *information*, and the main purpose of the editorial is to convey *opinion* or *interpretation*. Of course, this distinction is much too simplified: newspaper articles often convey opinion or bias, sometimes subtly, sometimes openly; and editorials often convey unbiased information, along with opinion. But as a practical matter, we can generally agree on the distinction between a newspaper article that *primarily* conveys information and an editorial that *primarily* conveys opinion.

We'll say, for the sake of convenience, that the newspaper article provides an *explanation* and that the editorial provides an *argument*. This is essentially the distinction we make between explanatory and argument syntheses.

As an example, read the following paragraph:

> Researchers now use recombinant DNA technology to analyze genetic changes. With this technology, they cut and splice DNA from different species, then insert the modified molecules into bacteria or other types of cells that engage in rapid replication and cell division. The cells copy the foreign DNA right along with their own. In short order, huge populations produce useful quantities of recombinant

DNA molecules. The new technology also is the basis of genetic engineering, by which genes are isolated, modified, and inserted back into the same organism or into a different one.*

Now read this paragraph:

Many in the life sciences field would have us believe that the new gene splicing technologies are irrepressible and irreversible and that any attempt to oppose their introduction is both futile and retrogressive. They never stop to even consider the possibility that the new genetic science might be used in a wholly different manner than is currently being proposed. The fact is, the corporate agenda is only one of two potential paths into the Biotech Century. It is possible that the growing number of anti-eugenic activists around the world might be able to ignite a global debate around alternative uses of the new science—approaches that are less invasive, more sustainable and humane and that conserve and protect the genetic rights of future generations.†

Both of these passages deal with the topic of biotechnology, but the two take quite different approaches. The first passage came from a biology textbook, while the second appeared in a magazine article. As we might expect from a textbook on the broad subject of biology, the first passage is explanatory and informative; it defines and explains some of the key concepts of biotechnology without taking a position or providing commentary about the implications of the technology. Magazine articles often present information in the same ways; however, many magazine articles take specific positions, as we see in the second passage. This passage is argumentative or persuasive. Its primary purpose is to convey a point of view regarding the topic of biotechnology.

While each of these excerpts presents a clear instance of writing that is either explanatory or argumentative, it is important to note that the sources for these excerpts—the textbook chapter and the magazine article—both contain elements of explanation and argument. The textbook writers, while they refrain from taking a particular position, do go on to note the controversies surrounding biotechnology and genetic engineering. They might even subtly reveal a certain bias in favor of one side of the issue, through their word choice, tone, and perhaps through devoting more space and attention to one point of view. Explanatory and argumentative writing are not mutually exclusive. The overlap in the categories of explanation and argument is also found in the magazine article: In order to make his case against genetic engineering, the writer has to explain certain elements of the issue. Yet, even while these categories overlap to a certain extent, the

---

*Cecie Starr and Ralph Taggart, "Recombinant DNA and Genetic Engineering," <u>Biology: The Unity and Diversity of Life</u> (New York: Wadsworth: 1998).

†Jeremy Rifkin, "The Ultimate Therapy: Commercial Eugenics on the Eve of the Biotech Century," <u>Tikkun</u> May–June 1998: 35.

second passage clearly has argument as its primary purpose, while the first passage is primarily explanatory.

In Chapter 2 we noted that the primary purpose in a piece of writing is either informative, persuasive, or entertaining (or some combination of the three). Some scholars of writing argue that all writing is essentially persuasive, and even without entering into that complex argument, we've just seen how the varying purposes in writing do overlap. In order to persuade someone of a particular position we typically must also inform them about it; conversely, a primarily informative piece of writing also must work to persuade the reader that its claims are truthful. Both informative and persuasive writing often include entertaining elements, and writing intended primarily to entertain also typically contains information and persuasion. For practical purposes, however, it is possible—and useful—to identify the *primary* purpose in a piece of writing as informative/explanatory, persuasive/argumentative, or entertaining. Entertainment as a primary purpose is the one least often practiced in purely academic writing—perhaps to your disappointment!—but information and persuasion are ubiquitous. Thus, while recognizing the overlap between these categories, we distinguish in this and the following chapter between two types of synthesis writing: explanatory (or informative), and argument (or persuasive). Just as distinguishing the primary purpose in a piece of writing helps you to critically read and evaluate it, distinguishing the primary purpose in your own writing helps you to make the appropriate choices regarding your approach.

In this chapter we'll first present some guidelines for writing syntheses in general, then we'll proceed to focus on explanatory syntheses. In the following chapter, we'll discuss the argument synthesis.

HOW TO WRITE SYNTHESES

Although writing syntheses can't be reduced to a lockstep method, it should help you to follow the guidelines listed in the box on pages 142–143.

THE EXPLANATORY SYNTHESIS

Many of the papers you write in college will be more or less explanatory in nature. An explanation helps readers understand a topic. Writers explain when they divide a subject into its component parts and present them to the reader in a clear and orderly fashion. Explanations may entail descriptions that recreate in words some object, place, emotion, event, sequence of events, or state of affairs. As a student reporter, you may need to explain an event—to relate when, where, and how it took place. In a science lab, you would observe the conditions and results of an experiment and record them for review by others. In a political science course, you might review research on a particular subject—say, the complexities underlying the debate over welfare—and then present the results of your research to your professor and the members of your class.

Your job in writing an explanatory paper—or in writing the explanatory portion of an argumentative paper—is not to argue a particular point, but rather *to present the facts in a reasonably objective manner*. Of course, explanatory papers, like other academic papers, should be based on a thesis. But the purpose of a thesis in an explanatory paper is less to advance a particular opinion than to focus the various facts contained in the paper.

DEMONSTRATION: EXPLANATORY SYNTHESIS— COMPUTERS, COMMUNICATION, AND RELATIONSHIPS

To illustrate how the process of synthesis works, we'll begin with a number of short extracts from several articles on the same subject.

Suppose you were writing a paper on a matter that many computer users are discussing these days: the ways in which communication via computers (that is, computer mediated communication, or CMC) is changing human patterns of interaction, communication, and relationships. In this Information Age when people all over the world can use various forums on the Internet to communicate with one another, many questions arise about this relatively new form of communication. Some writers and thinkers are excited about the world of possibilities opened up by this technological medium, while others are skeptical about whether the Internet will lead to more interaction and connection between people, or will harm the quality of such connections. Still others argue that this new mode of communication is likely to further isolate us from each other, and "real" human contact will become a rare and precious thing.

EXERCISE 4.1

Exploring the Topic

Before reading what others have written on the subject of computers, communication, and relationships, write several paragraphs exploring what you know and what you think about this topic. You might focus your first paragraph on discussing your own experience with computer communication and relationships. How much have you used e-mail, instant messaging, and other Internet-related activity? How have these technologies impacted your ability to communicate with others? What are some of the positive and negative impacts of such communication on relationships? In your second paragraph you might broaden the focus by discussing what you know about these issues in the world at large. What are some of the concerns people have about computers and their effects on communication? What do you think most interests journalists, professors, politicians, and businesspeople about computer communication and relationships?

GUIDELINES FOR WRITING SYNTHESES

- **Consider your purpose in writing.** What are you trying to accomplish in your essay? How will this purpose shape the way you approach your sources?
- **Select and carefully read your sources**, according to your purpose. Then reread the passages, mentally summarizing each. Identify those aspects or parts of your sources that will help you in fulfilling your purpose. When rereading, *label* or *underline* the sources for main ideas, key terms, and any details you want to use in the synthesis.
- **Take notes on your reading.** In addition to labeling or underlining key points in the readings, you might write brief one- or two-sentence summaries of each source. This will help you in formulating your thesis statement, and in choosing and organizing your sources later.
- **Formulate a thesis.** Your thesis is the main idea that you want to present in your synthesis. It should be expressed as a complete sentence. You might do some predrafting about the ideas discussed in the readings in order to help you work out a thesis. If you've written one-sentence summaries of the readings, looking these over will help you to brainstorm connections between readings and devise a thesis.

    When you write your essay drafts, you will need to consider where your thesis fits in your paper. Sometimes the thesis is the first sentence, but more often it is *the final sentence of the first paragraph*. If you are writing an *inductively arranged* synthesis (see page 201), the thesis sentence may not appear until the final paragraphs. (See Chapter 3 for more information on writing an effective thesis.)
- **Decide how you will use your source material.** How will the information and the ideas in the passages help you fulfill your purpose?
- **Develop an organizational plan**, according to your thesis. How will you arrange your material? It is not necessary to prepare a formal outline. But you should have some plan that will indicate the order

Because this is a topic that bears upon a broader subject—the ways that computers and the Internet affect our lives—you decide to investigate what has been written on the subject, both in print and electronic texts. In the following pages we present excerpts from the kinds of articles your research might locate.

Note: To save space and for the purpose of demonstration, the following passages are brief excerpts only. In preparing your paper, naturally you would draw upon the entire articles from which these extracts were made.

in which you will present your material and that will indicate the relationships among your sources.

- **Draft the topic sentences for the main sections.** This is an optional step, but you may find it a helpful transition from organizational plan to first draft.
- **Write the first draft** of your synthesis, following your organizational plan. Be flexible with your plan, however. Frequently, you will use an outline to get started. As you write, you may discover new ideas and make room for them by adjusting the outline. When this happens, reread your work frequently, making sure that your thesis still accounts for what follows and that what follows still logically supports your thesis.
- **Document your sources.** You must do this by crediting them within the body of the synthesis—citing the author's last name and page number from which the point was taken and by providing full citation information in a list of "Works Cited" at the end. (See Chapter 7 for more information on documenting sources.)
- **Revise your synthesis**, inserting transitional words and phrases where necessary. Make sure that the synthesis reads smoothly, logically, and clearly from beginning to end. Check for grammatical correctness, punctuation, spelling.

Note: The writing of syntheses is a recursive process, and you should accept a certain amount of backtracking and reformulating as inevitable. For instance, in developing an organizational plan (Step 6 of the procedure), you may discover a gap in your presentation that will send you scrambling for another source— back to Step 2. You may find that formulating a thesis and making inferences among sources occur simultaneously; indeed, inferences often are made before a thesis is formulated. Our recommendations for writing syntheses will give you a structure; they will get you started. But be flexible in your approach; expect discontinuity and, if possible, be comforted that through backtracking and reformulating you will eventually produce a coherent, well-crafted essay.

Cyberspace: A New Frontier for Fighting Words
Sanjiv N. Singh

Sanjiv N. Singh holds a J.D. from the UCLA School of Law. The article from which this piece is excerpted appeared in the Rutgers Computer and Technology Law Journal, *in 1999.*

Sanjiv N. Singh, "Cyberspace: A New Frontier for Fighting Words," <u>Rutgers Computer and Technology Law Journal</u> 25.2 (1999): 283.

[T]he Internet has begun to transform the way in which people interact. Various mediums now exist that allow for cheap and almost instantaneous communication via computer. For example, e-mail is now an increasingly common way to communicate with family, friends, and acquaintances. In fact, more than fifteen percent of the U.S. adult population use e-mail [. . .]. Technology research firms estimate that by the year 2001, fifty percent of the U.S. population will communicate via e-mail [. . .].

Many colleges and graduate schools routinely provide students with, and in some cases require, use of e-mail accounts. As a result, significant segments of our population are being socialized in an environment where cyberspace communication is an encouraged form of establishing and confirming social engagements or simply corresponding with friends.

Social Relationships in Electronic Forums: Hangouts, Salons, Workplaces and Communities
Rob Kling

Rob Kling is a professor of Information Systems and Information Science in the School for Library and Information Science at the University of Indiana at Bloomington. He has published numerous articles examining the impact of information technologies on organizations, the workplace, publishing and education, as well as on social life. His books include Computerization and Controversy: Value Conflicts and Social Choices *(1996), and* Computers and Politics: High Technology in American Local Governments *(1982). The following reading is excerpted from an essay that appeared in* CMC Magazine.

Enthusiasts for [Internet] forums argue that they are building new forms of community life (Rheingold, 1993). But other analysts observe that not every collection of people who happen to talk (or write) to each other form the sense of trust, mutual interest, and sustained commitments that automatically deserve to be labeled as communities (Jones, 1995). [. . .]

In the United States, communities seem to be deteriorating from a complex combination of causes. In the inner cities of big urban centers, many people fear street crime and stay off the streets at night. In the larger suburban and post-suburban areas, many people hardly know their neighbors and "latch key" children often have little adult contact after school. An African proverb which says that "it takes a whole village to raise a child" refers to a rich community life with a sense of mutual responsibility that is difficult to find in many new neighborhoods. Some advocates believe that computer technology in concert with other efforts could play a role in rebuilding community life by improving communication, economic opportunity, civic participation, and education (Schuler, 1994; Civille, Fidelman, and Altobello, 1993).

Rob Kling, "Social Relationships in Electronic Forums: Hangouts, Salons, Workplaces and Communities," CMC Magazine 22 July 1996, 4 Feb. 2000 <http://www.december.com/cmc/mag/1996/jul/kling.html>.

from Signs of Life in the USA
Sonia Maasik and Jack Solomon

Sonia Maasik is a member of the Writing Program faculty at UCLA, and Jack Solomon is an English professor at California State College, Northridge. In addition to their popular textbook (from which this excerpt comes) Signs of Life in the USA: Readings on Popular Culture for Writers *(3rd edition, 2000), the two have also collaborated on* California Dreams and Realities: Readings for Critical Thinkers and Writers *(1999).*

The emerging outlines of the Web's global village have some people very excited and others worried. The worried contingent are concerned that the relationships people are building on the Net lack an essential core of humanity. The unreal world of virtual culture, they believe, the world in which you can pretend to be just about anything, is being substituted for a social reality made up of real human beings. And such a world, based entirely on the transmission of electronic signals, is potentially a world in which human beings will be unable to conceive of others as human beings. When all interaction is electronic, they ask, where is the ground for true human empathy and relatedness?

Sonia Maasik and Jack Solomon, eds., <u>Signs of Life in the USA</u> (Boston: Bedford Books, 1997) 701.

Life at High-Tech U
Deborah Branscum

A contributing editor to Newsweek, *a columnist for* Fortune.com's *"Valley Talk," and a freelance technology writer, Deborah Branscum has written articles for a number of publications, including* Wired, The New York Times, Infoworld, *and* Yahoo Internet Life. *She operates a Web site called* MonsterBuzz.com *and founded its affiliated BUZZ executive conference.*

Some academics dismiss [e-mail] as an unhealthy substitute for human contact. But Stanford's Richard Holeton, who tracked e-mail discussions of first-year students in one dorm, found that 87 percent of their messages involved important social or critical dialogue. Those issues included "pornography, free speech, a potential grape boycott on campus and a sexual-harassment allegation," says Holeton. And the people who dominated dorm life in face-to-face encounters were not the same folks who ruled the e-mail debates. Electronic discourse, it seems, offered a voice to some students who might not otherwise be heard.

Deborah Branscum, "Life At High-Tech U," <u>Newsweek</u> 27 Oct. 1997: 78–80.

Developing Personal and Emotional Relationships Via Computer-Mediated Communication
Brittney G. Chenault

Brittney G. Chenault holds a degree from the Graduate School of Library and Information Science at the University of Illinois, Urbana-Champaign. This article appeared in the online journal, CMC Magazine, *and has been widely read and quoted since its publication in 1998.*

> The idea of a community accessible only via my computer screen sounded cold to me at first, but I learned quickly that people can feel passionately about e-mail and computer conferences. I've become one of them. I care about these people I met through my computer [. . .] (Rheingold, 1993, p. 1). [. . .]

People meet via CMC every day, exchange information, debate, argue, woo, commiserate, and support. They may meet via a mailing list or newsgroup, and continue the interaction via e-mail. Their relationships can range from the cold, professional encounter, to the hot, intimate rendezvous. Rheingold describes people in virtual communities as using the words they type on screens to exchange pleasantries and argue, engage in intellectual discourse, conduct commerce, exchange knowledge, share emotional support, make plans, brainstorm, gossip, feud, fall in love, find friends and lose them, play games, flirt, create a little high art and a lot of idle talk.

Brittney G. Chenault, "Developing Personal and Emotional Relationships Via Computer-Mediated Communication," CMC Magazine May 1998, 20 Mar. 2000 <http://www.december.com/cmc/mag/1998/may/chenault.html>.

Cyberspace Romances: Interview with Jean-François Perreault of *Branchez-vous*
John Suler

John Suler is a Professor of Psychology at Rider University in New Jersey, and a practicing psychologist. His publications include Contemporary Psychoanalysis *and* Eastern Thought *(1993) as well as the online hypertext book (Web site)* The Psychology of Cyberspace. *This excerpt comes from that Web site and represents a comment by the interviewee, Jean-François Perreault, of the Quebec, Canada based online magazine* Branchez-Vous.

Perreault: My guess is that in a "true" romance on the Internet, the couple eventually will want to meet each other face-to-face. They may HAVE to meet each other for the relationship to fully develop and to be fully satisfying. For these

John Suler, "Cyberspace Romances: Interview with Jean-François Perreault of Branchez-vous," The Psychology of Cyberspace, 11 Dec. 1996, 7 Apr. 2000 <http://www.rider.edu/users/suler/psycyber/psycyber.html>.

people, the Internet simply was a way to meet each other. I say "simply" but this feature of the Internet shouldn't be underestimated. It is a POWERFUL way for people with compatible interests and personalities to find each other.

There are some people who may NOT want to meet the lover face-to-face. My guess is that these people prefer living with the fantasy that they have created (consciously or unconsciously) about the cyber-lover [. . .]. They may not want to meet each other face-to-face because the fantasy might be destroyed by the hard facts of reality. Who can say whether this is "wrong" or "dangerous?" Many people allow themselves the luxury of fantasy—either through books, or TV, or movies. And most people don't confuse this fantasy with reality. A cyber-lover is just another type of "escape fantasy"—only it's much more interactive, and therefore much more exciting, than the more usual methods.

Click Here for Romance
Jennifer Wolcott

A staff writer for The Christian Science Monitor, *Jennifer Wolcott writes on a wide range of topics, including social issues, the arts, and popular culture.*

Online chat can sprout real-life romances that begin with surprisingly honest communication and realistic expectations, traits that many traditional relationships lack at first, according to an Ohio University sociologist who is studying relationships that begin in cyberspace. "I really feel the basis of these relationships is better and deeper than many real-life meetings because the couples are honest with each other in their writings," says Andrea Baker, assistant professor of sociology at Ohio University's Lancaster campus. [. . .] Baker's study suggests the written word tends to promote frank conversation in cyberspace, especially between couples who eventually want to meet face-to-face. Study participants said this immediate sincerity when meeting online was a pleasant switch from the typical blind date scenario. "Couples say this kind of honesty is absolutely necessary to forming a good relationship," Baker says. "In most cases, they are extremely honest and really cover the downsides as well as the upsides so there won't be any surprises when they meet." [. . .]

Honesty is what most appealed to California resident John Dwyer about the online approach. Disillusioned with the bar scene, he decided to give it a whirl. He posted a personal ad and photograph, got hundreds of responses, and eventually connected with Debbie. They married this past New Year's Eve—a year and a half after she answered his online ad. "If you are honest when talking online, you can strip away all the superficial stuff and really get to know someone," says Debbie. How did she know John was being honest? "I got a sense from the conversation whether it was real or contrived," she says. "I could tell after a while that he wasn't just someone trying to land a fish."

Jennifer Wolcott, "Click Here for Romance," <u>The Christian Science Monitor</u> 13 Jan. 1999, 23 Feb. 2000 <http://www.csmonitor.com/durable/1991/01/13/fp11s1-csm.shtml>.

You've Got Romance! Seeking Love Online: Net-Based Services Change the Landscape, If Not the Odds, of Finding the Perfect Mate
Bonnie Rothman Morris

Bonnie Rothman Morris is a journalist and screenwriter who writes frequently for The New York Times, *which is the source for this excerpt. Morris's screenplays include the comedies "Guy and Doll," and "Taking the Leap."*

Tom Buckley didn't have much use for a dating service, or so he thought. "I didn't need to pay a company to help set me up to get a date, a girlfriend, a fiancée, a wife," said Buckley, 30, a steel broker in Portland, Ore., who plays rugby in his spare time. But after a lonely Thanksgiving dinner where he was the only single adult at the family dinner table, Buckley signed up for a free week on Match.com. What ensued on the matchmaking service was an e-mail romance with Terri Muir, a schoolteacher on Vancouver Island in British Columbia. "Anybody who knew us would never have thought we would have gone down that road," Buckley said in a telephone interview. Reflecting on the couple's instant attraction, he said, "e-mail made it easier to communicate because neither one of us was the type to walk up to someone in the gym or a bar and say, 'You're the fuel to my fire.'"

Thirteen months after their first feverish exchanges, Buckley and Ms. Muir lied to their family and friends and sneaked away to Vancouver to meet for the first time. At their wedding one year later, they finally told the tale of how they had met to their 100 guests. More and more single people, used to finding everything else on the Internet, are using it to search for love. More than 2,500 Web sites for adults are now devoted to matchmaking, said Daniel Bender, founder of Cupid's Network, an Internet portal for personals sites. [. . .]

[Robert Spradling] struck up an online romance with a Ukrainian woman whom he had met on American Singles. The woman immediately asked him for money to pay the agency she was using to translate and send her romantic e-mails back to him. There are many such agencies in the former Soviet Union, Spradling said. Next she told Spradling she wanted to start her own matchmaking agency. Spradling, 42, an employee in the development office at Morehead State University in Kentucky, footed the bill for that, too. After sending her about $8,000, Spradling asked her to marry him, via e-mail. She said yes and invited him to Kiev. "When you meet somebody and you think you're in love, you never see any faults," said Spradling, who said the couple had made wedding plans when he was visiting. After his return to the United States, Spradling never heard from her again. He's sworn off finding love through the Internet for now [. . .]. "I caution a lot of guys to be careful and keep their head and learn a lot about who they're dating online," Spradling said.

Bonnie R. Morris, "You've Got Romance! Seeking Love Online: Net-Based Services Change the Landscape, If Not the Odds, of Finding the Perfect Mate," <u>New York Times on the Web</u> 26 Aug. 1999, 23 Feb. 2000 <http://www.nytimes.com/library/ tech/yr/mo/circuits/index.html>.

Consider Your Purpose

Here, then, are brief selections from eight sources on computer mediated communication. How do you go about synthesizing these sources?

First, remember that before considering the *how*, you must consider the *why*. In other words, what is your *purpose* in synthesizing these sources? You might use them for a paper dealing with a broader issue: the effects of computer technology on our daily lives, or on daily human interactions and relationships. If this were your purpose, these sources would be used for only one section of your discussion, and the paper as a whole would advance an *argument* for a particular viewpoint about technology in modern society. Or, for a communications course you might consider the impact technology is having on communication, comparing this kind of communication with other forms of written communication and/or with face-to-face, verbal communication. The various positions and uses of computer mediated conversation (CMC) would be important examples of how communication is changing. Or, moving out of the academic world and into the commercial one, you might be a computer consultant preparing a brochure for a new Internet application or matchmaking Web site. In this brochure, you might want to address the personal uses to which people put these kinds of applications, or for the Web site, you would focus on the positive aspects of forming relationships on the Internet.

But for now let's keep it simple: you want to write a paper, or a section of a paper, that simply explains the impact the Internet is having on relationships between people so that people who may be interested, but who know little or nothing about these issues, will understand some aspects of the CMC phenomenon. Your job, then, is to write an *explanatory* synthesis—one that presents a focused overview of computer mediated communication but does not advance your own opinion on the subject.

EXERCISE 4.2

Critical Reading For Synthesis

Look over the preceding readings and make a list of the different ways they address the overall topics of computers, communication, and relationships. Make your list as specific and detailed as you can. Then write several lists grouping together the readings that deal with similar aspects of the overall topics. You might imagine that you were planning to write a very short synthesis on one small aspect of the broad topics; in this case, for different aspects of the topic, which readings would you use?

We asked one of our students, Alyssa Mellott, to read these passages and to use them as sources in a short paper on some of the issues surrounding CMC. We also asked her to write some additional comments describing the process of developing her ideas into a draft. We'll draw upon some of these comments in the following discussion.

Formulate a Thesis

The difference between a purpose and a thesis is a difference primarily of focus. Your purpose provides direction to your research and focus to your paper. Your thesis sharpens this focus by narrowing it and formulating it in the words of a single declarative statement. (Refer to Chapter 3 for additional discussion on formulating thesis statements.)

Since Alyssa's purpose in this case was simply to summarize source material with little or no comment, her thesis would be the most obvious statement she could make about the relationship among these passages. By "obvious" we mean a statement that characterizes all of these readings' main points. Taken as a whole, what do they *mean*? Here Alyssa describes the process she followed in coming up with a preliminary thesis for her explanatory synthesis:

> I began my writing process by looking over all the readings and noting the main point of each reading in a sentence on a piece of paper.
>
> Then I reviewed all of these points and identified the patterns in the readings. These I listed underneath my list of main points: —All the readings focus on Internet communication, or CMC. —The readings address several different kinds of relationships the authors believe are affected by CMC: communal relationships, relationships between long-distance friends, those between students and instructors, and love relationships. —Some authors discuss positive views, others negative views, of CMC and relationships.
>
> Looking over these points, I drafted a preliminary thesis. This thesis summed up the different issues in the sources and stated how these interrelated.

> The Internet is changing the ways people interact and form relationships.

> This was a true statement, but it sounded too vague and too obvious. I didn't feel it adequately represented the readings' points, since the readings explored a number of specific kinds of interactions and relationships impacted by CMC. I wanted my thesis to more fully reflect the complexity of people's concern regarding technology and relationships. My next version followed:

> Computers and the Internet add new ways for people to interact, but we have yet to see whether or not these new modes of communication will improve human interaction.

This thesis was more comprehensive, but it still didn't quite work. It was vague, and the last part seemed bland; it didn't reflect the strong feelings the writers expressed about the possible effects of CMC on different kinds of relationships. In my next attempt, I tried to be more specific and a little more dramatic:

> With so many computer users forming a variety of online relationships, no one can deny that this new technology is affecting our modes of communication; however, reactions to these changes range widely from excitement over our abilities to forge global connections, to fear that such connections will prove much less satisfying than old-fashioned human interactions.

This sentence was quite long, but I felt the first part of the sentence introduced the real point of my essay: that people have certain mixed reactions to how CMC will impact relationships. I thought this would be a good working thesis because it would help me structure my essay around specific views on CMC. Now I proceeded to the next step in writing—organizing my material.

Decide How You Will Use Your Source Material

The easiest way to deal with sources is to summarize them. But because you are synthesizing *ideas* rather than sources, you will have to be more selective than if you were writing a simple summary. You don't have to treat *all* the ideas in your sources, only the ones related to your thesis. Some sources might be summarized in their entirety; others, only in part. Look over your earlier notes or sentences summarizing each reading, and refer back to the readings themselves. Focusing on some of the more subtle elements of the issues addressed by the authors, expand your earlier summary sentences. Write brief phrases in the margin, underline key phrases or sentences, or take notes on a separate sheet of paper or in a word processing file or electronic data filing program. Decide how your sources can help you achieve your purpose and support your thesis. For example, how, if at all, will you use the quotations by Rheingold contained in the passage by Chenault? How could you incorporate the personal experiences reported by some of the people who formed romantic attachments online?

Develop an Organizational Plan

An organizational plan is your map for presenting material to the reader. What material will you present? To find out, examine your thesis. Do the content and structure of the thesis (that is, the number and order of assertions) suggest an organizational plan for the paper? Expect to devote at least one paragraph of your paper to developing each section of this plan. Having identified likely sections, think through the possibilities of arrangement. Ask yourself: What information does the reader need to understand first? How do I build on this first section—what block of information will follow? Think of each section in relation to others until you have placed them all and have worked your way through to a plan for the whole paper.

Study your thesis, and let it help suggest an organization. Bear in mind that any one paper can be written—successfully—according to a variety of plans. Your job before beginning your first draft is to explore possibilities. Sketch a series of rough outlines: Arrange and rearrange your paper's likely sections until you develop a plan that both facilitates the reader's understanding and achieves your objectives as a writer. Think carefully about the logical order of your points: Does one idea or point lead to the next? If not, can you find a more logical place for the point, or are you just not clearly articulating the connections between the ideas?

Your final paper may well deviate from your final sketch, since in the act of writing you may discover the need to explore new material, to omit planned material, to refocus or to reorder your entire presentation. Just the same, a well-conceived organizational plan will encourage you to begin writing a draft.

Alyssa describes the process of organizing the material as follows:

Summary Statements

> In reviewing my sources and writing summary statements, I noted the most important aspects of the computer interaction issue, according to the authors:
>
> - An increasing number of people use the Internet to interact in new ways (Singh 144).
> - In this era when community life is threatened by social and economic hardships, advocates of Internet communication believe this technology could help improve community life by "improving communication, economic opportunity, civic participation, and education" (Kling 144).
> - Some fear the ways in which real human interaction is being taken over by "virtual culture" (Maasik and Solomon 145).
> - The Internet offers college students additional opportunities for meaningful "social or critical" discussions. It may be a useful outlet for otherwise quiet people (Branscum 145).

- Although the idea of interacting through the computer may sound impersonal, people who are involved in the many varieties of virtual communication come to form meaningful attachments to each other. (Rheingold qtd. in Chenault 146).

- Whether or not romances that begin over the Internet end up moving out into the real world, this form of communication has enormous potential for bringing together people with similar interests (Perreault qtd. in Suler 147).

- A sociologist studying Internet romances found that participants were generally quite honest and open with one another at the start of their relationships—perhaps even more honest than people beginning relationships in more traditional ways. (Wolcott 147).

- A large number of Web sites offer matchmaking services, and people using such services report both positive and negative outcomes. People should be cautious, however, as some experiences show that it's easy to be duped by a potential partner via computer (Morris 148).

I tried to group some of these topics into categories that would have a logical order. The first thing that I wanted to communicate was the growing prevalence of the Internet in our everyday lives and the variety of relationships that can develop online, which has sparked a debate over the quality of these.

Next, I thought I should explain what Internet enthusiasts are so excited about. I wanted to discuss the idea of using the Internet to rebuild community life.

I also wanted to explain the position of those who feel that Internet relationships will prove to be less satisfying than old-fashioned human interactions. In opposition to that, I wanted to explain that some people feel that the Internet can add additional qualities to communication that traditional human interaction lacks.

Next, I intended to counter this optimistic view with words of caution from Internet skeptics about romantic relationships that begin online.

> Finally, I planned to conclude with a short summary of the debate.

I returned to my thesis:

> With so many computer users forming a variety of online relationships, no one can deny that this new technology is affecting our modes of communication; however, reactions to these changes range widely from excitement over our abilities to forge global connections, to fear that such connections will prove much less satisfying than old-fashioned human interactions.

Based on her thesis, Alyssa developed an outline for a seven-paragraph paper, including introduction and conclusion:

> A. Introduction: explanation of the debate surrounding CMC.
>
> B. Enthusiasm over the possibilities that the Internet provides for communication.
>
> C. Skepticism about the quality of Internet relationships.
>
> D. Advantages of Internet relationships over old-fashioned relationships.
>
> E. Specific example of a relationship formed online.
>
> F. Words of caution and a negative example.
>
> G. Conclusion: summing up.

Write the Topic Sentences

This is an optional step, but writing draft versions of topic sentences will get you started on each main idea of your synthesis and will help give you the sense of direction you need to proceed. Here are Alyssa's draft topic sentences for sections based on the thesis and organizational plan she developed. Note that when read in sequence following the thesis, these sentences give an idea of the logical progression of the essay as a whole.

> · An increasing number of people are becoming Internet users every day.
>
> · Using the Internet to strengthen community life may sound like a good idea; however, skeptics warn that the quality of relationships formed through the Internet is not up to par with those formed through face-to-face human interactions.

- The argument has been taken a step further by those who contend that the Internet can provide certain advantages for communication that face-to-face human interactions cannot.
- Research indicates that at the start of a relationship, participants in Internet romances are often more honest and open with one another than their counterparts in traditional dating situations.
- With increasing numbers of people using Internet matchmaking services, skeptics remind us that people should exercise caution in getting to know people via CMC.

Write Your Synthesis

Here is the first draft of Alyssa's explanatory synthesis. Thesis and topic sentences are highlighted. Modern Language Association (MLA) documentation style, explained in Chapter 7, is used throughout. Note that for the sake of clarity, parenthetical references are to pages in *A Sequence for Academic Writing*.

Opposite each page of this first draft, we have included Alyssa's instructor's comments and suggestions for revision.

Model Essay

Advantages and Disadvantages of Computer Mediated Communication
Alyssa Mellott

1 From the home, to the workplace, to the classroom, the Internet has clicked its way into our everyday lives. On any given day, research papers may be e-mailed to professors, ads are posted to sell just about anything, and arrangements to meet significant others for dinner and a movie can be made—all with the help of the Internet. In addition to providing us with such conveniences, computer mediated communication (CMC) provides a medium for fostering new relationships. Whether you are looking for a business partner, fellow political enthusiasts, or a future spouse, the

Discussion and Suggestions for Revision

The following section summarizes the key points and suggestions for revision made during Alyssa's conference with her instructor.

Title and Paragraph 1
Your title could be more interesting and less mechanical. Your first paragraph introduces the subject with some good, specific examples, but you sound a bit too much like a proponent of the new technology, rather than a writer who is objectively presenting various positions on CMC's potential.

Your thesis statement could be shortened and tightened up. While it's good that you aim to specifically characterize the two overall positions regarding CMC, you end up over-simplifying things a bit.

Suggestions for Revision: Make the current title more interesting and less focused on a clear-cut set of oppositions.

In order to maintain an objective stance—since this essay is meant to be explanatory rather than argumentative—you might cut some of your examples here and get to the point sooner. You could then follow your introduction with a paragraph in which you

Internet can be a powerful tool for uniting people with similar interests. With so many computer users forming a variety of online relationships, no one can deny that this new technology is affecting our modes of communication; however, reactions to these changes range widely from excitement over our abilities to forge global connections, to fear that such connections will prove much less satisfying than old-fashioned human interactions.

2 An increasing number of people are becoming Internet users every day. It is estimated that by the year 2001, "fifty percent of the U.S. population will communicate via e-mail" (Singh 144). Is the growing popularity of the Internet as a form of communication and its effect on our modes of communication a positive trend? Champions of the Internet point out that in transforming the way people interact, the Internet has made communication faster, more efficient, and less expensive. Internet enthusiasts also feel that Internet forums "are building new forms of community life" (Kling 144). It has been suggested that CMC could play a role in "rebuilding [deteriorating] community life" in inner cities, suburban, and post-suburban areas of the United States. Kling quotes an African proverb "it takes a whole village to raise a child" to express the need for a "rich community life" based on "mutual responsibility" that seems to be lacking in our modern neighborhoods (144). Some observers feel CMC can improve "communication, economic opportunity, civic participation, and education" (Kling 144).

develop some of the background points you raise in your current introduction—that the Internet has enormous potential for "uniting people with similar interests," as you say. You could refer to points from the readings to make your discussion more objectively explanatory.

Shorten your thesis statement by separating the two ideas you've currently joined with a semicolon: the first clause introduces the thesis you state in the second clause, so separating these ideas will help emphasize your essay's main point. More important, rephrase your thesis so that it more accurately characterizes the positions offered in the readings. For example, none of the readings emphasize the "global" dimension to the connections forged on the Internet, nor does the notion of "fear" that Internet relations will be "less satisfying than old-fashioned . . . interactions" adequately account for the negative views regarding CMC. Back up a bit and formulate a slightly less specific—and more comprehensive—statement.

Edit your use of passive voice—*who* e-mails papers to professors? Avoid clichéd phrases such as "on any given day . . . ."

Paragraph 2
This paragraph starts with a good background point about the prevalence of the Internet in our lives; then you shift to one of the key reasons some people are excited about CMC. The first idea does lead to the second, but could bear more development, as could your second point about CMC's community-building potential.

Suggestions for Revision: Consider splitting this paragraph in two. As suggested in the comments on paragraph 1, some of the points raised in your introduction could be moved to a background paragraph—and the first two sentences in this current paragraph 2 would fit there. Look back over the readings for more ideas that would help you develop points about CMC's prevalence and its general, positive potential. After discussing that, you could begin a third paragraph focused upon the point about the Internet's potential for building communities. Spend more time defining "community" and explaining how, according to its advocates, CMC could replace lost community.

Edit your sentences—you have some repetitive and choppy sentence structures and passive constructions that could be rephrased in the active voice.

3   Using the Internet to strengthen community life may sound like a good idea; however, skeptics warn that the quality of relationships formed through the Internet is not up to par with those formed through face-to-face human interactions. Analysts have observed that not everyone who communicates via the Internet forms "the sense of trust, mutual interest, and sustained commitments" that characterize communities (Kling 144). Others are concerned that the relationships people are building through the Internet "lack an essential core of humanity" (Maasik and Solomon 145). They feel that our social reality made up of real people is being taken over by a virtual culture. It is within this virtual culture that a danger exists for people to become "unable to conceive of others as human beings," resulting in an environment lacking in "human empathy and relatedness" (Maasik and Solomon 145). Similarly, some teachers consider e-mail to be "an unhealthy substitute for human contact" (Branscum 145).

4   The argument has been taken a step further by some who contend that the Internet can provide certain advantages to communication that face-to-face human interactions cannot. In a study of first-year college students, Stanford's Richard Holeton found that students who were ordinarily reserved were often the most active participants in Internet discussions (Branscum 145). Similarly, the Internet can serve as a way for people who are having trouble dating to find romantic partners. For instance, Tom Buckley met his

Paragraph 3

Paragraph 3 follows logically from paragraph 2, and you make a clear transition in your topic sentence. However, this paragraph's points would be stronger if you had explained the arguments about the Internet's community-building potential in the last paragraph.

In your effort to paraphrase points from the Maasik and Solomon reading, and to intersperse their quoted words with your own, you end up producing wordy and awkward sentences. Furthermore, when you paraphrase the authors in the sentence "They feel that our social reality . . . ," you haven't changed the wording enough to qualify as a legitimate paraphrase.

In the last sentence of this paragraph you throw in another reference that doesn't really add anything to your points. Why do you need this point?

Suggestions for Revision: Once you've added development of your points in paragraph 2, rework the points expressed by the "skeptics" in this paragraph to more clearly relate back to the ideas of community you've just discussed.

Consider dealing with the ideas from Maasik and Solomon in a block quote, or else rework your sentences to more smoothly incorporate their ideas without using their sentence structures and wording.

If you feel the added point in your last sentence is important, then make that importance more clear; if it's really not necessary, then leave it out.

Paragraph 4

The topic sentence is confusing. You write, "The argument has been taken a step further . . . ," and this wording suggests that you're referring to the argument *against* CMC since this is the last argument about which you've written. In actuality, however, you seem to be referring to the entire argument over CMC, not just one side of it. Other than that, this paragraph contains interesting points and good examples.

Suggestions for Revision: Change your opening sentence to more accurately reflect the paragraph's focus.

wife after signing up with Match.com. Buckley noted that the Internet helped him to meet his wife because "neither one of us was the type to walk up to someone in the gym or a bar and say, 'You're the fuel to my fire'" (qtd. in Morris 148). Holeton's research and Tom Buckley's experience suggest that the Internet may provide an avenue of expression and opportunity for otherwise quiet or timid individuals.

5   Research indicates that at the start of a relationship, participants in Internet romances are often more honest and open with one another than their counterparts in traditional dating situations. Andrea Baker, assistant professor of sociology at Ohio University's Lancaster campus who is studying romances that start over the Internet, reports that relationships that start online are "better and deeper" than traditional relationships because the couples are honest in the words they write (qtd. in Wolcott 147). Like the participants in Baker's study, California resident John Dwyer found the sincerity present in online communication to be a pleasant change from more traditional dating scenes (Wolcott 147). After posting a personal ad on the Internet, Dwyer met his future wife, Debbie, who commented, "'If you are honest when talking online, you can strip away all the superficial stuff and really get to know someone'" (Wolcott 147).

6   With increasing numbers of people using Internet matchmaking services, skeptics remind us that people should exercise caution in getting to know people via CMC. After having his heart broken and his wallet

Paragraph 5

In paragraph 5 you do a nice job of extending the points in your last paragraph; however, your first sentence here doesn't make that relationship clear. By starting with "Research indicates . . ." you imply that you're moving on to a new element of CMC, rather than adding to the last point.

Suggestions for Revision: Write a topic sentence that spells out how your new points relate to the last ones. You also might add a sentence that sums up your overall point at the end of the paragraph to help improve the logical "flow" between this paragraph and paragraph 6.

Paragraph 6

Again, you're lacking an effective transition here, one that makes clear the way these new points qualify or limit the positive assessments offered in paragraph 5. The Spradling story provides a nice counterpoint to the happy couple's experience in the last paragraph, but as a drained by a romantic partner that he met online, Robert Spradling has sworn off using the Internet to find love and warns others to "be careful and keep their head and learn a lot about who they're dating online" (qtd. in Morris 148).

7   Wouldn't it be nice if the saying was "What you read is what you get"? Anyone who has spent even five minutes playing with e-mail cannot deny that the enthusiasm surrounding the possibilities posed for communication by the Internet is warranted. Nevertheless, we must constantly be reminded that the computer screen poses as an effective poker face for those with insincere intentions.

Works Cited

Branscum, Deborah. "Life At High-Tech U." <u>Newsweek</u> 27 Oct. 1997: 78-80.

Kling, Rob. "Social Relationships in Electronic Forums: Hangouts, Salons, Workplaces and Communities." <u>CMC Magazine</u> July 1996. 4 Feb. 2000. <http://www.december.com/cmc/mag/1996/jul/kling.html>.

Maasik, Sonia, and Jack Solomon, eds. <u>Signs of Life in the USA</u>. Boston: Bedford Books, 1997. 701.

Morris, Bonnie R. "You've Got Romance! Seeking Love Online: Net-Based Services Change the Landscape, If Not the Odds, of Finding the Perfect Mate." <u>New York Times on the Web</u> 26 Aug. 1999. 23 Feb. 2000 <http://www.nytimes.com/library/tech/yr/mo/circuits/index.html>.

Singh, Sanjiv N. "Cyberspace: A New Frontier for Fighting Words." <u>Rutgers Computer and Technology Law Journal</u> 25.2 (1999): 283.

Wolcott, Jennifer. "Click Here for Romance." <u>The Christian Science Monitor</u> 13 Jan. 1999. 23 Feb.2000 <http://www.csmonitor.com/durable/1991/01/13/fp11s1-csm.shtml>.

reader I don't get a complete picture of the actual events in Spradling's experience.

Suggestions for Revision: Write a better transitional sentence to open the paragraph. Slow down a little and tell Spradling's story more clearly. Review the reading by Suler: is there a way in which a cyberlove relationship might apply to Spradling's difficulties in moving his romance from the online to the off line realm?

Paragraph 7
Your conclusion focuses too much on the last issue raised in your essay, while failing to bring a sense of closure to the essay by pulling together all the points of the essay.

Suggestions for Revision: Think about what all these points add up to. Yes, as your current conclusion states, the Internet can help people hide malignant intentions—but is this the whole story? Are people able to lie and conceal things in real life as well as in the virtual world? And what about your earlier points about community-building and human connection? Try to wrap things up more comprehensively, rather than focusing narrowly on the one issue of deceit.

Revising the Sample Synthesis

Try your hand at creating a final draft of this essay by following the suggestions above, together with using your own best judgment about how to improve the first draft. After trying your own version of the essay, compare it to the revised version our student produced after the discussion on revision (below).

REVISED MODEL ESSAY

Computer Mediated Communication: New and Improved Human Relations Or The End of Real Interaction?
Alyssa Mellott

From the home, to the workplace, to the classroom, the Internet has clicked its way into our everyday lives. Today's students can e-mail as file attachments their end-of-term papers to their professors and can then turn around and use e-mail to gather a group of friends for a party or to celebrate the term's completion. These online exchanges, called CMC (or computer mediated communication) sound fairly commonplace at the turn of the millenium. But what we have yet to discover is how CMC might change both the ways we communicate and the quality of our relationships. While many praise CMC's potential to bridge barriers and promote meaningful dialogue, others caution that CMC's is fraught with dangers.

Very soon, half of America will communicat via e-mail, according to analysts (Singh 144). We can only assume that figure will grow—rapidly—as children who have matured in the Internet era move on to college and into careers. With e-mail becoming an increasingly common form of communication, people are discovering and conversing with one another in a variety of ways that bring a new twist to old, familiar patterns. Using e-mail, people meet "to exchange pleasantries and argue, engage in intellectual discourse, conduct commerce, exchange knowledge, share emotional support, make plans, brainstorm, gossip, feud, [and] fall in love" (Rheingold qtd. in Chenault 146). That is, through e-mail people do what they have always done: communicate. But the medium of that communication has changed, which excites some people and concerns others.

Advocates argue that the Internet has not only made existing types of communication faster, more convenient, more efficient, and less expensive; it has also made possible "new forms of community life," such as chat rooms and discussion lists, in which people from all over the country and the world gather to share information and exchange points of view (Kling 144). CMC is potentially so powerful a medium of exchange that some believe it can promote dialogue within communities that are declining. A community, after all, is built on people acting in the interests of their neighbors for the common good. Via e-mail, online news-groups, and e-forums, neighbors will have new ways of looking out for one another (Kling 144).

Still, skeptics aren't convinced that electronic communication can provide the basis of lasting personal relationships, primarily because relationships initiated on a cathode ray tube lack immediacy and physical presence. What may be missing in the electronic village, say the critics, is "an essential core of humanity" (Maasik and Solomon 145):

> The unreal world of virtual culture [. . .] is being substituted for a social reality made up of real human beings. And such a world, based entirely on the transmission of electronic signals, is potentially a world in which human beings will be unable to conceive of others as human beings. When all interaction is electronic, [the critics] ask, where is the ground for true human empathy and re-lated—ness? (Maasik and Solomon 145)

The fact that people communicate—via e-mail, snail (written) mail, or in person—does not guarantee that their exchanges lead to community. Members of a community trust and care for one another; they extend themselves and offer help (Kling 144). Critics of CMC argue that the supporters gloss over this important distinction when they assume that electronic forums are "building new forms of community life" (Kling 144). Talking, electronically or otherwise, marks only the *beginning* of a process. Community building is hard work and takes time.

Notwithstanding these concerns, proponents of CMC confidently point to examples in which the new

technologies of communication bring people together in meaningful, healthy ways. In a study of
first-year college students, researcher Richard
Holeton of Stanford University found that students
who were ordinarily reserved were often the most active participants in Internet discussions (Branscum
145). Similarly, the Internet can serve as a way for
people who are having trouble dating to find partners. For instance, Tom Buckley of Portland Oregon
met his wife after signing up with Match.com. Buckley noted that the Internet helped him to meet his
wife because "neither one of us was the type to walk
up to someone in the gym or a bar and say, 'You're
the fuel to my fire'" (qtd. in Morris 148). Holeton's research and Buckley's experience suggest that
the Internet may provide a way for otherwise quiet
or timid individuals to express themselves.

Beyond simply providing a safe and lower-
stress place to meet, the Internet may actually
promote honest communication. An Ohio University
sociologist, Andrea Baker, concluded from her research that individuals who begin their romance
online can be at an advantage: writing via e-mail
can promote a "better and deeper" relationship
than one begun in person because writing itself
promotes a frank, honest exchange (qtd. in Wolcott
147). Certainly this was the experience of John
Dwyer, a Californian who tired of meeting women in
bars and decided instead to post an advertisement
online. He eventually met the woman who would become his wife—Debbie, who said: "'If you are honest when talking online, you can strip away all
the superficial stuff and really get to know someone'" (Wolcott 147). When it works, CMC can promote a sincere exchange among those looking for
lasting relationships.

Skeptics are not so easily convinced, however. Show them an example of a relationship that
blossomed online and they will point to another in
which one party was betrayed emotionally or financially. Take, for instance, the experience of
Robert Spradling. He met and formed a romantic attachment to a Ukrainian woman online. She encouraged the romance via e-mail and eventually asked
for money to set up a business. He sent $8,000 and
later, again online, asked her to marry him. She
agreed, they met in Kiev, and after Spradling re-

turned home she disappeared—his money gone and his heart broken (Morris 148). Perhaps Spradling was one of the Internet romantics for whom it is wiser to avoid face-to-face meetings. That way, he could have enjoyed the interactive fantasy of a "cyber-lover" without ever having to ruin the fun with the uncomfortable truths of real life (Suler 147).

It is far from certain, then, that all or even most relationships begun online develop positively. Closer to the truth is that both online and offline, some relationships begin—and end—in deceit while others blossom. Experts do not yet know whether computer mediated communication, because of its electronic format, alters relationships as they are forming or, rather, is simply a new territory in which to find others. Time will tell. In the meantime, the advice that loved ones give us when we set off to find new friends—Be careful!—makes sense whether we are looking in the virtual world or down the street.

Works Cited

Branscum, Deborah. "Life at High-Tech U." <u>Newsweek</u> 27 Oct. 1997: 78-80.

Chenault, Brittney G. "Developing Personal and Emotional Relationships Via Computer-Mediated Communication." <u>CMC Magazine</u> May 1998. 20 Mar. 2000. <http://www.december.com/cmc/mag/1998/may/chenault.html>.

Kling, Rob. "Social Relationships in Electronic Forums: Hangouts, Salons, Workplaces and Communities." <u>CMC Magazine</u> 22 July 1996. 4 Feb. 2000. <http://www.december.com/cmc/mag/1996/jul/kling.html>.

Maasik, Sonia, and Jack Solomon, eds. <u>Signs of Life in the USA</u>. Boston: Bedford Books, 1997.

Morris, Bonnie R. "You've Got Romance! Seeking Love Online: Net-Based Services Change the Landscape, If Not the Odds, of Finding the Perfect Mate." <u>New York Times on the Web</u> 26 Aug. 1999. 23 Feb. 2000 <http://www.nytimes.com/library/tech/yr/mo/circuits/index.html>.

Singh, Sanjiv N. "Cyberspace: A New Frontier for Fighting Words." <u>Rutgers Computer and Technology Law Journal</u> 25.2 (1999): 283.

Suler, John. "Cyberspace Romances: Interview with Jean-Francois Perreault of *Branchez-vous*." <u>The Psychology of Cyberspace</u> 11 Dec. 1996. 7 Apr. 2000 <http://www.rider.edu/users/suler/psycyber/psycyber.html>.

Wolcott, Jennifer. "Click Here for Romance." <u>The Christian Science Monitor</u> 13 Jan. 1999. 23 Feb. 2000 <http://www.csmonitor.com/durable/1991/01/13/fp11s1-csm.shtml>.

Writing Assignment: An Expanded Explanatory Synthesis Drawing Upon More Sources

Now we'll give you an opportunity to practice your skills in planning and writing an explanatory synthesis. On pages 164–176 we provide eight additional sources on the issue of online communication and relationships.

EXERCISE 4.4

Exploring Internet Sources

Since online communication and relationships is such a "cutting-edge" topic—and, since the Internet itself provides a convenient forum for discussing these issues—many articles exploring the topic are available on the Internet. In addition to reading the sources we've provided, go to one of the search engines online (Google.com is a good one) and try searching for articles and discussions on computer mediated communication. You will find all sorts of more recent pieces than those we've been able to collect here. If you end up using any of the sources you find on the Internet for the explanatory synthesis assignment, you should review our cautionary discussion of using Web-based sources in Chapter 7 on Evaluating Sources (pages 281–282).

Read these additional sources; then plan and write an explanatory synthesis dealing with some aspect of their subject matter. You don't have to draw upon *all* of the sources. If you want to restrict your subject, as before, to the CMC issue, feel free to do that. And even with this highly focused subject, don't feel compelled to bring in every last source. Before reading, take a look at the reading tips presented in *Critical Reading for Synthesis* (page 165).

Will We Ever Log Off?
Robert Wright

Robert Wright is a senior editor at The New Republic *and a regular contributor to* Time *magazine, where the full text of this article originally appeared.* Wright's articles on science and technology for* The Sciences *magazine won the National Magazine Award for Essay and Criticism, and he has also written for* The New Yorker *and* The Atlantic Monthly. *His books include* Nonzero: The Logic of Human Destiny *(2001) and* The Moral Animal: Evolutionary Psychology and Everyday Life *(1995).*

During the past two years, the amount of time the average Internet user spends online each week has risen from 4.4 hours to 7.6 hours. [. . .] As cyberspace absorbs

---

Robert Wright, "Will We Ever Log Off?" Time 21 Feb. 2000: 56–58.

CRITICAL READING FOR SYNTHESIS

- **Use the tips from Critical Reading for Summary on page 6.** Remember to examine the context; note the title and subtitle; identify the main point; identify the subpoints; break the reading into sections; distinguish between points, examples, and counterarguments; watch for transitions within and between paragraphs; and read actively and recursively.
- **Establish the writer's primary purpose.** Use some of the guidelines discussed in Chapter 2; is the piece primarily informative, persuasive, or entertaining? Assess whether the piece achieves its purpose.
- **Read to identify a key idea.** If you begin reading your source materials with a key idea or topic already in mind, read to identify what your different sources have to say about the idea.
- **Read to discover a key idea.** If you begin the reading process without a key idea in mind yet, read to discover a key idea that your sources address.
- **Read for relationships.** Regardless of whether you already have a key idea, or whether you are attempting to discover one, your emphasis in reading should be on noting the ways in which the different readings relate to each other, to a key idea, and to your purpose in writing the synthesis.

---

more and more of our work, play, shopping and socializing, where will it end? What activities will still be off-line in 2025?

A few candidates spring to mind. Brushing your teeth. Eating. Playing tennis. Right? Not so fast. Even some of these seemingly solid barriers to the Internet's encroachment are shaky. A quarter-century from now, almost everything will in principle be doable online, and convenience will often argue for doing it there.

Bear in mind, for starters, that in 2025 the average American will have, as they say in technical circles, bandwidth out the wazoo. You won't just be able to monitor your child's day care by webcam (a service already offered by more than 100 day-care centers). You'll be able to monitor it in high-definition 3-D format, providing valuable perspective during slo-mo replays of block-throwing incidents.

And this is only the beginning. Just ask Jaron Lanier, who coined the term "virtual reality." Lanier is chief scientist for the "tele-immersion" project, part of the federally subsidized research program know as Internet2, which explores the upshot of massive bandwidth and computing power.

The standard virtual-reality experience, you may recall, involves donning a head-mounted display or special glasses—or, in principle, contact lenses—and thus entering a computer-generated fantasy world. As you turn your head or walk around, the computer adjusts your perspective accordingly. Tele-immersion is to videoconferencing as virtual reality is to Pac-Man. If it works, it will give you the visual experience of being in the same room with a person who is actually in another city.

"[Tele-immersion] will just become part of life," says Lanier. "It will be used by teenage girls to gossip, by business people to cut deals, by doctors to consult." And presumably by people who want to do long-distance lunch. Of course, there won't be any point in saying, "Pass the squash," but otherwise it will be a normal mealtime conversation. Eating online.

Speaking of squash, playing racquet sports at long distance is in principle simple. If you've got a squash-court-size space to run around in, you can play with your college buddy, wherever he or she may be. (And no more annoying collisions with opponent, walls or ball, since all three will be illusions.) In fact, using standard virtual-reality technology, people have already played tennis remotely, Lanier says. But each looked to the other like a cartoon character—an "avatar." Tele-immersion will let you see the agony of defeat on the face of your vanquished foe.

Obviously, some pastimes lose something when performed online. (No, I'm not going to talk about sex.) Consider hiking. True, you could don your head-mounted display and get on your treadmill while a friend did the same in another city. If you wanted a whiff of pine or cedar, you could crank up the computer-controlled aroma synthesizer that the company DigiScents has said it will market. Not too tempting, right?

Yet, even though hiking may remain reality-based, it will have its online elements. People are already finding new hiking buddies over the Internet. Here lies the biggest import of the expanding online experience. Even if tele-immersion is still crude in 2025, cyberspace will have reshaped life because it will have kept doing what it has been doing—nourishing shared enthusiasms. Even before most Americans had heard of e-mail, there were chat groups with names like alt.fetish.foot and some environmentalists were mobilizing online. But the more people online, the easier it is to find your own special interest, no matter how narrow. [. . .]

Lonesome Internet Blues, Take 2
Scott Rosenberg

For many years a theatre and movie critic at the San Francisco Examiner, *Scott Rosenberg helped found the online magazine* Salon.com, *and writes about technology and culture for that publication, which served as the source for this excerpt.*

Want your name on the front page of *The New York Times* and other newspapers? Just author a study concluding that Internet use is bad for you.

Scott Rosenberg, "Lonesome Internet Blues, Take 2," Salon.com 18 Feb. 2000, 3 Mar. 2000 <http://www.salon.com/tech/col/rose/2000/02/18/stanford_study/index>.

"A Newer, Lonelier Crowd Emerges in Internet Study," blared the *Times'* front page on Wednesday. *The Washington Post's* cover similarly trumpeted "A Web of Workaholic Misfits? Study Finds Heavy Internet Users Are Socially Isolated."

As with the widely discredited 1998 Carnegie-Mellon study that claimed Internet use made you sad and lonely, the findings of this new study—by the Stanford Institute for the Quantitative Study of Society—are highly questionable. But that hasn't stopped its conclusions from being reported as big news.

So once more, with an inevitable feeling of déjà vu, let us descend into the trenches of study-demolishing and identify the self-contradictions in this latest attempt to brand Internet users as bummed-out bums.

Point 1: Norman Nie, a Stanford professor who is the study's co-"principal investigator," identifies "a key finding" of the study: "The more hours people use the Internet, the less time they spend in contact with real human beings."

Point 2: The study reports that the overwhelmingly most popular use of the Internet—far more widespread than e-commerce, chat or even Web surfing—is e-mail. In other words: when it comes to human contact, in Nie's view, e-mail just doesn't count. I guess all those people you're exchanging e-mail with—your family, friends, co-workers, long-lost school buddies, new friends you made in an online discussion—aren't real human beings. Because you happen to be communicating with them via the Internet instead of the telephone or the postal service or a conversation on the street, they have become fake, and your "contact" with them has become a bogus exchange. [. . .]

All those headlines about "isolation" and "loneliness" drew on one of the study's most baleful findings—that people who use the Internet a lot spend less time with friends and family and don't go out as often. But when you look closely at the survey's numbers this conclusion seems pretty insignificant. [. . .] [F]or example, 27 percent of heavy Net users—10 or more hours a week—report that they spend less time talking to friends and family on the phone. But then, 9 percent of people who spend an hour or less online a week report the same thing. (Maybe people are looking for any excuse not to call Mom, or maybe the "less time" here isn't a lot less time.) Meanwhile, a total of 15 percent of the same heavy Net users report "spending less time with family and friends"; 13 percent say they spend "less time attending events outside the home."

Those figures are not landslide results—only 1 in 7 of the most avid Internet addicts is hanging out less with "real human beings." A "newer, lonelier crowd" this does not make. [. . .]

Nie interprets his findings in full-bore cautionary mode: "The Internet could be the ultimate isolating technology that further reduces our participation in communities even more than did automobiles and television before it," he argues. [. . .]

Are all these people knowingly choosing "social isolation" as they get to know the Net? Are they all helplessly enthralled by the new technology's seductive powers even as it is sucking their lives dry of human connection? Or do they understand the Net better than Nie—and realize that they aren't "reducing participation in communities" but rather spending time in different kinds of communities, whose members communicate online and group themselves based on choice and interests rather than accidents of geography?

Making Clones Among Us
Bob Gunn

As he states in this article, Bob Gunn is a substitute teacher and nature lover. The article from which this excerpt is taken appeared in the Sunday "Voices" section of the Santa Barbara News Press.

As a substitute teacher, mostly at the secondary level, I not only work with students, I also work with machines—primarily computers.

Many [. . .] students have become aware of my general abhorrence of the ongoing acceptance of the artificial at the expense of the natural. [. . .] It is in fact my concern for children that is at the heart of my arguments.

Children need to bond with nature. It is imperative that every child feel a part of the life force that created and nurtures that child, and is an essential part of that person—without which he or she could not continue to exist. Yet they don't.

Instead children are bonding more and more with the unreal—and artificial. We are teaching them to worship the machine, in all its limitations. Nature is fundamental! This has been obvious to indigenous peoples of the world for eons.

But no more. We have sold our souls for the sake of convenience, and our children will be the ones to pay the piper. None of technology's so-called marvels come free of baggage. Its by-products' destructive forces have wreaked havoc not only on our air, soil and water, they have also built walls of intolerance and deceit in the worldwide competition for its well-hyped products. [. . .]

Isn't it interesting how so-called primitive peoples lived in harmony with nature for thousands of years while so-called civilized peoples have brought us to the brink of self-destruction in a little over a century? And for what? Wealth? Power? Items to make us lazier, fatter and less connected to anything of real substance? [. . .]

But what do we care, we don't even go outside anymore. We've acquired the short-term data that enables us to convert natural resources into artificial contrivances, but we've lost the long-term wisdom that tells us those same natural resources allowed us to attain far deeper joys and insights when left in their natural state.

And what about choices? What about self-expression? What about singing and dancing and pretending? What about art and sports and talking and writing—in your own style rather than mechanical type?

And when school budgets center around more and more technology, which other programs suffer in the process? What about socialization? I mean isn't there a concern out there when your child opts to watch TV or play on a computer rather than interacting with another sentient being? [. . .]

It seems to me the central problem is that more and more now, computers are doing our thinking for us. We are trading in contemplation, intuition and creativity for mechanical analysis. We are becoming spectators rather than participants in this great adventure called life. [. . .]

Bob Gunn, "Making Clones Among Us," Santa Barbara News Press, 30 Apr. 2000: G1.

As for your children, make them go outside and climb a tree. Someday they'll thank you for it—with their own mouths rather than via e-mail.

The Net: It's the Unreal Thing
Gil Schwartz

Gil Schwartz is a senior vice president in charge of communications at CBS, and under the pseudonym Stanley Bing, he writes a column in Fortune *magazine. He has written for* Esquire *and* Computer Life, *from which this excerpt is taken. Schwartz/Bing is also the author of the humorous book* What Would Machiavelli Do? *(2000), and* Lloyd—What Happened: A Novel of Business *(1998).*

How much of what we find in cyberspace is tampered with, jiggered, clipped, morphed, and melded? I admit I'm obsessed with the existence of so many naked people on the Web, but I don't think I'm unique. Aside from convocations on bee pollen, nuclear physics in the kitchen, product information, and other scintillating effluvia never before available to the average groundling, the Internet is really all about sex. Talking about sex. Reading about sex. Seeing grotesque sex-related pictures and ragged video clips of things that make you wake up screaming later. For those with a high-speed modem and a taste for grunge, it's a bizarre and wonderful world.

But what is the nature of this stuff that we see? Is it real by any commonly accepted definition of reality? Does it have tangible existence in the world outside the realm of computing, telecommunications, and internodal fictional intercourse? Is it something you can touch, smell, meet for drinks, split a bucket of popcorn with? Is anything in there real?

I know what you're thinking: Who cares? Is reality important? What is this concept of real? If it exists, can we buy some? If we can't find it, where is it? Is it hiding? On vacation? Out to lunch? Does the concept of real have any meaning in a virtual landscape? And if nothing in there is real, what power does the medium have to evoke anything genuine in us, its users?

This train of thought pulled into my brain station yesterday when I grabbed a picture of Michelle Pfeiffer off the Web. I've always been a Michelle Pfeiffer fan. I think she's a good actress who seems like a serious person. That's why I was surprised to see a picture of her without clothes on in there. She seemed to be very young in the picture. Could it really be her? It sure looked like her. When would she have posed for such an image? I downloaded the shot, printed it on my color DeskJet, and showed it to my friend Werblin. "Are you sure it's real?" he asked. "It could be, you know, enhanced." This had not occurred to me, but now that he mentioned it . . . I looked at the image again. I noticed that underneath Ms. Pfeiffer's chin, where the recognizable head met the torso, there was a shadow, a thin, maroon line I hadn't noticed before. Was this a real picture of Michelle Pfeiffer? Or was it Michelle Pfeiffer's head on Arlene Crezoni's body? Arlene Crezoni is not her real name, but you know what I mean. It would certainly be easy to do, as anyone with a scanner and Photoshop knows.

How much of what we find in the virtual universe is tampered with, jiggered, clipped, morphed, smudged, melded, or artificially interlaced? And if it's not really a picture of what you think it is, is it still interesting? Or is it boring because it's not a record of something that exists objectively, in the physical world, but a mechanical figment of another person's software? [. . .]

My pal Brewster is about 30, with a jolly girth, a winning smile, and a trimmed beard [. . .]. He appears often on a chat line in the persona of a young woman with arcane interests. The boy spends hours trading stories with folks about stuff that never happened and never will. Who knows? Maybe the other "women" he's talking to are also chubby male account executives [. . .].

I, too, have been known to spend a few hours chatting with like-minded people about matters of mutual concern. Sometimes I'm myself. Other times I'm better looking, taller, smarter, faster, younger, hipper, softer, dryer. It doesn't matter. It's not real. Nothing is real in here. That's why it's so much fun, right?

Cyber Time: Living by the Credo 'Boot Up, Log On and Connect,' University Students are Mounting a Techno-Revolution
Joe Chidley

Joe Chidley is editor-in-chief of Canadian Business *magazine, and has served as a senior writer for* Maclean's, *a popular Canadian news magazine, and the source for this excerpt.*

Just about everything anybody would want to know about David Da Silva can be found at http://www.io.org/^dawds/. That is his Internet home-page address. There, a surfer on the World Wide Web will discover that Da Silva is a first-year arts student at McGill University in Montreal (his home page provides a link to the institution's own Web site), that he is a Roman Catholic (link provided to the Vatican), that he attended Lorne Park Secondary School in Mississauga, Ont. (link to Lorne Park Web site, which Da Silva helped design). They will also find out that Da Silva's father is a family physician, that his mother is a homemaker, that his sisters, Kathryn and Elizabeth, are age 15 and 12, respectively, and that his 17-year-old brother, Jonathan, works at McDonald's (link to the McDonald's Web site, as well as the Da Silva International Home Page, a site David designed "to keep my brothers and sisters happy"). The Da Silva Web pages—which have "sort of evolved over the past year," David says—constitute a cyber-domain, carefully tended by the 19-year-old from his dorm room on the edge of campus. And why does he do it? "I'm not exactly sure," he says. "It's sort of a personal scrapbook of things I find interesting—it's just a 'me' thing, really."

Joe Chidley, "Cyber Time: Living by the Credo 'Boot Up, Log On and Connect,' University Students are Mounting a Techno-Revolution," Maclean's 104.48 (25 Nov. 1996): 68–70.

Designing Web pages, e-mailing family and friends around the world, reading pixellated electronic newspapers and researching essays on the Internet's endless databases, university students are making their mark in cyberspace—and mounting a techno-revolution. In the words of Toronto communications guru Don Tapscott, they are part of the Net Generation: the new breed of computer-literate under-29-year-olds. While adults are still struggling with the concepts of www addresses, T1 lines, modems and mice (or are they "mouses"?), university students are just doing it. If the catchphrase of the '60s was "Turn on, tune in, and drop out," the Net Generation lives by a decidedly different credo: "Boot up, log on, and connect."

And as it transforms a generation, the Internet is transforming—oops, highlight that and hit delete—has already transformed life at university. An estimated 90 percent of college and university students in North America now have ready Internet access [. . .]. And with such a broad cross section of coeds cruising the information highway, some of the old computer-culture stereotypes—like the one about the antisocial geek who gets aroused looking at screen-savers and auto-exec files—are becoming in serious need of revision. If anything, the Web appears to be putting university students more in touch with the rest of the world than ever before. "In a way, the Internet has improved my social life," writes 22-year-old Christine Bhumgara, a fourth-year University of Waterloo environmental studies major, and one of dozens of students who replied by e-mail to a query posted recently on the chat forum of Maclean's own Web site (http://www.canoe.ca/macleans/). "I regularly e-mail my friends, which has subsequently pushed me to improve communication with people I only get to see once in a blue moon," she adds. [. . .]

What is remarkable about the Net Generation is how much the Web has become a part of their lives—and increasingly, their studies. Although students have yet to do away with books and journals, they are taking every chance they get to toss them out the window and onto the shoulder of the information on-ramp. [. . .]

[W]hen Andrea Marshall, a third-year environmental science major at Acadia University in Wolfville, N.S., heads to the campus library, it isn't to roam the stacks. It is "because they get subscriptions to hundreds of magazines and you can go and read them for free," she writes. When it does come time to hit the books, Marshall often wends her way Webward: many of the required readings in her environmental law course, for instance, are posted on the Internet.

10% of Students May Spend Too Much Time Online, Study Suggests
Leo Reisberg

Leo Reisberg is assistant editor for The Chronicle of Higher Education, *writing about college student life.*

Leo Reisberg, "10% of Students May Spend Too Much Time Online, Study Suggests," The Chronicle of Higher Education 5 June 2000, 5 June 2000 <http://chronicle.com/free/2000/06/2000060501t.htm>.

At least 10 percent of college students use the Internet so much that it interferes with their grades, their health, and their social lives, and the problem may run much deeper at science and engineering institutions, a psychologist at Rensselaer Polytechnic Institute said here Friday at the annual conference of the American College Health Association. Keith J. Anderson, a staff psychologist at Rensselaer's Counseling Center, reported on the findings of a survey of 1,300 college students at seven American institutions and one in Ireland, which he conducted in 1998-99. [. . .] Of the 1,078 participants who said they used the Internet, more than 100 of them fit the criteria—such as withdrawal from other activities—for Internet dependency.

The students who were identified as dependent spent an average of 229 minutes a day using the Internet for nonacademic reasons, compared with 73 minutes a day for others, Mr. Anderson said. As many as 6 percent of the students spent an average of over 400 minutes a day using the Internet. Dependent users reported negative consequences. "Grades decline, mostly because attendance declines. Sleep patterns go down. And they become socially isolated," Mr. Anderson said. [. . .]

As part of the study, students were asked to rate the degree to which their Internet usage affected their real-life relationships, academic success, participation in extracurricular activities, sleep patterns, and meeting new people. For the study, Mr. Anderson counted Internet activities not related to class work, including sending or receiving e-mail, browsing the World Wide Web, downloading software, and participating in cybersex, graphic interactive games, newsgroups, and online communities.

The participants were students from American International University, Black Hawk College, the New Jersey Institute of Technology, Rensselaer, Siena College, the State University of New York at Albany, SUNY at Buffalo, and one institution in Ireland. They were evenly divided among men and women, and they represented 18 different majors, from liberal arts to hard sciences. But the type of student most vulnerable to Internet dependency was clear: Of the 106 classified in this way, 93 were men. Seventy-six percent of those identified as dependent studied the hard sciences, with computer-science majors making up the majority of the dependents.

Mr. Anderson suggested that his study may underrepresent the extreme users—those students who are so consumed by the Internet that they rarely leave their rooms. Students filled out paper surveys while they were in class, and the extreme Internet users may have skipped class that day to remain in cyberspace, he said. [. . .]

Students don't generally walk into the counseling centers on their campuses and tell the staff that they are spending too much time on the Internet, Mr. Anderson said. He discovered the problem by asking two questions of students who see him because they're struggling with their classes: How much sleep do they get, and how much time do they spend on the Internet?

The survey was spurred by his encounter with a student who had flunked out of Rensselaer at the end of his sophomore year, in 1998. After three semesters of good academic progress, the student spent more time in his fourth semester logged on to the Internet than he did preparing for class or attending class. The student, whom Mr. Anderson identified as "Scott," came to the counseling center because of the academic problems, not because he believed he was hooked on the computer.

During that semester, Scott had experienced mild depression, sleeping problems, and conflict with his parents. Eventually he admitted to Mr. Anderson that he had spent about 2,000 hours from January to April participating in an online chat community. As he continued to withdraw from the campus community, the online group had become his primary form of interpersonal communication.

"By the end of April, Scott didn't know the first or last name of his next-door neighbor in his residence hall, but he drove to Tennessee, about 1,900 miles round-trip, to meet a woman that he met online," Mr. Anderson said in an interview after the session on excessive Internet use. "He would say that he had a lot of friends, but he never met the people he called his friends."

While an extreme case, Scott's situation motivated Mr. Anderson to conduct the study to gauge the prevalence of the problem. He said that many students who have difficulty with social interaction are susceptible to becoming Internet dependent. In fact, they often use the Internet as a coping mechanism to avoid problems in their lives or interpersonal communication. [. . .]

Romance on the Net
Ruth C. Eggett

This article appeared on a Web site devoted to Internet relationships.

Your date is just a mouse click away. [. . .]

Internet providers [. . .] provide hundreds of chat rooms where users congregate in a virtual reality environment in the convenience of their homes. ICQ and PowWow are two of many popular Net chat services available to users with Net access. PowWow was where Ruth Post, 20, met Jason, 23, last year. After chatting for two months, Post visited him in Vancouver and soon began dating him. Between three-hour commutes, long-distance phone calls, chat and e-mails, the two kept in touch. The relationship continued when Post went off to college in Alaska. Two months ago via telephone, Jason proposed to Post. She accepted. Since then, Jason has moved to Silverdale and Post has returned from Alaska to be with him.

"Long distance relationships are difficult," said Post, who plans to study at Olympic College this winter. "I've known Jason for one-and-a-half years. He makes my life happy."

[. . .]

Ruth C. Eggett, "Romance on the Net," An International Home for Internet Romance 13 June 1998, 24 Feb. 2000 <http://www.soft.net.uk/ashford/iromance/olymp.htm>.

Halfway around the world, Richard Hull and his fiancée, Lynda, maintain An International Home of Internet Romance, a support website for Net couples seeking to develop meaningful, long-term relationships. Hull, 26, met Lynda, 31, at the Christian Connections Matchmaker website in mid-April. Having established mutual interests, both began communicating via ICQ chat and e-mail. "Right from the start, there was that openness, respect and love for each other that has continued to grow and flourish," said Hull.

Three months later, Hull took a 24-hour flight from his home in Kent, England to Queensland, Australia to meet Lynda and her two children. Because the relationship went so well, Hull extended his two-week vacation by one week. "We experienced a whole range of emotions as we learned to be together and iron out all those culture differences," said Hull. "We saw the good and the bad side of each other. I knew what I liked and loved what I saw." "I feel complete," said Lynda. "I thank God every day for reaching across the other side of the world to bring me someone as wonderful, kind and compassionate as Richard." "The house and contents are up for sale," said Hull, who plans to move to Australia and marry Lynda. "Although it's a big step, it's the right step. [. . .]"

Those who have formed long-term relationships as a result of the Net quickly point out that honest communication and knowledge of the person are essential. "Without direct honesty up front, your Internet romance is in trouble straight off," said Lynda. "Both people get ripped off when you're not honest. You may be surprised that your partner loves you just how you are." [. . .]

Chat users scorned by dishonest behavior warn those seeking Net relationships to be extremely cautious when meeting anyone on the Net. "I met a man on [AOL] and we dated over nine months when he asked me to marry him," said AOL user NoFoolAmI. "We had our wedding planned when I found out he had a woman he was living with the whole time."

"Before I met Jason, I dated a guy from Seattle that I met in chat who [turned out to be] emotionally abusive," said Post. "It could've become physically abusive. Some people seem nice initially (on the Net) but then turn out to be really mean in person." [. . .]

Net chat rooms attract people who simply like meeting other people. "It's nice to talk to someone and see what it's like in different countries and all over the world," said Post. "Their lives are totally different than mine. It brings people closer together." "I enjoy meeting people without many of the assumptions that are placed on physical attraction," said Jeremy Wilson, 23. "I also enjoy watching and listening to people interact to see how they behave." [. . .]

Though savvy chat users enjoy the social interaction the Net provides, they know chat abusers take advantage of those who are too trusting. "I do believe in Internet romance to a certain extent," said Post. "I've also seen it destroy marriages where someone who thinks they've fallen in love leaves a relationship. I've seen it destroy families. I knew one girl who met a guy that tried to rape her. She ended up having to press charges." [. . .]

"Many people are not sincere," said Wilson. "I'd say six out of 10 on average. That depends on which chat rooms you're in. I try to be sincere. However, it is sometimes safer to remain neutral and anonymous."

Exploring Primary Sources on the Internet

Just for fun, you might go online and look at some of the dating Web sites mentioned in Eggett's article. In addition, look for homepages set up by couples who met on the Internet. If you were going to write a synthesis composed entirely of these kinds of primary sources—people's own accounts of their experience with CMC and relationships—on what kinds of points would you focus? In other words, in examining the material people post to the Internet regarding their Internet relationships, what are some of the common themes and patterns you notice?

Dear Ann Landers
Ann Landers

"Ann Landers" is the pseudonym of Esther Pauline Friedman Lederer, one of the most widely syndicated newspaper columnists in the world. On the basis of her charitable work and the service she's provided through her advice column, Landers has received numerous awards. Her books include Ann Landers Talks to Teenagers about Sex *(1963) and* The Best of Ann Landers: Her Favorite Letters of All Time *(1997).*

Dear Ann Landers: I really need your advice. Several months ago, my husband, "Archie," met a woman online. He chatted with her every day, then began to call her on the phone. He also sent her $3 cards, along with sweet poems and small gifts. When I confronted Archie about this coziness, he insisted that they were just "computer pals." So far as I know, they never met.

A few months ago, this woman married another man she met online. She sent Archie an e-mail to let him know about it, and then told him she would no longer be chatting with him. He was terribly upset when he learned of her marriage, which made me wonder about the intensity of their relationship. Archie insisted it was not an "affair," and that I am the only woman who ever interested him sexually. He swore he never did get together with her. So, I forgave him for the flirtation, and things seemed to be better between us.

I thought he was through with his chat-room shenanigans, but I was mistaken. Last month, Archie met a 28-year old woman online, and has been calling her and sending poems and gifts. He told me yesterday she is in a terrible marriage, and he is helping "recover" her self-esteem. Archie thinks if he stops communicating with her, she may do something drastic. I have told him he is betraying our marriage, but he insists since nothing physical is going on, I should not complain.

Am I overreacting? Archie says this flirtation is meaningless, but it is very upsetting to me. What can I do? —Need Advice Down South

Ann Landers, "Dear Ann Landers," <u>Santa Barbara News Press</u> 30 Mar. 2000: D 2.

Dear South: You can accept the fact that Archie operates at an adolescent level, and he is not going to change. You can insist, however, that he stop calling and sending gifts to his online cutie, and be very firm about it. Some joint counseling might be helpful. I recommend it.

EXERCISE 4.6

Summary Statements

Go back over these readings and write one- or two-sentence summary statements summing up the main point in each reading. Use these statements to start brainstorming issues and subtopics you might like to focus upon for the explanatory synthesis assignment.

5

Argument Synthesis

WHAT IS AN ARGUMENT SYNTHESIS?

The explanatory synthesis, as we have seen, is fairly modest in purpose. It emphasizes the materials in the sources themselves, not the writer's interpretation. Because your reader is not always in a position to read your sources, this kind of synthesis, if well done, can be very informative. But the main characteristic of the explanatory synthesis is that it is designed more to *inform* than to *persuade*. As we have said, the thesis in the explanatory synthesis is less a device for arguing a particular point than a device for providing focus and direction to an objective presentation of facts or opinions. As the writer of an explanatory synthesis, you remain, for the most part, a detached observer.

Recall the thesis our student devised for her final draft of the explanatory synthesis on computer mediated communication in Chapter 4:

> While many praise CMC's potential to bridge barriers
> and promote meaningful dialogue, others caution that
> CMC is fraught with dangers.

This thesis provides a summation of the viewpoints people espouse in regard to CMC, neither arguing for or against any one viewpoint.

In contrast to an explanatory thesis, an argumentative thesis is *persuasive* in purpose. Writers working with the same source material might conceive of and support other, opposite theses. So the thesis for an argument synthesis is a claim about which reasonable people could disagree. It is a claim with which—given the right arguments—your audience might be persuaded to agree. The strategy of your argument synthesis is therefore to find and use convincing *support* for your *claim*.

The Elements of Argument: Claim, Support, Assumption

Let's consider the terminology we've just used. One way of looking at an argument is to see it as an interplay of three essential elements: claim, support, and assumption. A *claim* is a proposition or conclusion that you are trying to prove. You prove this claim by using *support* in the form of fact or expert opinion. Linking your supporting evidence to your claim is your *assumption* about the subject. This assumption, also called a *warrant*, is—as we've discussed in Chapter 2—an underlying belief or principle about some aspect of the world and how it operates. By nature, assumptions (which are often unstated) tend to be more general than either claims or supporting evidence. What we do when we *analyze* is to apply the principles that underlie our assumptions to the specific evidence that we will use as support for our claims.

For example, here are the essential elements of an argument advocating parental restriction of television viewing for their high school children:

> *Claim*
> High school students should be restricted to no more than two hours of TV viewing per day.

> *Support*
> An important new study, as well as the testimony of educational specialists, reveals that students who watch more than two hours of TV a night have, on average, lower grades than those who watch less TV.

> *Assumption*
> Excessive TV viewing adversely affects academic performance.

As another example, if we converted the thesis for our explanatory synthesis into a *claim* suitable for an argument synthesis, it might read as follows:

> CMC threatens to undermine human intimacy, connection, and ultimately, community.

Here are the other elements of this argument:

> *Support*
> While the Internet presents us with increased opportunities to meet people, these meetings are limited by geographical distance.

> People are spending increasing amounts of time in cyberspace: In 1998, the average Internet user spent over four hours per week online, and by 2000, this figure had nearly doubled.

> College health officials report that excessive Internet usage threatens many college students' academic and psychological well-being
>
> New kinds of relationships fostered on the Internet often pose challenges to pre-existing relationships.
>
> *Assumptions*
> There is a fundamental difference between the communication skills used and the connections formed via the Internet and face-to-face contact.
>
> "Real" connection and a sense of community are sustained by face-to-face contact, not by Internet interactions.

For the most part, arguments should be constructed logically, or rationally, so that claims are supported by evidence in the form of facts or expert opinions. As we'll see, however, logic is only one component of effective arguments.

Exercise **5.1**

Practicing Claim, Support, and Assumption

Devise two sets of claims with support and assumptions for each. First, in response to the last example on computer mediated communication and relationships, come up with a one-sentence claim addressing the positive impact (or potential impact) of CMC on relationships—whether you personally agree with such a claim or not. Then list the support on which such a claim might rest, and the assumption that underlies these. Secondly, write a second claim, followed by support and assumption. This time make a claim that states your own position on any issue or topic you choose. Don't worry about the precision of your support; since this is a practice exercise, you can note the points of support that you think are out there in relation to your claim.

The Three Appeals of Argument: *Logos, Ethos, Pathos*

Speakers and writers have never relied upon logic alone in advancing and supporting their claims. More than 2,000 years ago, the Athenian philosopher and rhetorician Aristotle explained how speakers attempting to persuade others to their point of view could achieve their purpose primarily by relying on one or more *appeals*, which he called *logos*, *ethos*, and *pathos*.

Since we frequently find these three appeals employed in political argument, we'll use political examples in the following discussion. But keep in mind that these appeals are also used extensively in advertising, in legal cases, in business documents, and in many other types of argument.

LOGOS

Logos is the rational appeal, the appeal to reason. If they expect to persuade their audiences, speakers must argue logically and must supply appropriate evidence to support their case. Logical arguments are commonly of two types (often combined). The *deductive* argument begins with a generalization, then cites a specific case related to that generalization, from which follows a conclusion. A familiar example of deductive reasoning, used by Aristotle himself, is the following:

> All men are mortal. (*generalization*)
>
> Socrates is a man. (*specific case*)
>
> Socrates is mortal. (*conclusion about the specific case*)

In the terms we've just been discussing, this deduction may be restated as follows:

> Socrates is mortal. (*claim*)
>
> Socrates is a man. (*support*)
>
> All men are mortal. (*assumption*)

An example of a more contemporary deductive argument may be seen in President John F. Kennedy's address to the nation in June 1963 on the need for sweeping civil rights legislation. Kennedy begins with the generalizations that it "ought to be possible [. . .] for American students of any color to attend any public institution they select without having to be backed up by troops" and that "it ought to be possible for American citizens of any color to register and vote in a free election without interference or fear of reprisal." Kennedy then provides several specific examples (primarily recent events in Birmingham, Alabama) and statistics to show that this was not the case. He concludes:

> We face, therefore, a moral crisis as a country and a people. It cannot be met by repressive police action. It cannot be left to increased demonstrations in the streets. It cannot be quieted by token moves or talk. It is time to act in the Congress, in your state and local legislative body, and, above all, in all of our daily lives.

Underlying Kennedy's argument is the following reasoning:

> All Americans should enjoy certain rights.
>
> Some Americans do not enjoy these rights.
>
> We must take action to ensure that all Americans enjoy these rights.

Another form of logical argumentation is *inductive* reasoning. A speaker or writer who argues inductively begins not with a generalization, but with several pieces of specific evidence. The speaker then draws a conclusion from this evidence. For example, in a 1990 debate on gun control, Senator Robert C. Byrd (Democrat, Virginia) cites specific examples of rampant crime: "I read of young men being viciously murdered for a pair of sneakers, a leather jacket, or $20." He also offers statistical evidence of the increasing crime rate: "in 1951, there were 3.2 policemen for every felony committed in the United States; this year [1990] nearly 3.2 felonies will be committed per every police officer [. . .]." He concludes, "Something has to change. We have to stop the crimes that are distorting and disrupting the way of life for so many innocent, law-respecting Americans. The bill that we are debating today attempts to do just that."

Statistical evidence also was used by Senator Edward M. Kennedy (Democrat, Massachusetts) in arguing for passage of the Racial Justice Act of 1990, designed to ensure that minorities were not disproportionately singled out for the death penalty. Kennedy points out that 17 defendants in Fulton County, Georgia, between 1973 and 1980, were charged with killing police officers but the only defendant who received the death sentence was a black man. Kennedy also cites statistics to show that "those who killed whites were 4.3 times more likely to receive the death penalty than were killers of blacks," and that "in Georgia, blacks who killed whites received the death penalty 16.7 percent of the time, while whites who killed received the death penalty only 4.2 percent of the time."

Of course, the mere piling up of evidence does not in itself make the speaker's case. As Donna Cross explains in "Politics: The Art of Bamboozling,"* politicians are very adept at "card-stacking." And statistics can be selected and manipulated to prove anything, as demonstrated in Darrell Huff's landmark book *How to Lie with Statistics* (1954). Moreover, what appears to be a logical argument may, in fact, be fundamentally flawed. (See Chapter 2 for a discussion of logical fallacies and faulty reasoning strategies.) On the other hand, the fact that evidence can be distorted, statistics misused, and logic fractured does not mean that these tools of reason can be dispensed with or should be dismissed. It means only that audiences have to listen and read critically—perceptively, knowledgeably, and skeptically (though not necessarily cynically).

Sometimes, politicians can turn their opponents' false logic against them. Major R. Owens, a Democratic Representative from New York, attempted to counter what he took to be the reasoning on welfare adopted by his opponents:

> Welfare programs create dependency and so should be reformed or abolished.
>
> Aid to Families with Dependent Children (AFDC) is a welfare program.
>
> AFDC should be reformed or abolished.

---

*Donna Cross, <u>Word Abuse: How the Words We Use Use Us</u> (New York: Coward, 1979).

In his speech opposing the Republican welfare reform measure of 1995, Owens simply changes the specific (middle) term, pointing out that federal subsidies for electric power in the West and Midwest and farmers' low-rate home loan mortgages are, in effect, welfare programs ("We are spoiling America's farmers by smothering them with socialism [. . .]"). The logical conclusion—that we should reform or eliminate farmers' home loan mortgages—would clearly be unacceptable to many of those pushing for reform of AFDC. Owens thus suggests that opposition to AFDC is based less on reason than on lack of sympathy for its recipients.

EXERCISE 5.2

Using Deductive and Inductive Logic

Choose an issue currently being debated at your school, or a college-related issue about which you are concerned. Write down a claim about this issue. Then write two paragraphs addressing your claim—one in which you organize your points deductively, and one in which you organize them inductively. Some sample issues might include college admissions policies, classroom crowding, or grade inflation. Alternatively, you could base your paragraphs on the claim you generated in response to Exercise 5.1.

ETHOS

Ethos, or the ethical appeal, is an appeal based not on the ethical rationale for the subject under discussion, but rather on the ethical nature of the person making the appeal. A person making an argument must have a certain degree of credibility: That person must be of good character, be of sound sense, and be qualified to hold the office or recommend policy.

For example, Elizabeth Cervantes Barrón, running for senator as the peace and freedom candidate, begins her statement, "I was born and raised in central Los Angeles. I grew up in a multiethnic, multicultural environment where I learned to respect those who were different from me [. . .]. I am a teacher and am aware of how cutbacks in education have affected our children and our communities."

On the other end of the political spectrum, American Independent gubernatorial candidate Jerry McCready also begins with an ethical appeal: "As a self-employed businessman, I have learned firsthand what it is like to try to make ends meet in an unstable economy being manipulated by out-of-touch politicians." Both candidates are making an appeal to *ethos*, based on the strength of their personal qualities for the office they seek.

L. A. Kauffman is not running for office but rather writing an article arguing against socialism as a viable ideology for the future ("Socialism: No." *Progressive*, April 1, 1993). To defuse objections that he is simply a tool of capitalism, Kauffman begins with an appeal to *ethos*: "Until recently, I was executive editor of the journal *Socialist Review*. Before that I worked for the Marxist magazine, *Monthly Review*. My bookshelves are filled with books of Marxist theory, and I even have a picture of Karl Marx up on my wall."

Thus, Kauffman establishes his credentials to argue knowledgeably about Marxist ideology.

Conservative commentator Rush Limbaugh frequently makes use of the ethical appeal by linking himself with the kind of Americans he assumes his audiences to be (what author Donna Cross calls "glory by association"):

> In their attacks [on me], my critics misjudge and insult the American people. If I were really what liberals claim—racist, hatemonger, blowhard—I would years ago have deservedly gone into oblivion. The truth is, I provide information and analysis the media refuses to disseminate, information and analysis the public craves. People listen to me for one reason: I am effective. And my credibility is judged in the marketplace every day [. . .]. I represent America's rejection of liberal elites [. . .]. I validate the convictions of ordinary people.*

EXERCISE 5.3

Using **Ethos**

Return to the claim you used for Exercise 5.2, and write a paragraph in which either you or an imagined speaker use an appeal to *ethos* to make a case for that claim.

PATHOS

Finally, speakers and writers appeal to their audiences by use of *pathos*, the appeal to the emotions. There is nothing inherently wrong with using an emotional appeal. Indeed, since emotions often move people far more powerfully than reason alone, speakers and writers would be foolish not to use emotion. And it would be a drab, humorless world if human beings were not subject to the sway of feeling, as well as reason. The emotional appeal becomes problematic only if it is the *sole* or *primary* basis of the argument. This is the kind of situation that led, for example, to the internment of Japanese Americans during World War II or that leads to periodic political spasms to enact anti-flag-burning legislation.

President Reagan was a master of emotional appeal. He closed his first inaugural address with a reference to the view from the Capitol to the Arlington National Cemetery, where lie thousands of markers of "heroes":

> Under one such marker lies a young man, Martin Treptow, who left his job in a small-town barbershop in 1917 to go to France with the famed Rainbow Division. There, on the western front, he was killed trying to carry a message between battalions under heavy artillery fire. We're told that on his body was found a diary. On the flyleaf under the heading, "My Pledge," he had written these words: "America must win this war. Therefore, I will work, I will save, I will sacrifice, I

---

*Rush Limbaugh, "Why I Am a Threat to the Left," <u>Los Angeles Times</u>, 9 Oct. 1994.

> will endure, I will fight cheerfully and do my utmost, as if the issue of the whole struggle depended on me alone." The crisis we are facing today does not require of us the kind of sacrifice that Martin Treptow and so many thousands of others were called upon to make. It does require, however, our best effort and our willingness to believe in ourselves and to believe in our capacity to perform great deeds, to believe that together with God's help we can and will resolve the problems which now confront us.

Surely, Reagan implies, if Martin Treptow can act so courageously and so selflessly, we can do the same. The logic is somewhat unclear, since the connection between Martin Treptow and ordinary Americans of 1981 is rather tenuous (as Reagan concedes); but the emotional power of Martin Treptow, whom reporters were sent scurrying to research, carries the argument.

A more contemporary president, Bill Clinton, also used *pathos*. Addressing an audience of the nation's governors about his welfare plan, Clinton closed his remarks by referring to a conversation he had held with a welfare mother who had gone through the kind of training program Clinton was advocating. Asked by Clinton whether she thought that such training programs should be mandatory, the mother said, "I sure do." When Clinton asked her why, she said:

> "Well, because if it wasn't, there would be a lot of people like me home watching the soaps because we don't believe we can make anything of ourselves anymore. So you've got to make it mandatory." And I said, "What's the best things about having a job?" She said, "When my boy goes to school, and they say, 'What does your mama do for a living?' he can give an answer."

Clinton uses the emotional power he counts on in that anecdote to set up his conclusion: "We must end poverty for Americans who want to work. And we must do it on terms that dignify all of the rest of us, as well as help our country to work better. I need your help, and I think we can do it."

EXERCISE 5.4

Using Pathos

Return to the claim you used for Exercises 5.2 and 5.3, and write a paragraph in which either you or an imagined speaker use an appeal to *pathos* to make a case for that claim.

DEMONSTRATION: DEVELOPING AN ARGUMENT SYNTHESIS—THE WAL-MART CONTROVERSY

To demonstrate how to plan and draft an argument synthesis, let's consider another subject. If you were taking an economics or business economics course, you would probably at some point consider the functioning of the market economy. For consumers, one of the most striking trends in this economy in recent times has been the rise of superstores such as Wal-Mart, Home Depot, Costco, Staples, and Best Buy. Most consumers find these vast shopping outlets convenient and economical. Others find them an abomination, contending that these ugly and predatory outlets drive out of business the Mom-and-Pop stores that were the staple of small-town America.

Suppose, in preparing to write a short paper on Wal-Mart, you came up with the following sources. Read them carefully, noting as you do the kinds of information and ideas you could draw upon to develop an *argument synthesis*.

Note: To save space and for the purpose of demonstration, the following passages are excerpts only. In preparing your paper, naturally you would draw upon entire articles from which these extracts were made.

Ban the Bargains
Bob Ortega

Bob Ortega, reporter for the Wall Street Journal, *introduces the Wal-Mart debate with a particular slant: the involvement of aging activists from the 1960s and 1970s.*

"Ultimate Predator"

To denizens of the counterculture, Wal-Mart stands for everything they dislike about American society—mindless consumerism, paved landscapes and homogenization of community identity.

"We've lost a sense of taste, of refinement—we're destroying our culture and replacing it with . . . Wal-Mart," says Allan B. Wolf, a Kent State University alumnus now trying to keep Wal-Mart out of Cleveland Heights, Ohio, where he is a high-school teacher.

"We'd never have fought another business as hard as we've fought Wal-Mart," says Alice Doyle, of Cottage Grove, Ore., who calls the giant discounter "the ultimate predator."

At Wal-Mart headquarters in Bentonville, Ark., company officials characterize all opponents, ex-hippie and otherwise, as "a vocal minority." They deny that their store has become, for some activists, a kind of successor to Vietnam.

Don Shinkle, a Wal-Mart vice president, says "there are maybe eight to 10 sites where there is opposition." However, there are at least 40 organized groups actively opposing proposed or anticipated Wal-Mart stores in communities such as Oceanside, Calif.; Gaithersburg, Md.; Quincy, Mass.; East Lampeter, Penn.; Lake Placid, N.Y.; and Gallatin, Tenn.

Local opposition has delayed some stores and led the company to drop its plans in Greenfield, Mass., and two other towns in that state, as well as in Bath, Maine; Simi Valley, Calif.; and Ross and West Hempfield, Pa.

Bob Ortega, "Ban the Bargains," <u>Wall Street Journal</u> 11 Oct. 1994: B6.

Protest March

The residents of Cleveland Heights hope to join that list. On a recent Monday there, a large crowd, including some people who had been tear-gassed at Kent State 24 years ago for protesting the war, led a march on city hall and chanted, "One, two, three, four—we don't want your Wal-Mart store." Says Jordan Yin, a leader of the anti–Wal-Mart coalition, "Old hippies describes the whole town."

In Fort Collins, Colo., Shelby Robinson, a former Vietnam War protester and member of the George McGovern campaign, has little success these days persuading her old companions to join her lobbying for solar power, animal rights or vegetarianism. But when Wal-Mart proposed coming to town, the activist impulses of her old friends came alive, and many joined her in fighting the store.

"I really hate Wal-Mart," says Ms. Robinson, a self-employed clothing designer. "Everything's starting to look the same, everybody buys all the same things—a lot of small-town character is being lost. They disrupt local communities, they hurt small businesses, they add to our sprawl and pollution because everybody drives farther, they don't pay a living wage—and visually, they're atrocious."

In Boulder, Colo., Wal-Mart real-estate manager Steven P. Lane tried appeasing the city's ex-hippies by proposing a "green store" that he said would be environmentally friendly, right up to the solar-powered sign out front. But when city council member Spencer Havlick, who helped organize the first Earth Day in 1970, suggested that the whole store be solar-powered, Mr. Lane fell silent. Dr. Havlick, professor of environmental design at the University of Colorado, says, "Their proposal wasn't as green as they thought it was."

These activists have hardly slowed Wal-Mart's overall expansion—it expects to add 125 stores next year to its existing 2,504. But even so, some Wal-Mart sympathizers find them irritating. William W. Whyte, who bid good riddance to hippies when he graduated from Kent State in 1970, now finds himself annoyed by them again, as an analyst following Wal-Mart for Stephens Inc.

"The same types of people demonstrating then are demonstrating now," grumbles Mr. Whyte. "If they had to worry about putting food on the table, they'd probably be working for Wal-Mart instead of protesting them."

Some Wal-Mart supporters call the protesters elitists for opposing a purveyor of low-priced goods. But Tim Allen, who at age 26 has been active in the development of a "green" housing co-op and an organizer of the Wal-Mart protest movement in Ithaca, replies that "people aren't poor because they're paying 15 cents more for a pair of underwear."

Eight Ways to Stop the Store
Albert Norman

Albert Norman is a well-known opponent of Wal-Mart and a former anti-Vietnam activist. In this article, Norman outlines his strategies for blocking Wal-Mart. Norman's bias is clear—and will be balanced by some of the other selections that follow.

Albert Norman, "Eight Ways to Stop the Store," <u>Nation</u> 28 Mar. 1994: 10.

Last week I received another red-white-and-blue invitation to a Wal-Mart grand opening in Rindge, New Hampshire. I say "another" because Wal-Mart has already invited me to its new store in Hinsdale, New Hampshire, just twenty miles away. With over $67 billion in annual sales, and more than 2,000 stores, Wal-Mart holds a grand opening somewhere in America almost every other day. But it will never invite me to its new store in Greenfield, Massachusetts, my home town, because Greenfield voters recently rejected Wal-Mart at the ballot box.

The Arkansas mega-retailer has emerged as the main threat to Main Street, U.S.A. Economic impact studies in Iowa, Massachusetts, and elsewhere suggest that Wal-Mart's gains are largely captured from other merchants. Within two years of a grand opening, Wal-Mart stores in an average-size Iowa town generated $10 million in annual sales—by "stealing" $8.3 million from other businesses.

Since our victory in Greenfield, we have received dozens of letters from "Stop the WAL" activists in towns like East Aurora, New York; Palatine, Illinois; Mountville, Pennsylvania; Williston, Vermont; Branford, Connecticut—small communities fighting the battle of Jericho. If these towns follow a few simple rules of engagement, they will find that the WAL *will* come tumbling down:

Quote scripture: Wal-Mart founder Sam Walton said it best in his autobiography: "If some community, for whatever reason, doesn't want us in there, we aren't interested in going in and creating a fuss." Or, as one company V.P. stated, "We have so many opportunities for building in communities that want Wal-Marts, it would be foolish of us to pursue construction in communities that don't want us." The greater the fuss raised by local citizens, the more foolish Wal-Mart becomes.

Learn Wal-Math: Wal-Mathematicians only know how to add. They never talk about the jobs they destroy, the vacant retail space they create or their impact on commercial property values. In our town, the company agreed to pay for an impact study that gave enough data to kill three Wal-Marts. Dollars merely shifted from cash registers on one side of town to Wal-Mart registers on the other side of town. Except for one high school scholarship per year, Wal-Mart gives very little back to the community.

Exploit their errors: Wal-Mart always makes plenty of mistakes. In our community, the company tried to push its way onto industrially zoned land. It needed a variance not only to rezone land to commercial use but also to permit buildings larger than 40,000 square feet. This was the "hook" we needed to trip the company up. Rezoning required a Town Council vote (which it won), but our town charter allowed voters to seek reconsideration of the vote, and ultimately, a referendum. All we needed was the opportunity to bring this to the general public—and we won. Wal-Mart also violated state law by mailing an anonymous flier to voters.

Fight capital with capital: In our town (pop. 20,000) Wal-Mart spent more than $30,000 trying to influence the outcome of a general referendum. It even created a citizen group as a front. But Greenfield residents raised $17,000 to stop the store—roughly half of which came from local businesses. A media campaign and grass-roots organizing costs money. If Wal-Mart is willing to spend liberally to get into your town, its competitors should be willing to come forward with cash also.

Beat them at the grass roots: Wal-Mart can buy public relations firms and tele-marketers but it can't find bodies willing to leaflet at supermarkets, write dozens of letters to the editor, organize a press conference or make calls in the precincts. Local coalitions can draw opinion-makers from the business community (department, hardware and grocery stores, pharmacies, sporting goods stores), environmentalists, political activists and homeowners. Treat this effort like a political campaign: The Citizens versus the WAL.

Get out your vote: Our largest expenditure was on a local telemarketing company that polled 4,000 voters to identify their leanings on Wal-Mart. Our volunteers then called those voters leaning against the WAL two days before the election. On election day, we had poll-watchers at all nine precincts. If our voters weren't at the polls by 5 P.M., we reminded them to get up from the dinner table and stop the mega-store.

Appeal to the heart as well as the head: One theme the Wal-Mart culture has a hard time responding to is the loss of small-town quality of life. You can't buy rural life style on any Wal-Mart shelf—once you lose it, Wal-Mart can't sell it back to you. Wal-Mart's impact on small-town ethos is enormous. We had graphs and bar charts on job loss and retail growth—but we also communicated with people on an emotional level. Wal-Mart became the WAL—an unwanted shove into urbanization, with all the negatives that threaten small-town folks.

Hire a professional: The greatest mistake most citizen groups make is trying to fight the world's largest retailer with a mimeo-machine mentality. Most communities have a political consultant nearby, someone who can develop a media campaign and understand how to get a floppy disk of town voters with phone numbers. Wal-Mart uses hired guns; so should anti–Wal-Mart forces.

"Your real mission," a Wal-Mart executive recently wrote to a community activist, "is to be blindly obstructionist." On the contrary, we found it was Wal-Mart that would blindly say anything and do anything to bulldoze its way toward another grand opening in America. But if community coalitions organize early, bring their case directly to the public and trumpet the downside of mega-store development, the WALs will fall in Jericho.

Wal-Mart's War on Main Street
Sarah Anderson

Sarah Anderson is an economic analyst for a think tank in Washington, D.C.

Across the country, thousands of rural people are battling to save their local downtowns. Many of these fights have taken the form of anti–Wal-Mart campaigns. In Vermont, citizens' groups allowed Wal-Mart to enter the state only after the company agreed to a long list of demands regarding the size and operation of

Sarah Anderson, "Wal-Mart's War on Main Street," <u>The Progressive</u> Nov. 1994.

the stores. Three Massachusetts towns and another in Maine have defeated bids by Wal-Mart to build in their communities. In Arkansas, three independent drug-store owners won a suit charging that Wal-Mart had used "predatory pricing," or selling below cost, to drive out competitors. Canadian citizens are asking Wal-Mart to sign a "Pledge of Corporate Responsibility" before opening in their towns. In at least a dozen other U.S. communities, groups have fought to keep Wal-Mart out or to restrict the firm's activities.

By attacking Wal-Mart, these campaigns have helped raise awareness of the value of locally owned independent stores on Main Street. Their concerns generally fall in five areas:

- *Sprawl Mart*—Wal-Mart nearly always builds along a highway outside town to take advantage of cheap, often unzoned land. This usually attracts additional commercial development, forcing the community to extend services (telephone and power lines, water and sewage services, and so forth) to that area, despite sufficient existing infrastructure downtown.

- *Wal-Mart channels resources out of a community*—studies have shown that a dollar spent on a local business has four or five times the economic spin-off of a dollar spent at a Wal-Mart, since a large share of Wal-Mart's profit returns to its Arkansas headquarters or is pumped into national advertising campaigns.

- *Wal-Mart destroys jobs in locally owned stores*—a Wal-Mart-funded community impact study debunked the retailer's claim that it would create a lot of jobs in Greenfield, Massachusetts. Although Wal-Mart planned to hire 274 people at its Greenfield store, the community could expect to gain only eight net jobs, because of projected losses at other businesses that would have to compete with Wal-Mart.

- *Citizen Wal-Mart?*—in at least one town—Hearne, Texas—Wal-Mart destroyed its Main Street competitors and then deserted the town in search of higher returns elsewhere. Unable to attract new businesses to the devastated Main Street, local residents have no choice but to drive long distances to buy basic goods.

- *One-stop shopping culture*—in Greenfield, where citizens voted to keep Wal-Mart out, anti–Wal-Mart campaign manager Al Norman said he saw a resurgence of appreciation for Main Street. "People realized there's one thing you can't buy at Wal-Mart, and that's small-town quality of life," Norman explains. "This community decided it was not ready to die for a cheap pair of underwear."

Small towns cannot return to the past, when families did all their shopping and socializing in their hometown. Rural life is changing and there's no use denying it. The most important question is, who will define the future? Will it be Wal-Mart, whose narrow corporate interests have little to do with building healthy communities? Will it be the department of transportation, whose purpose is to move cars faster? Will it be the banks and suppliers primarily interested in doing business with the big guys? Or will it be the people who live in small towns, whose hard work and support are essential to any effort to revitalize Main Street?

Who's Really the Villain?
Jo-Ann Johnston

A freelance writer based in Greenfield, Massachusetts—a town that successfully fought off the construction of a Wal-Mart superstore—Jo-Ann Johnston challenges the logic of anti–Wal-Mart forces and argues that the store would have helped to address fundamental problems with the local economy.

Cheap underwear. That's all Wal-Mart Corp. contributes as it squeezes the life out of a community's downtown, according to Albert Norman, an outspoken Wal-Mart critic. His sentiment—and talent for rousing support—led folks in rural Greenfield, Massachusetts, to block the company's plans to build a store there. It also established the political consultant as one of the best known opponents to "Sprawl-mart" in the country. But fighting off Wal-Mart hasn't done much for the 18,845 residents of Greenfield.

As in numerous other communities during the past ten years, Wal-Mart simply found a site just a short distance away from its original target. In this case, it's in Orange, a smaller town located up the road about twenty-five minutes from downtown Greenfield. Meanwhile, this area ranks as the state's second poorest in per capita income. And in January, it posted an unemployment rate of 6.1 percent—attributable partly to the recent closings of a paper plant, a container factory, and a large store that sold liquidated merchandise. Wal-Mart would have brought to Greenfield 240 tax-paying jobs and increased retail traffic.

Set to open later this year, the store in Orange will be yet another example of how saying "go away" to the likes of Wal-Mart overlooks a much deeper problem facing small-town America: the need to change a way of doing business while maintaining, or improving, a deeply valued way of life. An increasing number of people are beginning to realize that small-town merchants need to adapt to changes in their communities, the economy, and their industries instead of chastising an outside company. That means accepting the fact that a Wal-Mart, or a similar retailer, may become a neighbor.

Such thinking is hogwash as far as anti–Wal-Marters are concerned. Consumerism has run amok if a town figures it needs a Wal-Mart, says Norman [see "Eight Ways to Stop the Store"], who today works with people in Illinois, Ohio, New England, and other regions to stop Wal-Marts and other large discount retailers from setting up shop. His list of reasons to fight such chain stores is lengthy, with perhaps one of the most popular being the potential loss of small-town quality of life. People move to small towns from urban or suburban America in part to escape from mall and shopping strip development, he says, not to see it duplicated.

That emotional argument carries weight, especially in New England, where twelve cities and one state, Vermont, have fought Wal-Mart. A current battle is taking place in Sturbridge, a historic town in eastern Massachusetts where community activists are fighting to keep Wal-Mart out. The town draws 60 percent of its general business from tourism-related trade, says local Wal-Mart opponent Carol Goodwin. "We

Jo-Ann Johnston, "Who's Really the Villain?" <u>Business Ethics</u> May-June 1995.

market history," she says. The town and its re-creation of an early American village are the state's second largest tourist attraction. A big cookie-cutter mart off the freeway could obscure this town of eight thousand's special appeal, she says.

Sturbridge may want to take a lesson from its neighbor to the northwest, however. Merchants in Greenfield face the possible loss of business due to the fact that Wal-Mart found a location "just over the hill" from where it was first looking to build. Kenneth Stone, an economist at Iowa State University and the country's leading researcher on the economic impacts of Wal-Marts, found that towns in the Midwest and East suffered a "retail leakage" of shoppers who instead drove to the closest regional shopping center with a discount store.

Does that mean Greenfield shoppers will now drive to Orange? Well, several of the town's shoppers complained during the Wal-Mart battle that area merchants could use competition because of their poor selection, high prices, limited hours, and lackluster service. Meanwhile, Wal-Mart has a good reputation for service. A *Consumer Reports* reader poll in late 1994 found that fifty thousand people rated Wal-Mart the highest in customer satisfaction of "value-oriented chains."

In many ways, what is happening to small-town retail corridors is similar to how mom-and-pop corporations were caught off guard during the takeover frenzy of the 1980s. Survivors became more efficient to avoid being picked off by raiders looking to maximize shareholder profits. With Wal-Mart, it's a matter of maximizing retailing opportunities for consumers.

By the time a community knows the demographically astute Wal-Mart has its eye on an area, it's virtually too late to stop *somebody* from coming into town, says Bill Sakelarios, president of the Concord-based Retail Merchants Association of New Hampshire. In Greenfield, for instance, the threat of competition to that town's small retailers didn't disappear with the Wal-Mart vote. BJ's Wholesale club is considering the town for a store.

Wal-Mart is viewed as a threat, though, because it uses bulk buying, discount pricing, and tight inventory and distribution management that smaller retailers can't keep up with. It also has the competitive advantage of size: The company's sales surged 22 percent to more than $82 billion, while net income climbed 15 percent to more than $2.6 billion in the year ended January 31, 1995, compared with year-earlier results.

Because it's so huge, the best defense against Wal-Mart for small-town retailers is to adapt, evolve, and create some stronghold that will make them viable and worth keeping, even in the face of new competition, says Robert Kahn, a Lafayette, California, management consultant who has worked with the chain and publishes a newsletter called *Retailing Today*. All kinds of stores have found ways to survive in the shadow of Wal-Mart, he says. Grocery stores have maintained check cashing, hardware stores and nurseries have offered classes, women's clothing retailers have filled in the gaps in the Wal-Mart line. Others point to pharmacies that have been able to compete with Wal-Marts. Stone met one druggist who kept a loyal clientele of shut-ins who spent $200 to $300 a month individually on prescriptions by offering home delivery, something Wal-Mart didn't do in his market.

The argument that self-improvement and change for small retailers may be the answer is definitely scorned in some circles. But stores that balk at such notions may not get much sympathy from customers who have had to change jobs or learn new skills—all because of shifts in the structure of the economies in the fields in which they work.

"You read stories about how towns don't want Wal-Mart, but in many cases that's a very few people getting a lot of publicity. And I may have on my desk a petition signed by fifteen thousand people saying, 'Please come, ignore the one hundred people who are trying to block the store,'" Wal-Mart President and CEO David Glass told a press gathering in December. "In retailing, you have a very simple answer to all that. Any community that didn't want a Wal-Mart store—all they've got to do is not shop there. And I guarantee a store, even if it's [just] built, won't be there long."

Another thing to consider is what happens if Wal-Mart, or a store like it, comes into town, stays for ten years, and then leaves. Where that's happened, retailers who found ways to adapt to Wal-Mart's presence still believe they're much better as a result. In Nowata, Oklahoma, Wal-Mart pulled up stakes last year and deserted a town of 3,900 people who had come to depend on it as their second largest taxpayer, as well as their major retailing center. But several local merchants survived Wal-Mart's stay of fourteen years because they learned to adjust their business practices. Wayne Clark, whose father opened Clark's Sentry Hardware in 1938, says he survived Wal-Mart's presence by providing better service and a more specialized inventory.

Nowata also brings up another interesting question on the Wal-Mart controversy: Could it be that old-time downtowns simply are obsolete and an impediment to efficient retailing? Many retailers have probably been in a precarious position for a long time, for a number of reasons, and then place the blame for problems or eventual demise on the highly visible Wal-Mart, says Sakelarios. "Wal-Mart is being singled out. Small-town business districts brought a lot of this on themselves," agrees Iowa State's Stone.

As cars have drawn shopping to other locales, downtown districts haven't worked hard enough to remain competitive and efficient, data suggest. "Small retailers often believe that the community *owes them* rather than *they owe* the community," Kahn wrote in his December newsletter.

He cites as evidence a recent survey of more than 1,500 Illinois retailers conducted by the state's merchant association. Kahn found it stunning that 54 percent reorder inventory for their stores only when they're already out of stock. That translates into poor selection and service, Kahn says, because small retailers often can't get priority shipments from vendors and most often wait for five to fifteen days to get fresh stock in, leaving customers without that selection in the interim. "That's not providing any service. If it's not in stock, eventually the customer is going to go somewhere else," Kahn points out.

Kahn also criticized the 63 percent of the retailers surveyed who claimed to know what their customers want, even though they didn't track customer purchases.

Apart from self-inflicted injuries, retailers are also pressured on other fronts, says John Donnellan, a member of the Consumer Studies faculty at the University of Massachusetts in Ames. The growth of the mail-order catalogs, cable TV shopping networks, specialized category stores such as Toys 'R' Us, and now, possibly, shopping via on-line computer services, all present more competition for small merchants that draw from local markets.

The only difference with Wal-Mart is that it's the biggest, most identifiable source of that new and increasing competition. As a result, it has become a lightning rod for all the angst and anxiety of struggling shop keepers—deserved or not.

Founded by Gary Hoover, this handbook provides detailed proprietary information on American companies.

Overview

Different cultures call the great omnipotent power by different names; retailers call it Wal-Mart. Bentonville, Arkansas-based Wal-Mart Stores operates about 4,000 stores, including discount stores (Wal-Mart), members-only warehouse stores (Sam's Club), and combination discount and grocery stores (Wal-Mart Supercenters and ASDA in the UK). It is the world's largest—and most feared—retailer. Although the chain touts a small-town flavor (with friendly People Greeters and simple trappings), it is best known for its breadth of merchandise and low prices.

Wal-Mart doesn't just complete in discount staples such as clothing—it is a force in many category-killer retailing operations, including auto parts, electronics, and toys, and it plans to start selling major appliances as part of a program with General Electric. Most of its approximately 750 Supercenters are open 24 hours a day, and it is adding about 150 of them in the US per year. More than 460 Sam's Club stores worldwide serve small-business and individual customers. It also sells products online.

Already a leading food retailer through its Supercenters, Wal-Mart is slowly expanding its Neighborhood Market supermarket format. (The stores are dedicated to groceries only.) Wal-Mart has stores in all 50 states and is expanding internationally; it has stores in China, Europe (including hypermarkets in Germany), and South Korea, as well as a majority interest in Mexico's #1 retailer, Wal-Mart de Mexico. In addition, Wal-Mart owns the largest US convenience store distributor, McLane Company.

One of the wealthiest families in the world, the heirs of late founder Sam Walton own about 38% of the company.

History

Sam Walton began his retail career as a J. C. Penney management trainee and later leased a Ben Franklin-franchised dime store in Newport, Arkansas, in 1945. In 1950 he relocated to Bentonville, Arkansas, and opened a Walton 5 & 10. By 1962 Walton owned 15 Ben Franklin stores under the Walton 5 & 10 name.

After Ben Franklin management rejected his suggestion to open discount stores in small towns, Walton, with his brother James "Bud" Walton, opened the first Wal-Mart Discount City in Rogers, Arkansas, in 1962. Growth was slow at first, but Wal-Mart Stores went public in 1970 with 18 stores and sales of $44 million.

Avoiding regional retailers, Walton continued to open stores in underserved small and midsized towns in the 1970s. The demise of state and federal "free trade" laws in the 1970s enabled discount retailers such as Wal-Mart to begin selling merchandise

Hoover's Handbook of American Business 2001 (Austin: Hoover's, 2000) 1504–05.

for less than manufacturers' suggested prices. By 1980 Wal-Mart's 276 stores had sales of $1.2 billion. The company bought and sold several operations in those years (selling off its Ben Franklin stores in 1976).

In 1983 Wal-Mart opened Sam's Wholesale Club, a concept based on the successful cash-and-carry, membership-only warehouse format pioneered by the Price Company of California.

The company started Hypermart*USA in 1987, originally as a joint venture with Dallas-based supermarket chain Cullum Companies (which later became Randall's Food Markets). The hypermarket, a huge 200,000-sq.-ft. discount store/supermarket hybrid, was later retooled as Wal-Mart Supercenters. Sam stepped down as CEO in 1988 and president David Glass was appointed CEO. Wal-Mart bought out Cullum the next year.

Wal-Mart acquired wholesale distributor McLane Company in 1990, and it launched deep-discounter Bud's Discount City (discontinued by 1999). In 1992, the year Sam died, the company expanded into Mexico by a joint venture to open Sam's Clubs with Cifra (renamed Wal-Mart de Mexico in 2000), that country's largest retailer. Co-founder Bud died in 1995.

The Windsor, Ontario, Wal-Mart became the first in the chain to negotiate under a union labor contract in 1997. The company also acquired German hypermarket chain Wertkauf that year.

Other international moves included the 1998 purchase of Brazilian retailer Lojas Americanas' 40% interest in their joint venture. Also in 1998 the company began testing Neighborhood Market, a 40,000-sq.-ft. grocery and drug combination store. In 1999 Wal-Mart bought 74 German-based Interspar hypermarkets and acquired ASDA Group, the UK's third-largest supermarket chain. In late 1999 the company partnered with America Online to unveil a co-branded Internet service provider that would primarily serve small towns.

COO Lee Scott succeeded Glass as CEO in early 2000. In August Wal-Mart announced plans to sell General Electric household appliances in selected stores to test consumer demand.

Officers

Chairman: S. Robson Walton, age 55

Chairman of the Executive Committee: David D. Glass, age 64, $3,946,154 pay (prior to title change)

President and CEO: H. Lee Scott Jr., age 51, $2,015,385 pay (prior to promotion)

EVP; President and CEO, Sam's Club Division: Thomas R. Grimm, age 55, $884,808 pay

EVP; President and CEO, Wal-Mart International Division: John B. Menzer, age 49, $1,372,693 pay

EVP; President and CEO, Wal-Mart Stores Division: Thomas M. Coughlin, age 51, $1,728,000 pay

EVP and CFO: Thomas M. Schoewe, age 47

SVP and Controller: James A. Walker Jr., age 53

SVP Merchandising: Hani Zayadi, age 52

VP Human Resources; VP Human Resources, Sam's Club: Coleman Petersen

CEO, Wal-Mart.com: Jeanne Jackson, age 48
President and CEO, McLane: W. Grady Rosier
President and CEO, Wal-Mart Europe: Dave Ferguson, age 55
COO, Wal-Mart Canada: Mario Pilozzi, age 53
Auditors: Ernst & Young LLP

Locations

HQ: 702 SW 8th St., Bentonville, AR 72716
Phone: 501-273-4000   **Fax:** 501-273-1917
Web site: http://www.walmart.com

Wal-Mart has 3,989 stores in Argentina, Brazil, Canada, China, Germany, Mexico, South Korea, the UK and the US.

Products/Operations

2000 Stores	No.
Discount stores	2,373
Supercenters	1,104
Sam's Club	512
Total	**3,989**

Selected Divisions

McLane Distribution Centers (about 15 regional wholesale distribution centers supplying convenience stores and Sam's Clubs, Supercenters, and Wal-Marts)
Sam's Club (members-only warehouse clubs)
Supercenters (large, combination general merchandise and food stores)
Wal-Mart Distribution Centers (45 regional centers, primarily supplying Wal-Marts and Supercenters)
Wal-Mart Stores (general merchandise)

Competitors

Ace Hardware
Albertson's
Army and Air Force
   Exchange
AutoZone
Best Buy
BJs Wholesale Club
Carrefour
Circuit City
CompUSA
Consolidated Stores
Core-Mark
Costco Wholesale
CVS

Dollar General
Eby-Brown
Family Dollar Stores
Home Depot
Hudson's Bay
J. C. Penney
Kmart
Kroger
Loblaw
Lowe's
Meijer
METRO AG
Office Depot
OfficeMax

Pep Boys
RadioShack
Rite Aid
Royal Ahold
Safeway
Sears
Service Merchandise
Staples
Target
TJX
Toys "R" Us
TruServ
Walgreen

Historical Financials & Employees

NYSE symbol: WMT FYE: January 31	Annual Growth	1/91	1/92	1/93	1/94	1/95	1/96	1/97	1/98	1/99	1/00
Sales ($ mil.)	19.7%	32,602	43,887	55,484	67,345	82,494	93,627	104,859	117,958	137,634	165,013
Net income ($ mil.)	17.2%	1,291	1,609	1,995	2,333	2,681	2,740	3,056	3,526	4,430	5,377
Income as % of sales	—	4.0%	3.7%	3.6%	3.5%	3.2%	2.9%	2.9%	3.0%	3.2%	3.3%
Earnings per share ($)	17.2%	0.29	0.35	0.44	0.51	0.59	0.60	0.67	0.78	0.99	1.21
Stock Price - FY high ($)	—	9.19	14.97	16.47	17.06	14.63	13.81	14.13	20.97	43.22	70.25
Stock price - FY low ($)	—	5.05	8.19	12.53	11.50	10.31	9.55	10.06	11.50	20.09	38.88
Stock price - FY close ($)	23.4%	8.25	13.47	16.28	13.25	11.44	10.19	11.88	19.91	43.00	54.75
P/E - high	—	32	43	37	33	25	23	21	27	44	56
P/E - low	—	17	23	28	23	17	16	15	15	20	31
Dividends per share ($)	19.6%	0.04	0.05	0.06	0.07	0.09	0.10	0.11	0.14	0.16	0.20
Book value per share ($)	19.4%	1.17	1.52	1.90	2.34	2.77	3.22	3.75	4.13	4.75	5.80
Employees	14.8%	328,000	371,000	434,000	528,000	622,000	675,000	728,000	825,000	910,000	1,140,000

Stock Price History

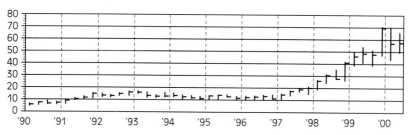

2000 Fiscal Year-End

Debt ratio: 39.2%
Return on equity: 22.9%
Cash ($ mil.): 1,856
Current ratio: 0.94
Long-term debt ($ mil.): 16,674
No. of shares (mil.): 4,457
Dividends
 Yield: 0.4%
 Payout: 16.5%
Market value ($ mil.): 244,021

Victorious Secret
Albert Norman

The following communities have either voted to reject a big box retail development at least once, or pressured the developer to withdraw. Developers don't want you to know that towns can beat sprawl, so this list is a victorious secret. Updated to August, 2001

Chandler, AZ	Colchester, CT	Naples, FL
Gilbert, AZ	Plainville, CT	St. Petersburg, FL
Glendale, AZ	Orange, CT	Temple Terrace, FL
Mesa, AZ	New Milford, CT	Atlanta, GA
Phoenix, AZ	Old Saybrook, CT	Athens, GA
Tucson, AZ	Tolland, CT	Hawaii Kai, HI
Eureka, CA	Fort Collins, CO	Mason City, IA
Grass Valley, CA	Jefferson County, CO	Hailey, ID
North Auburn, CA	Silverthorne, CO	Evergreen Park, IL
San Juan Capistrano, CA	Woodland Park, CO	Lake in the Hills, IL
Santa Rosa, CA	Rehobeth, DE	Wheaton, IL
Santa Maria, CA	Bonita Springs, FL	Lawrence, KS
Simi Valley, CA	Clermont, FL	New Albany, IN
S. San Francisco, CA	Hallandale, FL	Manhattan, KS
Yacaipa, CA	Lake Forest, FL	Overland Park, KS

Albert Norman, "Victorious Secret," <u>Sprawlbusters</u>, Sept. 2001, 3 Sept. 2001 <http://www.sprawl-busters.com/victoryz.html>.

Wichita, KS
Fort Wright, KY
Henderson, KY
Barnstable, MA
Billerica, MA
Boxboro, MA
Braintree, MA
Easthampton, MA
Greenfield, MA
Lee, MA
Northboro, MA
Plymouth, MA
Reading, MA
Saugus, MA
Somerset, MA
Westford, MA
Yarmouth, MA
Accokeek, MD
Chestertown, MD
Gaithersburg, MD
Paradise, MD
Kent Island, MD
Rockland, ME
Bangor, ME
Belfast, ME
Wells, ME
Fenton, MI
Buffalo, MN
Burnsville, MN
Olivette, MO
Springfield, MO
St. Louis, MO
Warsaw, MO
Lincoln, NB
Asheville, NC
Durham, NC
Hickory, NC

Claremont, NH
Peterboro, NH
Stratham, NH
Walpole, NH
Deptford, NJ
Englewood, NJ
Hamilton, NJ
Manalapan, NJ
Albuquerque, NM
Tijeras, NM
Reno, NV
Aurora, NY
Buffalo, NY
East Aurora, NY
Cazenovia, NY
Hornell, NY
Hyde Park, NY
Ithaca, NY
Lake Placid, NY
Leeds, NY
New Paltz, NY
North Greenbush, NY
New Rochelle, NY
Saranac Lake, NY
Beavercreek, OH
Broadview Hts. OH
Highland Hts, OH
Lorain, OH
North Olmstead, OH
Ottawa, OH
Strongsville, OH
Yellow Springs, OH
Westlake, OH
Warren, OR
Lower Gwynned, PA
Milford, PA
Mount Joy, PA

Warwick, PA
West Hempfield, PA
Barranquitas, PR
Utuado, PR
Middletown, RI
Clemson, SC
Arlington, TX
Cooleyville, TX
Fort Worth, TX
Kennedale, TX
Murphy, TX
Richardson, TX
Layton, UT
Taylorsville, UT
Accomac, VA
Ashland, VA
Charlottesville, VA
Fredericksburg, VA
Roanoke, VA
Warrenton, VA
Williamsburg, VA
Gig Harbor, WA
Port Townsend, WA
Brookfield, WI
Menomonee Falls, WI
Racine, WI
Waukesha, WI
Morgantown, WV
St. Albans, VT
St. Johnsbury, VT
Willison, VT
Brampton, ONT
Guelph, ONT
Oakville, ONT
Waterloo, ONT
Surrey, BC
Park Royal, BC

Shopping with the Enemy

This unsigned article first appeared in The Economist *on October 14, 1995.*

"Something there is that doesn't love a wall," wrote Robert Frost. "Or a Wal-Mart," he might add, were he to rise from his grave behind the Old First Church and look at the newly opened store just down the hill. Vermont is no longer the only state without a Wal-Mart, despite a five-year struggle by the company's opponents to keep it out.

Yet instead of protesting, the locals are pushing and shoving to get in. "The reaction has been tremendous," says Russ Walker, the manager. Mr. Walker recorded

23,000 transactions in his first week, and this in a town of 16,000 people. Drawn by such locally appealing bargains as red flannel shirts for $6.56, Vermonters are opening their hearts and their wallets to Wal-Mart.

Does that mean doom for downtown merchants? Not necessarily. Wal-Marts are usually huge, charmless boxes built on the outskirts of towns, where highways are handy and parking plentiful. But to crack the Vermont market and avoid the restrictions of the state's tough development-control law, Wal-Mart put a less-imposing, 50,000-square-foot store into an old Woolworth's building near the centre of town.

Bennington's downtown merchants seem to be adjusting to Wal-Mart; they are used to competing with other big discount chains such as KMart, already established in the local market. "I'm not really worried," says Catherine Mack, proprietor of the artsy-craftsy Pea Pod gift shop on Main Street. "I think we're building our own little niche as a specialty store." But not all Wal-Mart patrons are willing to venture downtown, despite a recent effort to spiff up the district. "I think the downtown in Bennington is doomed anyway, because of the lack of parking," Mary Lou Morris said firmly. "I go to malls."

Mall-going Vermonters have little patience with Wal-Mart's opponents. Mr. Walker, the store manager, blames the controversy on "a handful of non-natives" who care more about prettiness than economic development. But if they are a minority in blue-collar Bennington, the company's enemies are more influential elsewhere in the state. In Burlington, the state's biggest city, anxious officials are fighting a 115,000-square-foot Wal-Mart and a 132,000-square-foot Sam's Club planned for a largely undeveloped area outside the city.

Their battle appears lost, however. So far Vermont has largely avoided the suburban sprawl that blights so much of the American landscape. But too many people crave the low prices, large selection and convenient parking offered by the big discount chains. "Progress—can't stand in the way," said Wal-Mart shopper Jack Hodgeman, trundling several new refuse bins out to his pickup truck.

EXERCISE 5.5

Critical Reading for Synthesis

Look over the preceding readings and make a list of the different points they make regarding Wal-Mart. Make your list as specific and detailed as you can. Then make several more lists in which you group readings that take similar positions, noting the variations among them. Next go back over the readings, examining the kinds of arguments made by the writers. Do you see examples of faulty logic? (You might review the logical fallacies we discussed in Chapter 2 to help you here.) Do any of the writers use appeals to *ethos* or *pathos*? If so, are these effective or not, and why? Once you've critically examined the writer's arguments, look over the factual information presented in the charts and lists. How does this information fit into the claims made by the argumentative pieces? Lastly, spend some time freewriting what you think about this issue; which arguments do you find most persuasive, and how does your agreement with these arguments relate to your own experience with—or lack of experience with—Wal-Mart and other "megastores" of its ilk?

Consider Your Purpose

As with the explanatory synthesis, your specific purpose in writing an argument synthesis is crucial. What, exactly, you want to do will affect your claim, the evidence you select to support your claim, and the way you organize the evidence. Your purpose may be clear to you before you begin research, may emerge during the course of research, or may not emerge until after you have completed your research. (Of course, the sooner your purpose is clear to you, the fewer wasted motions you will make. On the other hand, the more you approach research as an exploratory process, the likelier that your conclusions will emerge from the sources themselves, rather than from preconceived ideas. For a discussion of the research process, see Chapter 7.)

Let's say that while reading these sources, your own encounters with Wal-Mart influence your thinking on the subject and you find yourself agreeing more with the supporters than with the detractors of Wal-Mart. Perhaps you didn't grow up in a small town, so you don't have much experience with or knowledge of the kind of retail stores that the megastores have been displacing.

On the one hand, you can understand and even sympathize with the viewpoints of critics such as Norman and Anderson. (You may have shopped in the smaller stores in towns you have visited, or seen them portrayed in movies, or perhaps even visited reconstructed small-town stores in museums such as the Smithsonian or in the "Main Street" area in Disneyland.) On the other hand, it seems to you unrealistic in this day and age to expect that stores like Wal-Mart can be stopped or should be. For you, the prices and the convenience are a big plus. Your purpose, then, is formed from this kind of response to the source material.

Making a Claim: Formulate a Thesis

As we indicated in the introduction to argument synthesis, one useful way of approaching an argument is to see it as making a *claim*. A claim is a proposition, a conclusion that you are trying to prove or demonstrate. If your purpose is to demonstrate that it is neither possible nor desirable to stop the spread of Wal-Mart, then that is the claim at the heart of your argument. The claim is generally expressed in one-sentence form as a *thesis*. You use the information—and sometimes appeals to *ethos* and *pathos* (see pages 182–184)—in sources to *support* your claim.

Of course, not every piece of information in a source is useful for supporting a claim. By the same token, you may draw support for your own claim from sources that make entirely different claims. You may use as support for your own claim—for example, that Wal-Mart is growing at an alarming rate—data from *Hoover's Handbook*, which indicates the exact opposite: that Wal-Mart's growth is good for both customers and stockholders.

Similarly, you might use one source as part of a *counterargument*—an argument opposite to your own—so that you can demonstrate its weaknesses and, in the process, strengthen your own claim. On the other hand, the author of one of your sources may be so convincing in supporting a claim that you adopt it yourself, either partially or entirely. The point is that *the argument is in your hands*: you must devise it yourself and must use your sources in ways that will support the claim expressed in your thesis.

You may not want to divulge your thesis until the end of the paper, to draw the reader along toward your conclusion, allowing the thesis to flow naturally out of the argument and the evidence on which it is based. If you do this, you are working *inductively*. Or you may wish to be more direct and *begin* with your thesis, following the thesis statement with evidence to support it. If you do this, you are working *deductively*. In academic papers, deductive arguments are far more common than inductive arguments.

Based on your reactions to reading the sources, you decide to concede that the case against Wal-Mart has some merit and certainly some homespun appeal, but that opponents of such megastores are being unrealistic in expecting most people to sacrifice convenience and economy for the sake of retaining a vanishing way of life. After a few tries, you arrive at the following provisional thesis:

> Opponents of the giant discount chains have made powerful arguments against them, and it's too bad that these megastores are helping to make a way of life extinct; but opponents should realize that stores such as Wal-Mart are so successful because most people prefer bargains and convenience to tradition and small-town charm.

Decide How You Will Use Your Source Material

Your claim commits you to (1) recognize the arguments made by opponents of Wal-Mart, and (2) argue that Wal-Marts will prevail because they offer people advantages that the traditional retail shops can't match. The sources provide plenty of information and ideas—that is, evidence—that will allow you to support your claim. Norman and Anderson sum up the anti-Wal-Mart case, one that is also described more objectively by Ortega and the anonymous author of the *Economist* article. Johnston offers the primary argument for Wal-Mart, and other data showing the growth of the chain are provided by the chart from *Hoover's Handbook*.

Develop an Organizational Plan

Having established your overall purpose and your claim, having developed a provisional thesis, and having decided how to use your source materials, how do you logically organize your essay? In many cases, including this one, a well-written thesis will suggest an overall organization. Thus, the first part of your synthesis will address the powerful arguments made by opponents of Wal-Mart. The second part will cover the even more powerful case (in your judgment) to be made on the other side. Sorting through your material and categorizing it by topic and subtopic, you might arrive at the following outline:

A. Introduction. The emotional anti–Wal-Mart case; conflict of values: consumerism vs. small-town America. *Thesis*.

B. Spectacular growth of Wal-Mart.

C. The case against Wal-Mart.

   1. Arguments against Wal-Mart.

   2. Al Norman's crusade

D. Transition: the case for Wal-Mart

E. Concession: charm of small-town stores. But— problems with small-town stores.

F. Changes in American economy and lifestyle and their effect on Main Street.

G. How traditionalists and store owners can deal with Wal-Mart.

   1. Fight it.

   2. Adjust by competing in ways that Wal-Mart can't.

H. Conclusion. Wal-Mart is not a "villain" because it offers what people want.

Argument Strategy

The argument represented by this outline deals with a claim of *value*, rather than a claim of *fact*. In other words, this is not an argument over whether Wal-Marts *are* better, according to some objective standard, than Main Street variety stores, since there is no such standard about which most people would agree. (Of course, if "better" were defined as more profitable, then this argument *would* become one of fact and would, in fact, be easily disposed of, since numbers would provide sufficient support for the claim.) Rather, it is an argument that turns on those values which for some people take priority—convenience and economy versus charm and traditional small-town life. This *claim*, therefore, is based not only upon the *supporting evidence*, but also upon *assumptions* about the relative value of convenience and economy, on the one hand, and charm and traditional small-town life, on the other. Accordingly, while some of the arguments are based upon an appeal to *logos*, most are based upon the appeal to *pathos*. Some are even based upon *ethos*, since the writer will occasionally imply that her view is representative of that of most people.

To *support* her *claim*, the writer will rely upon a combination of summary, paraphrase, and quotation—much of it *testimony* from either "average" customers or from proponents of one side or the other of the debate. Note that despite her own essentially pro–Wal-Mart position, the writer provides *counterarguments* and *concessions,* indicating that she is not afraid to fairly represent the views of the other side, and even to give them some credit (the concession) before she responds and reinforces her own argument.

Draft and Revise Your Synthesis

The final draft of a completed synthesis, based upon the above outline, follows. Thesis, transitions, and topic sentences are highlighted; Modern Language Association (MLA) documentation style, explained in Chapter 7, is used throughout. Note that for the sake of clarity, references in the following essay are to pages in *A Sequence for Academic Writing.*

MODEL ESSAY

A Vote for Wal-Mart

1   According to one critic, Wal-Mart is waging a "War on Main Street." Anti–Wal-Mart activists such as Bob Ortega think that we should "Ban the Bargains." A pro–Wal-Mart writer asks "Who's Really the Villain?" (Johnston 190). Obviously, the ever-expanding Wal-Mart brings some people's emotions to the boiling point. This seems strange. After all, Wal-Mart doesn't seem one of those hot-button issues like abortion or capital punishment. But for many, this is not just about discount department stores; it's about conflicting values: the values of small-town America versus the values of "mindless consumerism" (Ortega 185). I don't consider myself a mindless consumerist, but I happen to like Wal-Marts. Opponents of the giant discount chains have made powerful arguments against them, and it's too bad that these megastores are helping to make a way of life extinct; but opponents should realize that stores like Wal-Mart are so successful because most people prefer bargains and convenience to tradition and small-town charm.

2   Wal-Mart's growth has been spectacular. Launched in 1962, by 2000 Wal-Mart had about 4,000 stores, including 1,100 "Supercenters" (Hoover's 195). Al Norman, one of Wal-Mart's most vocal critics, reported that in 1994 Wal-Mart had over $67 billion in

sales (187). Six years later, Wal-Mart's annual sales climbed to over 165 billion (Hoover's 195). Wal-Mart also owns Sam's Club, another discount chain, which opened in 1983, and now numbers 512 stores (Hoover's 196).

3   To its critics, Wal-Mart seems to represent everything that's wrong with modern American society. Sarah Anderson, an economist and the daughter of a small-town retailer, argues that Wal-Mart encourages urban sprawl, drains money from local economies, kills downtowns and local jobs, and destroys the quality of small-town life (189). Others blame Wal-Mart for the "homogenization of community identity" (Ortega 185). One local resident complains, "Everything's starting to look the same, everybody buys all the same things—a lot of small-town character is being lost." She adds, "Visually, [Wal-Marts are] atrocious" (qtd. in Ortega 186). Wal-Marts' ugliness is a common theme: the stores have been described as "huge, charmless boxes" ("Shopping" 199).

4   Activist Al Norman has helped organize local communities to fight the spread of Wal-Mart. His Web site, "Sprawl-Busters," proudly lists 156 communities that have succeeded in beating back Wal-Mart's advance on their town. (He also lists communities that have rejected other large discounters like Home Depot, Costco, and K-Mart.) Norman argues that "Wal-Mart's gains are largely captured from other merchants" ("Eight Ways" 187). His rallying cry is that communities are "not ready to die for a cheap pair of underwear" (qtd. in Anderson 189).

5   But rhetoric like this is overkill. Norman might as well blame computer makers for the death of typewriters or automakers for the death of horse-and-buggy rigs. Horses and buggies may be more picturesque and romantic than cars, but most Americans drive cars these days because they're a lot faster and more convenient. If customers choose to buy underwear at Wal-Mart instead of the mom-and-pop store downtown, that's because it's easier to get to Wal-Mart—and to park there—and because cheapness is a quality that matters to them.

6   I agree that Wal-Marts are unattractive and "charmless." They just don't have the warmth or individuality of some of the small shops you find in downtown areas, especially the ones that have been in

business for generations. But like most people, I'm willing to sacrifice warmth and individuality if I can get just what I want at a price I can afford. As Jo-Ann Johnston points out, mom-and-pop stores have brought on a lot of their own problems by not being sufficiently responsive to what their customers need. She notes, "several of the town's shoppers complained during the Wal-Mart battle that area merchants could use competition because of their poor selection, high prices, limited hours, and lackluster service" (191). Johnston points out that if customers can't find what they want at the price they want at local stores, it's not surprising that they go to Wal-Mart. Even residents of Vermont, one of the areas most likely to resist the intrusion of Wal-Mart, come flocking to Wal-Mart for the bargains and the selection ("Shopping" 199). Russ Walker, store manager of the Bennington Wal-Mart, dismisses opposition to the discount chain as "'a handful of non-natives' who care more about prettiness than economic development" ("Shopping" 199).

7   As even opponents of Wal-Mart admit, American downtowns were in trouble long before Wal-Mart arrived on the scene. Changes in the economy and in the American lifestyle have contributed to the end of a traditional way of life. In other words, stores such as Wal-Mart are a symptom rather than a cause of the changes in Main Street. Blaming Wal-Mart "overlooks a much deeper problem facing small-town America," writes Jo-Ann Johnston: "the need to change a way of business while maintaining, or improving, a deeply valued way of life" (190). As Sarah Anderson admits, "Small towns cannot return to the past, when families did all their shopping and socializing in their hometown. Rural life is changing and there's no use denying it" (189).

8   In "Eight Ways to Stop the Store," Norman provides tips for community activists on how to fight Wal-Mart. I agree that if most people don't want Wal-Mart in their community, they should campaign against it and keep it out. I even think that the community might be a more pleasant place to live without the huge discount chains. But I also believe that residents of these communities should be aware of the price they will pay, both financially and in convenience, for maintaining their traditional way of doing

business. Even without Wal-Mart, local downtowns will have trouble holding on to their customers. A better plan than keeping the big discounters out would be for local retailers to adapt to the changing times and to the competition. Some store owners have found ways of offering their customers what Wal-Mart can't provide: personalized services, such as home delivery or special orders, along with merchandise not available in the chain stores (Johnston 191).

9   Wal-Mart did not become the huge success it is by forcing its products on an unwilling public. People shop there because they want to. They want to save money and they want to find what they're looking for. Who can blame them? Wal-Mart may not be pretty, but it's also not "the villain."

Works Cited

Anderson, Sarah. "Wal-Mart's War on Main Street." Progressive Nov. 1994: 19—21.

Hoover's Handbook of American Business. Austin: Hoover's, 2000.

Johnston, Jo-Ann. "Who's Really the Villain?" Business Ethics May—June 1995: 16—18.

Norman, Albert. "Eight Ways to Stop the Store." The Nation 28 Mar. 1994: 418.

———. "Victorious Secret." Sprawl-Busters Sept. 2001. 3 Sept. 2001 <http://www.sprawl-busters.com/victoryz.html>.

Ortega, Bob. "Ban the Bargains." The Wall Street Journal 11 Oct. 1994: 1.

"Shopping with the Enemy." Economist 14 Oct. 1995: 33.

Discussion

The writer of this argument synthesis on Wal-Mart attempts to support a *claim*—one that essentially favors Wal-Mart—by offering *support* in the form of facts (examples and statistics) and opinions (testimony of experts and "average" customers). However, since the writer's claim is one of *value*, as opposed to fact, its effectiveness depends partially upon the extent to which we, as readers, agree with the *assumptions* underlying the argument. (See our discussion of assumptions in Chapter 2, pages 66–68). An assumption (sometimes called a *warrant*) is a generalization or principle about how the world works or should work—a fundamental statement of belief about facts or values. In this particular case, the underlying assumption is that the values of cheapness and convenience are preferable, as a rule, to the values of charm and small-town tradition. Assumptions often are deeply rooted in people's psyches, sometimes deriving from lifelong experiences and observations, and are not easily changed, even by the most logical arguments. People who grew up in small-town America and remember it fondly are therefore far less likely to be persuaded by the support offered for this writer's claim than those who have lived in urban and suburban areas.

- **Paragraph 1:** The writer summarizes some of the most heated arguments against Wal-Mart by citing some of the titles of recent articles about the store. The writer goes on to explain the intensity of emotion generated by stores such as Wal-Mart by linking it to a larger conflict of values: the values of small-town America vs. the values of consumerism. The writer then states her own preference for Wal-Mart, which leads to her *claim* (represented in the *thesis* at the end of the first paragraph).

  Argument strategy: The writer sets up the argument as one of conflicting *values*, relying here upon summary and quotations that support an appeal to *pathos* (emotions of the reader). The writer also provides the beginning of an appeal to *ethos* (establishing herself as credible) by stating her own views as a consumer in the sentence before the thesis.

- **Paragraph 2:** Here the writer discusses the spectacular growth of Wal-Mart. This growth is indirectly, rather than directly, relevant to the debate itself, since it is this apparently unstoppable growth that has caused Wal-Mart to be perceived as such a threat by opponents.

  Argument strategy: This paragraph relies primarily upon the appeal to *logos* (logic) since its main purpose is to establish Wal-Mart's spectacular success. The argument here is supported primarily with statistics.

- **Paragraphs 3 and 4:** In these paragraphs, the writer discusses the case against Wal-Mart. The third paragraph covers the objections most commonly advanced by Wal-Mart critics. Three sources (Anderson, Ortega, and "Shopping with the Enemy") provide the source material for this paragraph. In the next paragraph, the writer focuses on Al Norman, one of the most prominent anti–Wal-Mart activists, who has helped localities organize campaigns against new Wal-Marts, some of them successful.

  Argument strategy: The third paragraph, part of the *counterargument*, attempts to support claims of value (that is, *pathos*) with a combination of summary (topic sentence), paraphrase (second sentence), and quotation (following sentences). The fourth paragraph, a continuation of the counterargument, relies on a combination of appeals to *logos* (the numbers of communities that, according to Norman, have rejected Wal-Mart) and *pathos* (the quotation in the final sentence of the paragraph).

- **Paragraph 5:** This paragraph begins the transition to the opposite side. The writer begins advancing her own claim—that people aren't willing to sacrifice convenience and price to charm and tradition. She also suggests that the small-town American Main Street that Wal-Mart is replacing was dying anyway.

Argument strategy: This paragraph makes a transition from the counterargument to the writer's own argument. Initially, the appeal is to *logos*: she draws an analogy between the passing of traditional Main Street stores and the passing of typewriters and horses and buggies. This is followed by another appeal to *pathos*—the importance of efficiency, convenience, and cheapness.

- **Paragraph 6:** The writer admits that Wal-Marts are not pretty, charming, or unique, but argues that the mom-and-pop stores have their own problems: small selection, nonresponsiveness to customer needs, indifferent service, and relatively high prices.

    Argument strategy: In this paragraph, the writer makes an important *concession* (part of the counterargument) that charm is important; but she continues to use the appeal to *pathos* to support the primary claim. Note that in the middle of the paragraph, the writer makes an appeal to *ethos* ("like most people, I'm willing to sacrifice warmth and individuality if I can get just what I want at a price I can afford"). This statement aligns the writer with what most people want from their shopping experiences. After all, the writer implies, this is a matter of good sense—a quality the reader is likely to think valuable, a quality that she or he appears to share with the writer.

- **Paragraph 7:** This paragraph deals more explicitly than the fifth paragraph with the passing away of traditional small-town America, owing to changes in the economy and in lifestyle.

    Argument strategy: In this paragraph the writer follows through with her strategy of relying upon a combination of *logos* and *pathos* to support her claim. Beginning by summarizing the reasons for the decline of Main Street, she concludes the paragraph with quotations focusing on the sad but inevitable passing of a way of life.

- **Paragraph 8:** Here the writer concedes that people are free to fight Wal-Mart coming to their town if they don't want the giant store; but a better course of action might be for local merchants to adjust to Wal-Mart by offering goods and services that the giant store is unwilling or unable to, such as home delivery and specialty merchandise.

    Argument strategy: At this point, the writer focuses almost all her attention on the appeal to logic: she summarizes both the essential nature of the conflict and suggestions offered by one source for counteracting the Wal-Mart threat.

- **Paragraph 9:** The writer concludes by reemphasizing her claim: Wal-Mart is successful because it gives customers what they want.

    Argument strategy: The writer wraps up her argument by reemphasizing the reasons offered for Wal-Mart's success. She rounds off her discussion by repeating, in quotation marks, the "villain" epithet with which the paper begins. The final sentence again combines the appeal to *pathos* (we admittedly cannot call Wal-Mart "pretty") and *logos* (in view of the evidence offered as support, it makes no sense to label Wal-Mart a "villain").

Of course, many other approaches to an argument synthesis would be possible based on the sources provided here. One, obviously, would be the opposite argument: that in embracing Wal-Marts and other giant chains, America is losing part of its soul—or, at a less profound level, small towns are losing part of their charm and distinctive character. Another might be to assess the quality of the various positions according, for example, to the nature of the evidence provided or the type of logic employed. Another might be to de-emphasize the more concrete issue of stores such as Wal-Mart and to focus on the broader issue of changes in small-town life. Whatever your approach to the subject, in first *critically examining* the various sources and then *synthesizing* them to support your argument, you are engaging in the kind of critical thinking that is essential to success in a good deal of academic and professional work.

DEVELOPING AND ORGANIZING THE SUPPORT FOR YOUR ARGUMENTS

Experienced writers seem to have an intuitive sense of how to develop and present the supporting evidence for their claims; this sense is developed through much hard work and practice. Less experienced writers wonder what to say first, and having decided on that, wonder what to say next. There is no single method of presentation. But the techniques of even the most experienced writers often boil down to a few tried and tested arrangements.

As we've seen in the model synthesis in this chapter, the key to devising effective arguments is to find and use those kinds of support that most persuasively strengthen your claim. Some writers categorize support into two broad types: *evidence* and *motivational appeals*. Evidence, in the form of facts, statistics, and expert testimony, helps make the appeal to *logos* or reason. Motivational appeals—appeals to *pathos* and to *ethos*—are employed to get people to change their minds, to agree with the writer or speaker, or to decide upon a plan of activity.

Following are some of the most common principles for using and organizing support for your claims.

Summarize, Paraphrase, and Quote Supporting Evidence

In most of the papers and reports you will write in college and the professional world, evidence and motivational appeals derive from summarizing, paraphrasing, and quoting material in the sources that either have been provided to you or that you have independently researched. (See Chapter 1 on when to summarize, paraphrase, and quote material from sources.) As we noted above, the third paragraph of the Wal-Mart synthesis offers all three treatments of evidence: in the first sentence, the writer *summarizes* anti–Wal-Mart sentiment in the sources; in the second sentence, she *paraphrases* Sarah Anderson; in the third sentence, she *quotes* Bob Ortega.

Provide Various Types of Evidence and Motivational Appeals

Keep in mind the appeals to both *logos* and *pathos*. As we've discussed, the appeal to *logos* is based on evidence that consists of a combination of *facts*, *statistics*, and *expert testimony*. In the Wal-Mart synthesis, the writer uses all of these varieties of evidence: facts (the economic decline of small-town America, as discussed in paragraph 7, statistics (the growth of Wal-Mart, as documented in paragraph 2), and testimony (the quotations in paragraph 3). The appeal to *pathos* is based on the appeal to the needs and values of the audience. In the Wal-Mart synthesis, this appeal is exemplified in the use of support (for example, the quotations in paragraph 6 about the limitations of mom-and-pop stores) that are likely to make readers upset or dissatisfied because they feel that they need greater selection, efficiency, and economy than the smaller stores can offer them.

Use Climactic Order

Organize by climactic order when you plan to offer a number of different categories or elements of support for your claim. Recognize, however, that some are more important—that is, are likely to be more persuasive—than others. The basic principle here is that you should *save the most important evidence for the end*, since whatever you have said last is what readers are likely to most remember. A secondary principle is that whatever you say first is what they are *next* most likely to remember. Therefore, when you have several reasons to support your claim, an effective argument strategy is to present the second most important, then one or more additional reasons, and finally, the most important reason.

Use Logical or Conventional Order

Using logical or conventional order means that you use as a template a preestablished pattern or plan for arguing your case.

- One common pattern is describing or arguing a *problem/solution*. Using this pattern, you begin with an introduction in which you typically define the problem, then perhaps explain its origins, then offer one or more solutions, then conclude.
- Another common pattern is presenting *two sides of a controversy*. Using this pattern, you introduce the controversy and (if an argument synthesis) your own point of view or claim, then explain each side's arguments, providing reasons that your point of view should prevail. This was the pattern of our argument synthesis: After an introduction to the controversy, the writer defined the problem by establishing the spectacular growth of Wal-Mart, then presented both sides of the controversy—taking care, because of the principle of climactic order, to present the pro–Wal-Mart side last.

- Another common pattern is *comparison-contrast*. In fact, this pattern is so important that we will discuss it separately in the next section.
- The order in which you present elements of an argument is sometimes dictated by the conventions of the discipline in which you are writing. For example, lab reports and experiments in the sciences and social sciences often follow this pattern: *Opening* or *Introduction*, *Methods and Materials* [of the experiment or study], *Results*, *Discussion*. Later in the Comparison-Contrast section of this chapter, we will see that legal arguments often follow the IRAC format: *Issue, Rule, Application, Conclusion*.

Present and Respond to Counterarguments

As we have seen in the Wal-Mart synthesis, people who develop arguments on a controversial topic can effectively use *counterargument* to help support their claims. When you use counterargument, you present an argument *against* your claim, but then show that this argument is weak or flawed. The advantage of this technique is that you demonstrate that you are aware of the other side of the argument and that you are prepared to answer it.

Here is how a counterargument typically is developed:

A. Introduction and claim
B. Main opposing argument
C. Refutation of opposing argument
D. Main positive argument

In the Wal-Mart synthesis, the writer gives a fair representation—using summary, paraphrase, and quotation—of the anti–Wal-Mart case for the purpose of showing that it is weaker than the pro–Wal-Mart case.

Use Concession

Concession is a variation of counterargument. As in counterargument, you present the opposing viewpoint, but instead of demolishing that argument, you concede that it does have some validity and even some appeal, although your own argument is the stronger one. This bolsters your own standing—your own ethos—as a fair-minded person who is not blind to the virtues of the other side.

Here is an outline for a concession argument:

A. Introduction and claim
B. Important opposing argument
C. Concession that this argument has some validity
D. Positive argument(s)

Sometimes, when you are developing a *counterargument* or *concession argument*, you may become convinced of the validity of the opposing point of view and change your own views. Don't be afraid of this happening. Writing is a tool for learning. To change your mind because of new evidence is a sign of flexibility and maturity, and your writing can only be the better for it.

Avoid Common Fallacies in Developing and Using Support

In Chapter 2, in the section on "Critical Reading," we considered some of the criteria that, as a reader, you may use for evaluating informative and persuasive writing (see pages 53–64). We discussed how you can assess the accuracy, the significance, and the author's interpretation of the information presented. We also considered the importance in good argument of clearly defined key terms and the pitfalls of emotionally loaded language. Finally, we saw how to recognize such logical fallacies as either/or reasoning, faulty cause-and-effect reasoning, hasty generalization, and false analogy. As a writer, no less than as a critical reader, be aware of these common problems and try to avoid them.

EXERCISE 5.6

Practicing Arguments

Devise a one sentence claim about the Wal-Mart controversy that differs from that made in the model essay or our other examples. Then write several paragraphs discussing what argument strategies you could use to develop this claim. What types of evidence—facts, statistics, and expert opinions—from the readings would you use? What motivational appeals (*ethos* and *pathos*) would be appropriate? Which counterarguments would you address, and how would you address them? What concessions would you make?

THE COMPARISON-AND-CONTRAST SYNTHESIS

A particularly important type of argument synthesis uses a comparison and contrast pattern. Comparison-and-contrast techniques enable you to examine two subjects (or sources) in terms of one another. When you compare, you consider *similarities*. When you contrast, you consider *differences*. By comparing and contrasting, you perform a multifaceted analysis that often suggests subtleties that otherwise might not have come to your (or the reader's) attention.

To organize a comparison-and-contrast argument, you must carefully read sources in order to discover *significant criteria for analysis*. A *criterion* is a specific point to which both of your authors refer and about which they may agree or disagree. (For example, in a comparative report on compact cars, criteria for *comparison and contrast* might be road handling, fuel economy, and comfort of ride.) The best criteria are those that allow you not only to account for obvious similarities and differences between sources but also to plumb deeper, to more subtle and significant similarities and differences.

Organizing Comparison-and-Contrast Syntheses

There are two basic approaches to organizing a comparison-and-contrast synthesis: organization by *source* and organization by *criteria*.

1. *Organizing by source.* You can organize a comparative synthesis as two summaries of your sources, followed by a discussion in which you point out significant similarities and differences between passages. Having read the summaries and become familiar with the distinguishing features of each passage, your readers will most likely be able to appreciate the more obvious similarities and differences. Follow up on these summaries by discussing both the obvious and subtle comparisons and contrasts, focusing on the most significant.

   Organization by source is best saved for passages that are briefly summarized. If the summary of your source becomes too long, your readers might forget the remarks you made in the first summary as they are reading the second. A comparison-and-contrast synthesis organized by source might proceed like this:

   I. Introduce the essay; lead to thesis.

   II. Summarize passage A by discussing its significant features.

   III. Summarize passage B by discussing its significant features.

   IV. Write a paragraph (or two) in which you discuss the significant points of comparison and contrast between passages A and B. Alternatively, you could begin the process of comparison-contrast in section III.

   End with a conclusion in which you summarize your points and, perhaps, raise and respond to pertinent questions.

2. *Organizing by criteria.* Instead of summarizing entire passages one at a time with the intention of comparing them later, you could discuss two passages simultaneously, examining the views of each author point by point (criterion by criterion), comparing and contrasting these views in the process. The criterion approach is best used when you have a number of points to discuss or when passages are long and/or complex. A comparison-and-contrast synthesis organized by criteria might look like this:

   I. Introduce the essay; lead to thesis.

   II. Criterion 1

       A. Discuss what author A says about this point.

       B. Discuss what author B says about this point, comparing and contrasting B's treatment of the point with A's.

   III. Criterion 2

       A. Discuss what author A says about this point.

       B. Discuss what author B says about this point, comparing and contrasting B's treatment of the point with A's.

And so on. Proceed criterion by criterion until you have completed your discussion. Be sure to arrange criteria with a clear method; knowing how the discussion of one criterion leads to the next will ensure smooth transitions throughout your paper. End with a conclusion in which you summarize your points and, perhaps, raise and respond to pertinent questions.

EXERCISE **5.7**

Comparing and Contrasting

Refer back to two of the readings on the Wal-Mart controversy that take opposing sides, such as Sarah Anderson's "Wal-Mart's War on Main Street on page 188 and Jo-Ann Johnston's "Who's Really the Villain?" on page 190. Identify at least three significant criteria for analysis—three specific points to which both authors refer, and about which they agree or disagree. Then imagine you are preparing to write a short comparison-and-contrast paper and devise two detailed outlines: the first organized by source, and the second organized by criteria.

A Case for Comparison-Contrast: Murder or Manslaughter?

We'll see how these principles can be applied to the following passages. Here are two cases dealing with "crimes of passion"—homicides arising out of a husband discovering that his wife is having an affair with another man. The texts, Rowland v. State and People v. Ashland are excerpted from the rulings of the courts to which they had been appealed. Rowland was a 1904 Mississippi case, Ashland a 1912 California case. Following these accounts, we present instructions of the kind that a judge would give to a jury in homicide cases. These instructions (written for California juries) deal with first- and second-degree murder and with involuntary manslaughter and are based on the applicable sections of the state Penal Code. In the original trial court, Rowland was found guilty of first-degree murder, but the appeals court reversed the murder conviction and ordered him retried on manslaughter charges. Ashland also was found guilty of first-degree murder by the trial court, but his murder conviction was upheld upon appeal.

Comparison-and-contrast is a very common technique among both prosecutors and defense attorneys, who, when researching their cases, look for precedents—prior cases with similar circumstances. If they want the verdict of the case they are trying to be the same as that of the precedent case, they will compare the cases and argue that they are similar enough so that the verdicts should be the same. But if they want the opposite verdict, they will contrast the cases and argue that the differences are sufficient to justify the opposite verdict.

In our model comparison-contrast essay—organized by criteria—we imagine that a prosecuting attorney is arguing that Rowland and Ashland are different enough that the final verdicts should be different. [Note: "References" after the essay follow "Blue Book" format for citing legal documents. Unless you are pursuing a law or pre-law curriculum you will not need to know the conventions of this style.]

Mose Rowland v. State

Supreme Court of Mississippi. Jan. 25, 1904.

The [defendant] was indicted for the murder of his wife, Becky Rowland, sentenced to imprisonment for life, and appeals. His story is as follows: His wife had been for about two months prior to the homicide living with Lou Pate, at whose house the killing occurred. The defendant and his wife were on good terms, and he was in the habit of visiting her and staying one night with her each week, or every two weeks. Lou Pate's house consisted of two rooms. In the front room were two beds—one occupied by Lou and her husband, and the other usually occupied by Becky Rowland. In the back room there was one bed. On the night of the killing, the defendant reached Pate's house about 10 o'clock, hitched his horse, and noticed John Thorn's also hitched to the fence. Coming up to the house, he heard a man and a woman talking in the back room, in which there was no light. Listening, he discovered that John Thorn and Becky Rowland (the defendant's wife) were in the room, and heard Thorn say, "Make haste." This aroused his suspicions, and he attempted to open the back door to the room; but it being latched, he went to the front door, pushed it open, and went into the front room, where, by the dim light of a lamp burning at the foot of their bed, he saw Lou Pate and her husband in bed asleep. He spoke to them, and also called his wife's name. Getting no answer, he stepped through the partition door into the back room, and discovered his wife and Thorn in the very act of adultery. They sprang up as they caught sight of him, and both rushed by him through the doorway into the front room; his wife blowing out the lamp as she passed the foot of the bed. The defendant fired at Thorn, and killed his wife. Lou Pate, the only eyewitness introduced by the state, corroborated the story of the defendant in its main features. She testified that Thorn came to the house about first dark, and, when she and her husband went to bed, Thorn and Becky were seated in the same room, talking; that she was awakened by hearing the defendant speak, and saw him standing in her room; that he went to the door between the rooms, and then Becky ran out of the back room into the front room, and blew out the lamp just as the defendant shot; that she did not see Thorn run out of the back room, and did not know how or when he got out of the house, but that after the shooting his horse was still hitched to the fence. Becky was in her nightclothes when killed.

Rowland v. State, 35 So. 826 (1904).

People v. Harry Ashland

California Court of Appeals, 1912

The facts and circumstances leading to and attending the commission of the homicide are undisputed, and are substantially as follows: The defendant was a married man, whose family consisted of his wife, aged 24 years, and four children,

People v. Ashland, 20 Cal. App. 168 (1912).

aged respectively, six, four, and two years and the youngest eight months. With his wife and family he came to California from Philadelphia in the year 1909, and a short time after his arrival in this state he purchased a twenty acre tract of land near a place called and known as Avena, in San Joaquin County. With his family he settled on this land. He owed something like six hundred dollars on the purchase price of the property and, after trying his hand at farming, he found that he was thus making no headway in the reduction of his indebtedness, and, therefore, in the month of June, 1911, went to San Francisco to seek employment, leaving his wife and children on the farm. He remained in and about San Francisco, making in the mean time one visit to his home, until about the thirtieth day of December, 1911, on which date he received a letter from his wife containing, among other things, the following: ". . .Well, dear, there is a lot of news around here and they are all concerning me. I got myself in all kinds of trouble. Well, I shall tell you when you come home, and then I guess you will get a divorce from me all right. Well I will take my medicine for my foolishness. I am sorry, but I can't do any more than that. I don't really understand myself; it is not like me at all. I will not ask forgiveness from you. You can judge for yourself when you hear it. Please write soon and tell me when you will come home. . . . I do wish I could see you and speak to you. I feel so miserable."

Upon reading the letter, Ashland immediately left San Francisco for his home, reaching the latter place at about midnight of the day on which he received and read said letter. His wife then told him that one John Gofield (the deceased) who had for some time been in the community where the Ashlands resided serving in the capacity of a United States squirrel inspector, had had sexual intercourse with her on two different occasions—the first time on the eighteenth day of December, 1911, and the second time a few days thereafter, or about Christmas day, and only a few days prior to the receipt by the defendant of the letter above referred to. She declared to her husband that the first sexual act with Gofield was forced upon her by threats and violence upon the part of the former; and that on both occasions the acts were committed on a cot situated in a bedroom in the defendant's house and where the children of the defendant were sleeping on both occasions.

It was about two o'clock in the morning when Mrs. Ashland finished detailing the story of the conduct of Gofield toward her. The defendant thereupon left his house and went to the house of a Mr. Gannon, a neighbor residing a distance of about half a mile from the defendant's home. He awoke Gannon and said that he desired to talk with him. Gannon opened the door and allowed the defendant to enter, whereupon the latter inquired whether there was a "squirrel man" boarding at his (Gannon's) house. Gannon replied that there were two "squirrel men" who had boarded with him, but that they had left his home some time prior to that day. Gannon, at the request of the defendant, described the men, and the defendant recognized the deceased as one of the two so described, and declared that he was the man he was looking for. Gannon asked him his reason for seeking Gofield and the defendant excitedly and in a loud tone of voice replied: "He raped my wife! He raped my wife! twice, two different times, four days apart." He then asked Gannon whether he was telling him the truth when he said that the deceased was not in his (Gannon's) house at that time. Gannon assured the defendant that Gofield had gone to his home in Stockton and allowed him to go into the bedroom to assure himself that the deceased was not then in any of the rooms. Gannon then advised the defendant to go to the sheriff and explain his trouble to that official. The defendant, tapping his breast, replied: "If I find him before the sheriff finds him the sheriff will have to do with me and not with him. California is not big enough to hide him."

The defendant then returned to his home, reaching there after two o'clock in the morning. At the hour of nine o'clock, he went to the home of a Mr. Ralph, another neighbor, whose home is situated about half a mile from that of the defendant. He excitedly told Mr. Ralph the story of the disgrace of himself and children by the conduct of his wife, and shortly thereafter returned to his home. At about eleven o'clock on the morning of the same day (Dec. 31, 1911), the defendant took the train at Avena, about half a mile distant from his house, and went to the city of Stockton. Arriving at Stockton, he immediately proceeded to make inquiries as to the location of the residence of Gofield and asked several persons whether they had seen him lately and where. Eventually he was given information as to the street and block in which Gofield's residence was situated and he immediately repaired to that neighborhood. This was about five o'clock P.M. He inquired of several persons whether they could point out to him the house of the deceased. It happened that a young son of the deceased overheard the defendant inquiring for Gofield and he thereupon volunteered to take the defendant to his father's house. The lad, upon reaching the house, followed closely by Ashland, opened the door and stepped inside, closing the door as he did so, but the defendant immediately opened the door and stepped into the hallway. The boy told his father that there was a man on the outside who desired to see him. The deceased, who was sitting at this time, arose and put on his coat and went into the hallway, meeting Ashland. The former asked Gofield if he was the "squirrel man," and the latter answered affirmatively. Thereupon Ashland took Gofield by the arm and together they walked out on the porch. After reaching the porch, Ashland asked the deceased if his name was Gofield, and the latter replied that it was. Ashland then said, "You talked to my wife," and the deceased replied, "Do you know who you are talking to?" Again Ashland said, "You talked to my wife," and at the same time fired a shot.

Mrs. Gofield, wife of the deceased, was at her husband's side when the fatal shots were fired. In her language may best be told what occurred following the first shot: "My husband kind of sank back and over again, and I was over my husband, and this man Ashland lowered the revolver and put it between my arm and side and shot my husband in the back, and I was down over him. . . . My husband turned and ran in the house and I turned to go, too, and Ashland ran between myself and husband. . . . My husband was running in the house, and I started to follow and just as we got in the hall we met my husband's mother—she was living with us—and she caught my husband and they both staggered back into the dining room, and he sank on the floor."

Gofield died shortly thereafter, not having uttered a word after being shot.

After the shooting Ashland fled from the house and was followed by Gofield's father-in-law, who was at the former's house when the shooting occurred, and by one F. J. Murray, a policeman, living near by, who had heard the shots and hastened to Gofield's house to learn the cause and the result of the shooting. Ashland ran down several streets, followed by Murray, who ordered him to stop and fired several shots in the air for the purpose of thus stopping him. Ashland, however, kept on running until he reached the office of the chief of police, located in the court house, into which he ran and there surrendered himself to the chief. The defendant was in a high state of excitement when he reached the police office and upon entering said that he was looking for the chief. The latter, who was standing in the office, told Ashland that he was the chief, and the defendant excitedly threw his arms about the officer, exclaiming that he had shot the "squirrel man," Johnnie Gofield, and explained that he did the act because Gofield had ruined his wife and broken up his home. He delivered the weapon with which he did the shooting to the chief, and for some time thereafter was in an exceedingly nervous and somewhat hysterical condition, crying and moaning and otherwise acquitting himself as one keyed up to a highly nervous state. A physician was called in and treated the defendant and finally restored him to comparative tranquility.

Instructions to the Jury

Murder—Defined

[Defendant is accused of having committed the crime of murder, a violation of Penal Code section 187.]

Every person who unlawfully kills a [human being] . . . [with malice aforethought] . . . is guilty of the crime of murder in violation of section 187 of the Penal Code.

[A killing is unlawful, if it [is] [neither] [justifiable] [nor] [excusable].]

In order to prove this crime, each of the following elements must be proved:

1. A human being was killed;
2. The killing was unlawful; and
3. The killing was done with malice aforethought.

"Malice Aforethought"—Defined

"Malice" may be either express or implied.

[Malice is express when there is manifested an intention unlawfully to kill a human being.]

[Malice is implied when:

1. The killing resulted from an intentional act,
2. The natural consequences of the act are dangerous to human life, and
3. The act was deliberately performed with knowledge of the danger to, and with conscious disregard for, human life.]

[When it is shown that a killing resulted from the intentional doing of an act with express or implied malice, no other mental state need be shown to establish the mental state of malice aforethought.]

The mental state constituting malice aforethought does not necessarily require any ill will or hatred of the person killed.

The word "aforethought" does not imply deliberation or the lapse of considerable time. It only means that the required mental state must precede rather than follow the act.

Deliberate and Premeditated Murder

All murder which is perpetrated by any kind of willful, deliberate and premeditated killing with express malice aforethought is murder of the first degree.

The word "willful," as used in this instruction, means intentional.

The word "deliberate" means formed or arrived at or determined upon as a result of careful thought and weighing of considerations for and against the proposed course of action. The word "premeditated" means considered beforehand.

If you find that the killing was preceded and accompanied by a clear, deliberate intent on the part of the defendant to kill, which was the result of deliberation and premeditation, so that it must have been formed upon pre-existing reflection and not under a sudden heat of passion or other condition precluding the idea of deliberation, it is murder of the first degree.

The law does not undertake to measure in units of time the length of the period during which the thought must be pondered before it can ripen into an intent to kill which is truly deliberate and premeditated. The time will vary with different individuals and under varying circumstances.

The true test is not the duration of time, but rather the extent of the reflection. A cold, calculated judgment and decision may be arrived at in a short period of time, but a mere unconsidered and rash impulse, even though it includes an intent to kill, is not deliberation and premeditation as will fix an unlawful killing as murder of the first degree.

To constitute a deliberate and premeditated killing, the slayer must weigh and consider the question of killing and the reasons for and against such a choice and, having in mind the consequences, [he] [she] decides to and does kill.

Unpremeditated Murder of the Second Degree

Murder of the second degree is . . . the unlawful killing of a human being with malice aforethought when the perpetrator intended unlawfully to kill a human being but the evidence is insufficient to prove deliberation and premeditation.

Manslaughter—Defined

The crime of manslaughter is the unlawful killing of a human being without malice aforethought. It is not divided into degrees but is of two kinds, namely, voluntary manslaughter and involuntary manslaughter.

Voluntary Manslaughter—Defined

. . . Every person who unlawfully kills another human being without malice aforethought but with an intent to kill, is guilty of voluntary manslaughter in violation of Penal Code section 192(a).

There is no malice aforethought if the killing occurred [upon a sudden quarrel or heat of passion] [or] [in the actual but unreasonable belief in the necessity to defend oneself against imminent peril to life or great bodily injury].

In order to prove this crime, each of the following elements must be proved:
1. A human being was killed;
2. The killing was unlawful; and
3. The killing was done with the intent to kill.
[A killing is unlawful, if it was [neither] [not] [justifiable] [nor] [excusable].]

Sudden Quarrel or Heat of Passion and Provocation Explained

To reduce an intentional felonious homicide from the offense of murder to manslaughter upon the ground of sudden quarrel or heat of passion, the provocation must be of the character and degree as naturally would excite and arouse the passion, and the assailant must act under the influence of that sudden quarrel or heat of passion.

The heat of passion which will reduce a homicide to manslaughter must be such a passion as naturally would be aroused in the mind of an ordinarily reasonable person in the same circumstances. A defendant is not permitted to set up [his] [her] own standard of conduct and to justify or excuse [himself] [herself] because [his] [her] passions were aroused unless the circumstances in which the defendant was placed and the facts that confronted [him] [her] were such as also would have aroused the passion of the ordinarily reasonable person faced with the same situation. [Legally adequate provocation may occur in a short, or over a considerable, period of time.]

The question to be answered is whether or not, at the time of the killing, the reason of the accused was obscured or disturbed by passion to such an extent as would cause the ordinarily reasonable person of average disposition to act rashly and without deliberation and reflection, and from passion rather than from judgment.

If there was provocation, [whether of short or long duration,] but of a nature not normally sufficient to arouse passion, or if sufficient time elapsed between the provocation and the fatal blow for passion to subside and reason to return, and if an unlawful killing of a human being followed the provocation and had all the elements of murder, as I have defined it, the mere fact of slight or remote provocation will not reduce the offense to manslaughter.

Murder or Manslaughter—Cooling Period

To reduce a killing upon a sudden quarrel or heat of passion from murder to manslaughter the killing must have occurred while the slayer was acting under the direct and immediate influence of the quarrel or heat of passion. Where the influence of the sudden quarrel or heat of passion has ceased to obscure the mind of the accused, and sufficient time has elapsed for angry passion to end and for reason to control [his] [her] conduct, it will no longer reduce an intentional killing to manslaughter. The question, as to whether the cooling period has elapsed and reason has returned, is not measured by the standard of the accused, but the duration of the cooling period is the time it would take the average or ordinarily reasonable person to have cooled the passion, and for that person's reason to have returned.

Comparison-Contrast (Organized by Criteria)

Here is a plan for a comparison-contrast synthesis, organized by *criteria*. The thesis (and the *claim*) is as follows:

> Ashland's case is not at all like Rowland's, and his first-degree murder conviction must be affirmed.

    A. Introduction. Background of the Ashland case. Initial comparison to apparently similar Rowland case. Rejection of comparison, leading to *thesis*.

    B. Facts of each case.

      1. Rowland.

      2. Ashland.

    C. The legal distinction between murder and manslaughter.

      1. Intentional killing under heat of passion—manslaughter.

      2. Intentional killing when heat of passion has had time to cool—murder.

    D. Ashland case contrasted to Rowland case.

      1. Whether there was premeditation and malice aforethought.

      2. Whether heat of passion had cooled.

    E. Conclusion: Ashland was no longer acting under heat of passion—unlike Rowland—and so is guilty of murder.

Following is a comparison-contrast synthesis by criteria, written according to the preceding plan. (Thesis and topic sentences are highlighted.)

MODEL ESSAY

Murder or Manslaughter?

1   On December 31, 1911, Harry Ashland shot and killed John Gofield in Gofield's house in Stockton, California. Ashland was enraged at Gofield, whom he accused of raping his wife. The defendant was then justifiably convicted of murder in the first degree. Now he appeals his murder conviction and argues that

if he is guilty of anything, it is, at most, voluntary manslaughter. He claims that the "heat of passion" defense should apply to him, just as it applied to Mose Rowland, whose murder conviction in 1904 was subsequently reversed and who was then retried and convicted of voluntary manslaughter. But Ashland's case is not at all like Rowland's, and his first-degree murder conviction must be affirmed.

2   Let us first review the facts of each case. In *Rowland*, the defendant "discovered his wife and [her lover] in the very act of adultery." They had been living apart, and she had been staying with another married couple. Late one evening, Rowland arrived at the house where Becky Rowland was staying, heard suspicious noises coming from the back bedroom, and upon entering the bedroom, found his wife in bed with another man. When the pair tried to flee, Rowland fired at the man. He missed, but the shot killed Becky Rowland. The killing occurred within seconds after Rowland had discovered his wife and her lover having sexual relations.

3   Contrast this series of events with those in *Ashland*. In this case, the defendant, who had been living and working in San Francisco, received a letter from his wife in which she strongly implied that she had been having an adulterous affair. When he arrived home in the town of Avena, his wife confessed that she had had sexual relations on two occasions with John Gofield. On the first occasion, she told him, she had been raped. Ashland then asked a neighbor about Gofield and discovered that he was living in Stockton. Ashland then returned home, told his story to another neighbor, then took a train to Stockton, where he tracked down Gofield. He went to Gofield's house, confronted the man, and then shot him in cold blood in front of his wife and son.

4   Is Harry Ashland guilty of murder or voluntary manslaughter? The law makes a clear distinction between these two crimes. Murder in the first degree is defined as "willful, deliberate and premeditated killing with express malice aforethought." "Deliberate" means "formed or arrived at or determined upon as a result of careful thought and weighing of considerations . . ." ("Jury Instructions"). A murder charge may be reduced to voluntary manslaughter if the killing was carried out under the influence of a

"heat of passion." However, the law requires that "Where the influence of . . . heat of passion has ceased to obscure the mind of the accused, and sufficient time has elapsed for angry passion to end and for reason to control [his] [her] conduct, it will no longer reduce an intentional killing to manslaughter" ("Jury Instructions").

5   Applying these rules, we find that the *Ashland* case is very different from *Rowland*. First consider the issue of premeditation and malice aforethought. In *Rowland*, there was no time for premeditation of homicide since, until seconds before the killing, Rowland had no idea that his wife was having an affair with another man. For this reason, he could not have had malice aforethought. Before the killing, he did not even know of the existence of Thorn, Becky Rowland's lover. On the other hand, Ashland had hours for premeditation after he learned of his wife's affair. His malice aforethought is shown by the statement he made to his neighbor, Mr. Gannon: "If I find him before the sheriff finds him, the sheriff will have to do with me and not with him. California is not big enough to hide him." This statement proves that Ashland was fully aware that he would be in trouble with the law if he killed Gofield. In planning the murder, he acted with "cold, calculated judgment and decision."

6   It is true that in both cases, the defendants had sufficient provocation "as would excite and arouse the passion." This "passion" would be the immediate reaction of most people in the same situation. However, when we consider and apply what the law says about a cooling off period, we find that unlike Rowland, Ashland had no legal justification for shooting Gofield. In the case of Rowland, there was not time for a cooling off period since Rowland fired the fatal shot almost immediately after he first discovered his wife's adultery. But this was not the case with Ashland. The law states that "whether the cooling period has elapsed and reason has returned is not measured by the standard of the accused, but the duration of the cooling period is the time it would take the average or ordinarily reasonable person to have cooled the passion, and for that person's reason to have returned." The "ordinarily reasonable person" should have had plenty of time to cool off during the

fifteen-hour period between the time Ashland learned of the adultery and his confrontation with Gofield. Moreover, the fact that he was rational enough to take a train to another town and then allow the deceased's own son to lead him to Gofield shows just how cold-blooded and malicious he was as he prepared to kill his victim.

7   For these reasons the defendant's contention that his case is like Rowland's, and so the charges against him should be reduced to manslaughter, is groundless. Both Rowland and Ashland were blameworthy, and both should pay the price for their crimes. But while Rowland can be partially excused by the fact that he was acting under the "heat of passion," Harry Ashland has no such excuse. Ashland is a "willful" and "deliberate" murderer, and his murder conviction should stand.

References

California Jury Instructions: Criminal [CALJIC]: Book of Approved Jury Instructions. 8th ed. (1994). Committee on Standard Jury Instructions, Criminal, of the Superior Court of Los Angeles County, California. West.

People v. Ashland, 20 Cal. App. 168 (1912).

Rowland v. State, 35 So. 826 (1904).

Discussion

The general organizational strategy of this argument can be described with the acronym IRAC—Issue, Rule, Application, Conclusion—a basic pattern of legal argument that also is applicable in other disciplinary areas. This strategy calls for the writer first to define the *issue*, or the essential question that must be decided, then to explain the *rule* or rules that apply when such an issue is to be decided, then to discuss how the rule *applies* or does not apply to the particular case(s) at hand, and finally to *conclude* by answering the question expressed in the issue.

In argument terms, this conclusion is the *claim* that the writer is making; the rule is the *assumption* or *warrant* underlying the argument; and the application draws upon the *support* that provides the evidence proving the claim. Specifically, the writer (whose *purpose* is to prosecute the defendant) makes a claim that Ashland is guilty of murder. His *assumption* or *warrant* is the rule that a premeditated homicide committed with malice aforethought is murder. For comparison-contrast purposes, an unpremeditated homicide committed under the heat of passion is manslaughter. The writer offers *support* for his claim by detailing the facts of the two cases, arguing that for the purpose of proving his claim, the differences outweigh the similarities, and that while Rowland's actions constitute manslaughter, Ashland's constitute murder.

- In the *first* paragraph, the writer introduces the two heat-of-passion cases, but maintains in the thesis that the cases are different enough that while Rowland's murder conviction was overturned, Ashland's murder conviction should be upheld.

- In the *second* and *third* paragraphs, the writer summarizes the key facts of each case, emphasizing the immediate act of homicide in *Rowland* and the delayed killing in *Ashland*.

- In the *fourth* paragraph, the writer reviews the legal criteria for arriving at verdicts of murder and manslaughter. In particular, the writer emphasizes that murder is "willful" and "deliberate" and is carried out "with malice aforethought," while voluntary manslaughter is carried out under the influence of a "heat of passion" that has had insufficient time to cool.

- In the *fifth* and *sixth* paragraphs, the writer applies these legal criteria to the two cases. Paragraph five deals with the elements of premeditation and malice aforethought, showing that these elements were not present in *Rowland* but were in *Ashland*. In supporting his argument, the writer cites specific actions of the defendant Ashland—such as his declaration to his neighbor that if he found Gofield before the sheriff did, then the sheriff would have reason to arrest him.

- In the *sixth* paragraph, the writer focuses on the cooling off period, showing that there was no such period in *Rowland* (where the killing immediately followed the discovery), but that there was in *Ashland* where the defendant had 15 hours to let his passion cool off.

- In the *seventh* and final paragraph, the writer reiterates his conclusion; he concedes that the cases do have certain similar elements; however, they are also different enough, he argues, that Ashland's murder conviction (unlike Rowland's) should be upheld.

SUMMARY

In this chapter and Chapter 4 preceding it, we've considered three main types of synthesis: the *explanatory synthesis*, the *argument synthesis*, and the *comparison-contrast synthesis*. Although for ease of comprehension we've placed them into separate categories, these types are not, of course, mutually exclusive. Both explanatory syntheses and argument syntheses often involve elements of one another, and comparison-contrast syntheses can fall into either of the previous categories. Which format you choose will depend upon your *purpose* and the method that you decide is best suited to achieve this purpose.

If your main purpose is to help your audience understand a particular subject, and in particular to help them understand the essential elements or significance of this subject, then you will be composing an explanatory synthesis. If your main purpose, on the other hand, is to persuade your audience to agree with your viewpoint on a subject, or to change their minds, or to decide upon a particular course of action, then you will be composing an argument synthesis. If one effective technique of making your case is to establish similarities or differences between your subject and another one, then you will compose a comparison-contrast synthesis—which may well be just *part* of a larger synthesis.

In planning and drafting these syntheses, you can draw upon a variety of strategies: supporting your claims by summarizing, paraphrasing, and quoting from your sources; using appeal to *logos*, *pathos*, and *ethos*; and choosing from among formats such as climactic or conventional order, counterargument, and concession, that will best help you to achieve your purpose.

The strategies of synthesis you've practiced in these last two chapters will be dealt with again in Chapter 7, on Research, where we'll consider a category of synthesis commonly known as the research paper. The research paper involves all of the skills in summary, critique, and synthesis that we've discussed so far, the main difference being, of course, that you won't find the sources you need in this particular text. We'll discuss approaches to locating and critically evaluating sources, selecting material from among them to provide support for your claims, and finally, documenting your sources in standard professional formats.

But first, we need to examine analysis, which is another important strategy for academic thinking and writing. Chapter 6, "Analysis," will introduce you to a strategy that, like synthesis, draws upon all the strategies you've been practicing as you move through *A Sequence for Academic Writing*.

6

Analysis

WHAT IS ANALYSIS?

In the last chapter we focused upon synthesis, which, as you may recall, means to combine separate things into a unified whole. In this sense, analysis is a kind of opposite to synthesis: To analyze something means to break it down into its constituent parts in order to understand it as a whole. For example, if you encountered a variety of flower with which you were unfamiliar, and you wanted to determine into which family of flowers this new flower fit—is it a kind of lily? a rose? a variety of poppy?—you would examine its various features or parts. What shape are its petals? How are the petals arranged around the center? What features does the flower's center have? What does the stem of the flower look like? Is it long and thin or does it branch off to many other smaller stems? Are there leaves on the plant? And so on. You would need to take the elements of the flower apart in order to compare it to other flower types.

Analysis is a key element of academic inquiry. We analyze things, or critically examine them, in order to identify their key elements as well as their causes, or (if they constitute an action of some sort) their possible results. In our daily lives we are constantly analyzing situations and people when we ask such questions as "why did the teacher frown at me?' or "how will I complete all my work by tomorrow?" Even the act of perceiving a teacher's frown is the result of a kind of analysis—one that you likely perform automatically now, but one that could be separated into its component parts. You look at a person's face, perceive the wrinkled brow, the negative cast to the eyes, the pursed or downward slanting lips, and you perceive all these elements as components that add up to "frown." Then, in order to analyze why the frown occurred—and why it seemed directed at you—again, you would take the elements of the situation apart, perhaps analyzing your own behavior to ascertain whether it might be of the type to inspire a teacher's frown. In your work as a student, you perform analysis when you respond to exam or homework questions asking you to describe a chemical process, to define something, or to explain the causes or effects of something. When you write essays in response to analytical questions such as these, your job usually involves more than simply making a descriptive statement of fact; instead, you typically must go deeper—stating why or how something is so. In other words, analysis doesn't simply ask you to break things down and describe them, but to go further and state what the information arrived at through analysis *means.*

WHERE DO WE FIND WRITTEN ANALYSES?

Here are just a few types of writing that involve analysis:

Academic Writing

- **Experimental and lab reports.** Analyze the meaning or implications of study results in the Discussion section.
- **Research papers.** Analyze information in sources; apply theories to material being reported.
- **Process analysis.** Break down the steps or stages involved in completing a process.
- **Literary analysis.** Analyze characterization, plot, imagery, or other elements in works of literature.
- **Essay exams.** Demonstrate understanding of course material by analyzing data using course concepts.

Workplace Writing

- **Grant proposals.** Analyze the issues you seek funding for in order to address them.
- **Reviews of the arts.** Employ dramatic or literary analysis to present assessments of artistic works.
- **Business plans.** Break down and analyze capital outlays, expenditures, profits, materials, and the like.
- **Medical charts.** Perform analytical thinking and writing in relation to patient symptoms and possible treatment options.
- **Legal briefs.** Break down and analyze facts of cases and elements of legal precedents; apply legal rulings and precedents to new situations.
- **Case-studies.** Describe and analyze the particulars of a specific medical, social service, advertising, or business case.

ANALYTICAL THINKING

While much of the analysis you perform in everyday life is automatic and intuitive, academic analysis requires some conscious and detailed activities—activities that, at their core, boil down to a process of asking questions of the object or phenomena being analyzed. While much analysis involves asking questions informed by specialized knowledge within a particular field, the underlying critical thinking in all analysis is essentially the same. The object or phenomena under inspection is "deconstructed": That is, you take it apart, look at those parts, determine how the parts relate to each other and to parts from related objects or phenomena, and, ultimately, how they combine to make up the whole.

A highly educated scholar in the field of literary studies, for example, brings to his or her analysis a specialized language and set of tools for analyzing works of fiction; nonetheless, a less experienced reader can also analyze a literary work by examining the elements within it—via specialized language and methods or not. The analysis performed in such a case may not go as far as one performed by the scholar, but such an analysis is still valuable in that it brings the reader to a deeper understanding of the literary work. The analytical thinking involved in understanding the literary work is then translated into an interpretive paper—which presents the student's interpretation as an argument to be supported. In humanities disciplines such as English, classics, comparative literature, art history, and film studies, students are often asked to write papers presenting an interpretation of a particular work of art.

ANALYSIS OF A TEXT

In this section we'll focus, for example's sake, on literary analysis, but the steps we present are similar to the steps one would take in analyzing other types of creative objects, such as paintings, performances, advertisements, and films. When dealing with long or complex works, you often will be asked to analyze specific elements of that work, such as its characters or use of particular settings or imagery, rather than the work as a whole. Every creative text you read or view will present a different challenge as you work to analyze it, but like any other skill, the ability to analyze improves with practice. Here are a few pointers to get you started. They represent possible stages, or steps, in the process of writing a literary analysis. These pointers are not meant as rigid prescriptions and should be modified to fit the analysis of different kinds of works. Although we have focused our discussion on literary analyses, with some modifications these steps are relevant to analysis of all kinds of cultural or creative texts. As such, the guidelines here are designed to encourage habits of thinking that will allow you to vary your technique as the situation demands. (Note: "Textual" as used here includes graphic, visual, and verbal material.)

GUIDELINES FOR WRITING ANALYSES

- *Read (or Study)* the object under analysis. Try to get a feel for the overall meaning, impressions, feelings that are conveyed during this initial reading.
- *Reread.* Once you have gotten an initial feel for the work, reread carefully. This time make notes in the margin or on paper, about elements that confuse you and elements that seem important. Look up words with which you are unfamiliar.
- *Take the work apart.* Break up the work into its constituent elements. If analyzing a poem, look closely at the imagery, metaphoric patterns, stanzas, lines, sentences and phrases, and words. In analyzing a film, consider the scenes, shots, camera movements, editing, sound elements, and characterization. Analyze each of these parts in turn, looking for patterns and arriving at an understanding of the work's elements. Make notes of your ideas, as these will be helpful when you begin drafting the paper.
- *Put the work back together again.* Use your understanding of the different parts of the work to arrive at an understanding of the work as a whole. How do these component parts create an overall meaning? This stage of the process can be the most challenging, and you might want to use freewriting or clustering to help you work out your ideas. Ask yourself *what, how,* and *why: What* is the work saying? *How* does it get this idea across? *Why* is this a significant idea?
- *Draft a preliminary thesis.* Your thesis will sum up your interpretation of the work. Often, you can construct your thesis to answer the what, how, and why questions mentioned in the last item. For example, "Through the use of metaphor and simile [*how*], poem X portrays the ideal of romantic love gone stale [*what*]." As in this example, the answer to the *why* part of the equation is implied—this is significant because it's a topic to which most people can relate in some way. Often writers leave the *how* part out of their the-

DEMONSTRATION I: ANALYZING A SHORT POEM

We'll now present a short poem to demonstrate some of the critical thinking and writing steps involved in writing textual analyses.

Read the Object under Analysis

Before we begin dissecting the poem, read it through, perhaps a couple of times. Note your initial impressions of the poem's mood, tone, and meaning. You might try reading the poem aloud to yourself, so that you can appreciate its rhythm and feeling.

sis as well, stating only their interpretation (the *what*), and elaborating on *how* the work generates this meaning in the body of their paper.

- **Work out the points that support your thesis.** In the simplest analysis of a text, your support comes from the elements of the work itself, combined with your reasoned understanding of those elements and the logical connection of the elements to one another. Consult the work under analysis, as well as your earlier notes on it, and determine the points you will need to make, selecting key examples to support your thesis.

- **Write an outline or plan.** In planning the structure of your paper, focus upon the points you want to make, not on the structure of the work you are analyzing. In other words, do not plan to present a line-by-line or section-by-section summary and analysis of the piece. Your job is to focus only on the elements that convey the interpretation you are presenting, and to cover these in the most logical order.

- **Write the first draft of your analysis.** Drawing upon the ideas generated in the last three steps, write a first draft. Don't worry about writing an introduction at first—start with your preliminary thesis and draft the body paragraphs.

- **Write the second draft of your analysis.** Refine your thesis statement based upon any new ideas generated thus far. Write an introduction to contextualize that thesis. Make sure you quote and paraphrase correctly from the work you're analyzing; refine your transitions throughout the paper; add or delete material as necessary to improve development of points and to avoid repetition.

- **Edit your analysis.** Combine sentences for a smooth, logical flow of ideas. Check for grammatical correctness, punctuation, and spelling.

Wild Nights! Wild Nights!
Emily Dickinson

Considered by many to be the greatest American woman poet—and some say she's the greatest American poet of either gender—Emily Dickinson spent her entire life, from 1830–1886, in Amherst, Massachusetts. While virtually none of her poems were published during her lifetime, Dickinson was a prolific, if intensely private, writer, producing nearly 2,000 finely crafted poems. Her work has had an enormous influence on twentieth-century poetry and American literature in general.

Emily Dickinson, Poem number 249, <u>The Complete Poems of Emily Dickinson</u>, ed. Thomas H. Johnson (Boston: Little Brown, 1960) 114.

> Wild Nights! Wild Nights!
> Were I with thee,
> Wild nights should be
> Our luxury!
>
> Futile the winds
> To a heart in port, —
> Done with the compass,
> Done with the chart!
>
> Rowing in Eden!
> Ah! the sea!
> Might I but moor
> Tonight in Thee!

Reread, Make Notes, Look Up Words

Here is how the poem might look after you had read it over several times and jotted down responses to it:

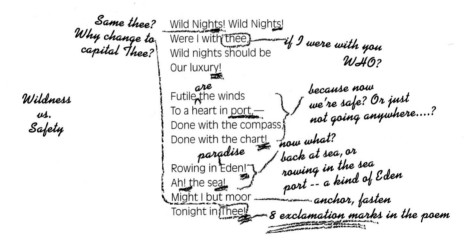

These kinds of notes can help you tease out the meaning of the poem. Notice how we've recorded our questions about the meaning of certain words or lines, we've underlined things we think might be important, and we've rephrased some of the lines to help make the poetic diction more comprehensible. For example, we rephrased line 2 and added the word "are" to line 5.

Take the Work Apart

To analyze the poem, we have to take apart its units; the units that make up a poem are words, sentences and phrases, lines, and stanzas.

STANZA 1

Here we have a three-stanza poem, with four lines per stanza. As our notes pointed out, the poem contains eight exclamation points. The first stanza consists of three sentences—two exclamations in the first line, and one sentence in the remainder of the stanza. In the second stanza we have one long sentence, ending with an exclamation. The third stanza moves back to a pattern similar to the first stanza—short exclamatory sentences followed by one longer sentence, which ends, again, with an exclamation point. Thus, before we even analyze the words of the poem, our analysis so far reveals that those exclamation points create a certain excited and energetic tone—although until we examine the words it's not clear whether this excitement is joyous or alarmed. In taking apart the structure of the sentences and lines in the stanzas, and in comparing them to other stanzas and lines, we see a pattern, with the first and last stanza following a similar structure. This kind of pattern might prove meaningful when we begin analyzing the words of the poem.

And what do we make of these words? They appear to be addressed to someone ("thee") in line 2; "Thee" reappears in line 12, but notice that this time it's capitalized. This leads to the question of whether the "thee" is the same in both lines. (In performing a less analytical reading of the poem, we might assume that the speaker is addressing the same person or entity throughout the poem, but our careful analysis shows this may not be a valid assumption.) Right away the first lines of the poem suggest to our modern minds an eroticism: We are likely to associate the term "Wild nights!" with something sexual or erotic. So the rest of the first stanza's words suggest the speaker of the poem is addressing a lover, one who is absent and with whom time spent (wildly at night) would be a luxury.

STANZA 2

The second stanza follows along with this reading; here we see the speaker likening her heart to a ship in port. If the winds are "futile" and compasses and charts are finished with when "a heart [is] in port," this suggests a range of possible meanings: that the ship/heart is safely anchored; it is unmoved by outside forces; it is a committed, constant heart, perhaps, and one that doesn't need the guidance of compass or chart since it knows where it belongs. Thus, following the meaning of the first stanza's words, we can conjecture that the speaker is either saying she is committed, even while absent from, the object of her affections, or she may be saying that were the absent lover there, she'd be safely in port. However, in keeping with the analytical practice of comparing parts of a piece to its other parts, this last reading with its emphasis on safety doesn't quite fit with the earlier abandon of "Wild Nights!"

STANZA 3

Now we find the speaker exclaiming in a seemingly joyous excitement ("Ah! the sea!" in line 10) about rowing either in or out to sea, and this return to joyous excitement suggests that perhaps safety in port is not what she seeks. In fact, the hope expressed in the last two lines of the poem suggests that she wants not to moor in a safe port but in the sea of " Eden." Why?

Put the Work Back Together

Once we have analyzed the poem's features, how do we then arrive at a cogent interpretation of the poem's meaning? Essentially, we now have to put all the pieces we analyzed in the last stage back together to form an overall sense of what the poem is saying.

Our analysis thus far has spurred us to ask many questions and offer preliminary answers to some. Based on observations so far, the central idea seems to involve the tension between safety and passion in love. The poem can be read as an exploration of the dual nature of romantic love (or perhaps even other kinds of love—including spiritual: God is all-powerful, awesome, even scary, and at the same time God is a safe port). Like the sea, love is wild and exciting as well as calming and potentially safe. A closely related idea is that perhaps the speaker's heart is constant. It can't be moved by the winds, it is safely in port, it knows where it belongs and needs to go (no need for compass or chart), but at the same time it contains the wilder impulses of passion that accompany love. This heart is drawn to the paradise (the "Eden") of love in the sea.

Draft a Preliminary Thesis

Now we must take our interpretation of the poem further, trying to sum it up as clearly as possible and making a claim about the poem's meaning that we can adequately support through examples in the text. This can be the most challenging part of the process, as it requires that we focus all the different ideas and possibilities we've been exploring into a single, declarative idea.

Complicating this process are the ways in which students sometimes feel intense pressure to come up with "the right" interpretation. Fortunately, however, there are usually a number of plausible interpretations for works of art, so instead of isolating one correct reading, our job is to come up with a reasonable interpretation, arrived at through careful thought, that can be supported through evidence—primarily evidence from the work itself.

For "Wild Nights! Wild Nights!" our analysis of the poem led us to some specific interpretations. Here are two possible theses that our analysis could support:

> In the poem "Wild Nights! Wild Nights!" Emily Dickinson uses the sea as a metaphor through which she examines the dual nature of romantic love, from its wild passion to its comforting safety.

> "Wild Nights! Wild Nights!" examines the ways in which a constant and loving heart can go forth into the world with joy and fearlessness.

What, How, and Why

Generally, textual analysis theses deal with some combination of the questions *what, how,* and *why.* Your textual analysis paper will need to address all three of these issues: 1) *What* is the meaning of the work under analysis? Or, in other words, *what* are you claiming this work is saying? 2) *How* does the work accomplish this? What features of the work construct this particular meaning? 3) *Why* is this idea, theme, message, or meaning significant? In other words, so what?

Because these are the issues typically addressed in your paper, your thesis statement can address some combination of these issues, with emphasis on the part of the what/how/why triad that is the focus of your paper. In most textual analysis assignments, you will focus on the *what*—what is your interpretation of the work. However, other, more advanced assignments might require you to focus more on the *how* or *why*. For example, in a film studies class you might be learning about a particular director's techniques, or in a literature class, the stylistic features of particular kinds of poetry might be the focus; you could be asked to write a paper demonstrating your learning and focused on these issues of *how*—how does the film director or how does this set of poems convey some sort of meaning. Take a look at these examples:

> Through his vivid depiction of such settings as orphanages and debtors' prisons, Charles Dickens's novels convey a powerful social message about the dark underside of nineteenth–century London society.

> The traditional Western film drew upon and further reinforced potent myths of American individualism through its emphasis on the lone hero who mediates conflict between "untamed" nature and encroaching civilization.

Sometimes the issue of *why* is the emphasis. If your paper focuses on the ways in which a particular work under analysis fits into the writer's body of work, or how it relates to historical trends of the time, or something along these lines, your thesis would emphasize this issue of *why*, or significance. Here is an example:

> William Carlos Williams's jealousy of T.S. Eliot, as well as his resistance to Eliot's negative view of the world, are displayed throughout his collection of poems *Spring and All*.

Notice in the above two sample thesis statements for Dickinson's "Wild Nights!" the first contains both the *what*—the poem examines the dual nature of love—and the *how*, through an extended sea metaphor. Neither thesis statement explicitly addresses the issue of *why*, but the significance is implied since the issue examined is itself significant, is a phenomenon with which many people must grapple. The second example mentions only the *what*; though, again, the *why* is implied, and both the *how* and *why* would be addressed in the paper as the thesis is supported.

EXERCISE 6.1

Planning a Textual Analysis

Choose one of the two preliminary thesis statements we came up with following our analysis of Dickinson's poem. Work together in small groups of your classmates to accomplish the next two planning stages involved in writing a literary analysis. (See the stages in the box "Guidelines for Writing Analyses," pages

230–31.) You don't need to actually write the paper, but write down the points such a paper would need to cover in developing one of the thesis statements we've generated. Then write an outline, placing those points in logical order.

Multiple Interpretations

The interpretation of Dickinson's poem at which we arrived based on this analysis is certainly not the only possible interpretation of this poem. Nor is the method of analysis we just delineated meant to represent some kind of rigid formula for analyzing poetry. Other readers might arrive at different understandings of the words of the poem—in fact, many literary critics and scholars have differing ideas about this particular poem's meaning. This doesn't mean, however, that a work has infinite possible meanings: You must be able to support any assertions about the meanings present in a poem—or any cultural artifact or "text"—with evidence. The first source for such evidence is found in the work itself—and indeed, this textual evidence was the only support on which our simple analysis relied. With their more specialized and in-depth knowledge, literary scholars might arrive at more sophisticated interpretations of the poem; and in addition to relying upon the elements of the poem itself, their interpretations might also rest on evidence from outside the poem. They might bring in knowledge of different forms and conventions in poetry; of common poetic devices such as rhythm, meter, and rhyme; figurative language like metaphor, simile, and imagery; and, with their knowledge of literature in general, they might recognize allusions to other works in the poem that the less informed reader might miss. Further, by utilizing their knowledge of Dickinson's poetry in general, the typical themes she addresses, knowledge of her interests and concerns, and the historical context in which she wrote, literary scholars' readings are more detailed and perhaps more persuasive than the simplified analysis we have generated. Nonetheless, even when they bring in their additional knowledge and more specialized methods of analysis, the essential task of explicating a poem still entails the kind of dissection of a poem's parts that we have just demonstrated. And, you'll notice, that our rudimentary analysis did produce a reasonable interpretation of the poem's meaning—one that is considerably more subtle and interesting than we would have attained without performing a careful analysis.

EXERCISE 6.2

Practicing Poetry Analysis

Try your hand at analyzing the Dickinson poem on your own, and see if you arrive at a different interpretation than the one our analysis produced. Look at the poem's words, sentences and phrases (including punctuation), its lines and stanzas. Put aside our analysis above so you won't be unduly influenced by the conclusions we've made, and write down your own impression of how the parts of this poem work to produce an overall meaning. You could then take this further and work out a thesis statement that sums up your interpretation.

Alternatively, or in addition to analyzing Dickinson's poem, read the following poem by twentieth-century poet Gwendolyn Brooks, and then proceed to analyze—in writing—the elements of the poem. What do all the pieces of the poem ultimately add up to for you? What do you think this poem is trying to say?

Kitchenette Building
Gwendolyn Brooks

A poet who was acclaimed for the ways in which her depictions of African-American lives and experiences resonated with universal themes, Gwendolyn Brooks won the 1950 Pulitzer Prize for her book of poetry, Annie Allen *and served for many years as poet laureate of Illinois. Her published works include collections of poetry such as* A Street In Bronzeville *(1945)—from which "Kitchenette Building" comes,* The Bean Eaters *(1960),* In the Mecca *(1968), and* Family Pictures *(1970). During her life, from 1917 to 2000, she also wrote a novel,* Maud Martha *(1950), and an autobiography entitled* Report From Part One *(1972).*

We are things of dry hours and the involuntary plan,
Grayed in, and gray. "Dream" makes a giddy sound, not strong
Like "rent," "feeding a wife," "satisfying a man."

But could a dream sent up through onion fumes
Its white and violet, fight with fried potatoes
And yesterday's garbage ripening in the hall,
Flutter, or sing an aria down these rooms,

Even if we were willing to let it in,
Had time to warm it, keep it very clean,
Anticipate a message, let it begin?

We wonder. But not well! not for a minute!
Since Number Five is out of the bathroom now,
We think of lukewarm water, hope to get in it.

ANALYZING VISUAL MEDIA

Scholars in the humanities and social sciences study advertising from a number of different angles: In the fields of cultural studies, literary studies, and American studies, scholars interpret the messages of advertisements much as they do the messages and meanings of artifacts from "high culture," such as literature and art. In opposition to high culture, advertisements (along with television shows, films, and the like) are considered examples of "popular culture" (or "pop culture"), and in the past 20 years or so, the study of these highly pervasive and influential works has attracted academic attention. Scholars in the fields of sociology, communications, and anthropology are also interested in studying such pop cultural artifacts, since they exert such powerful influences on our lives.

Analysis of advertisements has therefore become a fairly common practice in various fields of academia. Let's now take the analytical thinking skills we used in our poetry analysis, and apply them to a print advertisement. In this case, rather than lead you through the analytical process, we will show you an advertisement and provide you with some questions to apply so you can perform your own analysis of the ad's features, thereby arriving at a sense of its overall message or meaning.

The ad featured here is actually a parody of a print advertisement, produced by an organization called "Adbusters," a group whose mission, in part, is to use humor to expose some of the more potentially destructive forces in the advertising tactics employed by companies today (www.adbusters.org) . Even though we are not analyzing a real advertisement here, the kinds of questions we bring to our analysis of the ad's features are the same ones we would use to analyze any kind of print advertisement—it's just that in this case we have a level of parody and humor to add some fun to our exercise.

First, examine the ad carefully, and then proceed to the questions we've formulated to aid your analytical process.

Parody Ad: A Spoof on Mood-Enhancing Drugs
Adbusters

- What is depicted in the ad's images?
- What is the ad's text?
- How do text and images relate to each other in creating the ad's meaning?
- How are color/shading/different font styles used?
- How are words and various images in the ad placed in relation to one another, and how do these spatial relationships create meaning?
- What is the mood—i.e., the emotional output—of the ad? How does this mood help create the ad's meaning?
- How does the ad allude to images/ideas/events from our knowledge of advertising and of the world?
- Does the combination of text style and image remind you of advertising for any other type of product? If so, how does the relationship between that other product and the one being sold in the parody ad work to create a particular point or message?

EXERCISE 6.3

Analyzing an Advertisement

Work through the questions listed above, answering them in as much detail as you can. Then use your answers to write a paragraph or so proposing an overall interpretation of the ad's message.

After practicing this process by analyzing the ad parody, look through a popular magazine and find an ad that interests you—for whatever reason—and analyze the ad's features. Remember to be critical and detailed as you take apart the ad's elements and ultimately put them back together again to arrive at an interpretation of the ad's message. Describe both its explicit message (usually just "buy this product") as well as any implicit or covert messages about what kind of person the product might help you become, or what kinds of values the ad is portraying as desirable.

As these different exercises have demonstrated, analysis boils down to asking questions, observing patterns and relationships, and then deriving meaning from what you come up with in this process.

The type of object or phenomena you are analyzing helps determine the ways in which you look at it: A poem requires a different approach than a visual advertisement. In addition, your relationship to the object or phenomena under analysis further shapes your perspective on it. For example, a botanist will analyze a flower's features differently than an artist will—they are interested in the flower for different reasons, and their fields require different approaches and methods of study. The discipline of botany uses the scientific method (which we'll discuss in more detail below) and specialized tools and equipment, such as microscopes, aid in that method. Similarly, a sociologist examining data from the 2000 U.S. census will ask different questions of the data than a political scientist or economist—and their methods of analysis might vary as well. To take the example further, a sociologist studying racial segregation patterns will ask different questions than a sociologist studying religious affiliations of U.S. citizens. Thus, four major factors impact the way one performs academic analysis: (1) The type of object under analysis; (2) your purpose in studying it—that is, what you are trying to discover; (3) your disciplinary orientation and the methods appropriate to it; and (4) your level of specialized knowledge in the field within which you are acting.

THEORY AS A TOOL FOR ANALYSIS

We've mentioned the ways in which academic analysis often involves the application of specialized kinds of knowledge and methods. We've discussed how literary scholars, when analyzing a poem, bring with them a set of tools they have developed for literary analysis. One such tool is literary *theory.* A theory is a general statement about how things work. Every area of study has theories that practitioners use to explain a given phenomena. One typical way to conduct an analysis is to use a particular theory, like a lens, to study an object more closely: to examine the parts of a poem, for instance, or a plant, a star, a meeting, and so on. In each case, the observer/analyst would select a theory appropriate to the object being studied and then use that theory to identify and explore its various parts in an effort to arrive at some new, or more complete, understanding.

Consider the following sample analysis assignments:

> *Social-Psychology:* Describe the key features of the mother-son relationship as a Freudian psychologist might see it.

> *American Studies:* Explain how Herman Melville's "Benito Cereno" engages the issue of slavery as represented in the Abolitionist texts we've read this term.

> *Astronomy:* Explain how Newton's Laws of Motion and Gravitation apply to the shapes of orbits within the solar system.

> *Economics:* Using relevant principles of International Trade theory, support the proposition that unilateral free trade may not be the best policy for a country when other countries impose trade barriers.

Each of these examples calls for an analysis through application of theory. It is one thing to approach a given object or phenomenon with a completely open mind—to analyze the features of a flower, for example, without any prior knowledge of botany or other related sciences. With such an approach, you would be able to make a number of useful observations about the flower. But without an education in science, your observations would pretty much stop there. You would be able to *describe* the flower's features, but once you started wondering *why* certain features of the flower exist, your lack of botanical knowledge, of previously established facts or theories, would limit your ability to further analyze the flower.

WHAT IS THEORY?

A theory is a conceptual scheme that we invent or propose in order to explain to ourselves, and to others, observed phenomena and the relationships between them. Theories come in all shapes and varieties, from the broad to the narrow, from the serious to the silly. At one extreme are theories that are highly structured, focused, and comprehensive. A highly structured theory operates at several levels of specificity. A well-focused theory is one that is defined in more or less the same way no matter what practitioner applies it. A comprehensive theory is one that attempts to account for a broad range of human experience (e.g., the life of the mind, the way national economies function). Examples of such structured, focused, comprehensive theories include Darwin's theory of evolution, Marx's theory of capital, Freud's theory of the unconscious. As theories become less structured, focused, and comprehensive, their power to explain a wide variety of experience diminishes. These less ambitious theories may nonetheless prove very useful. Whether you are working with a carefully structured, comprehensive theory or a more casual one, you will follow essentially the same steps in applying elements of the theory when you engage in the process of analysis.

A brief discussion of the scientific method will help make clear how theories develop and how they function in academic thinking and discovery.

Theory in the Sciences: The Scientific Method

This method can be broken down into the following set of steps:

1. Observation and description of a phenomenon or group of phenomena.
2. Formulation of a *hypothesis* to explain the phenomena. A *hypothesis* is an informed estimate. As you know, a *thesis* is an assertion or argument about something, so a *hypothesis* is a provisional assertion, based on logic and prior knowledge.
3. Performance of new observations and/or experiments in order to test validity of the hypothesis.
4. Use of the hypothesis to predict existence of other phenomena or to predict results of new observations.
5. Performance of experimental tests of the predictions by independent researchers performing experiments using standard methods.
6. If the hypothesis is supported in repeated testing, it may come to be regarded as a theory or law of nature. If the experiments do not support the hypothesis, it must be modified or rejected.

Thus, a scientific theory or law represents a hypothesis (or a group of related hypotheses) that has or have been confirmed through repeated tests. Accepted scientific theories and laws become part of our understanding of the universe and form the basis for exploring less understood areas of knowledge. Scientists have often said that theories can never be proved, only disproved. A new observation or experiment may conflict with a long-standing theory, and result in its modification or refutation. Nevertheless, theories are not easily discarded; scientists first assume that new discoveries fit into the existing theoretical framework. It is only when, after repeated experiments, the new phenomenon cannot be accommodated, that scientists seriously question the theory and attempt to modify it.

Although scientific theories cannot be proven in the strictest sense, they are still valid representations of the physical world. For example, while the heat-transferring properties of iron are "only a theory," we know not to touch a skillet in which we've just been cooking.

To sum up then, theories function in academic inquiry in a kind of circular fashion: We observe the workings of things—the occurrence of particular phenomena—and develop theories inductively from those observations. The theories are meant to explain the phenomena under study. Then such theories are taken and applied deductively to other things or other instances of the same things. We see if we can establish a logical fit between the object or phenomena under study and the theoretical explanation of it.

EXERCISE 6.4

Exploring Theories

In order to see some examples of different kinds of theories, get on the Internet and go to a search engine such as Google.com. Type in several different combinations of the word *theory*, such as "psychological theories," "scientific theories," "sociological theories," and "engineering theories." Spend some time looking around at the different theories defined and discussed on the Web. Just for fun, here's a humorous (and fake) theory we found on the Internet. It won the Grand Prize in *Omni* magazine's contest for "new scientific theories":

> When a cat is dropped, it always lands on its feet, and when toast is dropped, it always lands with the buttered side facing down. It is proposed to strap buttered toast to the back of a cat; the two will hover, spinning inches above the ground. With a giant buttered cat array, pneumatic tires on cars and trucks could be replaced, and a high-speed monorail could easily link New York with Chicago.*

Theory in the Social Sciences and Humanities

General features of the scientific method form the basis for academic inquiry in disciplines outside the sciences. Knowledge is created within the social sciences and humanities by observing phenomena, asking questions about them, and developing provisional knowledge that is proposed, debated, tested, accepted, or refuted.

---

*Andrew Hughes, "Andy's Stupid Humor" 30 Jan. 2001, 19 Apr. 2001. <http://www.open.org/~hughesa/humor/theories.htm>.

However, the theories formed in some of the social sciences and much of the humanities are more provisional than those in the physical and biological sciences, because the objects of study in most of the social sciences and humanities—and consequently, the methods used to study them—are different than those in the physical and biological sciences. That is, since most social scientists study the human social world, and humanists study arts and texts produced by humans, scholars in these fields cannot subject their hypotheses or theories to all the kinds of rigorous testing available to most scientists. Of course, social scientists are more closely aligned with science and the scientific method, so the language of hypotheses and testing is employed there, while in the humanities such language and methodologies are largely absent. Nonetheless, theories are an important part of the work of scholars in the humanities as well as in the social sciences; they are just not usually the type of theories that attain the validity of natural laws. It should also be noted that not all theories in the sciences are testable, either.

Scholars in the social sciences observe phenomena and construct theories to explain them. In turn, they apply these theories to related phenomena, as tools for understanding how and why things work the way they do. Communications researchers, for example, have developed theories for understanding the ways in which media depictions of violence affect viewers. Some of these theories conflict with each other, but such conflicts may be resolved as more evidence is gathered that supports one theory over another. However, the most well-supported and accepted communications theory is unlikely to become a natural law since communications researchers can't conduct the kinds of tightly controlled experiments that would lead to absolute findings on human subjects' reactions to media violence. Nonetheless, the theories that many social scientists develop and test do provide powerful tools for explaining aspects of the human social world.

Theories sometimes function as particular orientations or perspectives through which people view the world. In fact, this is how theories most often function in the humanities. A literature professor who examines the ways in which gender roles are depicted in nineteenth-century American novels is approaching the object of study from a feminist theoretical perspective. A historian who focuses on the historical importance of economic issues may be coming from a Marxist (also known as materialist) theoretical orientation. These kinds of broad, conceptual theories are not of the type that one tests in order to prove or disprove; instead, they enable us to view things in a particular way, and thus to arrive at particular understandings of the ways things work. These understandings are relative and provisional, not factual, in nature.

Most scholars—and hence, most of your professors—have theoretical alignments that they may or may not state explicitly. Such alignments color how they view the world, what they choose to study, the questions they ask, and the planning and presentation of course materials. As a student, you don't necessarily have to know all the theoretical perspectives informing your professors' views of the world, but you ought to know *that* your professors possess such perspectives.

Theories are important outside the academic world, of course. Economic policies are informed by the theories to which different economists subscribe. For example, during Ronald Reagan's presidency, "supply-side" economic theories held sway, influencing the tax code and other aspects of economic policy. Such policies had direct effects upon our lives, although there is still some disagreement among economists about the negative or positive qualities of these effects.

A powerful example of the ways in which theories underlie the foundations of our society can be seen in the founding of the United States. Our nation's Constitution and our governmental system rest upon the theory that individuals are rational beings possessing free will. Thus, the ultimate purpose of government is thought to be protection of the rights of the individual. While it generally *feels* true that we are rational beings with free will, we cannot *prove* this is so. What if our every move is predetermined or fated? And if we have free will, was it endowed to us by a Creator, as many believe, or is it simply a function of neurons and brain chemistry? While we can't prove the theory of individual free will—nor prove where it might come from—we haven't disproved it either. But clearly, this isn't the kind of theory we can test through experimentation—at least not with the tools currently available to us.

HOW TO APPLY THEORY IN ANALYSIS PAPERS

Now we return to our focus upon writing. When you are asked to apply theories to particular phenomena, how do you go about it? Applying a specific theory, a theoretical perspective, or a set of theoretical concepts means that you must first understand the theory and/or concepts themselves, and this can be a challenging task, at times. Many theories are complex, and require you to apply skills you've been working on in this textbook, particularly the skills of critical reading and summary. Oftentimes when theories are presented to you by professors or in textbooks, the explanations will involve definition and example. Pay attention to the definitions of the theories, the concepts that comprise them, and then make sure you understand how they are represented in examples. Write brief summaries of the theories in your own words, and then check them against the original definitions.

Once you understand a theory, you must apply it. Theories usually apply to a limited kind of phenomena; typically, when a paper assignment or exam question asks you to apply a theory to some specific phenomenon, you can assume that the theory does apply in some way. Sometimes more complex assignments will require you to note the limited ways in which a theory applies to something—and this kind of limit can prompt you to propose a modification of the theory or, at the very least, to point out the theory's limits.

> ## CRITICAL READING FOR ANALYSIS
>
> - **Use the tips from Critical Reading for Summary on page 6.** Remember to examine the context; note the title and subtitle; identify the main point; identify the subordinate points; break the reading into sections; distinguish between points, examples, and counterarguments; watch for transitions within and between paragraphs; and read actively and recursively.
> - **Read to discover relationships within sources.** When analyzing a piece of fiction, such as a poem or story, watch for recurring images and ideas, similarities and contrasts between images and ideas, shifts or changes in portrayals of things, and cause and effect relationships between things.
> - **Read to discover relationships between sources.** When using theoretical perspectives to analyze specific phenomena, you must carefully consider the relationships between what the theory predicts and the phenomena itself.
> - **Read carefully.** Whether you are analyzing a work of fiction or a scientist's description of a chemical reaction, pay close attention to the ways in which things are described.

Once you have determined whether a theory applies—or to what extent it applies—to a specific object or phenomenon, your main task involves discussing the results of the theory's application. In other words, what understanding of the phenomenon are you able to gain through application of the theory? What are you able to see about the phenomenon through the lens of the theory? The answer to this kind of question should constitute the focus of your analysis. Analysis papers are thus the product of serious critical thinking.

DEMONSTRATION 2: APPLYING A THEORY TO A PARTICULAR PHENOMENON

Let's look now at a theory about American identity, "Of Individualism in Democratic Countries," by the famous nineteenth-century French political observer and theorist, Alexis de Tocqueville. Notice how Tocqueville's theory consists of a number of ideas—ideas that combine to produce a broad theoretical perspective on American identity and society. Following the selection by Tocqueville, a student will take us through her process of writing an analytic paper that applies this particular theoretical perspective to a social phenomenon with which she is familiar.

From *Democracy in America*
Alexis de Tocqueville

Born in 1805 in Paris, France, Alexis Charles Henri Clérel de Tocqueville is now regarded as one of the greatest political thinkers of all time, as well as one of the shrewdest observers of American society ever to live and write. Born an aristocrat, Tocqueville watched the fall of the French monarchy and the establishment of democracy in France; in 1831 he spent nine months traveling throughout the United States and later published his three-volume master-work, Democracy in America. *This work established him as an important political theorist in his time, and today his work remains influential in the fields of history, sociology, political science, and cultural studies. The following excerpt is taken from Volume 2, Part II: "The Influence of Democracy on the Sentiments of the Americans," Chapter 2, Of Individualism in Democracies; and Chapter 4, How the Americans Combat the Effects of Individualism by Free Institutions.*

Chapter 2: Of Individualism in Democratic Countries

I have shown how, in ages of equality every man finds his beliefs within himself, and I shall now go on to show that all his feelings are turned in on himself.

"Individualism" is a word recently coined to express a new idea. Our fathers only knew about egoism.

Egoism is a passionate and exaggerated love of self which leads a man to think of all things in terms of himself and to prefer himself to all.

Individualism is a calm and considered feeling which disposes each citizen to isolate himself from the mass of his fellows and withdraw into the circle of family and friends; with this little society formed to his taste, he gladly leaves the greater society to look after itself.

Egoism springs from a blind instinct; individualism is based on misguided judgment rather than depraved feeling. It is due more to inadequate understanding than to perversity of heart.

Egoism sterilizes the seeds of every virtue; individualism at first only dams the spring of public virtues, but in the long run it attacks and destroys all the others too and finally merges in egoism.

Egoism is a vice as old as the world. It is not peculiar to one form of society more than another.

Individualism is of democratic origin and threatens to grow as conditions get more equal.

Among aristocratic nations families maintain the same station for centuries and often live in the same place. So there is a sense in which all the generations are contemporaneous. A man almost always knows about his ancestors and respects them; his imagination extends to his great-grandchildren, and he loves them. He freely does his duty by both ancestors and descendants and often sac-

Tocqueville, Alexis de, <u>Democracy in America</u>, trans. George Lawrence (New York: Harper, 1966) 477–478; 481–483; 484.

rifices personal pleasures for the sake of beings who are not longer alive or are not yet born.

Moreover, aristocratic institutions have the effect of linking each man closely with several of his fellows.

Each class in an aristocratic society, being clearly and permanently limited, forms, in a sense, a little fatherland for all its members, to which they are attached by more obvious and more precious ties than those linking them to the fatherland itself.

Each citizen of an aristocratic society has his fixed station, one above another, so that there is always someone above him whose protection he needs and someone below him whose help he may require.

So people living in an aristocratic age are almost always closely involved with something outside themselves, and thus are often inclined to forget about themselves. It is true that in these ages the general conception of *human fellowship* is dim and that men hardly ever think of devoting themselves to the cause of humanity, but men do often make sacrifices for the sake of certain other men.

In democratic ages, on the contrary, the duties of each to all are much clearer but devoted service to any individual much rarer. The bonds of human affection are wider, but more relaxed.

Among democratic peoples new families continually rise from nothing while others fall, and nobody's position is quite stable. The woof of time is ever being broken and the track of past generations lost. Those who have gone before are easily forgotten, and no one gives a thought to those who will follow. All a man's interests are limited to those near himself.

As each class catches up with the next and gets mixed with it, its members do not care about one another and treat one another as strangers. Aristocracy links everybody, from peasant to king, in one long chain. Democracy breaks the chain and frees each link.

As social equality spreads there are more and more people who, though neither rich nor powerful enough to have much hold over others, have gained or kept enough wealth and enough understanding to look after their own needs. Such folk owe no man anything and hardly expect anything from anybody. They form the habit of thinking of themselves in isolation and imagine that their whole destiny is in their own hands.

Thus, not only does democracy make men forget their ancestors, but also clouds their view of their descendants and isolates them from their contemporaries. Each man is forever thrown back on himself alone, and there is danger that he may be shut up in the solitude of his own heart.

Chapter 4: How the Americans Combat the Effects of Individualism by Free Institutions

Despotism, by its very nature suspicious, sees the isolation of men as the best guarantee of its own permanence. So it usually does all it can to isolate them. Of all the vices of the human heart egoism is that which suits it best. A despot will lightly forgive his subjects for not loving him, provided they do not love one another. He does not ask them to help him guide the state; it is enough if they do not claim to manage it themselves. He calls those who try to unite their efforts to create a general prosperity "turbulent and restless spirits," and twisting the natural meaning of words, he calls those "good citizens" who care for none but themselves.

Thus vices originating in despotism are precisely those favored by equality. The two opposites fatally complete and support each other.

Equality puts men side by side without a common link to hold them firm. Despotism raises barriers to keep them apart. It disposes them not to think of their fellows and turns indifference into a sort of public virtue.

Despotism, dangerous at all times, is therefore particularly to be feared in ages of democracy.

It is easy to see that in such ages men have a peculiar need for freedom.

Citizens who are bound to take part in public affairs must turn from their private interests and occasionally take a look at something other than themselves.

As soon as common affairs are treated in common, each man notices that he is not as independent of his fellows as he used to suppose and that to get their help he must often offer his aid to them.

When the public governs, all men feel the value of public goodwill and all try to win it by gaining the esteem and affection of those among whom they must live.

Those frigid passions that keep hearts asunder must then retreat and hide at the back of consciousness. Pride must be disguised; contempt must not be seen. Egoism is afraid of itself.

Under a free government most public officials are elected, so men whose great gifts and aspirations are too closely circumscribed in private life daily feel that they cannot do without the people around them. It thus happens that ambition makes a man care for his fellows, and, in a sense, he often finds his self-interest in forgetting about himself. I know that one can point to all the intrigues caused by an election, the dishonorable means often used by candidates, and the calumnies spread by their enemies. These do give rise to feelings of hatred, and the more frequent the elections, the worse they are.

Those are great ills, not doubt, but passing ones, whereas the benefits that attend them remain.

Eagerness to be elected may, for the moment, make particular men fight each other, but in the long run this same aspiration induces mutual helpfulness on the part of all; and while it may happen that the accident of an election estranges two friends, the electoral system forges permanent links between a great number of citizens who might otherwise have remained forever strangers to one another. Liberty engenders particular hatreds, but despotism is responsible for general indifference.

The Americans have used liberty to combat the individualism born of equality, and they have won.

The lawgivers of America did not suppose that a general representation of the whole nation would suffice to ward off a disorder at once so natural to the body social of a democracy and so fatal. They thought it also right to give each part of the land its own political life so that there should be an infinite number of occasions for the citizens to act together and so that every day they should feel that they depended on one another.

That was wise conduct.

The general business of a country keeps only the leading citizens occupied. It is only occasionally that they come together in the same places, and since they often lose sight of one another, no lasting bonds form between them. But when the people who live there have to look after the particular affairs of a district, the same people are always meeting, and they are forced, in a manner, to know and adapt themselves to one another.

It is difficult to force a man out of himself and get him to take an interest in the affairs of the whole state, for he has little understanding of the way in which the fate of the state can influence his own lot. But if it is a question of taking a road past his property, he sees at once that this small public matter has a bearing on his greatest private interests, and there is no need to point out to him the close connection between his private profit and the general interest.

Thus, far more may be done by entrusting citizens with the management of minor affairs than by handing over control of great matters, toward interesting them in the public welfare and convincing them that they constantly stand in need of one another in order to provide for it.

Some brilliant achievement may win a people's favor at one stroke. But to gain the affection and respect of your immediate neighbors, a long succession of little services rendered and of obscure good deeds, a constant habit of kindness and an established reputation for disinterestedness, are required. [. . .]

The free institutions of the United States and the political rights enjoyed there provide a thousand continual reminders to every citizen that he lives in society. At every moment they bring his mind back to this idea, that it is the duty as well as the interest of men to be useful to their fellows. Having no particular reason to hate others, since he is neither their slave nor their master, the American's heart easily inclines toward benevolence. At first it is of necessity that men attend to the public interest, afterward by choice. What had been calculation becomes instinct. By dint of working for the good of his fellow citizens, he in the end acquires a habit and taste for serving them.

There are many men in France who regard equality of conditions as the first of evils and political liberty as the second. When forced to submit to the former, they strive at least to escape the latter. But for my part, I maintain that there is only one effective remedy against the evils which equality may cause, and that is political liberty.

EXERCISE 6.5

Critical Reading of de Tocqueville

Review the Critical Reading for Summary tips in Chapter 1, on page 6. Use these tips to go back over these Tocqueville excerpts. Write a one- to two-sentence summary of each of the two Tocqueville chapters presented here.

Applying Tocqueville's Perspective

Along with Tocqueville's perspective on identity, we gave our students a list of topics relating to the lives of American youth. We then asked the students to study Tocqueville's perspective and use it to write a 1,300 to 1,500 word analysis explaining the occurrence of a particular phenomenon in the lives of young people. The list of youth-related topics included the following:

Teenage membership in cliques and subcultures
College binge drinking
Popular culture and youth
Gender roles
Relationships and sexuality; "hooking up"
Low voting turnout among 18–30 year olds
Volunteerism and community service
Fraternity and sorority life
Career goals and/or attitudes toward education

EXERCISE 6.6

Practice Applying Tocqueville's Perspective

In small groups of your classmates, pick one of the topics listed above and discuss how Tocqueville's ideas might apply to aspects of the topic. Jot down your ideas so that you can share them with the class. If you need some help getting started, look over our discussion below of how one student applied Tocqueville's perspective to the phenomenon of voter apathy in young people.

Choose a Topic

One of our students, Lauren Stocks, chose the topic of low voter turnout among young people. Here she describes the process she used to decide which issue to analyze, to brainstorm ideas, and ultimately to write her analytical paper.

I had the opportunity to vote for the first time in the presidential election of 2000, so the topic of low voter participation among young people interested me. I had seen firsthand how many of my friends and acquaintances in college didn't seem to care very much about politics, and I had actually wondered about this.

Brainstorm

At first when I thought about how Tocqueville's ideas about individualism related to this social issue, I felt frustrated because he did not address my issue directly. Tocqueville's ideas related to political involvement, but not to young people specifically.

The reading was interesting to me, but since I couldn't immediately see how the ideas would apply to young people today—200 years after he wrote about America—I decided to start brainstorming by briefly summarizing the selection. I went back and reread it, making notes summing up the main points so that I could get a better handle on how they might connect to my issue.

Critical Reading and Summary

Here are my notes on the reading:

> The identity of Americans is characterized by individualism, which he says is a result of liberty and equality; in aristocratic societies people are more interdependent, while in democracies, people can withdraw easily into their own families since they are more free and independent. Individualism differs from egoism, or selfishness, but it can turn into egoism if unchecked. He goes on to say that despotism is a danger for individualistic societies since the lack of close ties between people makes them more vulnerable to control by an authoritarian leader. However, he believes that the system of local governance in various "free institutions" serves to bring people together, combating the negative effects of individualism. This works because people see that they have to work with others to get things accomplished in their communities, so they behave less selfishly than they otherwise might.

Freewrite

After summarizing Tocqueville's ideas in order to solidify her understanding, Lauren began some focused freewriting, attempting to work out how Tocqueville's ideas about individualism might apply to the issue of voter apathy. Notice how her freewriting sounds like a conversation with herself—conducted in writing.

> I looked over these notes and jotted down some thoughts about them:

> > Tocqueville's perspective on individualism is interesting. He doesn't explicitly mention identity, but he's describing the individualistic characteristics of American identity. I don't know

how individualistic people were in the nineteenth century, but I can see how we certainly are extreme individualists today. I don't see most people—young and old—that involved in local politics as Tocqueville implies many were then. Today it seems like we're so focused on our personal lives and our individual desires that we don't have time for politics.

Tocqueville pointed out that national politics is unlikely to interest citizens in general because they don't see its relevance; even local politics, for young people, holds little interest. If you're still in college and haven't yet gotten your life together—you don't have any property to be taxed or children in public schools, then local politics doesn't have much relevance either. As they get older I think people do become more interested in national politics than Tocqueville predicted (maybe because of the media?) because national issues like taxes and Social Security are relevant for a lot of people—but not for college students.

After doing this writing, I felt that the Tocqueville reading made quite a bit of sense in relation to my issue of nonvoting among youth. The ideas about individualism and involvement in public service explained my issue of voter apathy quite effectively, I thought. I decided to do some more freewriting to figure out the different points I might make about individualism and political apathy in young people.

- Okay, so Americans tend to be highly individualistic because we are free and live our lives independently of each other. We are dependent on each other in certain ways, but we just don't always see that very clearly. If we feel independent of others and are withdrawn into our private circles, it's easy to see how political involvement would suffer. It's also easy to see how individualism can lead to selfishness, and selfishness makes us even less interested in the public welfare and politics— unless we see that politics is directly affecting our lives.

- And when you're young, it's hard to see how politics really affects your life. The college students I know are busy focusing on their studies and their personal lives. They have no time or interest in politics.

- In the '60s, young people were involved in politics—why not now? Back then the big issues were the Vietnam War and civil rights. These issues directly affected young people. The issues today seem distant and irrelevant to young lives. The local political issues that Tocqueville thought would draw people out of their self-interested focus don't seem relevant for young people either. We let our parents' generation handle all that stuff.

- So without involvement in local or national politics, young people's individualism flourishes and easily becomes the egoism Tocqueville criticizes. Also, when we don't work together with others, and live our lives in isolation from each other, we're more vulnerable to control by politicians and potential despots. We could lose our treasured freedom and equality if we don't watch out.

Draft a Thesis

This freewriting helped give me a sense of my paper's focus, so I felt ready to try drafting a thesis.

> College students today are too individualistic to care about politics; thus, they stay on the outside of the political process and don't get involved. This is a kind of vicious cycle that just increases their individualism, and helps turn it into selfishness.

Whew, that was a mouthful. I knew I didn't need to say all this in my thesis, but it was helpful to do so at this point because this way I could see where I wanted my paper to go. Somehow I also needed to stress the idea that students don't think politics are relevant to their lives. In my next attempt I tried to include this idea, while also shortening my statement:

> College students today are too individualistic to care about politics, especially since they don't see its relevance in their lives.

This was simpler and more direct, and I felt more confident about the focus of this statement. I didn't like the use of "individualistic" in the statement, though. As I thought about my paper, and the context within which my thesis would fit, I knew I would follow the thesis with a discussion of Tocqueville's points about individualism, so I didn't want to use the term until after that discussion. I felt that in my thesis I needed to allude to individualism without using the term outright.

> College students today are focused narrowly on their own lives, and politics doesn't seem relevant to them so they leave it up to others to take care of.

This wording needed work, but now I felt as if I had hit on the key ideas to cover in my thesis. I reworded the sentence:

> Focused narrowly on what they think is relevant in their individual lives, today's college students are leaving politics to others.

Write an Outline

Based on her thesis, Lauren developed an outline for a nine-paragraph paper, including introduction and conclusion:

A. Introduction: Tell the story about Dad's political activism to set up a comparison between young people then and now. State thesis. Maybe split this introduction into two paragraphs.

B. Explain Tocqueville's ideas. Define individualism, and why it exists in America.

C. Describe the problem with individualism—how it can lead to selfishness. But Tocqueville believed involvement in local government would keep selfishness in check.

D. Discuss how Tocqueville's views on individualism apply to today's young people. They're focused on their own goals and their private lives.

E. Politics doesn't seem relevant to young people's private lives. Tocqueville saw that national politics wouldn't keep people involved, but believed local politics would do the job; however, young people don't have enough of a stake to be interested in either one.

F. In the '60s, political issues directly affected young lives, so they were more active. Find some statistics to compare voting rates.

G. When issues aren't seen as relevant, young people stay focused on themselves and let others run the country. Tocqueville believes this is the danger of individualism and could lead to the loss of our freedom.

H. Conclusion: Solutions?

Lauren went to the campus library and searched for some reputable sources containing statistics on voting rates of young people. She was then ready to write her paper.

Write the Analysis

Here is the final draft of Lauren's analysis, produced after two revisions of earlier drafts, which we haven't included here. Lauren uses Modern Language Association (MLA) documentation style, which is explained in Chapter 7. Note that for the sake of clarity, parenthetical references are to pages in *A Sequence for Academic Writing*. (Thesis and topic sentences are highlighted).

MODEL ESSAY

> **Youth and Politics: The Generation that Doesn't Care**
> *Lauren Stocks*
>
> On my one-year anniversary of being a proud, licensed driver with a clean record, I was pulled over by a police officer who was unreasonably harsh and issued me what I still consider to be an unfair ticket. A couple of days later, I was pouring my heart out to my father about how badly the policeman had treated me, and he told me that in his youth, he had been beaten by a police officer. I was shocked. What could my Dad have done to make an officer of the law resort to physical force? Apparently, he blocked off the Interstate Five freeway in protest with thousands of other people—in protest of what, I don't remember. But I couldn't

get over the fact that my father had felt strongly enough about something to make a statement like that. I couldn't imagine going out and blocking a whole freeway, even over something I strongly opposed or supported. Young people simply don't do that these days. They rarely act out politically. In fact, it's not uncommon to meet a young adult who has absolutely no interest in the government, and doesn't even bother to vote.

Why is it that today's young Americans are known as a generation that doesn't care about politics or fulfillment of their so-called "civic duty"? In the 1960's when my father was young, college students were directly affected by a number of political issues, while contemporary students don't see the relevance of politics to their lives. Instead, focused narrowly on what they think is relevant to their individual lives, today's college students are leaving politics to others.

This kind of individualistic focus is nothing new. In his analysis of American society and politics, the nineteenth-century political theorist Alexis de Tocqueville argued that the equality and liberty inherent in American democracy lead to the development of an individualistic identity. Writing in *Democracy in America,* Tocqueville defines individualism as a "feeling which disposes each citizen to isolate himself from the mass of his fellows and withdraw into the circle of family and friends"; he states further that American individualists tend to think of "themselves in isolation and imagine that their whole destiny is in their own hands" (246; 247).

Even while Tocqueville notes that this new individualism is better than its older, more widespread cousin, egoism, he argues that individualism does interfere with "public virtues," and "in the long run it attacks and destroys" all the other virtues, and "finally merges with egoism," or in other words, selfishness (246). Tocqueville goes on to describe a complex relationship between equality, freedom, public service, and individualism. He asserts that while equality and freedom tend to loosen the ties that hold people together, the American system of governance helps to alleviate the negative effects of individualism since citizen involvement in the "free institutions" that direct local, public affairs forces people to look beyond their narrow interests in order to work with others to obtain desired goals. Thus, paradoxically, self-interest can inspire individuals to direct their attention outside of themselves. Can these ideas, written by a Frenchman visiting America nearly 200 years ago, shed any light on the political behavior of young people today?

Tocqueville's ideas do provide a useful framework for understanding the relative lack of political involvement in contemporary college students. The individualism that Tocqueville predicted would spread as conditions became more equal has indeed become one of the most prevalent characteristics of American identity. College students are consummate individualists, focused on their private lives and goals. Things like studying hard to get good grades, working to pay their living expenses, or having fun and building social relationships tend to take priority over politics and participation in political institutions. This self-centered concern only with one's own life and immediate surroundings can be understood in the context of America's individualistic spirit. In extreme cases, all too prevalent among today's college students, this individualism has gone too far, turning into a feeling of utter indifference toward things that seem unrelated to one's personal life.

Many young people today say they have no interest in politics because they feel that it doesn't have a substantial impact on their lives. Issues such as Social Security, health care, campaign finance reform, and income taxes currently take center stage in national politics, and these issues seem irrelevant to the lives of young adults. Tocqueville believed that:

> It is difficult to force a man out of himself and get him to take an interest in the affairs of the whole state, for he has little understanding of the way in which the fate of the state can influence his own lot. But if it is a question of taking a road past his property, he sees at once that this small public matter has a bearing on his greatest private interests, and there is no need to point out to him the close connection between his private profit and the general interest. (249)

This is the kind of public involvement that Tocqueville believed would keep individualism in check and turn it outward toward the community. However, college students usually haven't yet established a tangible stake in the public affairs of the nation or their communities; thus they avoid politics and their individualism easily turns into egoism.

Thirty years ago, when more political issues directly affected the lives of young people than is currently the case, college students—like my father—were very politically active. When the lack of civil rights or the prospect of getting drafted into the Vietnam War were seen as barriers to personal fulfillment, many young people became politically active because it was the only means to make changes in society that they felt needed to be made in order to meet their needs. Today's young people are simply reaping the benefits of the political victories of their parents' generation. Now that most students don't feel that national political issues are seriously impeding their success in life, and with no tangible stake in local political issues, they are not forced to take action politically. So they focus upon their personal success and fulfillment, not upon public affairs. This private focus is reflected in declining voting rates. In his analysis of politics for Generation X, Ted Halstead, president of the New America Foundation, reports that while "as recently as 1972, half those aged eighteen to twenty-four voted," by the 1996 presidential election, the number shrank to 32 percent (34). If today's college students felt directly affected by political issues, that percentage would most likely rise.

As long as young individuals feel that politics has little impact on their lives, they seem content to let others run things. This is a danger Tocqueville foresees when he writes that people who withdraw into their "circle of family and friends" will gladly leave "the greater society to look after itself" (246). The danger here is that when we live in isolation and independence from one another, we become most vulnerable to control by despots or the politicians we let run things. While individualism has many positive facets, such as independent thinking and the freedom to pursue one's dreams, it is ironic that if Tocqueville is correct, our extreme individualism—our egoism—could ultimately lead to the loss of the liberty and equality that made it possible in the first place.

People frequently refer to "the government" as if it were an entirely separate entity, instead of seeing it as a place where they join in public governance for the general interest—which includes themselves. As Tocqueville predicted, the virtues of freedom and equality have led to individualism, but America's free institutions haven't held back the vice of selfishness as he believed they would (251). Somehow, we need to revitalize public life in such a way that all citizens—young and old—will feel its relevance in their lives and join together to work for the public good. Otherwise, we might lose our precious liberty and equality.

Works Cited

Halstead, Ted. "A Politics for Generation X." At-
    lantic Monthly Aug. 1999: 33—42.
Toqueville, Alexis de. Democracy in America.
    Trans. George Lawrence. Eds. J. P. Mayer and
    Max Lerner. New York: Harper, 1966.

Discussion

In this essay, Lauren develops an analysis: She applies Tocqueville's perspective on individualism to the specific phenomenon of low voting turnout among 18- to 30-year olds. Lauren makes a plausible argument that the individualistic attitudes Tocqueville foresaw as a result of equality and liberty help foster political apathy. Further, she shows how young people are uniquely vulnerable to extreme individualism since they don't have an investment in the public policies and institutions that might involve them in less selfish pursuits. Her systematically developed analysis (see outline on pages 254–255) relies entirely upon her own understanding of Tocqueville's complex ideas, her logical thinking, and a very small quantity of research on comparative statistics concerning voting patterns in the 1960s and the 1990s.

Writing Assignment: Analysis Paper

Refer back to the list of topics on page 250, and choose one of the following two theoretical perspectives by Erik H. Erikson and Kenneth J. Gergen, to write your own paper analyzing a phenomenon relevant to young peoples' lives. You may draw upon your own experiences and observations to help make your points. You also may want to consult some outside sources to help support your points (as did our student Lauren, in order to cite figures on youth voting rates), but don't treat this as a research paper. Stay focused on advancing your own argument explaining a social phenomenon through your systematic application of one of the theoretical perspectives on American identity.

From *Identity: Youth and Crisis*
Erik H. Erikson

A Harvard psychologist and one of the twentieth century's most influential theorists on child development and identity, Erik H. Erikson (1902–1994) theorized that humans develop through eight stages of life. Because of his extensive work and writings on identity formation, he has been called the "architect of identity," and he produced such texts as Childhood and Society *(1950);* Identity: Youth and Crisis *(1968), from which this reading is excerpted;* Dimensions of a New Identity *(1974); and* The Lifecycle Completed *(1987).*

As technological advances put more and more time between early school life and the young person's final access to specialized work, the stage of adolescing becomes an even more marked and conscious period [. . .]. Thus in the later school years young people, beset with the physiological revolution of their genital maturation and the uncertainty of the adult roles ahead, seem much concerned with faddish attempts at establishing an adolescent subculture with what looks like a final rather than a transitory or, in fact, initial identity formation. They are sometimes morbidly, often curiously, preoccupied with what they appear to be in the eyes of others as compared with what they feel they are, and with the question of how to connect the roles and skills cultivated earlier with the ideal prototypes of the day. In their search for a new sense of continuity and sameness, which must now include sexual maturity, some adolescents have to come to grips again with crises of earlier years before they can install lasting idols and ideals as guardians of a final identity. [. . .]

If the earliest stage bequeathed to the identity crisis an important need for trust in oneself and in others, then clearly the adolescent looks most fervently for men and ideas to have *faith* in, which also means men and ideas in whose service it would seem worthwhile to prove oneself trustworthy. [. . .] At the same time, however, the adolescent fears a foolish, all too trusting commitment, and will, paradoxically, express his need for faith in loud and cynical mistrust. [. . .] [T]he adolescent now looks for an opportunity to decide with free assent on one of the available or unavoidable avenues of duty and service, and at the same time is mortally afraid of being forced into activities in which he would feel exposed to ridicule or self-doubt. This, too, can lead to a paradox, namely, that he would rather act shame-

Erik Erikson, <u>Identity: Youth and Crisis</u> (New York: W. W. Norton, 1968) 128–129; 130; 132; 163; 165.

lessly in the eyes of his elders, out of free choice, than be forced into activities which would be shameful in his own eyes or in those of his peers. [. . .]

Adolescence [. . .] is least "stormy" in that segment of youth which is gifted and well trained in the pursuit of expanding technological trends, and thus able to identify with new roles of competency and invention and to accept a more implicit ideological outlook. Where this is not given, the adolescent mind becomes a more explicitly ideological one, by which we mean one searching for some inspiring unification of tradition or anticipated techniques, ideas, and ideals. And, indeed, it is the ideological potential of a society which speaks most clearly to the adolescent who is so eager to be affirmed by peers, to be confirmed by teachers, and to be inspired by worth while "ways of life." On the other hand, should a young person feel that the environment tries to deprive him too radically of all the forms of expression which permit him to develop and integrate the next step, he may resist with the wild strength encountered in animals who are suddenly forced to defend their lives. For, indeed, in the social jungle of human existence there is no feeling of being alive without a sense of identity. [. . .]

In general it is the inability to settle on an occupational identity which most disturbs young people. To keep themselves together they temporarily overidentify with the heroes of cliques and crowds to the point of an apparently complete loss of individuality. Yet in this stage not even "falling in love" is entirely, or even primarily, a sexual matter. To a considerable extent, adolescent love is an attempt to arrive at a definition of one's identity by projecting one's diffused self-image on another and by seeing it thus reflected and gradually clarified.

The final assembly of all the converging identity elements at the end of childhood [. . .] appears to be a formidable task [. . .]. [T]he adolescent, during the final stage of his identity formation, is apt to suffer more deeply than he ever did before or ever will again from a confusion of roles. [. . .] Whether or not a given adolescent's newly acquired capacities are drawn back into infantile conflict depends to a significant extent on the quality of the opportunities and rewards available to him in his peer clique as well as on the more formal ways in which society at large invites a transition from social play to work experimentation and from rituals of transit to final commitments, all of which must be based on an implicit mutual contract between the individual and society.

The Dissolution of the Self
Kenneth J. Gergen

Kenneth J. Gergen earned his Ph.D. in psychology from Duke University in 1962 and currently teaches psychology at Swarthmore University. He is author of numerous articles and books including An Invitation to Social Knowledge *(1999),* Realities and Relationships: Soundings in Social Construction *(1997), and* The Saturated Self: Dilemmas of Identity in Contemporary Life *(1991), from which this selection is excerpted.*

Kenneth Gergen, <u>The Saturated Self</u> (New York: Basic Books, 1991) 6–7; 170.

Cultural life in the twentieth century has been dominated by two major vocabularies of the self. Largely from the nineteenth century, we have inherited a romanticist view of the self, one that attributes to each person characteristics of personal depth: passion, soul, creativity, and moral fiber. This vocabulary is essential to the formation of deeply committed relations, dedicated friendships, and life purposes. But since the rise of the *modernist* world-view beginning in the early twentieth century, the romantic vocabulary has been threatened. For modernists, the chief characteristics of the self reside not in the domain of depth, but rather in our ability to reason—in our beliefs, opinions, and conscious intentions. In the modernist idiom, normal persons are predictable, honest, and sincere. Modernists believe in educational systems, a stable family life, moral training, and rational choice of marriage partners.

Yet, as I shall argue, both the romantic and the modern beliefs about the self are falling into disuse, and the social arrangements that they support are eroding. This is largely a result of the forces of social saturation. Emerging technologies saturate us with the voices of humankind—both harmonious and alien. As we absorb their varied rhymes and reason, they become part of us and we of them. Social saturation furnishes us with a multiplicity of incoherent and unrelated languages of the self. For everything we "know to be true" about ourselves, other voices within respond with doubt and even derision. This fragmentation of self-conceptions corresponds to a multiplicity of incoherent and disconnected relationships. These relationships pull us in myriad directions, inviting us to play such a variety of roles that the very concept of an "authentic self" with knowable characteristics recedes from view. The fully saturated self becomes no self at all.

I [. . .] equate the saturating of self with the condition of postmodernism. As we enter the *postmodern* era, all previous beliefs about the self are placed in jeopardy, and with them the patterns of action they sustain. Postmodernism does not bring with it a new vocabulary for understanding ourselves, new traits or characteristics to be discovered or explored. Its impact is more apocalyptic than that: the very concept of personal essences is thrown into doubt. Selves as possessors of real and identifiable characteristics—such as rationality, emotion, inspiration, and will—are dismantled. [. . .]

A century ago, social relationships were largely confined to the distance of an easy walk. Most were conducted in person, within small communities: family, neighbors, townspeople. Yes, the horse and carriage made longer trips possible, but even a trip of thirty miles could take all day. The railroad could speed one away, but cost and availability limited such travel. If one moved from the community, relationships were likely to end. From birth to death, one could depend on relatively even-textured social surroundings. Words, faces, gestures, and possibilities were relatively consistent, coherent, and slow to change.

For much of the world's population, especially the industrialized West, the small, face-to-face community is vanishing into the pages of history. [. . .] [A]s a result of technological developments [. . .], contemporary life is a swirling sea of social relations. Words thunder in by radio, television, newspaper, mail, telephone, fax, wire service, electronic mail, billboards, Federal Express, and more. Waves of new faces are everywhere—in town for a day, visiting for the weekend, at the Rotary lunch, at the church social—and incessantly and incandescently on television.

Long weeks in a single community are unusual; a full day within a single neighborhood is becoming rare. We travel to neighboring towns, cities, states; one might go thirty miles for coffee and conversation.

Through the technologies of the century, the number and variety of relationships in which we are engaged, potential frequency of contact, expressed intensity of relationship, and endurance through time all are steadily increasing. As this increase becomes extreme, we reach a state of social saturation. [. . .]

As belief in essential selves erodes, awareness expands of the ways in which personal identity can be created and recreated [. . .]. This consciousness of construction does not strike as a thunderbolt; rather, it eats slowly and irregularly away at the edge of consciousness. And as it increasingly colors our understanding of self and relationships, the character of this consciousness undergoes a qualitative change.... [P]ostmodern consciousness [brings] the erasure of the category of self. No longer can one securely determine what it is to be a specific kind of person...or even a person at all. As the category of the individual person fades from view, consciousness of construction becomes focal. We realize increasingly that who and what we are is not so much the result of our "person essence" (real feelings, deep beliefs, and the like), but of how we are constructed in various social groups [. . .]. [T]he concept of the individual self ceases to be intelligible.

Research

GOING BEYOND THIS TEXT

In this chapter we'll discuss how you can use the skills you've learned in writing summaries, critiques, syntheses, and analyses to conduct research and to compose research papers and reports. Research is a wide-ranging process that can result in a number of types of written documents (see box next page). When we need to find answers or to make discoveries, we engage in research. In your work as an undergraduate college student, you are usually asked to conduct research in order to produce a particular type of written document: the research paper. A research paper is generally considered a major academic endeavor, and frequently it is. But even a paper based on only one or two sources outside the scope of assigned reading has been researched. Research requires you to (1) locate and take notes on relevant sources and organize your findings; (2) summarize or paraphrase these sources; (3) critically evaluate them for their value and relevance to your subject; (4) synthesize information and ideas from several sources that best support your own critical viewpoint; and (5) analyze concepts and phenomena, often by applying theoretical concepts to them.

RESEARCH PAPERS IN THE ACADEMIC DISCIPLINES

Though most of your previous experience with research papers may have been in English classes, you should be prepared for instructors in other academic disciplines to assign papers with significant research components. Here, for example, is a sampling of research topics that have been assigned recently in a broad range of undergraduate courses:

Anthropology: Identify, observe, and gather data pertaining to a particular subculture within the campus community; describe the internal dynamics of this group, and account for these dynamics in terms of theories of relevant anthropologists and sociologists.

Art History: Discuss the main differences between Romanesque and Gothic sculpture, using the sculptures of Jeremiah (St. Pierre Cathedral) and St. Theodore (Chartres Cathedral) as major examples.

Asian-American Studies: Address an important socio-psychological issue for Asian-American communities and/or individuals—for example, the effects of stereotypes, mental health problems, gender relations, academic achievement, assertiveness, or interracial marriage. Review both the theoretical and research literature on the issue, conduct personal interviews, and draw conclusions from your data.

Environmental Studies: Choose a problem or issue of the physical environment at any level from local to global. Use both field and library work to explore the situation. Include coverage of the following: (1) the history of the issue

---

WHERE DO WE FIND WRITTEN RESEARCH?

Here are just a few types of writing that involve research:

Academic Writing

- **Research papers.** Research an issue and write a paper incorporating the results of that research.
- **Literature reviews.** Research and review relevant studies and approaches to a particular science or social-science topic.
- **Experimental reports.** Research previous studies in order to refine—or show need for—your current approach; conduct primary research.
- **Case studies.** Conduct both primary and secondary research.
- **Position papers.** Research approaches to an issue in order to formulate your own approach.

Workplace Writing

- **Reports in business, science, engineering, social services, medicine**
- **Market analysis**
- **Business Plans**
- **Environmental Impact Reports**
- **Legal Research: Memorandum of Points and Authorities**

or problem; (2) the various interest groups involved, taking note of conflicts among them; (3) critical facts and theories from environmental science necessary to understand and evaluate the issue or problem; (4) impact and significance of management measures already taken or proposed; (5) your recommendations for management of the solution.

Film Studies: Pick a particular period of British film and discuss major film trends or production problems within that period.

History: Write a paper analyzing the history of a public policy (for example, the U.S. Supreme Court's role in undermining the civil rights of African-Americans between 1870 and 1896), drawing your sources from the best, most current scholarly histories available.

Physics: Research and write a paper on solar cell technology, covering the following areas: basic physical theory, history and development, structure and materials, types and characteristics, practical uses, state of the art, and future prospects.

Political Science: Explain the contours of California's water policy in the last few decades and then, by focusing on one specific controversy, explain and analyze the way in which policy was adapted and why. Consider such questions as these: Where does the water come from? How much is there? Who uses it? Who pays for it? How much does it cost? Should more water resources be developed?

Psychology: Explore some issue related to the testing of mental ability; for example, the effects of time limits upon test reliability.

Religious Studies: Select a particular religious group or movement present in the nation for at least twenty years and show how its belief or practice has changed since members of the group have been in America or, if the group began in America, since its first generation.

Sociology: Write on one of the following topics: (1) a critical comparison of two (or more) theories of deviance; (2) a field or library research study of those in a specific deviant career: thieves, drug addicts, prostitutes, corrupt politicians, university administrators; (3) portrayals of deviance in popular culture—e.g., television accounts of terrorism, incest, domestic violence; (4) old age as a form of deviance in the context of youth culture; (5) the relationship between homelessness and mental illness.

WRITING THE RESEARCH PAPER

Here is an overview of the main steps involved in writing research papers. Keep in mind that, as with other writing projects, writing research papers is a recursive process. For instance, you will gather data at various stages of your writing, as the list below illustrates.

Data Gathering and Invention 1

- **Find a subject.** Decide what subject you are going to research and write about.
- **Develop a research question.** Formulate an important question that you would like to answer through your research.
- **Conduct preliminary research.** Consult knowledgeable people, general and specialized encyclopedias, overviews and bibliographies in recent books, the *Bibliographic Index*, and subject heading guides.
- **Refine your research question.** Based on your preliminary research, brainstorm about your topic and ways to answer your research question. Sharpen your focus, refining your question and planning the sources you'll need to consult.
- **Conduct focused research.** Consult books, electronic databases, general and specialized periodicals, biographical indexes, general and specialized dictionaries, government publications, and other appropriate sources. Conduct interviews and surveys, as necessary.

Data Gathering and Invention 2

- **Develop a working thesis.** Based on your initial research, formulate a working thesis that attempts to respond to your research question.
- **Develop a working bibliography.** Keep a working bibliography (either paper or electronic) of your sources. Make this bibliography easy to sort and rearrange.

Some of these research papers allow students a considerable range of choice (within the general subject); others are highly specific in requiring students to address a particular issue. Most of these papers call for some library research; a few call for a combination of library and field research; others may be based entirely on field research. As with all academic writing, your first task is to make sure you understand the assignment. Remember to critically read and analyze the specific task(s) required of you in a research paper assignment.

- **Evaluate sources.** Attempt to determine the veracity and reliability of your sources; use your critical reading skills; check *Book Review Digest*; look up biographies of authors.
- **Take notes from sources.** Paraphrase and summarize important information and ideas from your sources. Copy down important quotations. Note page numbers from sources of this quoted and summarized material.
- **Arrange your notes according to your outline.** Develop a working outline of topics to be covered in your paper. Arrange your notes according to this outline.

Drafting

- **Write your draft.** Write the preliminary draft of your paper, working from your notes, according to your outline.
- **Avoid plagiarism.** Take care to cite all quoted, paraphrased, and summarized source material, making sure that your own wording and sentence structure differ from those of your sources.
- **Cite sources.** Use in-text citations and a Works Cited or References list, according to the conventions of the discipline (e.g., MLA, APA, CBE).

Revision

- **Revise your draft.** Check that your thesis still fits with your paper's focus. Use transitional words and phrases to ensure coherence. Make sure that the research paper reads smoothly, logically, and clearly from beginning to end. Check for development.

Editing

- **Edit your draft.** Check for style, combining short, choppy sentences and ensuring variety in your sentence structures. Check for grammatical correctness, punctuation, and spelling.

FINDING A SUBJECT

When you are not assigned a specific subject to research, you're faced with finding your own subject (usually within the parameters of the course you're writing for). Within a course's broad subject area, you must narrow your focus. Review course readings and notes, and think back to issues of interest to you or questions you may have had. If you have trouble choosing a topic, do some writing to help free up your thoughts. Review the discussion of narrowing a subject in Chapter 3, pages 94–96.

THE RESEARCH QUESTION

Research handbooks generally advise students to narrow their subjects as much as possible. A ten-page paper on the modern feminist movement would be unmanageable. You would have to do an enormous quantity of research (a preliminary computer search of this subject would yield several thousand items), and you couldn't hope to produce anything other than a superficial treatment of such a broad subject. You could, however, write a paper on the contemporary feminist response to a particular social issue, or the relative power of current feminist political organizations. It's difficult to say, however, how narrow is narrow enough. (A literary critic once produced a twenty-page article analyzing the first paragraph of Henry James's *The Ambassadors*.)

Perhaps more helpful as a guideline on focusing your research is to seek to answer a particular question, a *research question*. For example, how did the Clinton administration respond to criticisms of bilingual education? To what extent is America perceived by social critics to be in decline? Did Exxon behave responsibly in handling the *Valdez* oil spill? How has the debate over genetic engineering evolved during the past decade? To what extent do contemporary cigarette ads perpetuate sexist attitudes? Or how do contemporary cigarette ads differ in message and tone from cigarette ads in the 1950s? Focusing on questions such as these and approaching your research as a way of answering such questions is probably the best way to narrow your subject and ensure focus in your paper. The essential answer to this research question eventually becomes your *thesis*; in the paper, you present evidence that systematically supports your thesis.

EXERCISE 7.1

Constructing Research Questions

Moving from a broad topic or idea to formulation of precise research questions is sometimes more challenging than it seems. Practice this skill by working with small groups of your classmates to construct research questions about the following topics (or come up with some topics of your own). Write at least one research question for each topic listed, then discuss these topics and questions with the other groups in class.

> Racial or gender stereotypes in television shows
> Drug addiction in the U.S. adult population
> Global environmental policies
> Employment trends in high-technology industries
> United States energy policy

PRELIMINARY RESEARCH

Once you have a research question, you want to see what references are available. You want to familiarize yourself quickly with the basic issues and generate a preliminary list of sources. This will help you refine your research question and conduct efficient research once you've attained more focus. There are many ways to go about finding preliminary sources; some of the more effective ones are listed in the box below. We'll consider a few of these suggestions in more detail.

HOW TO FIND PRELIMINARY SOURCES AND NARROW THE SUBJECT

- Ask your instructor to recommend sources on the subject.
- Ask your college librarian for useful reference tools in your subject area.
- Read an encyclopedia article on the subject and use the bibliography following the article to identify other sources.
- Read the introduction to a recent book on the subject and review that book's bibliography to identify more sources.
- Consult the annual *Bibliographic Index* (see page 274 for details).
- Use an Internet Search engine to explore your topic. Type in different key-word or search term combinations and browse the sites you find for ideas and references to sources you can look up later (see the box on pages 278–279 for details).
- If you need help in narrowing a broad subject, try one or more of the following:
  —search by subject in an electronic database to see how the subject breaks down into components;
  —search the subject heading in an electronic periodical catalog, such as *InfoTrac*, or in a print catalog such as the *Readers' Guide to Periodical Literature*;
  —search the *Library of Congress Subject Headings* catalog (see Subject-Heading Guides, page 274 for details).

Consulting Knowledgeable People

When you think of research, you may immediately think of libraries and print material. But don't neglect a key reference—other people. Your *instructor* probably can suggest fruitful areas of research and some useful sources. Try to see your instructor during office hours, however, rather than immediately before or after class, so that you'll have enough time for a productive discussion.

Once you get to the library, ask a *reference librarian* which reference sources (e.g., bibliographies, specialized encyclopedias, periodical indexes, statistical almanacs) you need for your particular area of research. Librarians won't do your research for you, but they'll be glad to show you how to research efficiently and systematically.

You can also obtain vital primary information from people when you interview them, ask them to fill out questionnaires or surveys, or have them participate in experiments. We'll cover this aspect of research in more detail below.

Encyclopedias

Reading an encyclopedia entry about your subject will give you a basic understanding of the most significant facts and issues. Whether the subject is American politics or the mechanics of genetic engineering, the encyclopedia article—written by a specialist in the field—offers a broad overview that may serve as a launching point to more specialized research in a particular area. The article may illuminate areas or raise questions that you feel motivated to pursue further. Equally important, the encyclopedia article frequently concludes with an *annotated bibliography* describing important books and articles on the subject.

Encyclopedias have certain limitations. First, most professors don't accept encyclopedia articles as legitimate sources for academic papers. You should use encyclopedias primarily to familiarize yourself with (and to select a particular aspect of) the subject area and as a springboard for further research. Also, because new editions appear only once every five or ten years, the information they contain—including bibliographies—may not be current. Current editions of the *Encyclopaedia Britannica* and the *Encyclopedia Americana*, for instance, may not include information about the most recent developments in biotechnology.

Some of the most useful general encyclopedias include the following:

American Academic Encyclopedia

Encyclopedia Americana

New Encyclopaedia Britannica

Keep in mind that the library also contains a variety of more *specialized encyclopedias*. These encyclopedias restrict themselves to a particular disciplinary area, such as chemistry, law, or film, and are considerably more detailed in their treatment of a subject than are general encyclopedias. Here are examples of specialized encyclopedias:

Social Sciences

Encyclopedia of Education

Encyclopedia of Psychology

Guide to American Law

International Encyclopedia of the Social Sciences

Humanities

Encyclopedia of American History
Encyclopedia of Art
Encyclopedia of Religion and Ethics
International Encyclopedia of Film
The New College Encyclopedia of Music

Science and Technology

Encyclopedia of Biological Sciences
Encyclopedia of Computer Science and Engineering
Encyclopedia of Physics
McGraw-Hill Encyclopedia of Environmental Science
Van Nostrand's Scientific Encyclopedia

Business

Encyclopedia of Banking and Finance
Encyclopedia of Economics

EXERCISE **7.2**

Exploring Specialized Encyclopedias

Go to the Reference section of your campus library and locate several specialized encyclopedias within your major or area of interest. Look through the encyclopedias, noting their organization, and read entries on topics that interest you. Jot down some notes describing the kinds of information you find. You might also use this opportunity to look around at the other materials available in the Reference section of the library, including the *Bibliographic Index, Biographical Indexes,* the *Book Review Digest,* and *Periodical Indexes* (see below).

Overviews and Bibliographies in Recent Books

If your professor or a bibliographic source directs you to an important recent book on your subject, skim the introductory (and possibly the concluding) material to the book, along with the table of contents, for an overview of key issues. Look also for a bibliography, works cited, and/or references list. These lists are extremely valuable resources for locating material for research. For example, Zvi Dor-Ner's 1991 book *Columbus and the Age of Discovery* includes a four-page annotated bibliography of important reference sources on Columbus and the age of exploration.

Keep in mind that authors are not necessarily objective about their subjects, and some have particularly biased viewpoints that you may unwittingly carry over to your paper, treating them as objective truth.* However, you may still be able to get some useful information out of such sources. Alert yourself to authorial biases by looking up the reviews of your book in the *Book Review Digest* (described on next page). Additionally, look up biographical information on the author (see Biographical Indexes, pages 286–287), whose previous writings or professional associations may suggest a predictable set of attitudes on the subject of your book.

Bibliographic Index

The *Bibliographic Index* is a series of annual volumes that enables you to lo-cate bibliographies on a particular subject. The bibliographies it refers to generally appear at the end of book chapters or periodical articles, or they may themselves be book or pamphlet length. Browsing through the *Bibliographic Index* in a general subject area may give you ideas for further research in particular aspects of the subject, along with particular references.

Subject-Heading Guides

Seeing how a general subject (e.g., education) is broken down in other sources also could stimulate research in a particular area (e.g., bilingual primary education in California). As in the table of contents of a book, the general subject (the book title) is analyzed into its secondary subject headings (the chapter titles). To locate such sets of secondary subject headings, consult:

- an electronic database
- an electronic or print periodical catalog (e.g., *InfoTrac, Readers' Guide, Social Science Index*)
- *The Library of Congress Subject Headings* catalog
- the *Propaedia* volume of the *New Encyclopaedia Britannica* (1998)

---

*Bias is not necessarily bad. Authors, like all other people, have certain preferences and predilections that influence the way they view the world and the kinds of arguments they make. As long as they inform you of their biases, or as long as you are aware of them and take them into account, you can still use these sources judiciously. (You might gather valuable information from a book about the Watergate scandal, even if it were written by former President Richard Nixon or one of his top aides, as long as you make proper allowance for their understandable biases.) Bias becomes a potential problem only when it masquerades as objective truth or is accepted as such by the reader. For suggestions on identifying and assessing authorial bias, see the material on persuasive writing (pages 56–64) and evaluating assumptions (pages 66–68) in Chapter 2.

FOCUSED RESEARCH

Once you've narrowed your scope to a particular subject and a particular research question (or set of research questions), you're ready to undertake more focused research. Your objective now is to learn as much as you can about your particular subject. Only in this way will you be qualified to make an informed response to your research question. This means you'll have to become something of an expert on the subject—or, if that's not possible, given time constraints, you can at least become someone whose critical viewpoint is based solidly on the available evidence. In the following pages we'll suggest how to find sources for this kind of focused research. In most cases, your research will be *secondary* in nature, based on (1) *books*; (2) *electronic databases*; (3) *articles*; and (4) *specialized reference sources*. In certain cases, you may gather your own *primary* research, using (5) *interviews, surveys*, structured observation, or content/textual analysis.

Books

Books are useful in providing both breadth and depth of coverage of a subject. Because they generally are published at least a year or two after the events treated, they also tend to provide the critical distance that is sometimes missing from articles. Conversely, this delay in coverage also means that the information you find in books will not be as current as information you find in journals. And, of course, books also may be shallow, inaccurate, outdated, or hopelessly biased; for help in making such determinations, see *Book Review Digest*, below. You can locate relevant books through the electronic or card catalog. When using this catalog, you may search in three ways: (1) by *author*, (2) by *title*, and (3) by *subject*. Entries include the call number, publication information, and, frequently, a summary of the book's contents. Larger libraries use the Library of Congress cataloging system for call numbers (e.g., E111/C6); smaller ones use the Dewey Decimal System (e.g., 970.015/C726).

Book Review Digest

Perhaps the best way to determine the reliability and credibility of a book you may want to use is to look it up in the annual *Book Review Digest*. These volumes list (alphabetically by author) the most significant books published during the year, supply a brief description of each, and, most importantly, provide excerpts from (and references to) reviews. If a book receives bad reviews, you don't necessarily have to avoid it (the book still may have something useful to offer, and the review itself may be unreliable). But you should take any negative reaction into account when using that book as a source.

Electronic Databases

Much of the information that is available in print—and a good deal that is not—is available in electronic form. Almost certainly, your library card catalog has been computerized, allowing you to conduct searches much faster and more easily than in the past. Increasingly, researchers are accessing magazine, newspaper, and journal articles and reports, abstracts, and other forms of information through *online* databases (many of them on the Internet) and through databases on *CD-ROMs*. One great advantage of using databases (as opposed to print indexes) is that you can search several years' worth of different periodicals at the same time.

Online databases—that is, those that originate outside your computer—are available through international, national, or local (e.g., campus) networks. The largest such database is DIALOG, which provides access to more than 300 million records in more than 400 databases, ranging from sociology to business to chemical engineering. Another large database is LEXIS-NEXIS (like DIALOG, available only through online subscription). LEXIS-NEXIS, and its "Academic Universe" version, provides access to numerous legal, medical, business, and news sources. In addition to being efficient and comprehensive, online databases are generally far more up-to-date than print sources. If you have an Internet connection from your own computer, you can access many of these databases—including those available through commercial online services such as CompuServe and America Online—without leaving your room.

Access to online databases often requires an account and a password, which you may be able to obtain by virtue of your student status. In some cases, you will have to pay a fee to the local provider of the database, based on how long you are online. But many databases will be available to you free of charge. For example, your library may offer access through its computer terminals to magazine and newspaper databases, such as MAGS and NEWS, as well as to the Internet itself.

Various sites and files on the Internet may be accessed through their *gopher* or *ftp* (file transfer protocol) addresses. (Once you locate a file, you may have to download it to your disk or to your e-mail address.) More user-friendly is the *World Wide Web*, which offers graphics, multimedia, and "hyperlinks" to related material in numerous sources. To access these sources, you can either browse (i.e., follow your choice of paths or links wherever they lead) or type in a site's address.

To search for Web information on a particular topic, try using one of the more popular search engines:

> *Google:* http://www.google.com
> *Yahoo:* http://www.yahoo.com
> *Alta Vista:* http://altavista.com
> *Northern Lights:* http://www.northernlights.com
> *WebCrawler:* http://webcrawler.com
> *SearchCom:* http://www.search.com
> *Lycos:* http://www.lycos.com

Review the "Help" and "Advanced Search" sections of search engines to achieve the best results. See the box on pages 278–279 for some general tips on searching online.

CD-ROMs (compact disk-read only memory) are useful sources for research. Many newspapers, magazines, and journals are available on

CD-ROM: for example, the *Readers' Guide to Periodical Literature, The New York Times, Film Index International, PAIS International,* and *America: History and Life,* as are other standard reference sources, such as *Statistical Abstract of the U.S., The Encyclopaedia Britannica, Bibliography of Native North Americans, Environment Reporter,* and *National Criminal Justice Reference Service.* Of particular interest is *InfoTrac,* which provides access to more than 1,000 general interest, business, government, and technological periodicals.

Keep in mind, however, that while electronic sources make it far easier to access information than do their print counterparts, they often do not go back more than fifteen years. For earlier information, therefore (e.g., contemporary reactions to the Milgram experiments of the 1960s), you would have to rely on print indexes.

EXERCISE | **7.3**

Exploring Electronic Sources

Go to the library and ask a Reference librarian how to access the available CD-ROMs (different libraries have different systems for finding these materials). Check out one or two CD-ROMs with information of interest to you, and spend some time familiarizing yourself with this method of finding information. Next, use the library's Internet connection (or use your home computer if you have Internet access) to access a search engine. Pick a topic/research question of interest to you, review the box on "Using Keywords and Boolean Logic to Refine Online Searches" (pages 278–279) and try different combinations of keywords and Boolean operators to see what sources you can find for your topic. Jot down notes describing the kinds of sources you find, which terms seem to yield the best results, etc. Effective searching on the Internet takes practice; you'll save time when conducting research if you have a good sense of how to use these search strategies.

The Benefits and Pitfalls of the World Wide Web

In the past few years, the Web has become not just a research tool, but a cultural phenomenon. The pop artist Andy Warhol once said that in the future everyone would be famous for fifteen minutes. He might have added that everyone would also have a personal Web site. People use the Web not just to look up information, but also to shop, to make contact with long-lost friends and relatives, to grind their personal or corporate axes, to advertise themselves and their accomplishments.

The Web makes it possible for people sitting at home, work, or school to gain access to the resources of large libraries and to explore corporate and government databases. In her informative book *The Research Paper and the World Wide Web,* Dawn Rodrigues quotes Bruce Dobler and Harry Bloomberg on the essential role of the Web in modern research:

> It isn't a matter anymore of using computer searches to locate existing documents buried in some far-off library or archive. The Web is

USING KEYWORDS AND BOOLEAN LOGIC
TO REFINE ONLINE SEARCHES

You will find more—and more relevant—sources on Internet search engines and library databases if you carefully plan your search strategies. *Note: Some search engines and online databases have their own systems for searching—review the "Help" section of different search engines, and use "Advanced Search" options where available. The following tips are general guidelines and their applicability in different search engines may vary somewhat.*

1. **Identify multiple keywords:**
   Write down your topic and/or your research question, then brainstorm synonyms and related terms for the words in that topic/question.

Sample topic: Political activism on college campuses.

Sample research question: What kinds of political activism are college students involved in today?

Keywords: Political activism; college students

Synonyms and related terms: politics; voting; political organizations; protests; political issues; universities; colleges; campus politics.

2. **Conduct searches using different combinations of synonyms and related terms.**

3. **Find new terms in the sources you locate and search with these.**

4. **Use quotation marks around terms you want linked.**
   "political activism"

providing documents and resources that simply would be too expensive to publish on paper or CD-ROM.

Right now—and not in some distant future—doing research without looking for resources on the Internet is, in most cases, not really looking hard enough. [...] A thorough researcher cannot totally avoid the Internet and the Web.*

---

*Dawn Rodrigues, <u>The Research Paper and the World Wide Web</u> (Upper Saddle River, NJ: Prentice Hall, 1997).

5. Use "Boolean operators" to link keywords:

The words AND, OR, and NOT are used in "Boolean logic" to combine search terms and get more precise results than using keywords alone.

AND: Connecting keywords with AND narrows a search by retrieving only sources that contain *both* keywords:

Political activism AND college students

OR: Connecting keywords with OR broadens a search by retrieving all sources that contain at least one of the search terms. This operator is useful when you have a topic/keyword for which there are a number of synonyms. Linking synonyms with OR will lead you to the widest array of sources:

Political activism OR protests OR political organizing OR voting OR campus politics

College OR university OR campus OR students

AND and OR: You can use these terms in combination, by putting the OR phrase in parentheses:

(political activism OR protests) AND (college OR university)

NOT: Connecting keywords with NOT (or, in some cases, AND NOT) narrows a search by excluding certain terms. If you want to focus upon a very specific topic, NOT can be used to limit what the search engine retrieves; however, this operator should be used carefully as it can cause you to miss sources that may actually be relevant:

College students NOT high school

Political activism NOT voting

And indeed, Web sites are increasingly showing up as sources in both student and professional papers. But like any other rapidly growing and highly visible cultural phenomenon, the Web has created its own backlash. First, as anyone who has tried it knows, for many subjects, systematic research on the Web is not possible. For all the information that is on the Internet, there's a great deal more that is not and never will be converted to digital format. One library director has estimated that only about 4,000 of 150,000 published scholarly journals are available online, and many of these provide only partial texts of relatively recent articles in the paper editions. *The New York Times* is available on the Web, but the online edition includes only a fraction of the content of the print edition, and online versions of the articles generally are abridged and often must be paid for. If you are researching the rise of McCarthyism in America during the early 1950s or trying to determine who else, since Stanley Milgram, has conducted psychological experiments on obedience, you are unlikely to find much useful information for your purpose on the Web.

Moreover, locating what *is* available is not always easy, since there's no standardized method—like the Library of Congress subheading and call number system—of cataloging and cross-referencing online information. The tens of thousands of Web sites and millions of Web pages, together with the relative crudity of search engines such as Yahoo, Google, AltaVista, and WebCrawler, have made navigating an ever-expanding cyberspace an often daunting and frustrating procedure.

Second, it is not a given that people who do research on the Web will produce better papers as a result. David Rothenberg, a professor of philosophy at New Jersey Institute of Technology, believes that "his students' papers had declined in quality since they began using the Web for research."* Neil Gabler, a cultural critic, writes:

> The Internet is such a huge receptacle of rumor, half-truth, misinformation and disinformation that the very idea of objective truth perishes in the avalanche. All you need to create a "fact" in the web world is a bulletin board or chat room. Gullible cybernauts do the rest.†

Another critic is even blunter: "Much of what purports to be serious information is simply junk—neither current, objective, nor trustworthy. It may be impressive to the uninitiated, but it is clearly not of great use to scholars."‡

Of course, print sources are not necessarily objective or reliable either, and in Chapter 2, Critical Reading and Critique, we discussed some criteria by which readers may evaluate the quality of information and ideas in *any* source (pages 54–68). Web sources, however, present a special problem. In most cases, material destined for print has to go through one or more editors and fact checkers before being published, since most authors don't have the resources to publish and distribute their own writing. But anyone with a computer and a modem can "publish" on the Web; furthermore, those with a good Web authoring program and graphics software can create sites that, outwardly at least, look just as professional and authoritative as those of the top academic, government, and business sites. These personal sites will appear in search-engine listings—generated through keyword matches rather than through independent assessments of quality or relevance—and uncriti-

---

*Steven R. Knowlton, "Students Lost in Cyberspace," Chronicle of Higher Education 2 Nov. 1997: 21.

†Neil Gabler, "Why Let Truth Get in the Way of a Good Story?" Los Angeles Times "Opinion," 26 Oct. 1997: 1.

‡William Miller, "Troubling Myths About On-Line Information," Chronicle of Higher Education 1 Aug. 1997: A44.

cal researchers, using their information as a factual basis for the claims they make in their papers, do so at their peril.

The Internet has also led to increased problems with plagiarism. Many college professors complain these days about receiving work copied directly off of Web sites. Such copying runs the gamut from inadvertent plagiarism of passages copied and pasted off the Web into notes and then transferred verbatim to papers, to intentional theft of others' work, pasted together into a document and claimed as the student's own. In one recent case, an instructor reports that she received a student paper characterized by a more professional writing style than usual for that student. The instructor typed a few keywords from the paper into an Internet search engine, and one of the first sources retrieved turned out to be a professional journal article from which the student had copied whole passages and pasted them together to create a "report." This student received an "F" in the course and was referred to a university disciplinary committee for further action.

The Internet sometimes proves a very tempting source from which to lift materials. But not only is such activity ethically wrong, it is also likely to result in serious punishment, such as permanent notations on your academic transcript or expulsion from school. One of the things all students should know is that, while cheating is now made easier by the Internet, the converse is also true: Instructors can often track down the sources for material plagiarized from the Internet just as easily as the student found them in the first place. (Easier, in fact, because now instructors can scan papers into software or Internet programs that will search the Web for matching text.) For more on plagiarism, see the section devoted to this subject later in the chapter, on pages 301 to 302.

We certainly don't mean to discourage Web research. There are thousands of excellent sites in cyberspace. The reference department of most college and university libraries will provide lists of such sites, arranged by discipline, and the most useful sites also are listed in the research sections of many handbooks. Most people locate Web sites, however, by using search engines and by "surfing" the hyperlinks. And for Web sources, more than print sources, the warning *caveat emptor*—let the buyer beware—applies.

Evaluating Web Sources

In their extremely useful site "Evaluating Web Resources" (http://www2.widener.edu/Wolfgram-Memorial-Library/webevaluation/webeval.htm), reference librarians Jan Alexander and Marsha Tate offer some important guidelines for assessing Web sources. First, they point out, it's important to determine what *type* of Web page you are dealing with. Web pages generally fall into one of six types, each with a different purpose: (1) entertainment, (2) business/marketing, (3) reference/information, (4) news, (5) advocacy of a particular point of view or program, (6) personal page. The purpose of the page—informing, selling, persuading, entertaining—has a direct bearing upon the objectivity and reliability of the information presented.

Second, when evaluating a Web page, one should apply the same general criteria as are applied to print sources: (1) accuracy, (2) authority, (3) objectivity, (4) currency, (5) coverage. As we've noted, when assessing the *accuracy* of a Web page, it's important to consider the likelihood that its information has been checked by anyone other than the author. When assessing the *authority* of the page, one considers the author's qualifications to write on the subject and the reputability of the publisher. In many cases, it's difficult to determine not just the qualifications, but the very identity of the author. When assessing the *objectivity* of a Web page, one considers the bias on the part of the author or authors and the extent to which they are trying to sway their reader's opinion. Many Web pages passing themselves off as informational are in fact little more than "infomercials." When assessing the *currency* of a Web page, one asks whether the content is up-to-date and whether the publication date is clearly labeled. Dates on Web pages often are missing or are not indicated clearly. If a date is provided, does it refer to the date the page was written, the date it was placed on the Web, or the date it was last revised? Finally, when assessing the *coverage* of a Web page, one considers which topics are included (and not included) in the work and whether the topics are covered in depth. Depth of coverage has generally not been a hallmark of Web information.

Other pitfalls of Web sites: Reliable sites may include links to other sites that are inaccurate or outdated. Web pages also are notoriously unstable, frequently changing or even disappearing without notice.

Finally, the ease with which it's possible to surf the net can encourage intellectual laziness and make researchers too dependent upon Web resources. Professors are increasingly seeing papers largely or even entirely based upon information in Web sites. While Web sources are indeed an important new source of otherwise unavailable information, there's usually no substitute for library or primary research, such as interviews or field study. The vast majority of printed material in even a small college library—much of it essential to informed research—does not appear on the Web, nor is it likely to in the immediate future. Much of the material you will research in the next few years remains bound within covers. You may well learn of its existence in electronic databases, but at some point you'll have to walk over to a library shelf, pull out a book, and turn printed pages.

Above all, remember that you must apply the critical reading skills you've been practicing throughout this textbook to all your sources—no matter what types they are or where you found them.

EXERCISE **7.4**

Practice Evaluating Web Sources

In order to practice applying the criteria for evaluating Web sources discussed in the section above, go to an Internet search engine and look for sources addressing a topic of interest to you (perhaps following completion of Exercise 7.3, page 277). Try to locate one source representing each of the six types listed above (i.e., entertainment, business/marketing, reference/information, etc.). Print out the main page of each of these sources and bring the copies to class. In small groups of your classmates look over the different sites each student found and make notes on each example's (1) accuracy; (2) authority; (3) objectivity; (4) currency; (5) coverage.

Periodicals: General

MAGAZINES

Because many more periodical articles than books are published every year, you are likely (depending on the subject) to find more information in periodicals than in books. By their nature, periodical articles tend to be more current than books. The best way, for example, to find out about the federal government's current policy on Social Security reform is to look for articles in periodicals and newspapers. However, periodical articles may have less critical distance than books, and they also may date more rapidly—to be superseded by more recent articles.

General periodicals (such as *Time*, *The New Republic*, and *The Nation*) are intended for nonspecialists. Their articles, which tend to be highly readable, may be written by staff writers, freelancers, or specialists. But usually they do not provide citations or other indications of sources, and so are of limited usefulness for scholarly research.

The most well-known general index is the *Readers' Guide to Periodical Literature*, an index of articles in several hundred general-interest magazines and a few more specialized magazines such as *Business Week* and *Science Digest*. Articles in the *Readers' Guide* are indexed by author, title, and subject.

Another general reference for articles is the *Essay and General Literature Index*, which indexes articles contained in anthologies.

Increasingly, texts and abstracts of articles are available on online databases. These texts may be downloaded to your floppy disk or e-mailed to your e-mail address.

NEWSPAPERS

News stories, feature stories, and editorials (even letters to the editor) may be important sources of information. Your library certainly will have the *New York Times* index, and it may have indexes to other important newspapers, such as the *Washington Post*, the *Los Angeles Times*, the *Chicago Tribune*, the *Wall Street Journal*, and the *Christian Science Monitor*. Newspaper holdings will be on microfilm (your library may have the *New York Times* on CD-ROM), and you will need a microprinter/viewer to get hard copies.

Note: Because of its method of cross-referencing, the *New York Times* index may at first be confusing. Suppose that you want to find stories on bilingual education during a given year. When you locate the "Bilingual education" entry, you won't find citations but rather a *"See also* Education" reference that directs you to seven dates (August 14, 15, and 17; September 11; October 20, 29, and 30) under the heading of "Education." Under this major heading, references to stories on education are arranged in chronological order from January to December. When you look up the dates you were directed to, you'll see brief descriptions of these stories on bilingual education.

Periodicals: Specialized

JOURNAL ARTICLES

Many professors will expect at least some of your research to be based on articles in specialized periodicals or "scholarly journals." So instead of (or in addition to) relying on an article from *Psychology Today* for an account of the effects of crack cocaine on mental functioning, you might (also) rely on an article from the *Journal of Abnormal Psychology*. If you are writing a paper on the satirist Jonathan Swift, you may need to locate a relevant article in *Eighteenth-Century Studies*. Articles in such journals normally are written by specialists and professionals in the field, rather than by staff writers or freelancers, and the authors will assume that their readers already understand the basic facts and issues concerning the subject.

To find articles in specialized periodicals, you'll use specialized indexes—that is, indexes for particular disciplines. You also may find it helpful to refer to *abstracts*. Like specialized indexes, abstracts list articles published in a particular discipline over a given period, but they also provide summaries of the articles listed. Abstracts tend to be more selective than indexes, since they consume more space (and involve considerably more work to compile); but, because they also describe the contents of the articles covered, they can save you a lot of time in determining which articles you should read and which ones you can safely skip. Don't treat abstracts alone as sources for research; if you find useful material in an abstract, you need to locate the article to which it applies and use that as your source of information.

Here are some of the more commonly used specialized periodical indexes and abstracts in the various disciplines.

Note: Lists of electronic databases follow the print indexes, but some listed print indexes (e.g., PAIS) also are available in electronic form, such as CD-ROM.

Social Science Indexes

Abstracts in Anthropology

Education Index

Index to Legal Periodicals

Psychological Abstracts

Public Affairs Information Service (PAIS)

Social Science Index

Sociological Abstracts

Women's Studies Abstracts

Social Science Databases

ERIC (Educational Resources Information Center)

PAIS (Public Affairs Information Service)

PSYCHINFO (psychology)

Psychological Abstracts

Social SciSearch

Sociological Abstracts

Humanities Indexes

Abstracts of English Studies

America: History and Life

Art Index

Cambridge Bibliography of English Literature

Essay and General Literature Index

Film/Literature Index

Historical Abstracts

Humanities Index

International Index of Film Periodicals

MLA International Bibliography of Books and Articles on Modern Languages and Literature

Music Index

Religion Index

Year's Work in English Studies

Humanities Databases

Arts and Humanities Citation Index

MLA Bibliography

Philosophers' Index

Historical Abstracts

Science and Technology Indexes

Applied Science and Technology Index

Biological Abstracts

Engineering Index

General Science Index

Index to Scientific and Technical Proceedings

Science and Technology Databases

Aerospace Database

Agricola (agriculture)

Biosis Previews (biology, botany)

Chemical Abstracts search (chemistry)

Compendex (engineering)

Environment Abstracts

MathSci

MEDLINE (medical)

ScienceCitation Index

SciSearch

WSPEC (physics, electronics, computer science)

Business Indexes
Business Index

Business Periodicals Index

Economic Titles/Abstracts

Wall Street Journal *Index*

Business Databases
ABI/INFORM

Econ Abstracts International

Labor Statistics

Standard & Poor's News

Law Databases
LEXIS-NEXIS

Westlaw

EXERCISE 7.5

Exploring Specialized Periodicals

Visit your campus library and locate the specialized periodical indexes for your major or area of interest (ask a Reference librarian to help you). Note the call numbers for specialized periodicals (also called academic journals) in your field, and visit the periodical room or section of the library where recent editions of academic journals are usually housed. Locate the call numbers you've noted, and spend some time looking through the different specialized periodicals in your field. The articles you find in these journals represent some of the most recent scholarship in your field—the kind of scholarship many of your professors are busy conducting. Write half a page or so describing some of the articles you find interesting, and why.

Biographical Indexes

To look up information on particular people, you can use not only encyclopedias but an array of biographical sources. (You can also use biographical sources to alert yourself to potential biases on the part of your source authors.) A brief selection follows:

Living Persons

Contemporary Authors: A Biographical Guide to Current Authors and Their Works

Current Biography

International Who's Who

Who's Who in America

Persons No Longer Living

Dictionary of American Biography

Dictionary of National Biography (Great Britain)

Dictionary of Scientific Biography

Who Was Who

Persons Living or Dead

Biography Almanac

McGraw-Hill Encyclopedia of World Biography

Webster's Biographical Dictionary

Dictionaries

Use dictionaries to look up the meaning of general or specialized terms. Here are some of the most useful dictionaries:

General

Oxford English Dictionary

Webster's New Collegiate Dictionary

Webster's Third New International Dictionary of the English Language

Social Sciences

Black's Law Dictionary

Dictionary of the Social Sciences

McGraw-Hill Dictionary of Modern Economics

Humanities

Dictionary of American History

Dictionary of Films

Dictionary of Philosophy

Harvard Dictionary of Music
McGraw-Hill Dictionary of Art

Science And Technology

Computer Dictionary and Handbook
Condensed Chemical Dictionary
Dictionary of Biology
Dorland's Medical Dictionary

Business

Dictionary of Advertising Terms
Dictionary of Business and Economics
Mathematical Dictionary for Economics and Business Administration
McGraw-Hill Dictionary of Modern Economics: A Handbook of Terms and Organizations

Other Sources/Government Publications

You also may find useful information in other sources. For statistical and other basic reference information on a subject, consult a *handbook* (example: *Statistical Abstracts of the United States*). For current information on a subject as of a given year, consult an *almanac* (example: *World Almanac*). For annual updates of information, consult a *yearbook* (example: *The Statesman's Yearbook*). For maps and other geographic information, consult an *atlas* (example: *New York Times Atlas of the World*). (Often, simply browsing through the reference shelves for data on your general subject—such as biography, public affairs, psychology—will reveal valuable sources of information.) And of course, much reference information is available on government sites on the Web.

Many libraries keep pamphlets in a *vertical file* (i.e., a file cabinet). For example, a pamphlet on AIDS might be found in the vertical file rather than in the library stacks. Such material is accessible through the *Vertical File Index* (a monthly subject-and-title index to pamphlet material).

Finally, note that the U.S. government regularly publishes large quantities of useful information. Some indexes to government publications include the following:

American Statistics Index
Congressional Information Service
The Congressional Record
Information U.S.A.

> ### CRITICAL READING FOR RESEARCH
>
> - **Use all the critical reading tips we've suggested thus far.** The tips contained in the boxes on Critical Reading for Summary on page 6, Critical Reading for Critique on page 76, Critical Reading for Synthesis on page 165, and Critical Reading for Analysis on page 245 are all useful for the kinds of reading used in conducting research.
> - **Read for relationships to your research question.** How does the source help you to formulate and clarify your research question?
> - **Read for relationships between sources.** How does each source illustrate, support, expand upon, contradict, or offer an alternative perspective to those of your other sources?
> - **Consider the relationship between your source's form and content.** How does the form of the source—specialized encyclopedia, book, article in a popular magazine, article in a professional journal, etc.— affect its content, the manner in which that content is presented, and its relationship to other sources?
> - **Pay special attention to the legitimacy of Internet sources.** Consider how the content and validity of the information on the Web page may be affected by the purpose of the site. Assess Web-based information for its (1) accuracy; (2) authority; (3) objectivity; (4) currency; and (5) coverage (Alexander and Tate).

Interviews and Surveys

Depending on the subject of your paper, some or all of your research may be conducted outside the library. In conducting such primary research, you may perform experiments in science labs, make observations or gather data in courthouses, in city government files, in shopping malls (if you are observing, say, patterns of consumer behavior), in the quad in front of the humanities building, or in front of TV screens (if you are analyzing, say, situation comedies or commercials, or if you are drawing on documentaries or interviews—in which cases you should try to obtain transcripts or tape the programs).

You may want to *interview* your professors, your fellow students, or other individuals knowledgeable about your subject. Before interviewing your subject(s), become knowledgeable enough about the topic that you can ask intelligent questions. You also should prepare most of your questions beforehand. Ask "open-ended" questions designed to elicit meaningful responses, rather than "forced choice" questions that can be answered with a word or two, or "leading questions" that presume a particular answer. (Example: Instead of asking "Do you think that men should be more sensitive to women's concerns for equality in the workplace?" ask, "To what extent do you see evidence that men are insufficiently sensitive to women's concerns for equality in the workplace?") Ask follow-up questions to elicit additional insights or details. If you record the interview (in addition to or instead of taking notes), get your subject's permission, preferably in writing.

Surveys or *questionnaires*, when well prepared, can produce valuable information about the ideas or preferences of a group of people. Before preparing your questions, determine your purpose in conducting the survey, exactly what kind of information you want to obtain, and whom you are going to ask for the information. Decide also whether you want to collect the questionnaires as soon as people have filled them out or whether you want the responses mailed back to you. (Obviously, in the latter case, you have to provide stamped, self-addressed envelopes and specify a deadline for return.) Keep in mind that the larger and more representative your sample of people, the more reliable the survey. As with interviews, it's important to devise and word questions carefully so that they (1) are understandable and (2) don't reflect your own biases. If you're surveying attitudes on capital punishment, for example, and you ask, "Do you believe that the state should endorse legalized murder?" you've loaded the questions to influence people to answer in the negative, and thus you've destroyed the reliability of your survey.

Unlike interview questions, survey questions should be short answer or multiple choice; open-ended questions encourage responses that are difficult to quantify. (You may want to leave space, however, for "additional comments.") Conversely, "yes" or "no" responses or rankings on a 5-point scale are easy to quantify. For example, you might ask a random sample of students in your residence hall the extent to which they are concerned that genetic information about themselves might be made available to their insurance companies—on a scale of 1 (unconcerned) to 5 (extremely concerned). For surveys on certain subjects (and depending on the number of respondents), it may be useful to break out the responses by as many meaningful categories as possible—for example, gender, age, ethnicity, religion, education, geographic locality, profession, and income. Obtaining these kinds of statistical breakdowns, of course, means more work on the part of your respondents in filling out the surveys and more work for you in compiling the responses. If the survey is too long and involved, some subjects won't participate or won't return the questionnaires.

FROM RESEARCH TO WORKING THESIS

The search strategy we've just described isn't necessarily a straight-line process. In other words, you won't always proceed from the kinds of things you do in "preliminary research" to the kinds of things you do in "focused research." You may not formulate a research question until you've done a good deal of focused research. And the fact that we've treated, say, biographical sources before specialized periodical articles does not mean that you should read biographical material before you read articles. We've described the process as we have for convenience; and, *in general*, it is a good idea to proceed from more general sources to more particular ones. In practice, however, the research procedure often is considerably less systematic. You might begin, for example, by reading a few articles on the subject, and continue by looking up an encyclopedia article or two. Along the way, you might consult specialized dictionaries, book review indexes, and a guide to reference books in the area. Or, instead of proceeding in a straight line through the process, you might find yourself moving in circular patterns—backtracking to previous steps and following up leads you missed or ignored earlier. There's nothing wrong with such variations of the basic search strategy, as long as you keep in mind the kinds of resources that are available to you, and as long as you plan to look up as many of these resources as you can—given the constraints on your time.

One other thing you'll discover as you proceed: research is to some extent a self-generating process. That is, one source will lead you—through references in the text, citations, and bibliographic entries—to others. Your authors will refer to other studies on the subject; and frequently they'll indicate which ones they believe are the most important and why. At some point, if your research has been systematic, you'll realize that you've already looked at most of the key work on the subject. This is the point at which you can be reasonably assured that the research stage of your paper is nearing its end.

As you progress in this, the "data-gathering" stage of your research and writing process, you will typically find yourself moving in and out of the next stage of the process, "invention" (see Chapter 3 for a complete discussion of the stages in a writer's process). Thus, as you locate and read your sources, you may find that your preliminary research question undergoes a change. Suppose you are researching bilingual education. At first you may have been primarily interested in the question of whether bilingual education is a good idea. During your research, you come across S. I. Hayakawa's controversial proposal that English be made the official language of the United States, and you decide to shift the direction of your research toward this particular debate. Or, having made an initial assessment that bilingual education is a good idea, you conclude that Hayakawa is wrong. Be prepared for such shifts: They're a natural—and desirable—part of the research (and learning) process. They indicate that you haven't made up your mind in advance, that you're open to new evidence and ideas.

You're now ready to respond to your modified research questions with a *working thesis*—a statement that controls and focuses your entire paper, points toward your conclusion, and is supported by your evidence. See our earlier discussion in Chapter 3 (pages 102–107) on the process of devising a thesis.

THE WORKING BIBLIOGRAPHY

As you conduct your research, keep a working bibliography—that is, a set of bibliographic information on all the sources you're likely to use in preparing the paper. Compile full bibliographic information as you consider each source. It's better to spend time during the research process noting information on a source you don't eventually use than to go back to retrieve information—such as the publisher or the date—just as you're typing your final draft.

Now that library catalogs and databases are available online, it's easy to copy and paste your sources' (or potential sources') bibliographic information into a document, or to e-mail citations to yourself for cutting and pasting later. A more traditional but still very efficient way to compile bibliographic information is on 3" x 5" cards. (Note, however, that certain software programs allow you to create sortable electronic cards.) You can easily add, delete, and rearrange cards as your research progresses. Whether you keep bibliographic information on 3" x 5" cards or in a document, be sure to record the following:

a. the author or editor (last name first)

b. the title (and subtitle) of the book or article

c. the publisher and place of publication (if a book) or the title of the periodical

d. the date of publication; if periodical, volume and issue number

e. the inclusive page numbers (if article)

You also may want to include:

f. a brief description of the source (to help you recall it later in the research process)

g. the library call number (to help you relocate the source if you haven't checked it out)

h. a code number, which you can use as a shorthand reference to the source in your notes

Your final bibliography, known as "Works Cited" in Modern Language Association (MLA) format and "References" in American Psychological Association (APA) format, consists of the sources you have actually summarized, paraphrased, or quoted in your paper. When you compile the bibliography, arrange your sources alphabetically by authors' last names.

Here is an example of a working bibliography notation or card for a book:

> Sale, Kirkpatrick. *The Conquest of Paradise: Christopher Columbus and the Columbian Legacy.* New York: Knopf, 1990.
>
> Attacks Columbian legacy for genocide and ecocide. Good treatment of Columbus's voyages (Chaps. 6–8).

Here is an example of a working bibliography record for an article:

> *Axtell, James. "Europeans, Indians, and the Age of Discovery in Ameri-
> can History Textbooks" American Historical Review 92.3 (1987): 621–32.*
>
> *Finds treatments of subjects in title of article inadequate in most college-
> level American history texts. Specifies "errors," "half-truths" and "mis-
> leading assertions." Recommends changes in nine areas.*

Some instructors may ask you to prepare—either in addition to or instead of a research paper—an *annotated bibliography*. This is a list of relevant
works on a subject, with the contents of each briefly described or assessed.
The bibliography cards shown provide examples of two entries in an annotated bibliography on the Columbian legacy. Annotations are different from
abstracts in that they do not claim to be comprehensive summaries; they indicate, rather, how the items may be useful to the researcher.

EVALUATING SOURCES

As you sift through what seems a formidable mountain of material, you'll
need to work quickly and efficiently; you'll also need to do some selecting.
This means, primarily, distinguishing the more important from the less important (and the unimportant) material. The hints in the box below can sim-
plify the task.

GUIDELINES FOR EVALUATING SOURCES

- **Skim** the source. With a book, look over the table of contents, the introduction and conclusion, and the index; zero in on passages that
  your initial survey suggests are important. With an article, skim the
  introduction and the headings.
- Be on the alert for **references** in your sources to other important
  sources, particularly to sources that several authors treat as important.
- Other things being equal, the more **recent** the source, the better. Recent work usually incorporates or refers to important earlier work.
- If you're considering making multiple references to a book, look up
  the **reviews** in the *Book Review Digest* or the *Book Review Index*. Also,
  check the author's credentials in a source such as *Contemporary Authors* or *Current Biography*.
- Draw on your **critical reading** skills to help you determine the reliability and value of a source (see the Box on Critical Reading for Research on page 289, and review Chapter 2 on Critical Reading and
  Critique).

NOTE-TAKING

People have their favorite ways of note-taking. Some use cards; others use legal pads or spiral notebooks; yet others type notes into a laptop computer, perhaps using a database program. We prefer 4" x 6" cards for note-taking. Such cards have some of the same advantages as 3" x 5" cards for working bibliographies: They can easily be added to, subtracted from, and re-arranged to accommodate changing organizational plans. Also, discrete pieces of information from the same source can easily be arranged (and re-arranged) into subtopics—a difficult task if you have three pages of notes on an entire article.

Whatever your preferred approach, we recommend including, along with the note itself,

   a. a topic or subtopic label, corresponding to your outline (see below)

   b. a code number, corresponding to the number assigned the source in the working bibliography

   c. a page reference at end of note

Here is a sample notecard for an article by Charles Krauthammer entitled "Hail Columbus, Dead White Male" (*Time*, May 27, 1991):

> *Defenses of Columbus* (III*ß*) ⑦
>
> *Defends Columbus against revisionist attacks. Our civilization "turned out better" than that of the Incas. "And mankind is the better for it. Infinitely better. Reason enough to honor Columbus and 1492" (74).*

Here is a notecard for the specialized periodical article by Axtell (see bibliography card on page 293):

> *Problems with Textbooks* (II *A*)
>
> *American history textbooks do not give adequate coverage to the Age of Discovery. An average of only 4% of the textbook pages covering first-semester topics is devoted to the century that accounts for 30% of the time between Columbus and Reconstruction. "The challenge of explain-ing some of the most complex, important, and interesting events in human history—the discovery of a new continent, the religious upheavals of the sixteenth century, the forging of the Spanish empire, the Columbian biological exchange, the African diaspora—all in twenty or twenty-five pages—is one that few, if any, textbook authors have met or are likely to meet" (623).*

The notecard is headed by a topic label followed by the tentative loca-tion in the paper outline where the information will be used. The number in the upper right corner is coded to the corresponding bibliography card. The note itself in the first card uses *summary* ("Defends Columbus against revisionist attacks") and *quotation*. The note in the second card uses *sum-*

mary (sentence 1), *paraphrase* (sentence 2), and *quotation* (sentence 3). Summary is used to condense important ideas treated in several paragraphs in the sources; paraphrase, for the important detail on textbook coverage; quotation, for particularly incisive language by the source authors. For general hints on when to use each of these three forms, see Chapter 1, page 49.

At this point we must stress the importance of using quotation marks around quoted language *in your notes*. Making sure to note the difference between your own and quoted language will help you avoid unintentionally using someone else's words or ideas without crediting them properly. Such use constitutes plagiarism—a serious academic offense—something that professors don't take lightly; you don't want to invite suspicion of your work, even unintentionally. See the discussion of plagiarism on pages 301–302 for more details.

INVENTION STRATEGIES

Brainstorming without Your Notes

As we've mentioned, while you're in the first, data-gathering stage of your research and writing process—as you're locating, reading, and taking notes on your sources—you usually move in and out of the next stage, invention. As you see what work has been conducted on your topic, as you read what others think and write about the topic, you are naturally led to revise and refine your own thinking on your topic and research question. So while these two stages in the process of conducting research and writing about it overlap, at some point you will have gathered enough materials (although you may not be finished gathering data yet) to be ready to make a more definite move from data-gathering to invention (but this doesn't mean you won't move back to data-gathering again!).

A useful strategy for making this transition is to put aside your notes and, based on the reading and note-taking you have done, sit down and write about your ideas. What have you learned about your topic? What answers to your research question have you generated? Try one of the invention strategies listed on pages 98–100 of Chapter 3 (freewriting, clustering, etc.) to generate ideas and sort out your thoughts about your topic. Spending time formulating and clarifying your thoughts *away* from your notes can help you retain ownership of the paper you ultimately write. That is, research papers are meant to represent *your synthesis* of your sources. Too often, students produce research papers that read like patchwork quilts of sources "sewn" together without a clear guiding point. It's up to you to have a point that is your own (the thesis, or answer to your research question), and to use your sources to make that point, rather than letting your sources take over and turn your paper into an "information dump."

Brainstorming with Your Notes

Once you have spent time clarifying your thoughts and your understanding of your sources, go back to your notes and check your understanding for accuracy. Revise your thoughts if necessary.

Now it's time to carefully and critically review your notes. Recall that your research originally was stimulated by one or more *research questions*, to which you may have made a tentative response in your *working thesis* (see page 103). As you review your notes, patterns should begin to emerge that either substantiate, refute, or otherwise affect your working thesis. These patterns represent the relationships you discern among the various ideas and pieces of evidence that you investigate. They may be patterns of cause and effect, of chronology, of logical relationships, of comparison and contrast, of pro and con, of correspondence (or lack of correspondence) between theory and reality. Once these patterns begin to emerge, you are ready to begin outlining the structure of your paper.

ARRANGING YOUR NOTES: THE OUTLINE

Working from your original working thesis—or a new thesis that you have developed during the course of data-gathering and invention, you can begin constructing a preliminary outline. This outline indicates the order in which you plan to support your thesis.

For example, on deciding to investigate new genetic technologies, you devise a working thesis focused on the intensity of the debate over the applications of such technologies. Much of the debate, you discover, focuses on arguments about the morality of (1) testing for genetic abnormalities in the fetus, (2) using genetic information to screen prospective employees, and (3) disrupting the ecosystem by creating new organisms. Based on this discovery, you might create a brief outline, numbering each of these three main categories (as examples of the pro-con debates) and using these numbers on your notecards to indicate how you have (at least provisionally) categorized each note. As you continue your research, you'll be able to expand or reduce the scope of your paper, modifying your outline as necessary. Your developing outline becomes a guide to continuing research.

Some people prefer not to develop an outline until they have more or less completed their research. At that point they will look over their notecards or notes, consider the relationships among the various pieces of evidence, possibly arrange their cards into separate piles, and then develop an outline based on their perceptions and insights about the material. They will then rearrange and code the notecards to conform to their newly created outline.

In the past, instructors commonly required students to develop multileveled formal outlines (complete with Roman and Arabic numerals) before writing their first drafts. But many writers find it difficult to generate papers from such elaborate outlines, which sometimes restrict, rather than stimulate, thought. Now, many instructors recommend only that students prepare an *informal outline,* indicating just the main sections of the paper and possibly one level below that. Thus, a paper on how the significance of Columbus's legacy has changed over the years may be informally outlined as follows:

> Intro: Different views of Columbus, past and
> present;
>
> —*thesis*: view of Columbus varies with
> temper of times
>
> Pre—20th century assessments of Columbus and
> legacy
>
> The debate over the quincentennial (1992)
>
> > —positive views
> >
> > —negative views
>
> Conclusion: How to assess Columbian heritage

Such an outline will help you organize your research and should not be unduly restrictive as a guide to writing.

The *formal outline* (a multileveled plan with Roman and Arabic numerals, capital and small lettered subheadings) may still be useful, not so much as an exact blueprint for composition—although some writers do find it useful for this purpose—but rather as a guide to revision. That is, after you have written your draft, outlining it may help you discern structural problems: illogical sequences of material; confusing relationships between ideas; poor unity or coherence; sections that are too abstract or underdeveloped. (See the discussion of *reverse outlines* in Chapter 3, pages 121–123.) Many instructors also require that formal outlines accompany the finished research paper.

The formal outline should indicate the logical relationships in the evidence relating to your particular subject (see example below). But it also may reflect the general conventions of presenting academic ideas. Thus, after an *introduction,* papers in the social sciences often proceed with a description of the *methods* of collecting information, continue with a description of the *results* of the investigation, and end with a *conclusion.* Papers in the sciences often follow a similar pattern. Papers in the humanities generally are less standardized in form. In devising a logical organization for your paper, ask yourself how your reader might best be introduced to the subject, be guided through a discussion of the main issues, and be persuaded that your viewpoint is a sound one.

Formal outlines are generally of two types: *topic* and *sentence outlines.* In the topic outline, headings and subheadings are indicated by words or phrases—as in the informal outline above. In the sentence outline, each heading and subheading is indicated in a complete sentence. Both topic and sentence outlines generally are preceded by the thesis.

Here is an example of a sentence outline:

Thesis: Assessment of Columbus, his voyages, and his legacy varies, depending on the values of the times.

   I. Early-19th century and late-20th century assessments of Columbus are 180 degrees apart.

     A. 19th-century commentators idolize him.

     B. 20th-century commentators often demonize him.

     C. Shifting assessments are based less on hard facts about Columbus than on the values of the culture that assesses him.

  II. In the 16th and 17th centuries, Columbus was not yet being used for political purposes.

     A. In the early 16th century, his fame was eclipsed by that of others.

       1. Amerigo Vespucci and Vasco da Gama were considered more successful mariners.

       2. Cortés and Pizarro were more successful in bringing back wealth from the New World.

     B. In the next century, historians and artists began writing of the achievements of Columbus, but without an overt political purpose.

       1. The first biography of Columbus was written by his son Fernando.

       2. Plays about Columbus were written by Lope de Vega and others.

     C. An important exception was that in 1542 the monk Bartolomé de las Casas attacked the Spanish legacy in the Americas—although he did not attack Columbus personally.

 III. In the 18th and 19th centuries, Columbus and his legacy began to be used for political purposes.

     A. During the late 18th century, Columbus's stature in America increased as part of the attempt to stir up anti-British sentiment.

       1. Columbus was opposed by kings, since he "discovered" a land free of royal authority.

       2. Columbus, the bold visionary who charted unknown territories, became symbolic of the American spirit.

     B. During the 19th century, Columbus's reputation reached its peak.

         1. For some, Columbus represented geographical and industrial expansion, optimism, and faith in progress.

         2. For others, Columbus's success was the archetypal rags-to-riches story at the heart of the American Dream.

         3. After the Civil War, Catholics celebrated Columbus as an ethnic hero.

         4. The 400th anniversary of Columbus's landfall both celebrated the past and expressed confidence in the future. Columbus became the symbol of American industrial success.

  IV. By the quincentennial of Columbus's landfall, the negative assessments of Columbus were far more evident than were positive assessments.

     A. Historians and commentators charged that the consequences of Columbus's "discoveries" were imperialism, slavery, genocide, and ecocide.

     B. The National Council of Churches published a resolution blasting the Columbian legacy.

     C. Kirkpatrick Sale's *The Conquest of Paradise* also attacked Columbus.

     D. Native Americans and others protested the quincentennial and planned counterdemonstrations.

  V. Conclusion: How should we judge Columbus?

     A. In many ways, Columbus was a man of his time and did not rise above his time.

     B. In his imagination and boldness and in the impact of his discoveries, Columbus stands above others of his time.

     C. When we assess Columbus and his legacy, we also assess our own self-confidence, our optimism, and our faith in progress.

WRITING THE DRAFT

Your goal in drafting your paper is to support your thesis by clearly and logically presenting your evidence—evidence that you summarize, critique, synthesize, and analyze. In effect, you are creating and moderating a conversation among your sources that supports the conclusions you have drawn from your exploration and analysis of the material. The finished paper, however, should not merely represent an amalgam of your sources; it should present your own particular critical perspective on the subject. Your job is to select and arrange your material in such a way that your conclusions seem inevitable (or at least reasonable). You also must select and arrange your material in a way that is fair and logical; remember that your paper will be evaluated to some degree on whether it meets the standards of logical argumentation discussed on pages 60–64. Try not to be guilty of such logical fallacies as hasty generalization, false analogy, and either/or reasoning.

As we suggested in the section on introductions (pages 107–113), when writing the first draft it's sometimes best to skip the introduction (you'll come back to it later when you have a better idea of just what's being introduced) and to start with the main body of your discussion. What do you have to tell your audience about your subject? It may help to imagine yourself sitting opposite your audience in an informal setting like the student center, telling them what you've discovered in the course of your research and why you think it's interesting and significant. The fact that you've accumulated a considerable body of evidence (in your notes) to support your thesis should give you confidence in presenting your argument. Keep in mind, too, that there's no one right way to organize this argument; any number of ways will work, provided each makes logical sense. And if you're working on a computer, it is particularly easy to move whole paragraphs and sections from one place to another, as logic dictates.

Begin the drafting process by looking at your notecards. Arrange the cards to correspond to your outline (or number entries in your notes, if you haven't used notecards). Summarize, paraphrase, and quote from your notecards as you draft. (If you write your first draft by hand, one timesaving technique is to tape photocopied quotations in the appropriate places in your draft.) If necessary, review the material on explanatory and argument syntheses in Chapters 4 and 5. In particular, note the Box "Guidelines for Writing Syntheses" (pages 142–143) and the section "Developing and Organizing the Support for Your Arguments" (pages 209–212). When presenting your argument, consider such rhetorical strategies as counterargument, concession, and comparison and contrast. The sample student papers in Chapters 4 and 5 on synthesis may serve as models for your own research paper.

As you work through your notes, be selective. Don't provide more evidence or discussion than you need to prove your point. Resist the urge to use *all* of your material just to show how much research you've done. (One experienced teacher, Susan M. Hubbuch, scornfully refers to papers with too much information as "memory dumps"—consisting of nothing but "mindless regurgitation of everything you have read about a subject.") Also avoid going into extended discussions of what are essentially tangential issues. Keep focused on your research questions and on providing support for your thesis.

At the same time, remember that you *are* working on a rough draft—one that will probably have all kinds of problems, from illogical organization to awkward sentence structure to a banal conclusion. Don't worry about it; you can deal with all such problems in subsequent drafts. The important thing now is get the words on paper or on your disk.

AVOIDING PLAGIARISM

Plagiarism is generally defined as the attempt to pass off the work of another as one's own. Whether born out of calculation or desperation, plagiarism is the least tolerated offense in the academic world. The fact that most plagiarism is unintentional—arising from ignorance of conventions rather than deceitfulness—makes no difference to many professors.

You can avoid plagiarism and charges of plagiarism by following the basic rules below:

RULES FOR AVOIDING PLAGIARISM

- Cite *all* quoted material and *all* summarized and paraphrased material, unless the information is common knowledge (e.g., the Civil War was fought from 1861 to 1865).
- Make sure that both the *wording* and the *sentence structure* of your summaries and paraphrases are substantially your own.

Following is a passage of text, along with several student versions of the ideas represented. (The passage is from Richard Rovere's article on Senator Joseph P. McCarthy, titled "The Most Gifted and Successful Demagogue This Country Has Ever Known."*)

> McCarthy never seemed to believe in himself or in anything he had said. He knew that Communists were not in charge of American foreign policy. He knew that they weren't running the United States Army. He knew that he had spent five years looking for Communists in the government and that—although some must certainly have been there, since Communists had turned up in practically every other major government in the world—he hadn't come up with even one.

One student version of this passage reads as follows:

> ```
> McCarthy never believed in himself or in anything
> he had said. He knew that Communists were not in
> charge of American foreign policy and weren't run-
> ning the United States Army. He knew that he had
> ```

---

*Richard Rovere, "The Most Gifted and Successful Demagogue This Country Has Ever Known," <u>New York Times Magazine</u> 30 Apr. 1967.

> spent five years looking for Communists in the
> government, and although there must certainly have
> been some there, since Communists were in practi-
> cally every other major government in the world,
> he hadn't come up with even one.

Clearly, this is intentional plagiarism. The student has copied the original passage almost word for word.

Here is another version of the same passage:

> McCarthy knew that Communists were not running
> foreign policy or the Army. He also knew that al-
> though there must have been some Communists in the
> government, he hadn't found a single one, even
> though he had spent five years looking.

This student has attempted to put the ideas into her own words, but both the wording and the sentence structure still are so heavily dependent on the original passage that even if it *were* cited, most professors would consider it plagiarism.

In the following version, the student has sufficiently changed the wording and sentence structure, and she uses a *signal phrase* (a phrase used to introduce a quotation or paraphrase, signaling to the reader that the words to follow come from someone else) to properly credit the information to Rovere, so that there is no question of plagiarism:

> According to Richard Rovere, McCarthy was cynical
> enough to know that Communists were running nei-
> ther the government nor the Army. He also knew
> that he hadn't found a single Communist in govern-
> ment, even after a lengthy search (192).

Apart from questions of plagiarism, it's essential to quote accurately. You are not permitted to change any part of a quotation or to omit any part of it without using brackets or ellipses (see Chapter 1, pages 45–48).

CITING SOURCES

When you refer to or quote the work of another, you are obligated to credit or cite your source properly. There are two types of citations—in-text citations and full citations at the end of a paper—and they work in tandem.

If you are writing a paper in the humanities, you probably will be expected to use the Modern Language Association (MLA) format for citation. This format is fully described in the *MLA Handbook for Writers of Research Papers*, 5th ed. (New York: Modern Language Association of America, 1999). A paper in the social sciences will probably use the American Psychological

Association (APA) format. This format is fully described in the *Publication Manual of the American Psychological Association*, 5th ed. (Washington, D.C.: American Psychological Association, 2001).

In the following section, we will focus on MLA and APA styles, the ones you are most likely to use in your academic work. Keep in mind, however, that instructors often have their own preferences. Some require the documentation style specified in the *Chicago Manual of Style*, 14th ed. (Chicago: University of Chicago Press, 1993). This style is similar to the American Psychological Association style, except that publication dates are not placed within parentheses. Instructors in the sciences often follow the Council of Biology Editors (CBE) format. Or they may prefer a number format: Each source listed on the bibliography page is assigned a number, and all text references to the source are followed by the appropriate number within parentheses. Some instructors like the old MLA style, which calls for footnotes and endnotes. Check with your instructor for the preferred documentation format if this is not specified in the assignment itself.

In-Text Citation

The general rule for in-text citation is to include only enough information to alert the reader to the source of the reference and to the location within that source. Normally, this information includes the author's last name and the page number (plus the year of publication, if using APA guidelines). But if you have already named the author in the preceding text, just the page number is sufficient.

TYPES OF CITATIONS

- Citations that indicate the source of quotations, paraphrases, and summarized information and ideas—these citations appear *in text*, within parentheses.
- Citations that appear in an alphabetical list of "Works Cited" or "References" following the paper.

Content Notes

Occasionally, you may want to provide a footnote or an endnote as a *content note*—one that provides additional information bearing on or illuminating, but not directly related to, the discussion at hand. For example

> [1]Equally well-known is Forster's distinction between story and plot: In the former, the emphasis is on sequence ("the king died and then the queen died"); in the latter, the emphasis is on causality ("the king died and then the queen died of grief").

Notice the format: The first line is indented five spaces or one-half inch and the note number is raised one-half line. A single space from there, the note begins. Subsequent lines of the note are flush with the left margin. If the note is at the bottom of the page (a footnote), it is placed four spaces below the text of the page, and the note itself is single-spaced. Content notes are numbered consecutively throughout the paper; do not begin renumbering on each page. Most word-processing programs have functions for inserting consecutive footnotes, formatting them, and placing them in the appropriate position on your pages.

Full Citations

In MLA format, your complete list of sources, with all information necessary for a reader to locate a source, is called "Works Cited." Entries in this listing should be double-spaced, with second and subsequent lines of each entry indented (a "hanging indent")—five spaces or one-half inch. In both styles, a single space follows the period. Here are two samples for comparison:

Sample MLA Full Citation (for a journal article)

> Haan, Sarah C. "The 'Persuasion Route' of the Law:
>
>   Advertising and Legal Persuasion." <u>Columbia</u>
>
>   <u>Law Review</u> 100.5 (June 2000): 1281–1326.

Sample APA Full Citation (for a journal article)

> Haan, S. C. (2000). The "persuasion route" of the
>
>   law: Advertising and legal persuasion. *Columbia*
>
>   *Law Review 100* (5). 1281–1326.

The main difference between MLA and APA styles is that in MLA style, the date of the publication follows the name of the publisher; in APA style, the date is placed within parentheses following the author's name. Other differences: In APA style, only the initial of the author's first name is indicated, and only the first word (and any proper noun) of the book or article title and subtitle is capitalized. The first letter of any word after a colon in a title is also capitalized. In MLA style, all words following the first word (except articles and prepositions) are capitalized. For APA style, do *not* place quotation marks around journal/magazine article titles. However, do use "p." and "pp." to indicate page numbers of newspaper articles. In APA format, italicize titles of books and journals, extending italics to include punctuation and volume (but not issue) numbers. When citing books, both MLA and APA rules dictate that publishers' names should be abbreviated; thus, "Random House" becomes "Random"; "William Morrow" becomes "Morrow."

Note: While the hanging indent (second and subsequent lines indented) is the recommended format for APA style references in student papers, manuscripts intended for publication follow paragraph indent format, in which only the first line of each reference is indented.

Provided below are some of the most commonly used citations in MLA and APA formats. For a more complete listing, consult the MLA *Handbook,* the APA *Manual,* or whichever style guide your instructor has specified.

MLA STYLE

In-Text Citation

Here are sample in-text citations using the MLA system:

> From the beginning, the AIDS antibody test has been
>
> "mired in controversy" (Bayer 101).

Notice that in the MLA system there is no punctuation between the author's name and the page number within the parentheses. Notice also that the parenthetical reference is placed *before* the final punctuation of the sentence, because it is considered part of the sentence.

If you have already mentioned the author's name in the text—in a *signal phrase*—it is not necessary to repeat it in the citation:

> According to Bayer, from the beginning, the AIDS an-
>
> tibody test has been "mired in controversy" (101).

In MLA format, you must supply page numbers for summaries and paraphrases, as well as for quotations:

> According to Bayer, the AIDS antibody test has been
>
> controversial from the outset (101).

Use a block, or indented form, for quotations of five lines or more. In block quotations, place the parenthetical citation *after* the period:

> Robert Flaherty's refusal to portray primitive people's
>
> contact with civilization arose from an inner conflict:
>
>> He had originally plunged with all his heart into
>>
>> the role of explorer and prospector; before Nanook,
>>
>> his own father was his hero. Yet as he entered the
>>
>> Eskimo world, he knew he did so as the advance guard

> of industrial civilization, the world of United
>
> States Steel and Sir William Mackenzie and railroad
>
> and mining empires. The mixed feeling this gave him
>
> left his mark on all his films. (Barnouw 45)

Again, were Barnouw's name mentioned in the sentence leading into the quotation, the parenthetical reference would be simply (45).

Usually parenthetical citations appear at the end of your sentences; however, if the reference applies only to the first part of the sentence, the parenthetical information is inserted at the appropriate points *within* the sentence:

> While Baumrind argues that "the laboratory is not
>
> the place to study degree of obedience" (421), Mil-
>
> gram asserts that such arguments are groundless.

There are times when you must modify the basic author/page number reference. Depending on the nature of your source(s), you may need to use one of the following citation formats:

Quoted Material Appearing in Another Source

> (qtd. in Garber 211)

An Anonymous Work

> ("Obedience" 32)

Two Authors

> (Bernstein and Politi 208)

A Particular Work by an Author, When You List Two or More Works by That Author in the List of Works Cited

> (Toffler, <u>Wave</u> 96–97)

Two or More Sources as the Basis of Your Statement

> (Butler 109; Carey 57)

The Location of a Passage in a Literary Text

> for example, Hardy's <u>The Return of the Native</u> (224; ch. 7)

> [Page 224 in the edition used by the writer; the chapter number, 7, is provided for the convenience of those referring to another edition.]

A Multivolume Work

(3:7–12) [volume number: page numbers]

The Location of a Passage in a Play

(1.2.308–22) [act.scene.line number(s)]

The Bible

(John 3.16) [book.chapter.verse]

(Col. 3.14)

In-Text Citation of Electronic Sources (MLA)

Web sites, CD-ROM data, and e-mail generally do not have numbered pages. Different browsers may display and printers may produce differing numbers of pages for any particular site. You should therefore omit both page numbers and paragraph numbers from in-text citations to electronic sources, unless these page or paragraph numbers are provided within the source itself. For parenthetical citations of electronic sources, MLA style dictates that you cite the author's name. In APA style, cite the author's name and the year of publication.

Examples of MLA Citations in Works Cited List

BOOKS (MLA)

One Author

> Kolodny, Annette. <u>The Land Before Her: Fantasy and Experience</u>
>
> <u>of the American Frontiers, 1630–1860</u>. Chapel Hill: U of
>
> North Carolina P, 1984.

Note: MLA convention dictates abbreviating the names of university presses (e.g. Oxford UP for Oxford University Press or the above for University of North Carolina Press). Commercial publishing companies are also shortened by dropping such endings as "Co.," or "Inc."

Two or More Books by the Same Author

> Gubar, Susan. <u>Critical Condition: Feminism at the Turn of the</u>
>
> <u>Century</u>. New York: Columbia UP, 2000.

> ———. <u>Racechanges: White Skin, Black Face in American Culture</u>.
>
> New York: Oxford UP, 1997.

Note: For MLA style, references to works by the same author are listed in alphabetical order of title.

Two Authors

Chambliss, William J., and Thomas F. Courtless. <u>Criminal Law,</u>

<u>Criminology, and Criminal Justice: A Casebook</u>. Pacific

Grove: Brooks/Cole, 1992.

Three Authors

Young, Richard E., Alton L. Becker, and Kenneth L. Pike.

<u>Rhetoric: Discovery and Change</u>. New York: Harcourt,

1970.

More than Three Authors

Maimon, Elaine, et al. <u>Writing in the Arts and Sciences</u>.

Boston: Little, 1982.

Book with an Editor

Grant, Michael, ed. <u>T. S. Eliot: The Critical Heritage</u>.

Boston: Routledge, 1982.

Later Edition

Houp, Kenneth W., and Thomas E. Pearsall. <u>Reporting Technical</u>

<u>Information</u>. 8th ed. Boston: Allyn, 1995.

Republished Book

Dreiser, Theodore. <u>An American Tragedy</u>. 1925. Cambridge:

Bentley, 1978.

One Volume of a Multivolume Work

Bailey, Thomas A. <u>The American Spirit: United States History as</u>

<u>Seen by Contemporaries</u>. 6th ed. 2 vols. Lexington: Heath, 1987.

Translation

Kundera, Milan. <u>The Book of Laughter and Forgetting</u>. Trans.

Michael Henry Heim. New York: Penguin, 1987.

Selection from an Anthology

Rueckert, William. "An Experiment in Ecocriticism." <u>The Eco-</u>
<u>criticism Reader: Landmarks in Literary Ecology</u>. Ed.
Cheryll Glotfelty and Harold Fromm. Athens: U of Georgia
P, 1996. 105—121.

Reprinted Material in an Edited Collection

McGinnis, Wayne D. "The Arbitrary Cycle of <u>Slaughterhouse-</u>
<u>Five:</u> A Relation of Form to Theme." <u>Critique: Studies</u>
<u>in Modern Fiction</u> 17.1 (1975): 55—68. Rpt. in <u>Contem-</u>
<u>porary Literary Criticism</u>. Ed. Dedria Bryfonski and
Phyllis Carmel Mendelson. Vol. 8. Detroit: Gale, 1978.
530—31.

Government Publication

United States Commission on Child and Family Welfare. <u>Parent-</u>
<u>ing our Children: In the Best Interest of the Nation: A</u>
<u>Report of the U. S. Commission on Child and Family Wel</u>
<u>fare</u>. Washington: GPO, 1996.

United States. Congress. House. Committee on Energy and Commerce. Subcommittee on Health and the Environment. <u>Health</u>
<u>Consequences of Smoking: Nicotine Addiction: Hearing Be-</u>
<u>fore the Subcommittee on Health and the Environment of</u>
<u>the Committee on Energy and Commerce</u>. 100th Cong., 2nd
sess. Washington: GPO, 1988.

The Bible

<u>The New English Bible</u>. New York: Oxford UP, 1972.

Signed Encyclopedia Article

Lack, David L. "Population." <u>Encyclopaedia Britannica: Macro-</u>
<u>paedia</u>. 15th ed. 1998.

Unsigned Encyclopedia Article

"Tidal Wave." <u>Encyclopedia Americana</u>. 1982 ed.

PERIODICALS (MLA)

Continuous Pagination throughout Annual Cycle

Binder, Sarah. "The Dynamics of Legislative Gridlock, 1947–

1996." <u>American Political Science Review</u> 93 (1999): 519–31.

Separate Pagination Each Issue

O'Mealy, Joseph H. "Royal Family Values: The Americanization

of Alan Bennett's <u>The Madness of King George III</u>." <u>Litera-

ture/Film Quarterly</u> 27.2 (1999): 90–97.

Monthly Periodical

Davison, Peter. "Girl, Seeming to Disappear." <u>Atlantic Monthly</u>

May 2000: 108–11.

Signed Article in Weekly Periodical

Gladwell, Malcolm. "The New-Boy Network." <u>New Yorker</u> 29 May

2000: 68–86.

Unsigned Article in Weekly Periodical

"GOP Speaker Admits 'Exaggerations.'" <u>New Republic</u> 14 Aug.

2000: 10–11.

Signed Article in Daily Newspaper

Vise, David A. "FBI Report Gauges School Violence Indicators."

<u>Washington Post</u> 6 Sept. 2000: B1+.

Unsigned Article in Daily Newspaper

"The World's Meeting Place." <u>New York Times</u> 6 Sept. 2000: A11.

Review

Barber, Benjamin R. "The Crack in the Picture Window." Rev. of

<u>Bowling Alone: The Collapse and Revival of American Com-

munity</u>, by Robert D. Putnam. <u>Nation</u> 7 Aug. 2000: 29–34.

OTHER SOURCES (MLA)

Interview

Emerson, Robert. Personal interview. 10 Oct. 1998.

Dissertation (Abstracted in Dissertation Abstracts International)

Sheahan, Mary Theresa. "Living on the Edge: Ecology and Econ-
omy in Willa Cather's 'Wild Land': Webster County
Nebraska, 1870-1900." Diss. Northern Illinois U, 1999.
DAI 60/04 (1999): 1298.

Note: If the dissertation is available on microfilm, give the University Micro-
films order number at the conclusion of the reference. Example, in MLA format: UMI, 1999. 9316566.

Lecture

Osborne, Michael. "The Great Man Theory: Caesar." Lecture.
History 41. University of California, Santa Barbara, 5
Nov. 1999.

Paper Delivered at a Professional Conference

Worley, Joan. "Texture: The Feel of Writing." Conference on College Composition and Communication. Cincinnati, 21 Mar. 1992.

Film

Howard's End. Dir. James Ivory. Perf. Emma Thompson and Anthony Hopkins. Merchant/Ivory and Film Four International, 1992.

Recording of a TV Program or Film

Legacy of the Hollywood Blacklist. Dir. Judy Chaikin. One Step
Productions and Public Affairs TV. Videocassette. 1987.

Audio Recording

Hersh, Kristen. "Rock Candy Brains." Strange Angels. Rykodisc,
1998.

```
Schumann, Robert. Symphonies 1 & 4. Cond. George Szell. Cleve-

    land Orchestra. Columbia, 1978.
```

[Or, to emphasize the conductor rather than the composer:]

```
Szell, George, cond. Symphonies 1 & 4. By Robert Schumann.

    Cleveland Orchestra. Columbia, 1978.
```

ELECTRONIC SOURCES (MLA)

According to guidelines in the 1999 *MLA Handbook for Writers of Research Papers*, writers of research papers should credit the electronic sources they use by following these general conventions: 1. Name of the author (if given); 2. Title of the work, underlined; 3. Name of editor, compiler, or translator (if relevant); 4. Electronic publication information, including edition, volume number, release, or version (if relevant); 5. Date of electronic publication or latest update; 6. Name of any sponsoring organization or institution; 7. Date of access; 8. Pathway or method of access. Include a full and accurate URL for any source taken from the Internet (with access-mode identifier—*http, ftp, gopher, or telnet*). Enclose URLs in angle brackets(<>). When a URL continues from one line to the next, break it only after a slash. Do not add a hyphen; 9. *For portable sources:* City of publication and name of publisher (e.g., Redmond: Microsoft), or name of the vendor (e.g., SilverPlatter), and electronic publication date.

If you cannot find some of this information within your sources, cite what is available. Note that the order of this information may vary depending upon the type of source cited. Follow the formatting conventions illustrated by the following models:

An Online Scholarly Project or Database

```
The Walt Whitman Hypertext Archive. Eds. Kenneth M. Price and

    Ed Folsom. 16 Mar. 1998. College of William and Mary. 3

    Apr. 1998 <http://jefferson.village.Virginia.EDU/ whitman/>.
```

1. Title of project or database; 2. name of the editor of project; 3. electronic publication information; 4. date of access and URL

A Short Work within a Scholarly Project

```
Whitman, Walt. "Crossing Brooklyn Ferry." The Walt Whitman

    Hypertext Archive. Ed. Kenneth M. Price and Ed Folsom. 16

    Mar. 1998. College of William and Mary. 3 Apr. 2001

    <http://jefferson.village.virginia.edu/whitman/works/

    leaves/1891/text/index.html>.
```

A Personal or Professional Site

Winter, Mick. <u>How to Talk New Age</u>. 6 Apr. 2000 <http://
www.well.com/user/mick/newagept.html>.

An Online Book Published Independently

Smith, Adam. <u>The Wealth of Nations</u>. New York: Methuen, 1904.

3 Mar. 2001 <http://www.mk.net/~dt/Bibliomania/NonFiction/
Smith/Wealth/index.html>.

An Online Book within a Scholarly Project

Whitman, Walt. <u>Leaves of Grass</u>. Philadelphia: McKay, 1891–2.

<u>The Walt Whitman Hypertext Archive</u>. Ed. Kenneth M. Price
and Ed Folsom. 16 Mar. 1998. College of William and Mary.
3 Apr. 1998 <http://jefferson.village.virginia.edu/whitman/
works/leaves/1891/text/title.html>.

An Article in a Scholarly Journal

Jackson, Francis L. "Mexican Freedom: The Idea of the Indigenous State." <u>Animus</u> 2.3 (1997): 15 pars. 4 Apr. 1998
<http://www.mun.ca/animus/1997vol2/jackson2.htm>.

An Unsigned Article in a Newspaper or on a Newswire

"Drug Czar Wants to Sharpen Drug War." <u>TopNews</u> 6 Apr. 1998.

6 Apr. 1998 <http://news.lycos.com/stories/
TopNews?19980406_NEWS-DRUGS.asp>.

A Signed Article in a Newspaper or on a Newswire

Davis, Robert. "Drug May Prevent Breast Cancer." <u>USA Today</u> 6 Apr.

1998 8 Apr. 1998 <http://www.usatoday.com/news/ nds14.htm>.

An Article in a Magazine

Pitta, Julie. "Un-Wired?" <u>Forbes</u> 20 Apr. 1998. 12 May 1998

<http://www.forbes.com/Forbes/98/0420/6108045a.htm>.

A Review

Beer, Francis A. Rev. of <u>Evolutionary Paradigms in the Social</u>
<u>Sciences. Special Issue, International Studies Quarterly</u>
40.3 (1996). <u>Journal of Mimetics</u> 1 (1997). 4 Jan. 1998
<http://www.cpm.mmu.ac.uk/jomemit/1997/vol1/beer_fa.html>.

An Editorial or Letter to the Editor

"The Net Escape Censorship? Ha!" Editorial. <u>Wired</u> 3.09. 1
Apr. 1998. 22 Aug. 2000 <http://www.wired.com/wired/3.09/
departments/baker.if.html>.

An Abstract

Maia, Ana Couto. "Prospects for United Nations Peacekeeping:
Lessons from the Congo Experience. <u>MAI</u> 36.2 (1998): 400.
Abstract. 6 Apr. 1998 <http:/www.lib.umi.com/
dissertations/fullcit?289845>.

A Periodical Source on CD-ROM, Diskette, or Magnetic Tape

Ellis, Richard. "Whale Killing Begins Anew." <u>Audubon</u> [GAUD]
94.6 (1992): 20–22. <u>General Periodicals Ondisc–Magazine</u>
<u>Express</u>. CD-ROM UMI-Proquest. 1992.

A Non-Periodical Source on CD-ROM, Diskette, or Magnetic Tape

Clements, John. "War of 1812." <u>Chronology of the United States</u>.
CD-ROM. Dallas: Political Research, Inc. 1997.

Electronic Mail

Mendez, Michael R. "Re: Solar power." E-mail to Edgar V.
Atamian. 11 Sept. 1996.

Armstrong, David J. E-mail to the author. 30 Aug. 1996.

An Online Posting

For online postings or synchronous communications, try to cite a version
stored as a Web file, if one exists, as a courtesy to the reader. Label sources

as needed (e.g., Online posting, Online defense of dissertation, etc., with neither underlining nor quotation marks). Follow the following models as appropriate.

Message from an Electronic Mailing List

> Kosten, A. "Major update of the WWWVL Migration and Ethnic Relations." Online posting. 7 Apr. 1998. ERCOMER News. 7 May 1998 <http://www.ercomer.org/archive/ercomer-news/ 0002.html>.

Message from an Online Forum or Discussion Group

> Dorsey, Michael. "Environmentalism or Racism." Online posting. 25 Mar. 1998. 1 Apr. 1998 <news:alt.org.sierra-club>.

Synchronous Communication

> Mendez, Michael R. "Solar Power Versus Fossil Fuel Power." Online debate. 3 Apr. 1998. CollegeTownMOO. 3 Apr. 1998 <telnet://next.cs.bvc.edu.7777>.

Computer Software on CD-ROM

> Gamma UniType for Windows 1.5. Vers. 1.1. San Diego: Gamma Productions, Inc., 1997.

[Note: If software is downloaded, include the date of download in the citation.]

APA STYLE

In-Text Citation

Here are the sample in-text citations using the APA system:

> From the beginning, the AIDS antibody test has been "mired in controversy" (Bayer, 1989, p. 101).

Notice that in the APA system, there is a comma between the author's name, the date, and the page number, and the number itself is preceded by "p." or "pp." Notice also that the parenthetical reference is placed *before* the final punctuation of the sentence.

If you have already mentioned the author's name in the text, it is not necessary to repeat it in the citation:

> According to Bayer (1989), from the beginning, the
> AIDS antibody test has been "mired in controversy"
> (p. 101).

or:

> According to Bayer, from the beginning, the AIDS
> antibody test has been "mired in controversy"
> (1989, p. 101).

When using the APA system, provide page numbers only for direct quotations, not for summaries or paraphrases. If you do not refer to a specific page, simply indicate the date:

> Bayer (1989) reported that there are many precedents for the reporting of AIDS cases that do not unduly violate privacy.

For quotations of 40 words or more, use block (indented) quotations. In these cases, place the parenthetical citation *after* the period:

> Robert Flaherty's refusal to portray primitive people's contact with civilization arose from an inner conflict:
>
> > He had originally plunged with all his heart into the role of explorer and prospector; before Nanook, his own father was his hero. Yet as he entered the Eskimo world, he knew he did so as the advance guard of industrial civilization, the world of United States Steel and Sir William Mackenzie and railroad and mining empires. The mixed feeling this gave him left his mark on all his films. (Barnouw, 1974, p. 45)

Again, were Barnouw's name mentioned in the sentence leading into the quotation, the parenthetical reference would be simply (1974, p. 45) for APA style.

If the reference applies only to the first part of the sentence, the parenthetical reference is inserted at the appropriate points *within* the sentence:

```
While Baumrind (1963) argued that "the labora-

tory is not the place to study degree of obedi-

ence" (p. 421), Milgram asserted that such argu-

ments are groundless.
```

There are times when you must modify the basic author/page number reference. Depending on the nature of your source(s), you may need to use one of the following citation formats:

Quoted Material Appearing in Another Source

```
(cited in Garber, 2000, p. 211)
```

An Anonymous Work

```
("Obedience," 1993, p. 32)
```

Two Authors

```
(Bernstein & Politi, 1996, p. 208)
```

A Particular Work by an Author, When You List Two or More Works by That Author in the List of References

```
(Toffler, 1973, pp. 96–97)
```

Two or More Sources as the Basis of Your Statement (Arrange Entries in Alphabetic Order of Surname)

```
(Butler, 1990, p. 109; Carey, 1987, p. 57)
```

A Multivolume Work

```
(Vol. 2, p. 88)
```

In-Text Citation of Electronic Sources (APA)

Web sites, CD-ROM data, and e-mail generally do not have numbered pages, and different printers may produce different numbers of pages for any particular site. You should therefore omit both page numbers and paragraph numbers from in-text citations to electronic sources, unless these page or paragraph numbers are provided within the source itself.

Examples of APA Citations in References List

BOOKS (APA)

One Author

 Kolodny, A. (1984). *The land before her: Fantasy and experi-*

   ence of the American frontiers, 1630-1860. Chapel Hill,

   NC: University of North Carolina Press.

Two or More Books by the Same Author

 Gubar, S. (1997). *Racechanges: White skin, black face in Amer-*

   ican culture. New York: Oxford UP.

 Gubar, S. (2000). *Critical condition: Feminism at the turn of*

   the century. New York: Columbia UP.

Note: For APA style, references to works by the same author are listed in
chronological order of publication, earliest first.

Two Authors

 Chambliss, W. J., & Courtless, T. F. (1992). *Criminal law,*

   criminology, and criminal justice: A casebook. Pacific

   Grove, CA: Brooks/Cole.

Three Authors

 Young, R. E., Becker, A. L., & Pike, K. L. (1970). *Rhetoric:*

   Discovery and change. New York: Harcourt.

More than Three Authors

 Maimon, E., Belcher, G. L., Hearn, G. W., Nodine, B. N., &

   O'Connor, F. W. (1982). *Writing in the arts and sciences.*

   Boston: Little.

Book with an Editor

 Grant, M. (Ed.). (1982). *T. S. Eliot: The critical heritage.*

   Boston: Routledge.

Later Edition

Houp, K. W., & Pearsall, T. E. (1995). *Reporting technical information* (8th ed.). Boston: Allyn and Bacon.

Republished Book

Dreiser, T. (1978). *An American tragedy*. Cambridge, Mass.: R. Bentley. (Original work published 1925).

One Volume of a Multivolume Work

Bailey, T. A. (1987). *The American spirit: United States history as seen by contemporaries* (6th ed., Vol. 2). Lexington, MA: Heath.

Translation

Kundera, M. (1987). *The book of laughter and forgetting*. (M. H. Heim, Trans.). New York: Penguin.

Selection from an Anthology

Rueckert, W. (1996). An experiment in ecocriticism. In C. Glotfelty & H. Fromm (Eds.), *The ecocriticism reader: Landmarks in literary ecology*. (pp. 105–121). Athens, GA: University of Georgia Press.

Reprinted Material in an Edited Collection

McGinnis, W. D. (1975). The arbitrary cycle of *Slaughter house-five:* A relation of form to theme. In D. Bryfon ski and P. C. Mendelson (Eds.), *Contemporary literary criticism* (Vol. 8, pp. 530–531). Detroit: Gale. (Reprinted from *Critique: Studies in modern fiction 17* (1), 1975, pp. 55–68.)

Government Publication

U. S. Commission on Child and Family Welfare. (1996). *Parenting our children: In the best interest of the nation: A* report of the U. S. commission on child and family wel-

fare. Washington, DC: U. S. Government Printing Office.

U. S. Congress. House. Committee on Energy and Commerce.

Subcommittee on Health and the Environment. (1988).

Health consequences of smoking: nicotine addiction:

Hearing before the subcommittee on health and the envi-

ronment of the committee on energy and commerce. 100th

Congress, 2nd session. HR. Washington, DC: Government

Printing Office.

Signed Encyclopedia Article

Lack, D. L. (1998). In *The new encyclopaedia Britannica.*

(Vol. 20, pp. 368–372). Chicago: Encyclopaedia

Britannica.

Unsigned Encyclopedia Article

Tidal wave. (1982). In *The encyclopedia Americana.* (Vol. 28,

pp. 213–216). New York: Americana.

PERIODICALS (APA)
Continuous Pagination throughout Annual Cycle

Binder, S. (1999). The dynamics of legislative gridlock, 1947–

1996. *American Political Science Review, 93,* 519–531.

Separate Pagination Each Issue

O'Mealy, J. H. (1999). Royal family values: The Americaniza-

tion of Alan Bennett's *The Madness of King George III.*

Literature/Film Quarterly, 27 (2), 90–97.

Monthly Periodical

Davison, P. (2000, May). Girl, seeming to disappear. *Atlantic*

Monthly, 108–111.

Signed Article in Weekly Periodical

> Gladwell, M. (2000, May 29). The new-boy network. *The New*
>
> *Yorker,* 68–86.

Unsigned Article in Weekly Periodical

> GOP speaker admits 'exaggerations.' (2000, August 14). *New*
>
> *Republic,* 10–11.

Signed Article in Daily Newspaper

> Vise, D. A. (2000, September 6). FBI report gauges school vio-
>
> lence indicators. *The Washington Post,* pp. B1, B6.

Unsigned Article in Daily Newspaper

> The world's meeting place. (2000, September 6). *The New York*
>
> *Times,* p. A11.

Review

> Barber, B. R. (2000, August 7). The crack in the picture win-
>
> dow. [Review of the book *Bowling alone: The collapse and*
>
> *revival of American community].* The Nation, 29–34.

OTHER SOURCES (APA)

Dissertation (Abstracted in Dissertation Abstracts International)

> Pendar, J. E. (1982). Undergraduate psychology majors: Factors
>
> influencing decisions about college, curriculum and
>
> career. *Dissertation Abstracts International, 42,* 4370A.

Note: If the dissertation is available on microfilm, give the University Micro-
films order number in parentheses at the conclusion of the reference: (UMI
No. AAD9315947).

Lecture

> Baldwin, J. (1999, January 11). *The self in social interactions.*
>
> Sociology 2 lecture, University of California, Santa Barbara.

Paper Delivered at a Professional Conference

```
Worley, J. (1992, March). Texture: The feel of writing. Paper

    presented at the Conference on College Composition and

    Communication, Cincinnati, OH.
```

Film

```
Thomas, J. (Producer), & Cronenberg, D. (Director). (1991).

    Naked  lunch [Motion picture]. United States: 20th Cen-

    tury Fox.
```

TV Series

```
Chase, D. (Producer). (2001). The Sopranos [Television se-

    ries]. New York: HBO.
```

Music Recording

```
Hersh, K. (1998). Rock candy brains. On Strange Angels [CD].

    Salem, MA: Rykodisc.
```

ELECTRONIC SOURCES (APA)

The general APA order of items for electronic sources is as follows: 1. Name of the author (if given); 2. Date of publication; 3. Title of electronic source, in italics; 4. Edition, volume number, release, or version (if relevant); 5. Date source was retrieved; 6. Pathway or method of access. 7. *For portable sources:* City of publication and name of publisher (e.g., Redmond: Microsoft), or name of the vender (e.g., SilverPlatter).

If the electronic source includes a previously published printed source or analogue for which you have given the date, do not include the date of electronic publication; also do not include the page numbers of the printed source or analogue. As with MLA citation, include as much of the pertinent information as is available.

The general APA format for online periodical sources is as follows:

> Author, I. (date). Title of article. *Name of Periodical. Volume number.* Retrieved month day, year, from source

Remember: For online sources do not add periods or other punctuation immediately following path statements; such extra marks may prevent you from accessing the source.

An Article in an Internet-Only Scholarly Journal

```
Sheehan, K. B. & Hoy, M. G. (1999). Using e-mail to survey in-
    ternet users in the United States: Methodology and as-
    sessment. Journal of Computer-Mediated Communication. Re-
    trieved August 14, 2001, from http://www.ascusc.org/jcmc/
    vol4/issue3/sheehan.html
```

Note: The APA guidelines distinguish between Internet articles that are based on a print source, and those that appear in Internet-only journals. When an Internet article is reproduced from a print source, simply follow the usual journal article reference format, and include the phrase "Electronic version" in brackets following the title of the article. In such a case, you don't need to include the URL or date retrieved from the Internet.

A Personal or Professional Site

```
Winter, M. (n.d.) How to talk new age. Retrieved April 6,
    1998, from http://www.well.com/user/mick/newagept.html
```

Note: When no date of publication is given, indicate this with n.d. for "no date" in parentheses where the date usually would appear.

An Unsigned Article in a Newspaper or on a Newswire

```
Drug czar wants to sharpen drug war. (1998, April 6) Retrieved
    April 6, 1998, from http://news.lycos.com/stories/
    TopNews?19980406_NEWS-DRUGS.asp
```

A Signed Article in a Newspaper or on a Newswire

```
Davis, R. (1998, April 6). Drug may prevent breast cancer.
    USA Today. Retrieved April 8, 1998, from http://
    www.usatoday.com/news/nds14.htm
```

An Article in a Magazine

```
Pitta, J. (1998, April 20). Un-wired? Forbes. Retrieved May
    12, 1998, from http://www.forbes.com/Forbes/98/
    0420/6108045a.htm
```

An Abstract

> Maia, A. C. (1998). Prospects for United Nations peacekeep-
>
> ing: Lessons from the Congo experience. *MAI 36* (2) Ab-
>
> stract retrieved April 6, 1998, from http://www.lib.umi.com/
>
> dissertations/fullcit?289845

A Periodical Source on CD-ROM, Diskette, or Magnetic Tape

> Ellis, R. (1992). Whale killing begins anew. *Audubon 94* (6),
>
> 20–22. Retrieved from *General Periodicals Ondisc-Magazine*
>
> *Express* [CD-ROM] UMI-Proquest.

A Non-Periodical Source on CD-ROM, Diskette, or Magnetic Tape

> Clements, J. (1997). War of 1812. Retrieved from *Chronology of*
>
> *the United States* [CD-ROM]. Dallas: Political Research, Inc.

An Online Posting

For online postings or synchronous communications, the APA recom-
mends only referencing those sources which are maintained in archived
form, since non-archived postings are not retrievable by your readers. If
you must include sources that are not archived—and this includes e-mail
communications between individuals—the APA suggests citing them
as personal communications in the text of your work, but leaving them
out of the References list. For archived sources, follow these models as
appropriate.

Message from an Electronic Mailing List

> Kosten, A. (1998, April 7). Major update of the WWWVL migra
>
> tion and ethnic relations. Message posted to ERCOMER
>
> News, archived at http://www.ercomer.org/archive/
>
> ercomernews/ 0002.html

Message from an Online Forum or Discussion Group

> Pagdin, F. (2001, July 3). New medium for therapy [Msg 498].
>
> Message posted to http://www.groups.yahoo.com/group/
>
> cybersociology/message/498

Computer Software on CD-ROM

```
Gamma UniType for Windows 1.5 (Version 1.1) [Computer soft-

    ware]. (1997). San Diego: Gamma Productions, Inc.
```

Writing Assignment: Short Research Paper

Using the methods we have outlined in this chapter—and incorporating the skills covered in this textbook as a whole—conduct your own research on a topic and research question that falls within your major or your area of interest. Your research process should culminate in a 1500–1700 word research paper in which you use your sources to present an answer to your research question.

Credits

Graham: "The Future of Love: Kiss Romance Goodbye, It's Time for the Real Thing" by Barbara Graham, *Utne Reader*, January–February 1997, 20–23. Reprinted by permission of the author.

Miller: "Why I Will Never Have a Girlfriend" by Tristan Miller, <http://www.nothingisreal.com/girlfriend/>.

Hetsroni: "Choosing a Mate in Television Dating Games: The Influence of Setting, Culture, and Gender" by Amir Hetsroni, Figures 1.1 and 1.2, and Table 1.1, *Sex Roles*, 2001, 42:1. Reprinted by permission of Plenum Publishing.

Feldman: "The (Un)Acceptability of Betrayal: A Study of College Students' Evaluations of Sexual Betrayal by a Romantic Partner and Betrayal of a Friend's Confidence" by S. Shirley Feldman, *et al.*, Figure 1, p. 511, *Journal of Youth and Adolescence*, 2000, 29:4, 498–523. Reprinted by permission of Plenum Publishing.

Capron: "Body, Body Double: Cloning Infants a Distant Fantasy" by Alexander M. Capron, *Boston Globe*, 11 January 1998, Focus section. Copyright *Boston Globe*. Used with permission.

Davis: "A Message to President Clinton and the 105th Congress: A Simple One-Step Plan to Solve the Education Crisis" by Morton J. Davis, *New York Times*, 18 January 1998, Week in Review section. Reprinted by permission of J. Morton Davis.

Olson: Excerpted from *The School-to-Work Revolution* by Lynn Olson, Perseus Books. Reprinted by permission of Perseus Books Publishers, a member of Perseus Books, L.L.C.

Schlafly: "School-to-Work Will Train, Not Educate" by Phyllis Schlafly, <IntellectualCapital.com/>. Reprinted with permission of *The Phyllis Schlafly Report*.

On-line Postings: <http://www.IntellectualCapital.com/>.

Weinberg: Response to Phyllis Schlafly's "School-to-Work Will Train, Not Educate" by Russ Weinberg. Reprinted with permission of Russ Weinberg.

Smith: Comments by Lloyd Smith, <http://www.IntellectualCapital.com/>. Reprinted with permission of Lloyd Smith.

Morris: "You've Got Romance! Seeking Love Online: Net Based Services Change the Landscape, If Not the Odds, of Finding the Perfect Mate" by Bonnie Rothman Morris, *New York Times on the Web*, 26 August 1999.

Wright: "Will We Ever Log Off?" by Robert Wright, *Time*, 21 February 2000, 56–58. Copyright 2000 Time Inc., reprinted by permission.

Rosenberg: "Lonesome Internet Blues, Take 2" by Scott Rosenberg, <http://www.salon.com/tech/cod/rose/2000/02/18/Stanford_study/index. html>. Reprinted by courtesy of Salon.com.

Gunn: "Making Clones Among Us" by Bob Gunn, *Santa Barbara News Press*, 30 April 2000.

Schwartz: "The Net: It's the Unreal Thing" by Gil Schwartz, *Computer Life*, 1995, 2:7, 65. Reprinted by permission of Gil Schwartz.

Chidley: "Cyber Time: University Students Are Mounting a Techno Revolution" by Joe Chidley, *Maclean's*, 25 November 1996. Reprinted by permission of *Maclean's Magazine*, Canada.

Reisberg: "10% of Students May Spend Too Much Time Online, Study Suggests" by Leo Reisberg, *Chronicle of Higher Education*, 5 June 2000. Copyright 2000, the *Chronicle of Higher Education*. Reprinted with permission.

Eggett: "Romance on the Net" by Ruth C. Eggett, *An International Home for Internet Romance*, 13 June 1998.

Landers: "Husband Met Online" by Ann Landers. Permission granted by Ann Landers and Creators Syndicate.

Ortega: "Ban the Bargains" by Bob Ortega *The Wall Street Journal*, 11 October 1994. Reprinted by permission of the *Wall Street Journal*. Copyright 1994 by Dow Jones and Company, Inc. All rights reserved worldwide.

Albert: "Eight Ways to Stop the Store" by Norman Albert, *The Nation*, 28 March 1994. Reprinted with permission of *The Nation*.

Anderson: "Wal-Mart's War on Main Street" by Sarah Anderson, *The Progressive*, November 1994, 19–21. Reprinted with permission of *The Progressive*.

Johnson: "Who's Really the Villain?" by Jo Ann Johnson, *Business Ethics*, May–June 1995. Reprinted with permission from *Business Ethics*, P.O. Box 8439, Minneapolis, MN 55408; www.business-ethics.com.

Hoover's: "Wal-Mart Stores, Inc." from *Hoover's: Handbook of American Business, 2001*. Courtesy of Hoover's, Inc. (Nasdaq:Hoov).

Norman: "Sprawl-Busting Victories—to Aug. 2001" by Al Norman, <http://www.sprawl.busters.com>. Reprinted with permission of Al Norman.

The Economist: "Shopping With the Enemy," *The Economist*, 14 October 1995, 33. Copyright 1995 by The Economist Newspaper Group, Inc.; www.economist.com. Reprinted by permission. Further reproduction prohibited.

California Jury Instructions: Excerpted from *Criminal (CALJIC, 6th ed. 1996) Committee on Standard Jury Instructions, Criminal, of the Superior Court of Los Angeles County, CA* Vol.1, St. Paul, Minn.: West Publishing Company, 1996. Used by permission. *People v Ashland*, 20 Cal. Appl. 168 (1912). Used by permission. *Rowland v State*, 35 so. 826 (1904). Used by permission.

Index